The Politics of the Crucified

The Politics of the Crucified

The Cross in the Political Theology of Yoder, Boff, and Sobrino

JOHN C. PEET

☙PICKWICK *Publications* • Eugene, Oregon

THE POLITICS OF THE CRUCIFIED
The Cross in the Political Theology of Yoder, Boff, and Sobrino

Copyright © 2021 John C. Peet. All rights reserved. Except for brief quotations in critical publications or reviews, no part of this book may be reproduced in any manner without prior written permission from the publisher. Write: Permissions, Wipf and Stock Publishers, 199 W. 8th Ave., Suite 3, Eugene, OR 97401.

Scripture quotations are from Common Bible: New Revised Standard Version Bible, copyright © 1989 National Council of the Churches of Christ in the United States of America. Used by permission. All rights reserved worldwide. http://nrsvbibles.org

Pickwick Publications
An Imprint of Wipf and Stock Publishers
199 W. 8th Ave., Suite 3
Eugene, OR 97401

www.wipfandstock.com

PAPERBACK ISBN: 978-1-7252-8865-2
HARDCOVER ISBN: 978-1-7252-8866-9
EBOOK ISBN: 978-1-7252-8867-6

Cataloguing-in-Publication data:

Names: Peet, John C.

Title: The politics of the crucified : the cross in the political theology of Yoder, Boff, and Sobrino / John C. Peet.

Description: Eugene, OR : Pickwick Publications, 2021 | Includes bibliographical references.

Identifiers: ISBN 978-1-7252-8865-2 (paperback) | ISBN 978-1-7252-8866-9 (hardcover) | ISBN 978-1-7252-8867-6 (ebook)

Subjects: LCSH: Jesus Christ—Crucifixion. | Political theology. | Yoder, John Howard. | Boff, Leonardo. | Sobrino, Jon.

Classification: BT453 .P34 2021 (paperback) | BT453 .P34 (ebook)

07/29/21

Contents

Preface		vii
Chapter 1	Introduction	1
Chapter 2	The Context of the Political Theology of the Cross in Yoder, Boff, and Sobrino	20
Chapter 3	The Historical and Political Causation of the Crucifixion in Yoder, Boff, and Sobrino	40
Summary 1	Towards a Political Theology of the Cross—Foundations	61
Chapter 4	The Cross as a Definitive Source of Christian Political Ethics	68
Chapter 5	The Cross and Political Discipleship	82
Chapter 6	The Cross and a Response to Violence	96
Summary 2	Towards a Political Theology of the Cross—Discipleship and Peacemaking	114
Chapter 7	The Cruciform People—The Church and Political Responsibility	126
Chapter 8	The Crucified People—Solidarity between the Poor and the Crucified Christ	154
Summary 3	Towards a Political Theology of the Cross—Community, Crucifixion and Responsibility	172
Chapter 9	Hope, Eschatology, and the Cross	188
Chapter 10	Power, Providence and the Cross	200
Summary 4	Towards a Political Theology of the Cross—Hope and Power	213
Chapter 11	The Cross and Political Power	219
Chapter 12	The Cross, the Church, and the Crucified People	259
Bibliography		297

Preface

Politics, in essence, is about power—who holds the power, what kind of power is held, how it is used, to whom it is accountable. The most pressing issues in today's world—and the major challenges to Christian political theology—have power at their root: globalization, with its concomitant agenda of neo-imperial power and domination; the ecological crisis, which has at its heart the question of whether certain nations will use their power for the good of the world rather than for narrowly national interests; and, most of all, war, which brings to sharp and ultimate focus the dilemma of applying violent power in reaction to threat. For the Christian, behind and within these questions of power stands the figure of the crucified Jesus, the ultimate symbol of powerlessness. I make a plea that the cross be taken seriously in constructing and living out a distinctively Christian political theology to meet these challenges.

Can the twenty-first century avoid the tragedies of the twentieth? Jonathan Glover, in *Humanity: a Moral History of the twentieth century* writes, "I assume that a central part of morality should be concerned with avoiding repetition of man-made disasters of the kind the Nazis brought about." (Glover, 2001: 41) Twenty-first- century political theology has as its immediate context the crisis in the present dominant ideology, liberal capitalism, but has constantly to look over its shoulder at the totalitarian ideologies of the last century, which show dangerous signs of re-emergence All this forms the background of my attempt to outline a cruciform political theology which has power as its focus.

Until recently I worked as an Anglican/Methodist Vicar/Minister in two small communities between the Bradford conurbation and the Yorkshire Dales. My main work was pastoral, but I have long been excited (and disturbed) by the relevance of the cross to the big issues of political power. I hope that the exploration contained in this book might contribute to a more effective prophetic ministry by the church in its social witness to the crucified and living Jesus in the light of these issues. My overall purpose is to provide some pointers towards how the church worldwide can reposition itself in the light of the cross so that a cruciform social theology can be more effectively enacted. I hope most of all that this study might provide an impetus to a better informed praxis—as the Peruvian philosopher Mariategui observed, "It is not sufficient in life to think of an ideal: we must make every effort to achieve its realization. . . . .the value of thought is measured by the social action it engenders."[1] Using Sobrino's words, taking the crucified from their cross (and repenting of the times when in history or in the present we have been complicit in crucifixion) is the over-riding aim of Christian social ethics—all else is commentary.

Anyone who attempts to write theology realizes that he or she is building on what has gone before and sees a little beyond their own horizon by standing on the shoulders of the giants of the past. I am particularly aware of standing on the shoulders of such giants of twentieth-century theology as Barth, Bonhoeffer, Rahner and Moltmann. I thank God for their wisdom and hope that the ways in which I have tentatively developed their insights would not meet with too much disapproval from them! I am equally aware of the delicate position occupied by the Christian theologian vis-à-vis practical politics. David Martin usefully describes the potentially confusing distinction in roles between the Christian, who deals with absolutes; the politician, who deals with pragmatics; and the journalist, or commentator, who analyses the situation from the outside.[2] I hope that an incarnational and thus realistic political theology can ameliorate the absolutist / pragmatist distinction, and that the role of the Christian theologian as committed participant as well as observer may overcome the criticism of a commentator's lack of responsibility.

I am very grateful to my son Andrew and daughter Susan for their loving encouragement; to Dr.Kevin Ward, my supervisor for my PhD thesis at Leeds University, for his wise guidance; and to the churches of St. John's Cononley and St. Mary's Bradley, for providing a stimulating and down to earth context for this work. Most of all I thank my wife Mary for her help and support which, as always, goes far beyond proof reading! Her engineer's eye for detail, her ability to detect a weak argument, and her patience in living with such a long term project has meant that this book could not have been written without her.

---

1. Pastoral Team of Bambamarca, *Vamos*, 223.
2. Martin, "Christian," 341–56.

Chapter 1

Introduction

THE CROSS AND POLITICAL THEOLOGY

Alternative histories delight in "what if?" What difference would it have made had Abraham Lincoln not been assassinated? if Halifax had succeeded Chamberlain as the British Prime Minister in May 1940, rather than Churchill? What difference would it have made had the Persians won the battle of Salamis in 479 BCE? Often such alternative histories are merely an academic game—but sometimes they usefully illustrate the contingencies of the past, which, had they turned out another way, could have made the present very different.

It is an established historical fact that Jesus died on a Roman cross outside Jerusalem probably in 33 CE. But what difference would it have made had Jesus died in bed, of old age or illness? The history of the Christian church, if one had arisen, might have been radically different. Possibly the history of the world might have taken a different course. All this is in the realm of conjecture, and, in the end, undiscoverable. What I wish to explore is something rather different, starting from the following thought experiment: What difference would it have made to political theology had Jesus not died, as a political prisoner, on the instrument of execution used by the imperial power of the time to keep potential disturbers of the established order in their place? The fact that Jesus was crucified on a Roman cross automatically put him on the underside of the Roman imperial project, as a threat and challenge to the system of power which constituted the Roman Empire. But could it be that political theology has largely ignored this elephant in the room, especially at those times when the church's political theology and state (or imperial) theology became almost co-terminous, when (in Roger Mitchell's words) the Caesar Christ replaced the counter-political Jesus?[1] Has the cross, in reality, been irrelevant to much political theology? Would political theology really have been significantly different had the resurrection been of one who died of natural causes? These disturbing questions have made me attempt to re-explore the relationship between the cross and political theology.

There is nothing new in using the motif of the cross in political theology. For example, a century ago P.T. Forsyth in 1916 wrote that "the cross of Christ, eternal and universal, immutable and invincible, is the moral goal and principle of nations and affairs."[2] Any Barthian theology (and Forsyth has been widely acknowledged as a proto-Barthian) is bound to emphasize the centrality of the cross. But has the cross remained merely a symbol of suffering disconnected from the actual political events which surrounded it? The cross has certainly played a more general role in illustrating the depths of human sinfulness, but the particular political circumstances in which the crucifixion took place have too often been ignored and their revelatory value neglected.

The dominant tradition in political theology since the mid-nineteenth century has been based upon a reading of more general biblical themes, such as love, incarnation, justice, and sovereignty, and has attempted to construct a prudential political theology from them. In the Anglican tradition, especially in the liberal Anglo-Catholic theology which perhaps disproportionately influenced Anglican social theology in the twentieth century, the focal points were the creation and incarnation, rather than the cross. The influence of F.D. Maurice and *Lux Mundi* remained strong throughout much of the twentieth century. Donald McKinnon in the nineteen sixties valiantly attempted to incorporate a theology of the cross in his Christology and ecclesiology, but it is probably true that, as Atherton observed, "An age of atonement that lasted through to the 1920's [gave way] to an age of incarnation for the rest of the twentieth century."[3] This has been no less true for Anglican political theology than for mainstream liberal theology in general. Evangelicalism, by contrast, has always put the cross at the centre, but has not necessarily translated this into a social theology, and its social activism

---

1. Mitchell, *Church*, 83.
2. Forsyth, *Justification*, 235.
3. Brown, *Divine Humanity*, 7.

has not particularly rested on a theology of the cross. It could therefore be argued that the crucifixion has, in fact, been largely downplayed in the political theology of the first three quarters of the twentieth century, until the huge impact of Moltmann's *The Crucified God*.

I wish, standing on the shoulders of such giants as Barth, Bonhoeffer and Moltmann, to explore what happens when the cross is placed at the centre of a political theology, not to the detriment of an incarnational theology, but as its culmination—I regard the cross as the ultimate expression of incarnation. I intend to investigate the difference made to political theology by the fact that Jesus did not die peacefully, of natural causes, but was crucified, in common with tens of thousands of others, on a Roman cross. How should the crucifixion affect the way in which political theology is formulated and lived out? What are the implications of this for the political role of the church?

I also wish to take up Bonhoeffer's challenge to concreteness. Bonhoeffer, as a recent biographer observed, "sought to rescue the experience of Christ from metaphysical abstraction and capture the fullness of embodied life for the church."[4] Doctrine and ethics have to be worked out in the real encounters of human beings with each other, and cannot rightly be dealt with as abstractions. With reference to the atonement, this insight encourages exploration both of the historical and human factors in the atoning death of Jesus and of the social consequences of that death. Simply to state that Jesus died for our sins, without exploring the particular sins which caused his death is likely to lead to an abstract, rather than a concrete doctrine of atonement, where the social consequences of that atonement can be downplayed. Atonement is thus separated from a huge area of human activity—the political. This is not a retreat into a Kantian cul-de-sac, where doctrine is justified by the ethics it produces—it is simply an attempt to be true to the human history of the divine atonement.

I seek therefore to develop, in critical conversation with three theologians, Yoder, Boff, and Sobrino, a political theology where the significance of the cross is given due weight. I aim not to analyze and bring into dialogue the whole of the teaching of the above theologians, which would be a task far beyond the limits of this study, but to focus on what they have to contribute to its main point—the crucifixion of Jesus and its relevance for political theology. Why these three interlocutors? The obvious interlocutor would be Moltmann, whose work on the cross and political theology has been groundbreaking and inspirational. But as a European belonging to a mainline Protestant church, I wish to look a little beyond those boundaries.

---

4. Marsh, *Strange Glory*, 57.

Since the issues facing Christian political theology and social ethics are increasingly global in their extent, there is a growing need for a global and ecumenical theology, drawing on theological insights and contributions from a variety of cultural and ecclesiastical settings. While issues in social and political theology have ultimately to be interpreted locally and contextually, this is best informed by drawing on as universal and catholic a theology as possible. Boff, a Franciscan Roman Catholic working in Brazil, Sobrino, a Jesuit Roman Catholic working in El Salvador, and Yoder, a Mennonite working in the USA (but also with wide experience of Latin America, including a year teaching in Argentina) represent a wide ecclesiastical and geographical range of background and experience.

Theologically, the truth of God is expressed through a tortured, humiliated, and powerless victim, the crucified Jesus. Since this would seem to indicate a perspective from below, I have chosen as the chief interlocutors two liberation theologians working in Latin America who consciously attempt to do their theology from the perspective of the seemingly powerless victims of history and a Mennonite theologian who stands consciously outside the establishment of political and ecclesiastical power. All three have, moreover, written specifically and extensively about the significance of the cross for political theology.

THE SCANDAL OF YODER'S SEXUAL MISCONDUCT

The publishing agency of the Mennonite Church, Herald Press, has included the following at the beginning of all books by Yoder:

> John Howard Yoder (1927—1997) was perhaps the most well-known Mennonite theologian in the twentieth century. While his work on Christian ethics helped define Anabaptism to an audience far outside the Mennonite Church, he is also remembered for his long-term sexual harassment and abuse of women. At Herald Press we recognize the complex tensions involved in presenting work by someone who called Christians to reconciliation and yet used his position of power to abuse others. We believe that Yoder and those who write about his work deserve to be heard; we also believe readers should know that Yoder engaged in abusive behavior.

As someone engaged in a study of Yoder, I am painfully aware of his sexual misconduct and abuse of women. Over a long period Yoder sexually abused and intimidated, with psychological and sometimes physical violence, over a hundred women, involving both what may have been consensual adultery and, more often, opportunistic or pre-planned non consensual sexual harassment. Some of this abuse appears to have been under the guise of "theological experiments" regarding the sexuality of single women. Anyone who studies Yoder must be horrified by the violence and breach of trust and by the glaring inconsistency with his teaching on peace and nonviolence. Yoder's abuse of women has led admirers to write of "the paradox of how the theology I love coexists with the behavior I hate."[5]

It should hardly need stating, but Christian faith and practice necessitates the absolute physical and psychological inviolability of any human being, and particularly those who are relatively powerless and vulnerable. Such an abusive transgression of this inviolability cannot be dismissed, trivialized, or ignored, and has caused justifiable anger against both Yoder and the Mennonite Church. This must be seen in the continual and disturbing context of the imbalance of male and female power within the worldwide church, which is only just beginning to emerge, slowly and painfully, from the sin of patriarchy. Stephanie Krehbiel notes that "there's always been something oddly masculinist about the way Mennonites teach nonviolence. Mennonite pacifist discourse evolved as a response to the dominant ideal of warrior masculinity, a way for men to justify not going to war; it has never been as fully formed or as celebrated for its challenge to interpersonal violence."[6]

Does this affect an assessment of Yoder's theological work? Yes, without doubt, since, especially for a theological ethicist, actions and teaching cannot easily be separated. Christian theology is not a theoretical science, but a reflection on past and present experience, with the aim of a more truthful and Christ-like living. At what point does our flawed behavior cancel any good we teach in our theology? Or, to put it another way, how far down the scale of human sinfulness does someone have to go to disqualify themselves from being a theologian? This is a perennial problem for theology—in the early church, such heroes of orthodoxy as Cyril of Alexandria and Jerome can hardly be said to have been Christ-like in dealing with theological and political opponents. Two giants of twentieth-century Protestant theology, Barth and Tillich, did not live exemplary lives with regard to their sexual relationships. Beyond theology, the principal author of the Declaration of Independence, Thomas Jefferson, was a slave owner. Carl Schmitt continues to exercise great influence in political philosophy, yet he was a Nazi whose legal work underpinned much of the early Nazi regime. He has been

---

5. Weaver, *John Howard Yoder*, 344.
6. Krehbiel, "Woody Allen Problem," para. 21.

described as the "crown jurist" of the Third Reich, and exercised a pernicious influence in the consolidation of Nazism in the 1930's.

All these brilliant and seminal thinkers had feet of clay, and it is wise to remember that every theologian in the history of the church has been a sinner in need of God's grace, forgiveness, and healing. Not that a general doctrine of sinfulness absolves the individual theologian, such as Yoder, of personal responsibility. One of the themes to be explored in this book is that the reality of sin is never merely general, but exists in specifics, for which the individual is culpable, to a greater or lesser degree.

How do we handle this inevitable gap between orthodoxy and orthopraxis? From the perspective of the theologian or preacher looking honestly at himself or herself, there is an inevitable, realistic, and healthy sense of falling far short of one's beliefs. However, from the perspective of the reader, although he or she knows that the theologian is not perfect, a degree of consistency is rightly expected between their words and actions. A theological teacher is a witness—the important question is whether or not that person is a credible witness.

Can we separate the ideas from the person? Not entirely, as I have argued above. But there is a sense that certain ideas have epistemic value regardless of the character of the person who uttered them. It is not reasonable or possible to ignore truths because the person who discovered or enunciated them was badly flawed. There is a choice—refraining from admitting the source of a truth (thus, in effect, plagiarizing); abandoning some part of a truth because of the moral status of the source; or openly using that person's work, and attempting to build in as many safeguards and warnings as possible. It could be argued that there is a limit to this latter course of action—for example, scientists would baulk at using the results gained from the Nazi concentration camp experiments. But in that case it was not just the persons conducting the experiments but the methods themselves that were corrupt. The fact is that it is impossible to make a study of twentieth-century social ethics, especially with regard to pacifism and peace church theology, without referencing Yoder.

Can we, then, continue to use Yoder as a theological source, or even a theological authority? The key question is this—did what Yoder wrote corroborate and facilitate his behavior, or did he behave in contradiction to his theological writings? If the former is true, then his work is severely vitiated. It seems likely that at least some of his abuse (to what extent, it is impossible to tell) seems to have been justified by Yoder as part of a long standing "legitimate" theological and pastoral enterprise—Yoder's writings on sexuality parallel his better known writings on social ethics over a long period. If the latter is true, and there is a fundamental contradiction between his actions and the main themes of his overall theology, then he is certainly placed on the high end of the continuum of failing to live up to his ideals, but his theological work is not in itself invalidated. I believe, at least in the works I have used in my analysis, which have been concerned with political theology rather than sexual ethics, that the latter is true, that his writings did not serve to corroborate his behavior, and that it is possible profitably to continue to use Yoder's work, at least in this area. Perhaps, though, it might not be so straightforward. There may be elements in Yoder's political theology that make his abuse more possible—and there is the sad fact that exceptionally intelligent people can often persuade themselves that what they are doing, however abusive, is justified. It may be that Yoder used his considerable intellectual powers to that end in rationalizing the unacceptable.

There are clear risks in using Yoder as a theological source which must be honestly faced. I discuss this under three headings—first, aspects of Yoder's political theology which might have facilitated his abuse; second, the danger of normalizing abuse; and, third, the effect on the abused.

At first sight, the inconsistency between Yoder's teaching on nonviolence and his abuse of power seems to be grotesque and inexplicable. Hauerwas, a friend and admirer of Yoder, however, adds the proviso: "We cannot avoid the question of whether his justification for his sexual behavior is structurally similar to his defense of Christian nonviolence."[7] Most notoriously, with his doctrine of revolutionary subordination, Yoder "seems to veer dangerously close to setting up frameworks that would not just allow abuse to happen, but make it somehow noble."[8] This is perhaps one example of the tunnel vision which, as we will see, can sometimes be identified in Yoder's theology, that isolates one element to the detriment of others. This, of course, is not something peculiar to Yoder. More generally, Yoder saw his theological quest as being that of a radical Christian nonconformist in the context of a church with values different from those of society as a whole. Whereas that allowed bold new insights into Christian belief and practice, it also may have led Yoder into the temptation of making his own rules and attempting new paths without the correction of a broader attention to Christian tradition. Unconventionality is not a guarantee of truth. Allied to this is Yoder's overconfidence in the church, which may be paralleled by overconfidence in his own ability to judge the rightness of untried courses of action. As we will see, Yoder can treat the church unrealistically as a sufficiently self critical and coherent body, rather than a sinful group of fallible

7. Hauerwas, "In Defence," para. 15.
8. Weaver, *John Howard Yoder*, 344.

human beings. Any reading of Yoder's theology must take this potentially dangerous tendency into account

Next, there is a danger that by using Yoder's theology as an authoritative source we are somehow normalizing abuse. It could be argued that Yoder committed abuse alongside his theological work, but that was dealt with (eventually) by the church's disciplinary measures, and therefore Yoder can continue as an honored teacher and representative of the church's theology with his theological legacy untouched. Yoder alive might have been a danger to women—Yoder, as a figure of the past, can have this aspect of his life quietly forgotten and he can resume his position as theological genius. However, to glamorize an abuser is to perpetuate both the abuse and the possibility of further abuse by others. The slowness of the Mennonite church to take action (in similar ways to the child abuse scandals in the Roman Catholic Church) illustrates the danger of ecclesiastical self defensiveness and the sense of double betrayal, both by the original act and the church's hesitancy in taking action. It is good that the Mennonite Church has publicly recognized that Yoder's theological legacy is not untouched, in particular by the acknowledgment of Yoder's abuse by the Herald Press as quoted above. If Yoder as a theologian is idolized and his work regarded as somehow canonical within political theology without such an acknowledgment, it would add further hurt and insult to those already affected by his abuse. One of the themes of this book is that the victim's perspective must be privileged, and one of my chief fears in analyzing (and sometimes praising) Yoder's theology is the effect that might have on Yoder's victims who might read such an analysis. I can only say that I am in no way an apologist for his actions, nor do I see him as a theological paragon. Rather, I seek to analyze Yoder's theology critically, in conversation with other theologians. It should be possible to acknowledge the truth in Yoder's theology (and the good in his life) while being painfully conscious of the evil and the destructiveness. I would agree with Lisa Schirch in her comment: "Yoder has a place on our bookshelves, but not on a pedestal. The integrity of pacifist theology does not depend on Yoder."[9]

SOME PRELIMINARY DEFINITIONS

At its simplest, Christian political theology is an attempt to be faithful to the God revealed in Jesus Christ in the arena of politics and reflection upon politics. I would happily endorse the definition of political theology given by Cavanaugh and Scott in the *Blackwell Companion to Political Theology*:

---

9. Weaver, *John Howard Yoder*, 387.

> Theology is broadly understood as discourse about God, and human persons as they relate to God. The political is broadly understood as the use of structural power to organise a society or community of people . . . Political theology is, then, the analysis and criticism of political arrangements (including cultural-psychological, social and economic aspects) from the perspective of differing interpretations of God's ways with the world.[10]

If politics is, in general terms, the gaining and use of power, political theology takes place at the intersection between divine revelation and the interrelationships of human structures of power. All theology is, ultimately, political, in that it reflects the political *sitz im leben* of its practitioners and has political ramifications. Political theology, more specifically, involves doing theology consciously in the light of politics, and politics consciously in the light of theology. While ecclesiology is important in political theology—my concluding chapter discusses how a cruciform political theology can be embodied in the community of the church—the horizon for political theology is not the church, but the kingdom of God.

I have refrained from giving a tight definition to terms such as "the poor," or "the oppressed." The use by liberation theologians of such language describes both the context in which they work and the interpretation they put on that context. Poverty, whether the absolute poverty of lack of food and shelter, or the relative poverty of exclusion from good things taken for granted by large sections of society, forms the background to much of their writing and therefore to much of this study. Oppression implies the existence of both oppressed and oppressors—at its simplest, the oppressed being those who, by the working of a political or economic system are coerced into, or forced to remain in a position of deprivation and suffering by those above them on the socio-economic ladder. Oppression entails the human infliction of needless suffering whether deliberately or through neglect. In the discourse of liberation theology, the oppressed are those who suffer such oppression—oppressors are those who inflict it, deliberately, or through culpable and uncritical participation in an unjust political, social, sexual, or economic system. I am content to utilize this discourse, with which I am in substantial agreement.

---

10. Scott and Cavanaugh, *Blackwell Companion*, xi.

AN AMBIVALENCE TOWARDS THE CROSS, AND A NEW VISION FOR THE CHURCH

In order to establish a genuine political theology of the cross it is necessary to recover the power of the cross to shock. In the ancient world the cross was regarded, understandably, with horror, and the loss of that sense of horror in the modern world has perhaps diminished its power in political theology. The cross, as used by the Romans, was a bloody and obscene act of savagery perpetrated by a cruel and arrogant (if often well meaning) people whose imperial agenda made them ruthless defenders of their power. Crucifixion served to keep in check those outside the imperial power structure who threatened their rule, through the deliberate infliction of the maximum degree of pain and humiliation. The cross, when seen from this perspective, should elicit similar shock and revulsion to that elicited by Auschwitz or the lynch rope. To use the cross as an object of devotion is to enter into a dangerous area of cognitive dissonance and to risk at best sentimentalizing or at worst making God complicit in such suffering. To use the cross as a badge of political success, as in Constantine's *in hoc signo vinces* (in this sign you will conquer) or as a slogan of conquest, as in the Crusaders' *negotium crucis* (the business, or affair, of the cross) is to indulge in a gross contradiction in terms. The cross, rather, must be seen as a protest against suffering, the "cross against the crosses," a protest in which God participates no less than does crucified humanity. A further danger arises for the theologian—that of conceptualizing the cross and failing to translate it into bloody reality. The end point of any theology of the cross is not a felicitous theological formula or a satisfying conceptual statement, but the removal of human beings from the crosses of alienation from God or political and economic oppression.

I have argued that the horizon for political theology must be the kingdom of God, rather than the church. But within the kingdom of God the church's task is to embody an alternative social vision, where the cross must be central. As Moltmann observed, *crux probat omnia* (the cross criticizes everything) and this criticism must begin, but not end, with the church. In the important symposium, *Anglican Social Theology,* Malcolm Brown writes that "a serious social theology for the Church of England, in the sense of a living tradition that can evolve with the changing context while continuing to be informative, has been elusive."[11] He suggests a need for theological and social repositioning, so that a truly Anglican social theology can meet the needs of today's society:

---

11. Brown, "Case for Anglican," 3.

> The test of Anglican social theology is whether it will in the end make the claims of Christ, the vision of Scripture and the rich Christian understanding of being human within community audible to the world at large. As the integration of faith, culture and politics, epitomized in the concept of Christendom, recedes into history, the crucial question is whether the remaining, if residual, elements of Christendom provide sufficient foundations upon which to erect something new, or are merely relics that should be jettisoned as an encumbrance.[12]

In terms of political theology, we do indeed live in interesting times, as the past dominance of the Christendom tradition fades, at least in Europe, with ever accelerating rapidity. My purpose is to sketch a basis for a social theology for this new situation, relevant to the mainstream churches of the west, and to suggest some hints, rooted in the revelation of Christ in the scriptures, as to how those churches might reposition themselves as a result of that theology.

QUESTIONS OF METHODOLOGY

My theological methodology is christocentric—in other words, primarily dependent on God's self-revelation in Jesus Christ. If God's nature and purposes for humankind are revealed in the historical life, death, and resurrection of Jesus, the fact that Jesus' life was ended, not naturally or peacefully, but by a violent political act, must have significant revelatory value in terms of political theology. The crucifixion and the political events which preceded the crucifixion should be seen not as a general and fluid metaphor for human sinfulness as a whole, but as an indication of a particular type of human sinfulness, and Jesus' response provides both a revelation of the divine nature and a model for Christian political action.

Traditionally, theories of the atonement and redemption have centered (rightly) upon the death of Christ on the cross. The concrete political nature of the crucifixion has, however, been sadly neglected. I attempt to explore the particularity of that mode of death, concentrating upon the relevance of this for political theology, but not in isolation from the doctrines of atonement and redemption, which, if they are to be holistic, must include the political. At the very least, the fact that political factors feature so strongly in God's way of atonement and redemption indicates that any such doctrine which does not include a political element must be deficient. A non-political doctrine of atonement, with political elements as, at best,

12. Brown, "Anglican Social Theology," 188.

an optional extra, cannot be sufficient. It is not enough to say that Jesus died violently as a result of human sinfulness, as might perhaps be exemplified by a mugged traveler on the Jericho road who did not have the good fortune of being aided by a Good Samaritan. The violence of the crucifixion was the result of political choices, and it is against the background of those particular political choices, and Jesus' response to them, that both a Christian doctrine of atonement and a Christian political theology must primarily be formulated. This is not, however, to restrict Christian political theology or, indeed, the atonement, to a historical study of first-century Palestinian politics. The political choices which led to the crucifixion are paradigmatic. They continue to be worked out in today's world, and demand a response which, if it is to be Christian, must follow the pattern of Jesus' response. It might be argued that this methodology privileges the cross to the detriment of other aspects of Jesus' life and ministry and, indeed, of other elements of Christian belief. In answer to this, I would stress that the uniqueness and power of the Christian revelation rests primarily upon the scandal of the cross and the subsequent resurrection. The cross is the ultimate consequence of the incarnation and the defining point of any theology which calls itself Christian.

LIMITATIONS AND OMISSIONS

It is perhaps worthwhile to indicate at the outset the limitations of this study. I am not attempting to draw out political implications from certain models of the atonement. This has been widely discussed, for example by Jersak and Hardin in their symposium *Stricken by God? Nonviolent identification and the victory of Christ*. It is impossible to go directly back to Jesus' cross in a manner totally unmediated by subsequent historical and theological interpretations, but I aim to concentrate on the historical crucifixion and its political implications rather than on subsequent more general models of the atonement. Nor do I explore at any great length the political implications of the resurrection, as has been done, for example, by Scott in *Theology, Ideology and Liberation*. I realize that, in the New Testament witness, cross and resurrection go closely together, and a theology which concentrates on one rather than the other runs the risk of imbalance. I emphasize the negatives rather than the positives—removing the crucified from their crosses—while being aware that a more positive *telos* (end in view) for politics is also needed—the peace, wholeness and justice of human flourishing. I am also aware of the dangers of a one-sided theology which errs towards the critical and away from the constructive.

A stringent hermeneutic of suspicion engendered by the cross is necessary, but an over emphasis on the negative can merely lead to stagnation and hopelessness. The cross without the resurrection is not enough, for either soteriology or political theology—but the resurrection must always be that of Jesus crucified, and crucified for political reasons. I am conscious of the dangers of imbalance, and so would present my argument with the proviso that it is inevitably incomplete. Similarly, I make little reference to the Holy Spirit, while recognizing that pneumatology is a necessary component of a full political theology. What follows is not a comprehensive political theology where the whole of biblical revelation is brought to bear in a grand vision of Christian politics, as in O'Donovan's *Desire of the Nations*. I simply attempt to emphasize a neglected, though central, aspect of the Christian revelation vis-à-vis political theology. And I set this not merely in the context of contemporary liberal capitalism, the present dominant ideology, but against the background of the whole twentieth century, when the dominant ideologies were not necessarily liberal or democratic, but fascist or communist.

SOME QUESTIONS THAT ARISE IN THIS STUDY

It may be useful at this point to sketch out eight fundamental questions around which this study revolves.

1. What has the Christian revelation distinctively to offer to political theology?

Does political theology in fact merely baptize secular or pragmatic ideologies with a Christian veneer? What is the place for natural theology in relation to a distinctively Christian revelation? I attempt to incorporate both what could be called a natural and a revelational standpoint. Jesus' humanity means that his political impact can be analyzed historically and sociologically in the same way, for example, as that of Julius Caesar or the Zealots. His crucifixion differed in no human way from that of the multitude of others crucified by the Romans. The politics around Jesus involve human responsibility, analysis and decision making no less than any other politics. Jesus' divinity means that his political actions, and their defining point, the cross, indicate something of God and of God's intentions for human politics. They are thus revelational, distinctive and programmatic for the Christian. In Christian political theology there has been a divide between the christologically based absolutism of theologians such as Yoder, and the non-christological (apparent) compromises of the mainstream. I seek a *via media* between the two.

2. Is Jesus' death necessary or contingent?

If the circumstances of Jesus' death are wholly contingent, then there can be no necessary political theology of the cross. If they are necessary (in the sense of inevitable, both with regard to the character of God and the nature of sinful human power) then a political theology of the cross is not only possible, but essential.

3. What does the suffering of God mean for political theology?

Pascal's observation, that "Jesus will be in agony until the end of the world, and we cannot sleep during this time,"[13] is at the root of this study. Can Christ be "uncrucified" (as in Edwin Muir's poem *The Transfiguration*) while there is human suffering? Does God suffer on the cross in the person of Jesus and then, as it were, leave such suffering behind, or is the cross of Jesus the expression of continuing and eternal divine suffering, which broke into human, and therefore, political history in 33AD? Moltmann's insistence that the suffering of God plays a central role in political theology was a huge and revolutionary breakthrough. I seek to explore this theme further.

4. What is the focus of political theology—the church or the world?

The horizon of political theology must be the kingdom of God, and hence the world. In a sense the cross, being originally a totally secular event, breaks down the division between the religious and the secular. But what is the focal task of political theology? Should it be directed to the church or to the world? This is, ultimately, an unreal distinction, since the church, as a social organization, must embody or at least adumbrate God's will for society as a whole. What is right for the church must be right for the world, and vice versa. But in a post-Christendom situation, where the church / society synthesis has broken down, a starker choice is presented. Is Christian political theology (and Christian ethics as a whole) intended primarily to educate the church, or to provide guidelines for all people—guidelines which will invariably, and increasingly, be seen as irrelevant as the memory of Christianity recedes further into the distance? I attempt a political theology with a double horizon—church and kingdom. Political theology cannot solely be focused on the church, as a reflection on the political nature of Christian practice, which can at its worst be a recipe for self absorbed navel gazing. Nor can it be presented to the world as something universal to which all sensible people can assent, whatever their religious beliefs. This tension, or dialectic, inevitably pervades all twenty-first-century political theology.

---

13. Pascal, *Pensees*, 313.

5. How far does the atonement rest on the historic circumstances of the cross?

Traditional soteriology—whether that of Athanasius, Anselm, Luther or Tridentine Catholicism—rests solely on the fact that Jesus was crucified by sinful humanity, while neglecting the actual history of the cross and the political acts of Jesus which preceded it. The fact that Jesus died seems to be somehow more important than how his death actually occurred. Is this sufficient? Or is this diminished view of the cross positively dangerous? Jennings argues that the old models, which isolate the cross from the mission and ministry of Jesus, "risk a sort of generic victimage that, rather than unleashing the transformation of the world, serves as an alibi for the perpetuation of the structures of domination, division and death."[14] While certainly not discarding the traditional models, I argue that a holistic soteriology gains immeasurably through being fleshed out by a connection both to the historic mission and ministry of Jesus and to the wholeness of the human predicament, which includes corporate as well as individual sin.

6. How far can we use Marxist analysis?

One of the chief criticisms of liberation theology has been its use of Marxist analysis and categories. How far can such a use of Marxism be justified, especially in Britain and the USA where the Marxist traditions have not played, at least overtly, a leading role in political theology? I argue that a critical and selective use of Marxism is possible, in terms of at least some of Marx's analyses, if not his forecasts or solutions. Alongside this criticism is the alleged problem of using liberation theology in countries such as Britain, which (ignoring such churches as the Primitive Methodists and working class Catholicism) has supposedly never had a "church of the poor." The present middle class nature of British Christianity is well established, although given the predominance in the churches of the elderly and female, the economic status of British Christians may well not correspond to their perceived wealthy image. In Britain and the USA, it is argued, the church is one of the institutions of social and cultural power—but does not Latin American Roman Catholicism play a similar role? Also, the church, through its international nature, is in closer touch with the world's poor than virtually any other large scale British and American social organization. While Latin American liberation theology cannot be neatly transferred to a British or American context (it would be contrary to its contextual nature to attempt to do so) the insights gained and the analyses used by the liberation theologians are certainly transferable.

---

14. Jennings, *Transforming*, 223.

7. Is the present marginalization of the church a danger or an opportunity—or both?

A Christian social ethic must continually tread a tightrope, balancing between the comparative purity of the New Testament church, which lacked any political power, and the necessary compromises of the post-Constantinian church, loosely described as Christendom, where Christians were faced with the dilemma of how to use political power. For the British and European churches, Christendom is very definitely over—less so for the American churches, as we shall see. What are the consequences of this for political theology? I argue that the magnitude of the consequences has often been underestimated and the new situation in which the British and European churches find themselves necessitates a new approach to political theology. In many ways, this is an opportunity for the church to rediscover its definitive mission, as its sociological reality approaches more closely that of the New Testament church—with the dying of Christendom there is an increasing convergence between the political position of the early church and that of the marginalized churches of Western Europe (perhaps in contrast with the comparative strength of American Christianity). I am, however, aware of the dangers of what O'Donovan has called a "catacomb consciousness."[15] There is a strong temptation, influenced by the convenience of this convergence, to write off the social ethics of the Christendom period as irrelevant. This is particularly true of Yoder's theology, which involves a radical suspicion of, if not power itself, then certainly the church's accommodation with and chaplaincy to political power, which he labels Constantinianism. (Liberation theology, although utilizing a hermeneutic of suspicion vis-à-vis power, tends more to a pragmatic use of political power when used for the ends of justice and freedom.) But the fact that there happens to be a good sociological fit between the early church and the postmodern church does not necessarily mean that the early church's political ethic is sufficient for today.

Billings writes of the post Christendom church, "The church's rediscovery of the tradition of nonviolence was as much a sign of its own weakness as of any recovery of virtue."[16] A minority status does not automatically ensure spiritual health, and the benefits of distinctiveness must be balanced by a loss of political relevance which, though it may make the church more sure of itself, does not necessarily benefit the kingdom of God. The Yoderian stance has been severely criticized, for example by Millbank, who asks if anti-Constantinianism actually risks a form of Marcionism in concentrating

---

15. Doerksen, *Beyond Suspicion*, 149.
16. Billings, *Dove*, 152.

on the person of Jesus without regard for a fuller political theology found in the Old Testament.

8. Christology or Jesuology?

A similar criticism is made powerfully by O'Donovan,[17] who finds Yoder's view of power too narrow and dependent on a Jesuology, rather than a Christology, arguing furthermore that the resurrection, rather than the political circumstances around the cross, is the key to Christian politics. To move too automatically from Jesus' political context to today's is seen as naïve and narrow—narrow in that following Jesus must involve political discipleship beyond the church. A cross based theology which merely engenders suspicion of political power is an insufficient basis for a holistic Christian doctrine of power, which must, somehow, recognize a "hidden counsel of God which worked also through Caiaphas and Pilate."[18]

I fully acknowledge the strength of O'Donovan's criticism and, in my study of Yoder, seek to keep it in mind as a reminder of the need for a comprehensive doctrine of political power and practice. However, I am equally aware of the fact that while Christ, through the resurrection is King, he is Crucified King; that O'Donovans' emphasis on how to rule justly is best exercised by testing that rule from the perspective of the crucified; that while an exaggerated suspicion of political power is indeed a danger, throughout its post-Constantinian history the church has consistently erred in the other direction; and that a Christology that is not firmly anchored in a historical Jesuology can become dangerously free floating.

A PRELIMINARY OUTLINE

My argument can be sketched in outline as follows. In the first part (chapters 2 to 10) I engage in dialogue with the three chosen theologians, Yoder, Boff, and Sobrino, and attempt a close analysis and criticism of their political teaching concerning the cross. In the second part (chapters 11 and 12) I seek a wider perspective, attempting to use insights gained in the first part to construct, first, a theology of power and, second, a framework for a corporate outworking of a cruciform political theology.

In more detail—in order that a subsequent theology of the cross might be securely grounded, I begin in chapters 2 and 3 by examining the foundations. I pay particular regard to coherence—in chapter 2, the coherence of the cross based political theologies of Yoder, Boff, and Sobrino with the

---

17. O'Donovan, *Desire*, esp. chapter 4.
18. O'Donovan, *Desire*, 121–22.

totality of their theologies; in chapter 3, the coherence of their accounts of the historical circumstances in which the crucifixion took place with the historical evidence. In particular, I ask whether they are justified in constructing a definitive theology from those accounts. These foundations I regard as essential, in that a political theology of the cross cannot be firmly established unless it coheres with an overall theological schema and can be firmly rooted in history, as far as that can be accurately ascertained. At the end of these two chapters I summarize what can be carried forward to form a basis for a constructive political theology of the cross. (A reader who wishes to proceed quickly to the heart of this study might prefer to begin at chapter 4 and read chapters 2 and 3 later.)

In the next three sections I attempt to build on the foundations. First, in chapters 4, 5, and 6, I draw from Yoder, Boff, and Sobrino a cruciform response to suffering and oppression. In chapter 4 I examine how each theologian treats the cross as definitive for Christian political ethics. In Yoder, I indicate the necessity of redefining the nature of Christian politics as cruciform; in Boff and Sobrino the cross as a protest against suffering in the name of the crucified God revealed by Jesus. In chapter 5 I describe the three theologians' interpretation of the cross and political discipleship: in Yoder, the cross as a mark of radical nonconformity in imitation of the crucified; in Boff and Sobrino, the cross as inculcating a sacrificial spirituality of martyrdom. In chapter 6 I discuss the cross in relation to violence and the appropriate response for a Christian: in Yoder, his christological and cruciform pacifism (alongside comparisons with other forms of pacifism); in Boff and Sobrino the question of violence in response to political oppression. Again, at the end of these chapters I summarize the above and outline a theology and spirituality of cruciform and costly imitation of the nonviolent crucified God.

In the next section, in chapters 7 and 8, I analyze the theologies of Yoder, Boff, and Sobrino in relation to two overlapping sociological communities: in chapter 7, the cruciform people, the church in its political responsibility, and in chapter 8, the crucified people, those who suffer oppression and injustice. In my discussion of the cruciform people, I concentrate chiefly on Yoder's doctrine of a new way of doing politics through a cruciform church. In my discussion of the crucified people I concentrate on Sobrino's emphasis on solidarity between the poor and the crucified Christ. Again, at the end of this section I draw together themes which emerge from the above—the meaning of Christian responsibility in the light of the cross, how the cross is manifested in community, the nature and use of powerlessness, and the crucified people as a criterion for political action.

In the third section of building on the foundations, chapters 9 and 10, I examine the cross in relation to eschatological hope and to divine and human power and powerlessness—Christian hope rests on the power of God manifested in the resurrection of the crucified. In chapter 9 I discuss Yoder's eschatological ethic of faith and hope in the "lamb who was slain," and Boff and Sobrino's proclamation of hope for the oppressed through the cross and resurrection. Chapter 10 moves to a discussion of the cruciform divine providence which forms the ground for that hope. Yoder's kenotic teaching on the cross as the key to God's providential action in overcoming "the powers" is paralleled by a discussion of Boff and Sobrino's doctrine of power in the light of the cross. I conclude this section, as before, by summarizing the themes of hope, power and the cross in the light of the resurrection and by outlining a theology of a cruciform hope based on a kenotic doctrine of divine power.

In the second part of the study I depart from a close analysis of the three theologians, and attempt to gain a wider perspective on some of the themes which have been identified. First, in chapter 11, I discuss the cross in relation to divine power and political power. and argue that the cross exercises a critical function vis-à-vis political power, and defines the *telos*, or end-in-view of political power. I analyze the nature of power, using the distinction between power *over* and power *to*, and then turn again to the Pauline doctrine of kenosis, describing the kenotic power and "weakness" of God in the light of the cross, before attempting to construct a kenotic and cruciform political ethic.

In chapter 12 I conclude by discussing how a cross based theology might be socially embodied. I return to the themes of the cruciform and crucified people, with special reference to the church in Britain and the USA, and end with a description of a cruciform church, based upon the beatitudes, as a community of solidarity, resistance, and hope.

Chapter 2

The Context of the Political Theology of the Cross in Yoder, Boff, and Sobrino

Before proceeding to an analysis of the use of the cross in the political theology of Yoder, Boff, and Sobrino, it is necessary to set this in the context of the totality of their theologies. How far do their more general theologies of the cross cohere with their more specifically political theologies? As will be seen, such a distinction is not always clear cut, since, methodologically, the political cannot be neatly separated from the rest. I do not attempt a detailed exposition of each theologian's doctrine of the cross, but pay special attention to the role of Christology (the significance of the person on the cross); to soteriology (how the cross is instrumental in salvation); and to the political and ecclesiological context of their work.

As a basis for what follows in this study, I seek to demonstrate first that their political readings of the cross are not arbitrary additions to their theologies, but firmly situated within and coherent with their overall theological stance and second, that the political nature of the cross has definite revelatory value and is not simply contingent to a transactional soteriological purpose. (My use of the word transactional describes a doctrine of atonement seen primarily in terms of the intra-trinitarian relationship between God the Father and Jesus the Son, its historical outworking in the cross and resurrection, and its application to humanity through the Holy Spirit. I would not wish in any way to deny the truth and validity of such a view of atonement, which I regard as basic to salvation, but seek to extend its meaning.)

A) THE CONTEXT OF THE CROSS IN YODER

The Importance of Community—Mennonite and Ecumenical

Yoder is particularly concerned to root his theology in the church community, and regards it as his aim that his ethics should mould and guide that community. His nonfoundationalism can perhaps be read most accurately in his taking the church community, rather than a preconceived philosophical position, as his epistemological and hermeneutical starting point. His is explicitly a church theology, shaped by and intended to shape his context. For his social ethics, the distinction between church and world is crucial— Christian social ethics are primarily for Christians, and only of secondary and indirect relevance to those outside the ecclesiastical body, which he sees as a voluntary organization, freely constituted rather than imposed by the authority of the state.

Yoder writes as a Mennonite, and that allegiance is closely bound up with his theology. The cross, both in Mennonite soteriology and in the history of a community which has frequently suffered persecution, has always been central to Mennonite belief. Yoder's membership of a believers' church, a church visibly identified as other by "baptism, discipline, morality and martyrdom"[1] provides themes which run through his theology. His theological privileging of freedom and choice, and the willingness of a non-coercive God to respect that freedom, which, it will be argued, is one of the major themes of his theology (especially with regard to the cross) is firmly rooted in the free choice of adult baptismal membership of the church. The distinctive and demanding cross bearing discipleship advocated by Yoder is undergirded and reinforced by a strong church discipline. The Mennonite sense of a morality, both personal and social, which is not necessarily shared by the world and which may be antithetical to the world's values, necessitates a refusal to participate in the generally accepted violence of the world, and hence involves a readiness to accept the often painful consequences of that refusal. This leads to one of the most significant Yoderian marks of the church—martyrdom, both in the sense of the inevitable suffering of the distinctively Christian church and in the powerful witness inherent in that suffering. It is difficult to conceive of Yoder's theology, especially with regard to the cross, divorced from its Mennonite context.

Yoder, however, cannot be read solely as a Mennonite theologian. An authoritative study of Yoder by Mark Nation, entitled *Mennonite Patience, Evangelical Witness, Catholic Convictions* illustrates the breadth of Yoder's theology. As a contributor to the radical Evangelical community/magazine

---

1. Yoder, *Royal Priesthood*, 56.

Sojourners and keynote speaker at the founding meeting of Evangelicals for Social Action in Chicago in 1973 Yoder was sufficiently trusted by evangelicals to address that section of the church which is notoriously suspicious of outsiders.[2] His seminal work, *Politics of Jesus* was a major influence on the revival of a more socially conscious and left wing evangelicalism. Yoder was (not always to his satisfaction) identified as an evangelical by both evangelicals and non-evangelicals.[3] With regard to his theology of the cross, this is highly significant, given the stress placed by evangelicalism on the centrality of the cross and the emphasis on penal substitution as the privileged interpretation of the cross. Yoder in fact diverges significantly from this mainstream evangelical substitutionary reading of the cross, but continues to engage evangelicals by emphasizing both the centrality of the cross for Christian faith in general and the broader significance of the cross for social ethics (which has been a historic gap in evangelical soteriology, the acknowledgment of which has contributed to the growth of a politically more radical evangelicalism). Yoder's catholic sympathies are seen explicitly in his teaching for thirty years at the (Roman Catholic) University of Notre Dame, but more generally in his insistence that his theology is not sectarian but for the whole church, and that his social ethics are an interpretation of what is inherent in the Chalcedonian formulations.

Barthian Christocentrism

If the church, in its present form as community and in its doctrinal formulations from the past, gives the context for Yoder's theology, his methodology, at least for his social ethics, can most appropriately be described as a Barthian christocentrism. For Yoder, as for Barth, traditional Christendom, with Christianity the default position for society as a whole, is over. The church is a distinctive minority community, marked out from the rest of society by its confession of faith. In this, Yoder shares one of Barth's core beliefs in social ethics. He writes:

> The definition of the gathering of Christians is their confessing Jesus Christ as Lord. The definition of the whole of human society is the absence of that confession.[4]

From a European viewpoint of radically declining church membership and influence, it seems significant that neither Yoder nor Barth seem to

2. Carter, *Politics*, 15.
3. Nation, *John Howard Yoder*, xx–xxi.
4. Yoder, *Politics*, 108.

envisage a situation where the Christian church is in a very small minority position. Barth wrote at a time when the Christian churches in Europe were certainly in a numerical minority, but retained a considerable degree of strength and influence. The American churches which form Yoder's theological backdrop still retain that position of strength and influence. For a more radical (and realistic) critique, Bonhoeffer's teaching on the powerlessness of a sidelined church speaks perhaps more relevantly to the contemporary European church.

Yoder's social ethic is based on uncompromising obedience to the Lordship of Jesus Christ—especially the crucified Christ—and an exploration of the radical implications of his exemplarity. Christian social ethics, if they are to be Christian and not just "natural human ethics as held to by Christians among others,"[5] must be controlled, firmly and definitively, by the example of Jesus. The centrality of the example of Jesus for social ethics cannot be overemphasized in Yoder's theology, and this exemplarity, Yoder insists, must not be diluted by any other authority or ethical norm, whether "nature, reason, creation, or reality"[6] or by an appeal to "trinitarian" social ethics, which removes, or at least weakens, the definitiveness of Jesus. The incarnation is the ultimate revelation of the nature and purpose of God, and is normative in its historical particularity. Yoder criticizes the incarnationalist reading (popular in certain Anglican traditions) according to which God, by taking on human nature, thereby ratifies human nature as revelation. Rather, "God broke through the borders of our standard definition of what is human, and gave a new, formative definition in Jesus."[7] This means that the historical deeds, attitudes, intentions, and strategies of Jesus (as far as we can read them) have revelatory value. Moreover, if the whole life of Jesus is revelatory, the cross, as the culmination and inevitable result of Jesus' actions and teaching, has supreme revelatory significance. The cross must not be isolated as an ahistorical symbol either of sin or of sacrifice, as is the tendency (paradoxically) in both Christian realism and the liberal optimism of much twentieth-century pacifism. Rather, the historical choices made by Jesus which led to the crucifixion have no less revelatory value than the fact of the crucifixion itself. To see the cross in isolation, solely as an expiatory sacrifice, a substitutionary penalty, in terms simply of an intra-trinitarian transaction, or merely as a symbol, however important, of human sinfulness, is seriously to detract from both its salvific and revelatory value. Yoder attacks this approach by describing it as follows: "Jesus had to die for

---

5. Yoder, *Politics*, 10.
6. Yoder, *Politics*, 19.
7. Yoder, *Politics*, 99.

reasons unrelated to his social humanity. Therefore the social humanity of how that necessity came to be carried out is unimportant"[8]—unimportant, that is, apart from as a broad brush illustration of the general sinfulness of humanity. Yoder characterizes this approach as one of the "docetic ways of avoiding the political Jesus," and hence stresses the need to take the cross into account when formulating social ethics.

Chalcedonian Christology

If, for Yoder, the cross is central to Christian theology and social ethics, the question of the identity of the crucified is also of the utmost importance. For Yoder, an orthodox Chalcedonian reading of the incarnation, grounded in the historical acts and teaching of Jesus, is at the root of his Christology:

> What becomes of the meaning of the incarnation if Jesus is not normative man? If he is a man but not normative, is this not the ancient ebionitic heresy? If he is somehow authoritative but not in his humanness, is this not a new Gnosticism?[9]

Yoder repeatedly looks back to the orthodox Christology expounded in the early creeds. His social ethic, he claims, is a drawing out of the implications of the church's credal confessions, not by propounding a new Christology but by taking the Nicene and Chalcedonian definitions with the utmost seriousness. For Yoder, if Jesus is not, in Chalcedonian terms, true God (in that he definitively reveals the eternal purposes of God) and true man (in that those eternal purposes are revealed in a fully human life) his theology, and especially his social ethic, becomes weak and rootless. Since his social ethic depends upon the fact that God reveals himself definitively in Christ, any diminution of a high Christology is fatal to his project, and removes both divine authority and a sense of being in accord with, as Hauerwas put it in another context, "the grain of the universe."[10] For Yoder, ethics is a reflection on reality as intended by God, a reality which in turn flows from the divine nature as exemplified in the human life and death of Jesus. His theological method, in essence, is to return continually to the narrative of the life of Jesus as represented in the gospels and interpreted in the epistles, and to develop a theology from a reading of that narrative. Discipleship is the process of corresponding faithfully in the present time to the divine action in Jesus Christ in history. For Yoder's political theology, the notion of

8. Yoder, *Politics*, 99.
9. Yoder, *Politics*, 10.
10. Hauerwas, *Grain*.

correspondence between the disciple (and the disciple's cross bearing) and the cross bearing action of God in Christ is central.

Soteriology

How does Yoder's overall soteriology cohere with his political reading of the cross? Three themes recur—first, the elimination of any hiatus between the cross and preceding events; second, the incorporation into soteriology of the need for a potentially costly discipleship; and third, the emphasis on Christ's (and God's) respect for human freedom. In accordance with his conversational style of theology, Yoder is reluctant to set out a definitive and systematic soteriology. The closest he comes is in a repeated series of lectures to the Mennonite Biblical Seminary collected in *Preface to theology: Christology and Theological Method*. It is worthwhile examining this in some detail, as it demonstrates the coherence, even identity, of Yoder's political theology of the cross with his overall theology. Yoder's political theology is not even to be seen as a deduction from what could be described as his more doctrinal theology—both are of one piece. Yoder lists New Testament and post-biblical models for explaining why Christ had to die.[11] He is especially critical of the Anselmian satisfaction theory, in that it sees God as the object, rather than the agent of reconciliation, and uses a substitutionary doctrine not supported by the New Testament. Salvation in the New Testament is not so much concerned with guilt or punishment, but "reconciliation (reestablishment of communion) and obedience, i.e., discipleship."[12]

Yoder's chief criticism of the Anselmian theory is that it has little to say about discipleship and obedience. Moreover, the actual historical life and death of Jesus—the circumstances of the crucifixion, the reasons why Jesus' opponents brought about his death, his teaching and actions which led to his death—have little relevance to the Anselmian theory. According to this theory, "the only obedience that is required of him is that he committed no sin."[13] While admitting the moral and spiritual force of the Anselmian soteriology, Yoder describes it as "not a biblically satisfactory theory."[14] An alternative theory, suggests Yoder, while taking sin as seriously as Anselm, has to include those themes neglected by Anselm, particularly the faith union with Christ, and most of all must take Jesus seriously as a teacher

---

11. Yoder, *Preface*, 209.
12. Yoder, *Preface*, 221.
13. Yoder, *Preface*, 224.
14. Yoder, *Preface*, 224.

and moral leader within his contemporary culture and against his political background:

> We would seek some relationship between atonement and his talking about the kingdom, his forgiving people, his teaching people, his making of people a church—a body of disciples—his sending people into mission. We would see his getting crucified and his being raised from the dead as a social process.[15]

Also integral to a full soteriology is a cruciform discipleship, central to the biblical account but absent in Anselm:

> The cross of Christ demands and enables the cross of the Christian. We might try to affirm the unity of obedience, sanctification with justification . . . the unity of these in biblical thought links the unity of our obedience with God's work in Christ, his cross with our cross, his death, our dying with him.[16]

Yoder characteristically declines to set out a definitive model for atonement, but offers the following presuppositions or components necessary for an adequate doctrine.[17] First, a real identification-communion with God in Christ is necessary for the believer, expressed by such terms as "faith union," "abide in me," and "in Christ." Second, God's way of dealing with evil is through an agape which expresses itself in non-resistance. And, third, there is a real difference between church and world, and the Christian faith is distorted if this is not clearly kept in mind. It is significant that this part of Yoder's work dates from 1954 and can be seen directly to prefigure themes which emerge strongly in *Politics of Jesus* and thereafter—discipleship, non-resistance, and the world-church separation. Another presupposition is the freedom of humanity to choose, and God's respect for that choice. Humanity is always given the freedom to choose whether to obey or disobey, and God's honoring of that freedom is basic to the divine-human relationship. God takes the risk of disobedience, since "God is agape and agape respects the freedom of the beloved"[18] —with no exceptions. God's total respect for that freedom leads to humanity's lost state, since overcoming that freedom by a divine fiat would contradict the nature of agape. This tension between God's desire both to save and to respect human freedom is central to Yoder's soteriology. Yoder identifies two expressions of agape in God's salvific work—first, restoring sinful humanity to communion and obedience while,

15. Yoder, *Preface*, 226.
16. Yoder, *Preface*, 226.
17. Yoder, *Preface*, 227.
18. Yoder, *Preface*, 228.

at the same time respecting humanity's freedom to sin: "How, in short, to reveal love to man without forcing it upon him, which forcing would contradict love."[19] We will see that a similar tension is found in Yoder's social ethics between the church's necessary loving involvement in political issues and a non-resistant refusal to take political responsibility, between the demand actively to express love in political and social ethics and the necessity of "letting be" the sinner.

The Obedient Non-resistance of Jesus

The answer to the human predicament lies in Christ's obedience (within the social and political circumstances of his time) to the absolute, freedom-respecting, agape of God, which necessarily involves his non-resistance to those who would do him harm. Yoder sees the obedience of the perfect human being, Jesus Christ, living in free communion with God and loving humankind with divine love, as the focal point of atonement. Jesus respected the liberty of sinful humanity to the extent that he did not resist their sinfulness but himself bore the consequence of that sinfulness. This non-resistance demonstrates the fullness of divine agape in respecting to the utmost human freedom to sin against God and God's human representative. In Yoder's interpretation of the temptations, Jesus is faced with a series of short cuts which would undermine human freedom to reject him and thus to reject God. Yoder locates this within the political choices available to Jesus. One possibility was to use violent means of self defense. Another was the defenselessness of the cross:

> Since murder is the worst sin, as it takes away freedom most utterly, so the utmost in agape is the utmost in non-self-defense, to undergo murder, respecting the other's freedom to commit the worst sin out of love for the sinner-murderer. Which is what Jesus did.[20]

Jesus died a (self) sacrificial death in allowing God to express agape through his non-resistance, which culminated in the crucifixion. "His sinlessness, his obedience, is what he offered to God, and that sinlessness, utter faithfulness to love, cost his life in a world of sinners."[21]

If some of the strengths of Yoder's subsequent theology are prefigured here, so also are some weaknesses; Yoder can justly be accused of

---

19. Yoder, *Preface*, 229.
20. Yoder, *Preface*, 230.
21. Yoder, *Preface*, 230.

the tendency to isolate and absolutise certain concepts, and hence to lose perspective. It could be argued that Yoder makes this "agape-respect" for freedom a mechanistic, legalistic concept, unrelated to any realistic human analogy of agape; a parent would, out of genuine agape, override the ideal of absolute freedom in order to restrain (and punish) a child who might hurt itself or others.

Resurrection and Faith

The resurrection is not to be detached from what precedes it—rather, it ratifies this sacrifice of the cross, and

> vindicates the rightness, the possibility, the effectiveness of the way of the cross. But our present concern is the place of the resurrection in the dialectic of God's love, *which sought to save man by respecting his freedom to sin so far as to die at his hands.*[22]

These words (in my italics) seem to sum up Yoder's soteriology. The resurrection is the ultimate endorsement of God's love which persists even when human beings do their worst to the agent of that love. The resurrection of the crucified Jesus thus preserves both elements of the salvific love of God; it overcomes sin without denying freedom to the sinner. This act of God in Christ has to be appropriated by human faith; a faith identified not merely as intellectual assent, but as faith union. The Christian appropriates by repentance and faith the obedience of Christ, repentance being interpreted as an ethical "turning round of the will."[23] In a similar way, faith is not merely the acceptance of something external which has been done on one's behalf, but rather an obedient discipleship and faith union with the one who has, by his obedience, made that relationship possible. Forgiveness is interpreted not as a transactional cancelling of sin, but as a restoration of obedient relationship. Yoder concludes: "This view of salvation as restored communion and consequently restored capacity to obedience fits, better than Anselm's view, all the New Testament figures for atonement."[24] Salvation, as restored communion with God affording the capacity for costly and obedient discipleship, based upon the sacrificial and non-resistant obedience of the crucified Christ, is the starting point of Yoder's political theology.

Can the cross bear the hermeneutical weight Yoder places upon it?

---

22. Yoder, *Preface*, 251.
23. Yoder, *Preface*, 251.
24. Yoder, *Preface*, 231.

As one who adopts the christocentric, Barthian, methodology, Yoder regards the person and acts of Christ, and especially the crucified Christ, as the key to his interpretation of Christian politics. Yoder is concerned to stress that he is not propounding a new Christology, but merely exploring the political implications of the orthodox Christology as traditionally taught and accepted by the church. The exemplarity of Christ, in the tradition of "every act of Christ is for our instruction" is at the heart of his theology. Logically, therefore, Yoder must draw his theology from the totality of Christ and his impact on first-century society, without isolating certain aspects to the detriment of others. Does he, in fact, over-isolate the cross? Or does Yoder treat as definitively revelatory aspects of the cross which are merely contingent to its salvific purpose? We have already noted Yoder's possible tendency to overemphasize and absolutise. Against this criticism, Yoder strives to locate the cross as an integral and inevitable consequence of Jesus' ministry. The cross, for Yoder, is not an accident or a divine transaction worked out in isolation from the rest of Jesus' ministry, but the culmination and consummation of the whole. In *Politics of Jesus* Yoder is at pains to stress the cross as the inevitable consequence of the political choices of Jesus. Moreover, he shows that this is precisely how the cross was interpreted by his first followers, as evidenced by them adopting a similar cruciform and cross-risking lifestyle. The political cross is also at one with the overall salvific purpose of God—the pattern of non-resistant respect for human freedom is as much part of Yoder's doctrine of atonement as of his political theology. Given the traditional christological framework of Christ the revealer of the divine nature and purposes, Yoder's emphasis on the cross as essential to understanding and formulating a doctrine of Christian politics is justifiable. The cross is the radicalization of the incarnation, where the incarnation comes to its sharpest point. Yoder recognizes this and seeks to draw out its implications.

B) THE CONTEXT OF THE CROSS IN BOFF AND SOBRINO

Theology in the Service of Liberation

As with Yoder, the ecclesial and social background against which Boff and Sobrino write significantly colors their theology. Both work as liberation theologians in Latin America, where poverty, violence and political oppression form a constant theme. Boff lived through the military dictatorship in Brazil, one of the more prosperous of the Latin American countries, but still divided by gross inequality. Sobrino is rooted in the context of the bloody civil war in El Salvador which claimed thousands of lives, mostly of innocent peasants, at the hands of military and paramilitary death squads.

Boff's work is intended to be a practical theology designed for use in Christian liberative praxis. The ultimate criterion for the truth of theology is practical—for Boff, the accent throughout is on discipleship exercised with a prior commitment to human liberation, praxis being the essence of spirituality. Despite the Marxist influenced terminology, this need mean no more than James' "faith by itself, if it has no works, is dead."(Jas 2:17, NRSV) Boff, however, goes beyond this to the distinctive emphasis of liberation theology that praxis, commitment to liberation, is epistemologically prior to doxa, and that the standpoint from which theology is done decisively affects the content of that theology, the perspective being that of the poor, who provide the key to interpreting the gospel.

The setting for Boff's theology of the cross is the suffering of the poor of Latin America, which Boff links intimately with the suffering of the crucified Jesus. His theology is consciously and intensely contextual, in that it both reflects and serves its context. For Boff, the cross cannot be understood or interpreted without constant reference to its parallels today in the suffering of the poor and in their struggle for liberation from that poverty. The fact that God continues to suffer in the poor and oppressed is integral to Boff's theology of the cross, and crucial to his methodology. In his introduction to *Way of the Cross, Way of Justice*, he makes his programmatic statement: "Theology is *ante et retro oculata*; it has two eyes. One looks back toward the past, where salvation broke in; the other looks toward the present, where salvation becomes reality here and now."[25] This is not peculiar to Boff or to liberation theology, but it is given extra meaning by Boff's insistence that there is a continuity and even an equivalence between the sufferings of Jesus and those of the poor and oppressed today. The cross bearing of Jesus is paralleled by the contemporary cross bearing of Jesus' brothers and sisters, in whom Jesus' passion is replicated in history. This is the basis for Boff's spirituality of the cross, emphasizing the present encounter with God which is the basis of any spirituality.

Boff's writings on the cross and Christology are chiefly directed not so much to the poor themselves as to those within the church who serve the poor. A possible exception is *Way of the Cross, Way of Justice*, which can perhaps best be read as a popularization of Boff's work on Christology and soteriology. It takes the form of meditations on the fifteen Stations of the Cross, a theme familiar in Catholic devotion, in simple, non-technical

---

25. Boff, *Way*, viii.

language and blank verse. However, in general, it is true to say that the poorest themselves are not the most likely readers of Boff's work. For example, in chapter 10 of *Passion of Christ, Passion of the World*, which summarizes the themes of the work, emphasis is given to preaching the cross. This emphasis may relate to Boff's membership of the Franciscan order, where proclamation and action are not finely differentiated. Of equal significance is the intended audience for Boff's work—not so much the poor themselves (for whom poverty is not a choice) but those Christians who have made a decision to place themselves alongside the poor (i.e., the practitioners of liberation theology) and act, in the Gramscian sense, as organic intellectuals.

Although originating from Spain, Sobrino, like Boff, is a Latin American liberation theologian, differing in spiritual background (Jesuit rather than Franciscan), geographical location (El Salvador rather than Brazil), and language (Spanish rather than Portuguese). Both Sobrino and Boff share in a theology influenced by Moltmann and Marx, but, far more important than these, share a *locus theologicus* of ministry in a context of suffering and poverty. This, especially, gives Sobrino's theology of the cross a radically personal edge, springing as it does from his close acquaintance with those martyred in El Salvador, especially Archbishop Romero, assassinated in 1980, and Sobrino's six Jesuit colleagues who together with their housekeeper and her daughter were murdered by a death squad in 1989. Sobrino's theology of the cross is thus formed not in a position of detachment, but through involvement in the struggles for liberation. If, as Sobrino argues, the best location for a *theologia crucis* is in the midst of those experiencing similar crosses, his personal propinquity to contemporary crosses give his theology a certain hermeneutical privilege. Whereas European theology takes place, necessarily, against a post Auschwitz background, Latin American theology is constructed actually within an Auschwitz like situation where contemporary "crucifixions" are an ever present reality.[26]

An Orthodox Christology from Below

In chapter 1 of *Passion of Christ, Passion of the World* Boff begins by setting out the presuppositions that inform his work. There are two perspectives from which he is writing, both giving him a viewpoint from below. Theologically, he interprets the person of Christ from the point of view of a synoptic, Antiochene, Franciscan Christology, beginning from the humanity of Jesus, rather that his divinity. Sociologically, his *locus* is the poor, in both

---

26. Sobrino, *Jesus the Liberator*, 195.

their oppression and their resistance to oppression.[27] This orientation is in line with his role as a liberation theologian, doing his theology and interrogating the scriptures from the perspective and for the benefit of those at the grassroots. His motivation is twofold—the uncovering of those factors that caused Jesus' rejection and execution, especially his "praxis that threatened the status quo of his time,"[28] and the application of the significance of the historical crucifixion to the faith of today

It is important to note that from below describes the perspective, rather than the content, of Boff's Christology, which can best be described as traditionally orthodox. His method is of great importance, as he sees the New Testament interpretation of Jesus, and especially the cross, as developing in response to the various pastoral challenges (most of all the challenge of persecution) faced by the early Christian community. The corollary Boff draws from this is a freedom to develop a Christology and soteriology in response to contemporary challenges to Christian community. This development of doctrine emerges very clearly in Boff's interpretation of the cross—not denying the biblical and traditional explanations, but extending the meaning to answer contemporary questions.

Similarly, Sobrino's Christology can be described as essentially orthodox and traditional, but with an emphasis on contextuality. Sobrino is concerned to describe a "Latin American historical Jesus"—that is, his Christology begins, not from above but from the historical Jesus as interpreted with the special insights of Latin America. This is especially relevant to what is probably the most significant contribution Sobrino has made to Christology, linking Jesus to the contemporary "crucified people" in a reciprocal relationship. The nature and theological significance of the crucified people is derived from the crucified Jesus, and a theology arising out of the crucified people provides insights into the nature and significance of the crucified Jesus. Sobrino is much influenced by the philosopher Zubiri, for whom a subject's status is constituted by the relations in which that subject is embedded. Hence relationality plays an important part in Sobrino's Christology, which begins by analyzing the historical relations in which Jesus is embedded. The two basic christological relations are to "the kingdom of God and to the God of the kingdom." Also of great significance are Jesus' relations with his subsequent followers, which, in the light of the cross, can be seen in history as that reciprocal relationship between the crucified Jesus and the crucified people.

---

27. Boff, *Passion*, xi.
28. Boff, *Passion*, 2.

Again, as with Boff, "from below" describes the perspective, rather than the content, of Sobrino's Christology. Sobrino certainly makes a distinction between the eternal Sonship of Christ, confessed in the christological creeds and dogmas, and the realization of that Sonship in history, expressed in the historical Jesus' relationship with God. It is true, also, that the Vatican document detailing criticisms of Sobrino's theology, the *Notification on the works of Father Jon Sobrino, SJ,* censures Sobrino for tending towards assumptionism, a form of adoptionism whereby the historical human Jesus was "assumed" by the divine Son of God. These criticisms, however, can be leveled at many Christologies which begin from the perspective of below, and would seem to be a matter of perspective and emphasis rather than content. A more serious criticism is that Sobrino downplays Christ's uniqueness, especially the uniqueness of his cross. This arises, most of all, from Sobrino's linking of the theme of the crucified people to Christology. If the historical community which derives from Christ through relationality with him crucified is not solely the church, but a more diffuse and general crucified people, then such an interpretation of Christ is more vulnerable to the charge of pluralism or lack of specificity than a Christ whose being is tightly defined by ecclesiastical tradition and is confined to a community of explicit faith. This criticism points to an important fault line between liberation and more traditional theologies which will be explored later at greater depth. If Jesus is portrayed merely as one of the millions of crucified people in history, even as an "elder brother," this continuity between his crucifixion and theirs, it is argued, might detract from his uniqueness. In fact, however, the converse would appear to be true. The reciprocal relationship between Jesus and the crucified peoples certainly would not be possible without a radical continuity between them. Yet without a traditionally orthodox Christology there would be little point in Sobrino describing the suffering of people as crucified, rather than machine gunned, starved, impoverished, etc. Although much of the theological importance of the crucified people is intrinsic to them and their sufferings (and does not depend on a relationship to anyone else) the *theologoumenon* "crucified people" derives from their relationship with Jesus, the definitive son of God, who was crucified in a way that parallels their sufferings. If Sobrino did not consider Jesus to be the Son of God much of the force and meaning of his specifically crucifixion language would be lost.

Soteriology

The relationship between Boff's overall soteriology and his political reading of the cross is best seen in chapters 6 and 7 of *Passion of Christ, Passion of the world*, where he sets out and criticizes biblical, patristic and scholastic interpretations of the crucifixion. He begins with the earliest Christian communities, who interpreted Christ's death in terms of the death that awaited any prophet, thus needing no special explanation. However, the suffering and persecution experienced by the early Christian community caused them to use the suffering servant figure in interpreting Christ's death, introducing new meanings of expiation and vicarious atonement, reinforced by a sacrificial, expiatory reading of the Last Supper in eucharistic theology. Paul's theology of the cross is seen in the light of his pastoral involvement with those pneumatics or "spiritual" Christians of Corinth who downgraded the earthly, crucified Jesus and boasted of their wisdom. Against this, Paul sets the cross as the criterion of Christian wisdom, the criterion against which all else is to be measured. This cross–wisdom is not based on worldly power, but on apparent weakness.

Boff now turns to the ways in which the crucifixion has been interpreted in post-biblical tradition. The criterion he uses is highly significant for political theology. He asks whether those theological and liturgical motifs used to describe Jesus' ministry and its climax in the crucifixion actually express what is liberative in Christ's death and resurrection. Or do they do the opposite?[29] Boff stresses the fact that the images used to express Christian interpretation of the cross are culturally conditioned, and convey ideological interests—hence, these images need to be re-examined, or perhaps deconstructed, to convey liberative meaning today. There is a clear political corollary—do these images assist in the present liberative purpose of the church, or do they contribute to oppression? First, Boff returns to an earlier theme in refusing to isolate the death of Christ as redemptive. He describes redemption as a praxis in which the whole of Jesus' life, not merely the moment of death, is redemptive and liberative.[30] Boff is, like Yoder, concerned to avoid a solely transactional account of redemption—he seems to see redemption (although he does not put it in these terms) in function and process rather than ontological status. Redemption is the process of being redeemed in the totality of life (including the political), as a consequence of the totality of the life of Jesus. It is not to be reduced to a transaction of a single moment. And so Boff criticizes both the Greek and

29. Boff, *Passion*, 86.
30. Boff, *Passion*, 89.

the Latin approaches for separating parts of the earthly life of Jesus from the totality: the Greek for concentrating on the fact alone of the incarnation (and downplaying the actual redemptive details of Jesus' life), the Latin for concentrating on the death of Christ to the detriment of the life which went before. Boff's target is a mechanical doctrine of the atonement, where traditionally used concepts veil rather than express the liberative nature of Jesus' death.[31] He does, however, seek to salvage what he can from these images of redemption in a process of demythologization. For example, the first model is that of expiatory sacrifice for the sins of his people, which Boff re-interprets as self-surrender for the sake of the Other, and for others.[32] The relevance of this for a spirituality of committed political action is evident—discipleship has an outward orientation, both towards God and humanity, and this necessitates a commitment of the self away from the self, which expresses itself in costly service.

Boff concludes this survey by asking how Christ's salvific solidarity with humanity connects with humanity today.[33] He appeals to a sense of universal human solidarity, across geography, time and history. The incarnation, the divine-human unity is the key to (or the model of) the divine-human unity achieved by Christ in his solidarity with humankind. This solidarity means that "when he touches them he opens to them the possibility of redemption and liberation . . . he activates the forces that can shake off the yoke of all manner of servitude."[34] The cross fits into this schema as the end point of the incarnation, as an ultimate revelation both of God's nature and human openness.[35] As elsewhere, Boff is determined not to isolate the cross, but to see it in close relationship with the rest of Jesus' incarnate life.

This is also very much a theme of Sobrino's soteriology—the totality of Jesus' life-and-death is salvific, and it is a mistake to isolate Jesus' death in an ahistorical soteriology. For Sobrino, salvation is deeply related to a primary conflict between, as he puts it, "the God of life and the gods of death." Salvation takes place within the one history and is centered on the holistic coming of the kingdom of God in its concreteness. Salvation is not something performed by God alone, but by the co-operation of humans in forwarding the acts of healing, liberation and peacemaking that are specific to each situation where God's kingdom is challenged.

31. Boff, *Passion*, 91.
32. Boff, *Passion*, 94.
33. Boff, *Passion*, 99.
34. Boff, *Passion*, 101.
35. Boff, *Passion*, 100.

Sobrino writes that "the salvation brought by the Kingdom—*though this is not all the Kingdom brings*"[36] (my italics) involves actual historical acts of liberation determined by the context of the oppressed peoples involved. The kingdom of God is not an ahistorical theory, but something worked out in human history. Sobrino appears to recognize, from those words in italics, that the totality of salvation means more than a reactive response to political and social oppression, but, given his context, this is where he chooses to place the emphasis of his soteriology. Jesus is the salvific mediator of the kingdom, as the Son of God who promotes authentic humanization and divinization (humanity and divinity being not mutually incompatible).

For Sobrino, as for Yoder and Boff, there is an intimate relationship between the historical reasons for Jesus' death and its soteriological significance. The bare fact of Jesus' crucifixion means little in isolation from the historical facts which caused that crucifixion. Jesus' death is not a contextless sacrifice at the hands of those whose sin is general and ahistorical. It was a historical scandal, a crime, a deliberate ending of a life lived in the service of a liberative kingdom by those who were threatened by that kingdom. Sobrino describes the soteriological role of Christ in traditional terms—as sacrifice, new covenant, suffering servant, liberation from the law,[37] and emphasizes two aspects of the salvific role of the cross. First, the sacrificial death of Jesus is "pleasing to God," not in itself in isolation, but as the culmination of a life lived in love.[38] The suffering in itself is not a good thing pleasing to God—there is no deification of suffering. Rather, what is pleasing to God is a love that is willing, if necessary, to suffer. The manifestation of this, of Jesus as the true human being, is salvific in that it invites and engenders true humanity.[39] Second, the cross shows that God's love is credible in real, concrete terms.[40] The cross does not change God's attitude to humanity. Jesus' life and cross are that in which God's love for human beings is expressed and made as real as possible.[41] In Sobrino's context of suffering in Latin America, the credibility of God's love needs to be demonstrated in the most radical way possible. Sobrino quotes the famous words of Bonhoeffer which form a sub-text to much of his own writing on the cross: "Only the suffering God

---

36. Sobrino, *Jesus the Liberator*, 125.
37. Sobrino, *Jesus the Liberator*, 223–27.
38. Sobrino, *Jesus the Liberator*, 227–28.
39. Sobrino, *Jesus the Liberator*, 230.
40. Sobrino, *Jesus the Liberator*, 230–31.
41. Sobrino, *Jesus the Liberator*, 230.

can help."⁴² God's love can only be credible to the suffering if God himself has undergone the depths of suffering.

Various criticisms can be made of this soteriology, de-emphasizing as it does certain aspects of the atonement familiar in more traditional interpretations—most notably the nature of sin being an offence, primarily, against God. The "Notification on the Works of Father Jon Sobrino, SJ," criticizes him for an exemplarist soteriology that "reduces redemption to moralism," the goal being "the appearance of the *homo verus*, manifested in fidelity unto death." Salvation and redemption "cannot be reduced to the good example that Jesus gives us."⁴³ However, Sobrino can be defended in two ways. First, in general it is in the nature of liberation theology not to present the whole of Christian doctrine at any one point, but only that which is most relevant to the particular context in which the theologian teaches. Second, it is misleading simply to portray Sobrino's soteriology as exemplarist. The cross does not only reveal the love of God but unleashes its reality in concrete situations. Sobrino looks to the cross of Jesus not merely as an example, but as a present and active force of suffering love.

The Necessity of the Cross

The question of the necessity of the cross is important to Boff, in seeking a theology of the cross which avoids a deification and glorification of suffering. This is exemplified in *Way of the Cross, Way of Justice* where Boff translates necessity into inevitability through Jesus' fidelity both to his Father and to his contemporaries.⁴⁴ God did not prevent the suffering of Jesus, but given the nature of Jesus' mission, he would inevitably face the cruelty of human opposition.⁴⁵ It is certainly not the case that God actively willed the crucifixion, but, given the human propensity to reject Jesus' mission, the establishment of the kingdom made something like the crucifixion inevitable.⁴⁶ The necessity or inevitability of the crucifixion, which is stressed in the Synoptic accounts (as in Mark 8:31 and parallels) lies in the fact that given the sin of the world, Jesus' obedience to his Father would inexorably lead to his death at the hands of sinners.⁴⁷ Jesus feely accepted this inevitable sacrifice. But the inevitability lies in the sinfulness and hardness of heart of

42. Bonhoeffer, *Letters*, 361.
43. "Notification," 9, 10.
44. Boff, *Way*, ix.
45. Boff, *Way*, 11.
46. Boff, *Way*, ix.
47. Boff, *Way*, ix.

human beings who refused to accept God's call to conversion and to participate in the present and coming kingdom.[48]

Boff is attempting to indicate a place for the cross in the divine purpose without implicating God as actively willing the crucifixion. The cross is a crime, and Boff is determined not to minimize its criminal nature, or to make God an accomplice in the crime. God the Father is determined to realize his "project in history," the "kingdom of God," the "divine revolution,"[49] even though it will inevitably cost the life of his Son. Given the nature of the world in its hostility to God's ways, any "historical project" of God will inevitably risk God's agent's suffering and death. God, loving humankind, freely accepts this sacrifice as a tragic necessity. This seems to be the way in which Boff, at least in *Way of the Cross, Way of Justice* understands the salvific nature of the cross. The kingdom of God will be realized through the death of Jesus—he died for our sins in the sense that human rejection of God's purposes caused his death.[50] Boff is content to use traditional language to describe the crucifixion, Jesus taking the sins of humanity upon himself in solidarity with sinners, but with a crucial addition—"In particular, he established solidarity with all the *victims* of human sinfulness." This theme of solidarity with humanity is an important and recurring theme in Boff's political theology of the cross.

A similar doctrine of the necessity of the cross is found in Sobrino. Again, necessity is probably better rendered as inevitability. Sobrino regards the cross not as a chance happening or a contingent aspect of God's action, but as the necessary outcome of the incarnation, God's "primordial option." He describes the cross as "the outcome of an incarnation situated in a world of sin that is revealed to be a power working against the God of Jesus."[51]

In such a world, given the nature of sin and evil, the cross is historically inevitable. If there is to be an incarnation into the processes of human history, the cross is necessary. This is not so much a theological necessity as an inevitable consequence of human history. Although God's design of incarnation makes that crucifixion inevitable, human sin, not the will of God crucified Jesus. Here, again, Sobrino is careful not to deify or to privilege suffering in itself. God's suffering in Christ is not for its own sake, but for the sake of a diminution of human suffering. A spirituality of dolorism is futile, if by that suffering the suffering of humankind is not diminished.

---

48. Boff, *Way*, 6, 89.
49. Boff, *Way*, 29.
50. Boff, *Way*, 90.
51. Sobrino, *Christology*, 201.

C) CONCLUSION

Contextless theology, done in a social and ecclesiastical vacuum, is impossible. For Yoder, Boff, and Sobrino the background against which they do their theology is highly significant, though in differing ways. Yoder's ecclesiastical setting in the Mennonite tradition of a non-resistant martyr church, and Boff's and Sobrino's situation of ministering to the suffering poor of Latin America determine the content of much of their theologies of the cross. All three theologians attempt to integrate their political theologies of the cross with their overall theologies—Yoder, with his insistence on a non-coercive God respecting (and permitting) human freedom, Boff with his liberative reinterpretation of traditional categories of atonement, Sobrino with his interweaving of Christology with the theme of the crucified people. All three profess an orthodox Christology and seek to draw out the implications of an already well established theology for political and social ethics. All three have been criticized by more conservative members of their denominations for a defective (i.e., non-traditional) Christology, but have insisted that any divergence from the traditional is a matter of christological perspective, rather than content. All three are concerned not to isolate the cross from its political causation in an ahistorical manner but to ascribe revelatory and salvific value to events preceding the actual crucifixion.

Soteriology is, perhaps, less easy to assess. Yoder's soteriology diverges significantly from the Evangelical doctrine of penal substitutionary atonement. Boff and Sobrino shelter behind liberation theology's tendency to emphasize only those parts of the Christian faith which serve the particular liberative purpose, with the result that it is difficult to ascertain the full content of their soteriological beliefs. Boff, in his reinterpretation of the traditional models of atonement, elicits from these models images of use to current liberative practice, but it is difficult to ascertain which model he would use to express a more traditional form of atonement, where the focus is the restoration of relationship between God and humanity, broken by sin, rather than simply restoration of just relationships within humanity. Both Boff and Sobrino stress, however, the holistic or integral nature of salvation, and the fact that the kingdom of God, the goal of salvation, cannot be simply reduced to political activity, even though this is the main focus of their concern.

Chapter 3

The Historical and Political Causation of the Crucifixion in Yoder, Boff, and Sobrino

In the previous chapter I examined in outline the theologies of Yoder, Boff and Sobrino, in order to test the coherence of their general interpretations of the cross with their specifically political theologies. In this chapter I discuss an equally fundamental question—how does each theologian present the causation for Jesus' crucifixion as an historical phenomenon? What political causes do they identify? It is important to note that the causation of the crucifixion cannot neatly be separated into the theological and the historical. When we claim that Jesus was crucified by the sin of humankind, this sin has no meaningful reality except in the concrete historical acts committed in reaction to him. Likewise, the revelatory quality of Jesus' reaction to human sin was actualized in historically analyzable strategies. Hence the theological and the historical necessarily overlap.

I pose the question—are the accounts given by our three interlocutors of the crucifixion and its causation justifiable in the light of the evidence of the New Testament, especially as evaluated by current scholarship? A full and detailed examination of the coherence of the theologians' accounts with biblical scholarship is beyond the scope of this study. What needs to be shown, however, is that their accounts of the crucifixion are reasonably consistent with a possible historical reconstruction.

EXCURSUS—IDENTIFYING THE POLITICAL

It is important to consider what is meant by political, as there is a sense in which most moral teaching has political ramifications, if pushed far enough. Socrates, for example, was a member of the politically participating class in Athens (i.e., free adult male citizen), took part in at least one of the significant political events of his time (the Arginusae debate in the Peloponnesian War), and was executed partly for political reasons, because some of his aristocratic followers had become involved as leaders in the oligarchic revolution of 404 BCE. His teaching, by his own admission, was intended to make Athenian society re-examine its presuppositions, and in that sense was potentially subversive. In fact, one of the charges on which he was condemned was "corrupting the youth." His concern for the truth and his pursuit of self-knowledge would, no doubt, in the end lead to a better society if widely practiced. However, this was only of tangential political significance, in the sense of direct engagement in the power politics of his day. It is difficult to penetrate beyond the Platonic overlay, where Plato uses Socrates as a mouthpiece for his own thoughts, but it is unlikely that Socrates' teaching could be interpreted as having such direct political content. Although Socrates' indirect political relevance was a crucial factor in his trial and condemnation, his teaching was, as far as we can tell, directed primarily to the individual, and he does not seem to have been particularly interested in the business of political power or authority or in causing social or economic change. This, of course, is precisely how Jesus has been portrayed in certain strands of theology and spirituality. By contrast, the theologians studied in this investigation present Jesus as having much more direct political aims and influence.

The difficulties surrounding this issue are exemplified by controversies over the interpenetration of religion and politics in the twentieth century. The argument over the political/religious martyr status of Bonhoeffer will be mentioned later. More recently, the murders of Fr. Jerzy Popieluszko and Bishop Oscar Romero indicate the difficulties in dividing religion and politics into rigidly separate compartments. From the perspective of the murderers, the assassinations were political, in that they were a reaction of threatened power to those who constituted a threat. From the perspective of the murdered, the politically adversarial actions that led to their deaths were a consequence of their religious convictions and cannot be separated from them. Perhaps there is a parallel here with Jesus, especially in the context of first century Galilee and Judaea, where religion and politics were so closely intertwined.

A) THE HISTORICAL AND POLITICAL CAUSATION OF THE CROSS IN YODER

Jesus' Ministry as Inescapably Political

Yoder certainly presents the ministry of Jesus in political terms. Most notably, his seminal work *Politics of Jesus* is an explicit attempt to demonstrate the political nature of much of Jesus' ministry and its relevance for contemporary Christians. Yoder recognizes that Jesus has often been presented as only possessing marginal political relevance and insists that Jesus' ministry was much more directly political. Two examples suffice, from the beginning and end of Jesus' ministry. First, Yoder describes the jubilee influenced "Nazareth manifesto" in Luke 4 as "a visible socio-political economic restructuring of relations among the people of God, achieved by his intervention in the person of Jesus as the one anointed and endued with the Spirit."[1] Second, the "cleansing of the temple" is described by Yoder as "the symbolic takeover of the temple precinct by One who claims jurisdiction there." The attempt of the chief priests and other religious and political power holders to destroy him "is linked to the messianic claim acted out in the nonviolent seizure of the holy place, and not simply to the offence against order which might have been involved in his driving out the bulls."[2] In both instances, Jesus is represented by Yoder as deeply involved as an agent in questions of political power and change.

Nor is Jesus, according to Yoder, merely a solitary and individualistic prophet. The political and social change latent in Jesus' words and deeds must find its reality in a new community. In describing the course of Jesus' ministry, and the opposition to him by the power-holders, Yoder writes, "To organized opposition he responds with the formal founding of a new social reality."[3] This alternative social reality is not another political party, but a whole new social order marked by the cross. Jesus, Yoder writes, is building a community "to share in that style of life of which the cross is the culmination."[4] Jesus broadens the cross bearing from himself to his community. He does not "reprimand his disciples for trying to establish some new social order—he reprimands them for misunderstanding the character of the social order that is to be established."[5] If cross bearing is the mark of

---

1. Yoder, *Politics*, 32.
2. Yoder, *Politics*, 41.
3. Yoder, *Politics*, 33.
4. Yoder, *Politics*, 37–38.
5. Yoder, *Politics*, 38.

this new social order/community, the function of the community is political and social change. Yoder describes Jesus' new community as having

> those sociological traits most characteristic of those who set about to change society. . .a nonconformed quality of 'secular' involvement in the life of the world . . . an unavoidable challenge to the powers that be and the beginning of a new set of social alternatives.[6]

A Different Kind of Politics

The new order taught, practiced, and inaugurated in community by Jesus is intensely and directly political. But Yoder emphasizes that it is a different kind of politics which Jesus promulgates. Again, the cross—or, more accurately, an approach to politics which would inevitably lead to the cross—is central. For example, Yoder reads the temptation narrative as a choice between different kinds of kingship, the acceptance or refusal of which would define the nature of the mission and purpose of Jesus—in other words, the nature of the politics in which he was engaged. Similarly, Yoder sees the episode of the "bread in the desert" (Luke 9:10–17) as the turning point of Jesus' ministry, in that Jesus was dealing not merely with a small group of disciples but "the first wave of inquirers coming to see if this kingdom which the twelve was announcing was for real."[7] Jesus rejects definitively a certain kind of kingship or politics for himself and his followers. The crowd wishes to acclaim Jesus as the new Moses, "the provider, the welfare king." Yoder observes that

> his withdrawal from their acclamation is . . . the occasion for his first statement that his ministry was to be one of suffering and that his disciples would need to be ready to bear with him that cross."[8] There is thus a clear choice between cross and crown. But Yoder stresses that this choice is not situated outside of, but within the arena of politics. It is a choice of a certain mode of politics, not a rejection of the political. Yet what he proposes is not withdrawal into the desert or into mysticism: it is a renewed messianic claim . . . The cross is beginning to loom not as a

---

6. Yoder, *Politics*, 39.
7. Yoder, *Politics*, 34.
8. Yoder, *Politics*, 35.

ritually prescribed instrument of propitiation, but as the political alternative to both insurrection and quietism.⁹

This last sentence sums up Yoder's interpretation of the political choices of Jesus—a different way, certainly involving a challenge to the powerful, but not violent insurrection. That way, if not inevitably leading to the cross, certainly risked that outcome.

An example of this occurs at the climax of Jesus' activity in Jerusalem. After the cleansing of the temple, the next step would be to "storm the Roman fortress next door. But it belongs to the nature of the new order that, though it condemns and displaces the old, it does not do so with the arms of the old."¹⁰ In Gethsemane, too, the choice is not between political engagement and withdrawal, but between two options of engagement. Yoder asks what would "remove this cup from me" mean in the actual historical circumstances, and interprets this prayer in terms not of a withdrawal from a challenge to power but of a renewed temptation to messianic violence in pursuit of power, i.e., a zealot-type campaign.¹¹ Jesus resists this very real option, and chooses a renunciation of zealot-type means, in favor of the nonviolent resistance which ends in, and is symbolized by, the cross. This, Yoder insists, does not imply the rejection of the need to pursue a kingdom. On the Emmaus road, Jesus rebukes the disciples not because they had been looking for a kingdom and should not have been. Rather, "their fault is that, just like Peter at Caesarea Philippi, they were failing to see that the suffering of the Messiah is the inauguration of that kingdom."¹² Yoder concludes: "The cross is not a detour or a hurdle on the way to the kingdom; it is the kingdom come." Jesus is not concerned with seizing power by violent means according to the old politics. Rather, his is a new politics, no less a challenge to the powers of his day, but reliant on nonviolent means and hence vulnerable to the violence of the powerful.

Jesus as Politically Subversive

The subversive (and hence, in the political situation vis-à-vis the Romans, cross-risking) nature of Jesus' ministry is, according to Yoder, historically well established. Even before the climax of his ministry in Jerusalem, "Herod cannot be seeking to kill Jesus for heresy or prophecy; sedition would be the

9. Yoder, *Politics*, 35.
10. Yoder, *Politics*, 43.
11. Yoder, *Politics*, 45.
12. Yoder, *Politics*, 51.

only possible charge."[13] The language Jesus uses about taking up the cross is interpreted not in terms of a general self denial or dying to self but as a warning to the disciples about the standard punishment for insurrection or refusal to confess Caesar's lordship—even as an echo of a phrase possibly used in zealot recruiting. "The disciples' cross is not a metaphor for self-mortification or even generally for innocent suffering—if you follow me, your fate will be like mine, the fate of a revolutionary."[14] To use such a phrase metaphorically without taking into account its inevitably political connotations would be, at the very least, unlikely. The subversive nature of Jesus' ministry has a parallel with the zealots, but with the difference that the zealots' subversion was exercised violently, whereas Jesus, though equally subversive was nonviolent. Reflecting the scholarly controversy current in the nineteen sixties over Jesus' possible zealot links, Yoder agrees with Brandon, a proponent of the "Jesus as zealot" theory, that Jesus was executed for sedition, was socially close to the zealot movement, and had his revolutionary nature concealed through apologetic motives in early Christianity. Yoder, however, argues that Jesus' revolutionary initiative was, in contrast to the zealots, nonviolent: "The fault we find with Brandon is not that he interprets Jesus as politically relevant, but that he assumes violence is the only model for such relevance."[15] (Because of the doubts concerning the existence of a group specifically named zealot in the time of Jesus I have throughout put the word zealot in lower case. It is, however, almost certain that there existed zealot-*type* groups at this time, even if not bearing the name zealot.)

The primary evidence for the politically subversive nature of Jesus' ministry is the cross itself. Any denial of this subversive nature and its consequence in the crucifixion (by what Yoder calls spiritualistic-apologetic exegesis) must depend on a huge (and historically incomprehensible) misunderstanding. The cross itself demonstrates the real threat which both Pilate and Caiaphas believed Jesus posed to the established order, unless they totally misread his actions.

> That the threat was not one of armed, violent revolt, and that it nonetheless bothered them enough to resort to irregular procedures to counter it, is a proof of the political relevance of nonviolent tactics, not a proof that Pilate and Caiaphas were exceptionally dull or dishonorable men.[16]

---

13. Yoder, *Politics*, 37.
14. Yoder, *Politics*, 38.
15. Yoder, *Politics*, 42.
16. Yoder, *Politics*, 49.

Yoder omits the possibility that Pilate and Caiaphas may have mistaken Jesus for a violent insurrectionist, not realizing that his approach was radically different from the zealots. Evidence such as the gathering of the crowds in the wilderness, the cleansing of the temple, and the fact that Jesus' close associates included at least one zealot sympathizer make that an understandable mistake. This does not vitiate Yoder's main argument, that Jesus' nonviolent politics led to the cross—it simply means that Jesus' politics were sufficiently close to the zealot option in their subversive capacity as to make Pilate's and Caiaphas' postulated mistake credible.

Coherence with Historical Evidence

How far is this interpretation coherent with the modern historical reconstructions of the New Testament evidence? On one level Yoder takes what has become known since his first writing of *The Politics of Jesus* as a canonical approach, dealing with the evidence of the surface text rather than historical reconstructions of what lies behind the text. However, in the second edition of *The Politics of Jesus* he admits that his argument would be seriously diminished "if the historical questers were to come up with solid demonstrations that the 'real Jesus' they find is quite incompatible with what we find in the canonical account."[17] Yoder defends his position by examining the tendencies of the evidence on which a historical reconstruction can be based. He claims that "any . . . serious attempt at hypothetical reconstruction does move toward taking more seriously the economic-political threat Jesus posed to the Romans than does the traditional ecclesiastical interpretation."[18] The more one digs beneath the surface of the text, the more political and social motivation in Jesus' ministry is unearthed, not less. This is a point corroborated by New Testament scholarship of the late twentieth century, which has increasingly seen Jesus' teaching and actions earthed in first-century Palestinian economics and politics and not as something floating in a quasi timeless void (as Yoder observes in his comments on the contribution of Bammel and Moule, in their symposium *Jesus and the politics of his day* and the various writers of the third quest[19]).

When considering the social and economic background, Yoder rightly insists that his thesis is proved by a very low level of evidence:

---

17. Yoder, *Politics*, 12.
18. Yoder, *Politics*, 50.
19. Yoder, *Politics*, 13.

> All that needs to be affirmed to make our point is that Jesus' career had been such as to make it quite thinkable that he would pose to the Roman Empire an apparent threat serious enough to justify his execution.[20]

Starting from the fact that the cross was the mode of execution for those who threatened the existing political and economic order, it is legitimate to read back into the preceding career of Jesus elements which would indicate such a threat. The only argument against such a reading is that Jesus was totally misunderstood, or misrepresented, and that his execution was based completely on mistaken premises. That is, of course, a possibility, but Yoder rightly argues that his political interpretation is overwhelmingly more likely. Moreover, in Chapter 5 of *The Politics of Jesus*, which he entitles "The possibility of nonviolent resistance" Yoder provides copious evidence of contemporary parallels to the type of non violent resistance with which he associates Jesus. Such teaching and actions were, at the very least, not unknown or unfeasible in the context of first-century Palestine, and corroborate Yoder's historical reconstruction. He concludes his argument (in the original edition) with this summary:

> Jesus was, in his divinely mandated prophethood, priesthood, and kingship, the bearer of a new possibility of human, social and therefore political relationships. *At this one point* there is no difference between the Jesus of historie and the Christ of Geschichte, or between Christ as God or Jesus as man, or between the religion of Jesus and the religion about Jesus. No such slicing can avoid his call to an ethic marked by the cross, a cross identified as the punishment of a man who threatens society by creating a new kind of community leading to a radically new kind of life.[21]

A similar point is made later, when Yoder points out that the episodes in the gospels which contain the most political significance are precisely those places where the "historic" and the "historical" Jesus most coincide, "where there is least distinction between what the critic thinks must actually have happened and what the believing witnesses reported."[22] In other words, whichever interpretation is adopted, whether it is of the Jesus of history or the Christ of faith, the *sine qua non* is the crucifixion with all its political implications. In his epilogue, added in the second edition of *The Politics of Jesus*, Yoder asserts:

---

20. Yoder, *Politics*, 50.
21. Yoder, *Politics*, 52.
22. Yoder, *Politics*, 101–2.

> It is noteworthy that within that debate [i.e., concerning the historical Jesus] what is least open to debate, in all of the Gospel accounts and in all the critical reconstructions, is the historical/political dimension of what Jesus did. It is with regard to the Zealot option, that is, to the prospect of anti-Roman violence, that the gospel text is closest to the issues of historical conflict.[23]

Yoder summarizes his argument in his second edition of *The Politics of Jesus*: "Scholarly developments have not had the effect of discovering an apolitical Jesus."[24] More specifically, "it does not follow . . . .that Jesus seen as sage, as rabbi, or as incarnate Wisdom, would be any less politically relevant than Jesus the nonviolent Zealot." This is perhaps overstating the case. Given that, as argued above with the example of Socrates, the political nature of a teacher can be implicit or explicit, direct or indirect, there is a great difference between a teacher of moral (and mainly religious) aphorisms which are not necessarily directed to specific political, social and economic issues, but are only tangentially political, and one whose teachings (and actions) are more directly political. Hays notes correctly that "the politically detached Cynic Jesus imagined by the historical critics of the Jesus Seminar would stand in fundamental tension with Yoder's work."[25] He points out that although Yoder disclaims reliance on historical reconstructions behind the text, his thesis does actually depend on a particular reconstruction of the events underlying the text. This is a fair criticism insofar as an individualist Socratic or Cynic type Jesus would significantly weaken Yoder's argument—as would a "Jesus the magician," if the miracles are understood merely (and wrongly) as cases of individual healing without further social relevance. However, the tendency of Yoder's argument is that the need for direct historical evidence for much of Jesus' ministry is not great in order for his case to be proved, given the overwhelmingly political nature of the crucifixion and the political, social, and economic threat which can be read back from that into the rest of his ministry—that is, of course, unless the crucifixion was a complete mistake caused by a gross misunderstanding or misrepresentation. The work of, for example, Borg, Wright, or Sanders certainly does not rule out the political import of Jesus' ministry—Jesus is directly political to a varying degree in their reconstructions, but the political nature of the crucifixion and the ministry which preceded it is certainly not excluded by such scholarly reconstruction. Such a political interpretation is strongly corroborated

---

23. Yoder, *Politics*, 55.
24. Yoder, *Politics*, 15.
25. Hays, *Moral Vision*, 286n141.

by scholars such as Crossan and Horsley without necessarily ascribing to Jesus a strictly pacifist strategy.

Conclusion

Yoder's strength is realistically to situate Jesus within the politics of his day, and to argue for a dangerously subversive, but nonviolent strategy. In Yoder's account, Jesus was seen as such a political threat to the Romans that he suffered the penalty for challenging the imperial order. Although close, in many ways, to the zealots, he decisively rejected their violence. He set himself against the Sadducean and Herodian parties, who collaborated with Rome in order to preserve at least some of their power. He rejected strategies of political withdrawal, whether the monasticism of the Essenes or the personal piety of the Pharisees. The alternative was a strategy which, if not leading inevitably to the cross, at least seriously risked that outcome.

B) THE HISTORICAL AND POLITICAL CAUSATION OF THE CROSS IN BOFF AND SOBRINO

Jesus' Death as a Consequence of His Life

As a liberation theologian, Boff is naturally concerned to establish Jesus' political relevance. He recognizes, however, that the political agenda he brings to the gospels is not directly found in the gospels themselves, the interest of the gospel writers being primarily theological, rather than political. The gospels do not set out to analyze in any great depth the political causation of events in Jesus' ministry—their interest is more in divine causation. Any political Jesus has to be found, either indirectly in the oblique political implications of his actions (such as his healing, or breaking of the Sabbath rules), or by arguing that a more directly political Jesus lies concealed by the other interests of the evangelists. Boff argues that the almost exclusively theological reading of the passion, with its emphasis on God's role, causes the gospel writers to downplay the actual historical causes and the political factors involved. The Passion is historically inexplicable if those causes and factors are ignored. Boff suggests that an analysis of such causes and factors do not diminish a "religious, transcendent" interpretation of the crucifixion, but adds another crucial dimension that forms the foundation of the religious meaning. He reminds us of the role of human responsibility in the crucifixion. Jesus, after all, did not "die in bed."[26]

By sifting through the interplay of fact and interpretation, Boff believes that there is sufficiently reliable material available to reconstruct some of the political factors which led to Jesus' crucifixion: first, Jesus' overturning of religious traditions and systems of power in the name of humanity and justice (emphasized by Boff with regard to his own struggles with religious authority); second, Jesus' eschatology which, although not directly political, used potentially political categories (e.g., the kingdom of God) and which posited the coming of the kingdom as something which calls into question human structures of power; and third, the passion narrative, in which Jesus is seen directly challenging the powers of his time (e.g., in the cleansing of the temple).

For Sobrino also, the political nature of Jesus' ministry comes to a climax in his death as a political prisoner at hands of the occupying power whose political dominance rested on the threat and actuality of crucifixion.[27] This, in itself, does not prove beyond doubt the political nature of Jesus' ministry—theoretically, as we have seen in our discussion of Yoder, a historical reconstruction could be made whereby Jesus' death was due to the political authorities misinterpreting Jesus and ascribing to him non-existent political relevance—but Sobrino sets Jesus' trial and death in the overall context of a political, or quasi-political confrontation between what he describes as two "mediations," the kingdom of God and the Roman empire, played out in a "total encounter" between Jesus and Pontius Pilate. Jesus' message was, undoubtedly, religious—but to dismiss the political danger inherent in his religious message would be to betray a gross underestimation of the way religion underpinned the society of Jesus' day.[28] Jesus' death is the sharpest point of this underlying confrontation which shaped his whole ministry.

We have seen how both Boff and Sobrino, like Yoder, stress that Jesus' death must not be viewed in isolation from his life, either theologically or historically. A person's life gives meaning to their death, and vice versa. Hence Jesus' death does not stand on its own as a salvific entity. Historical causation, including the events preceding Jesus' death, is an essential component in constructing a theology of the cross. Boff implicitly criticizes the tendency of the creeds, and certain soteriologies, to treat Jesus' life as relatively unimportant (other than the fact that he was incarnate) compared

---

26. Boff, *Passion*, 7.
27. Sobrino, *Jesus the Liberator*, 206.
28. Sobrino, *Jesus the Liberator*, 209.

to his death and resurrection. Hence the title of chapter 2 of *Passion of Christ, Passion of the World*—"Jesus' death as consequence of a praxis and a message." It is a deficient soteriology—and one which severely downplays the actual incarnation of Jesus as revelatory—to focus on the divine drama of the crucifixion but to ignore the human causation. Boff is concerned to root Jesus' death in the concrete political history of his time. Like Yoder, he resists a dehistoricisation which sees the cross solely in terms of a divine transaction in which the preceding ministry of Jesus is neglected. Jesus' death can be understood only in the context of the concrete circumstances of his time, the conflictual politics and his role in them through his teaching and actions.[29] Boff goes on to describe Jesus' "historical project," beginning with the challenges Jesus faced—a general regime of dependency, socio-economic oppression, and religious oppression. Although Boff does not make the parallels explicit, the terms used to describe the situation of first-century Palestine would seem to be intended to evoke his *sitz im leben* of Latin America and his own struggles with the Roman Catholic hierarchy.

Jesus' Death as a Political Execution

It is significant that Boff does not attempt to make Jesus an explicitly political figure, certainly not a zealot or Bar Kochba like guerrilla, a temptation especially attractive to a liberation theologian writing, at least in part, for those involved in a struggle analogous to that of the zealots. Nor, on the other hand, does Boff regard Jesus' message as being confined to the individual conscience, as he interprets that of John the Baptist.[30] Jesus' message is broader and, Boff argues, further reaching, encompassing "an absolute, all-comprehending, all-transcending meaning . . . the reign of God" which "calls into question social, political, and religious interests"

And not only does Jesus make the proclamation, which could be seen as merely one of a series of utopian proclamations—he actualizes the kingdom, the reign of God, he lives it out, he anticipates the future. This is the focal point of Jesus' ministry, and his death was caused by his faithfulness to proclaiming and living out that reign. Boff indicates various "redemptive, liberative" aspects of that reign: a change from an oppressive religion of cults and sacrifices to one where the criteria of salvation are found in the love of neighbor; liberation from a society divided by wealth, class, race, disease, and gender to a new solidarity; a respect for the freedom and rights of others, and an insistence on the need for justice, forgiveness, and mercy;

29. Boff, *Passion*, 9.
30. Boff, *Passion*, 14.

and a commitment to living life as a gift to others, as sacrifice on behalf of others.[31] These aspects of the reign of God are potentially politically and religiously subversive and, ultimately, caused Jesus to be crucified at the hands of those threatened by his praxis and message. The causes of Jesus' death are the same causes as the death of any prophet—self sacrifice for the sake of his message. In this, Jesus is joined not simply by those who preach a religious message, but by those others who have made a similar commitment to the "creation of a human society more marked by a communion of brothers and sisters and by a greater openness to the Absolute."[32]

We are surely meant to see in this a reference to contemporary political activity and suffering in Latin America, not only in the church with its preferential option for the poor, but also in those working from a Marxist commitment. The terms Boff uses are familiar in contemporary struggles against oppressive regimes in Latin America. However, while using such language, which would suggest affinity with the zealots (or their forerunners), Boff's analysis of the political nature of Jesus' ministry avoids trapping him in a zealot framework, while giving him both a genuine political relevance in first-century Palestine and also a deeper, more lasting political relevance.

Sobrino's analysis is very similar. Jesus' death is represented not in ahistorical isolation, but as an inevitable consequence of his life and ministry—inevitable in the eyes of those who see contemporaries murdered for pursuing similar ends. The reasons for Jesus death—his words and actions—were and are totally comprehensible, because they are paralleled so many times in history and in the contemporary world.[33] Nor was Jesus death an accident, but a fully understandable outcome of the particular circumstances of the incarnation, in reaction to what Sobrino describes as an "anti-kingdom."[34] This anti-kingdom presents itself in various facets of oppression of the powerless by the powerful, some religious and only implicitly political, others more obviously of a political nature. The direct threat was to the religious authorities, but was not confined to them, extending, more indirectly, to tyrannical power as a whole.[35] The crucifixion was the culmination of the persecution Jesus encountered throughout his life from the oppressors because of his words and actions on

---

31. Boff, *Passion*, 16–21.
32. Boff, *Passion*, 22.
33. Sobrino, *Jesus the Liberator*, 209.
34. Sobrino, *Jesus the Liberator*, 210.
35. Sobrino, *Jesus the Liberator*, 196.

behalf of the oppressed. This manifested itself in a variety of ways, but the common factor was a resistance to and a condemnation of oppression.[36]

What differentiates Jesus from a contemporary revolutionary, whether a Camillo Torres (who described himself as a Christian revolutionary) or a Che Guevara (a Marxist revolutionary whose motivation was not explicitly Christian)? Much of what Boff and Sobrino write about the self giving, freely chosen passion of Jesus and the defense of the oppressed against oppressors could just as well be applied to either of the above, and to many others less well known. Sobrino draws close parallels between the death of Jesus and contemporary events in El Salvador. He describes Jesus as a "man in conflict [who] got in the way" and, as Archbishop Romero observed, "those who get in the way get killed." This "getting in the way" is the simple and overriding cause of Jesus' death.[37]

What difference, then, is there between Jesus' crucifixion and the judicial murder of thousands throughout history? Boff gives two answers—first, the resurrection, and second, Jesus' new experience of God as gracious Father and his radical incarnation of the divine love and forgiveness—"the concretization of the Father's love."[38] Boff seems at first to be treading a tightrope between holding to a Christology of uniqueness, and indicating the points of contact between Jesus and contemporary figures who strive for liberation. This is, however, a false dichotomy given the logic of Boff's argument. There is no reason why Jesus' crucifixion should be any different in nature or historical cause from any other judicial murder perpetrated by authorities who felt their power threatened. If it were different, it would lessen the self-identification of Jesus (and God) with those who suffer similarly today. The uniqueness of Jesus crucifixion lay in its theological meaning, in Jesus' role in God's plan to establish the kingdom. The fact that Jesus, as God's Son, confirmed by the resurrection, fulfilled this salvific purpose differentiates Jesus' death, theologically, from the other crucifixions—although, considered from the point of view of historic causation, no differentiation can (or should) be made.[39]

In chapter 3 of *Passion of Christ, Passion of the World* Boff investigates the Passion narratives and attempts to reconstruct the events which led to the crucifixion. He begins with the Bultmannian warning that presuppositionless, neutral exegesis is not possible. Not only were the facts of the events leading up to the crucifixion interpreted in a certain way by the

---

36. Sobrino, *Jesus the Liberator*, 200.
37. Sobrino, *Jesus the Liberator*, 196.
38. Boff, *Passion*, 24.
39. Boff, *Way*, 88–90.

evangelists for the communities for which they were writing, but subsequent exegesis of those texts is conditioned by the situation, mind-set, and beliefs of the exegete. This is a commonplace in biblical interpretation, but Boff emphasizes it here to legitimize his re-interpretation of the Passion and to introduce interests different from those of the evangelists, i.e., political, rather than solely theological. Boff represents Jesus as a prophet who makes the journey to Jerusalem as the place of crisis, where the history of God's revelation comes into sharpest focus.[40] He goes expecting the fate of the prophets, a violent death. The Last Supper is seen in terms of "covenant and sacrificial self-surrender."[41] The Gethsemane experience is interpreted as anguish occasioned by Jesus' awareness of the coming apocalyptic conflict. Jesus is tried on religious and political grounds: by the Sanhedrin, for blasphemy, and by Pilate as a guerrilla subversive. Jesus' death was "religio-political murder via an abuse of justice."[42]

It is interesting that, on Boff's account, the Jewish authorities and the Pharisees, rather than the Romans, appear to be the prime motivators of Jesus' crucifixion. Boff takes a view, which does not sit easily with modern biblical scholarship, that the Romans needed to be coerced into crucifying Jesus. Because of Jesus' perceived subversion of the law and the national religion, the Pharisees and the powers that be in Jerusalem join together to pressurize Pilate into ordering the crucifixion.[43] On this account the Romans may not have felt Jesus to be so much a subversive threat as simply a victim whose sacrifice was worthwhile for the preserving of political order. This is bound to weaken the argument, adduced by Yoder and Sobrino (and Boff in other passages) that Jesus was crucified as a subversive of the Roman *imperium*. It is interesting, again, that Boff (along with Sobrino) takes a traditional view of the trial and death of Jesus in not allowing himself the tempting path of portraying Jesus as a zealot, for which historical evidence is at best dubious. He insists, however, that political and quasi-political factors (i.e., structures of socio-religious power being threatened) played a significant role in Jesus' condemnation. What is undeniable is that Jesus suffered the death meted out to those who were seen to threaten the established order —the *servile supplicium*, the punishment inflicted on those outside the prevailing power structures by those who wished to preserve those structures.

---

40. Boff, *Passion*, 30.
41. Boff, *Passion*, 35.
42. Boff, *Passion*, 41.
43. Boff, *Passion*, 40–41.

Jesus' Interpretation of His Death

Boff, in chapter 4 of *Passion of Christ, Passion of the World*, attempts to shed light on the question of the historical causation of the crucifixion by examining the question of the meaning Jesus himself ascribed to his death, one of the principal questions at the juncture of history, Christology and soteriology. First, he asks the essential prior question—did Jesus anticipate his crucifixion?

In general terms Jesus, as a prophet, knew the fate that traditionally befell prophets, the execution of John the Baptist being a recent example, and Jesus would surely have been aware that he was challenging vested interests in a similarly dangerous manner. In that sense, Boff argues, Jesus would have been alert to the possibility of his death. But in other senses he was not. Boff discounts the various passion predictions as *vaticinia ex eventu*, or as more general statements. In fact, Boff suggests that an awareness of the inevitability of imminent death only came to Jesus on the cross, with the cry of dereliction. This suggestion short-circuits the question of Jesus' interpretation of his violent death. It would be unlikely, to say the least, for Jesus to attempt to interpret something that he did not (at least immediately) anticipate would happen to him. As to the question of what Jesus actually expected in Jerusalem, Boff suggests the following scenario: Jesus, as an eschatological prophet, preaching that the kingdom of God was at hand and was, in fact, present in him and his ministry, expected his challenge to the theological and sociological heart of his people to result in a time of apocalyptic trial, through which he (and the kingdom of God) would be vindicated. It was only on the cross that this expectation ceased—hence the terrible cry of dereliction—although Boff does not seem to be sure whether Jesus died with a shattering awareness of dereliction or in faith, freedom and trust in God. At one point he treats the Lucan and Johannine words from the cross as non-historical, post-resurrection additions—later, he appears to build from them a theology of Jesus' final trust in God. What Boff stresses is that Jesus' persistence in and loyalty to his preaching of the kingdom of God brought about his death. In that lies much of the political significance of his death, the kingdom being a challenge to the political powers, with a "preferential love for the poor, the weak, the insignificant and the sinful."[44] What differentiates Jesus from any secular prophet is his intimate relationship with God, and the divine, all-embracing, and eschatological nature of the reign he proclaimed and lived. Boff returns to an earlier theme in stressing that Jesus' death is not to be seen in isolation from the rest of his

---

44. Boff, *Passion*, 58.

life, since it is Jesus' whole life, his commitment to both God and fellow humanity, and not just his death, which is redemptive. His mode of death is the climax and consequence of his life, and cannot be seen in isolation from what came before.[45] Faithfulness to God's cause, not a consciousness of any further redemptive meaning, formed the basis of Jesus' own interpretation of his death.

This theme is echoed in Sobrino, whose interpretation of Jesus' death closely resembles that of Boff. Sobrino discounts any self-interpretation of his death by Jesus in terms of models such as expiation, sacrifice, or satisfaction. He finds no evidence that Jesus gave to his death an "absolute transcendent meaning"[46] noting, however, that he looked for some meaning in his death as a consequence of the cause in which he was engaged. Jesus saw, from the history of the prophetic protest and from the contemporary power structures which he faced, the likely consequences of his ministry. But his faithfulness was such that he persisted and, in his last actions in Jerusalem (especially the cleansing of the temple) seems to have deliberately and consciously intensified his challenge. In his undergoing of suffering he knew the reason and the consequence. This consciously and faithfully accepted suffering made possible the biblical interpretation that his death expressed a freely bestowed love and also demonstrated that Jesus knew that he was in conflict with those elements which, in the biblical account, killed the prophets.[47] Sobrino stresses the conflictual nature of Jesus' ministry and Jesus' determination not to shrink from the conflict. This faithful service is sacrificial and ends in the sacrifice of death—not a deliberate self immolation, but a willingness to risk the almost inevitable consequences, in order that good might come. This is the meaning of the eucharistic *huper* (on behalf of) words in the Last Supper—his death will be a sign and consequence of sacrificial, prophetic, and compassionate service which will bring benefit to others.[48] The "transcendent meaning" of Jesus' death is interpreted in terms not of a divine transaction, sealed by the blood of sacrifice, but of self-sacrificial and faithful service, which is not in itself unique but provides an example for others to follow.

---

45. Boff, *Passion*, 63.
46. Sobrino, *Jesus the Liberator*, 201.
47. Sobrino, *Jesus the Liberator*, 201.
48. Sobrino, *Jesus the Liberator*, 203–4.

Coherence with Historical Evidence

How far do Boff and Sobrino's interpretation of Jesus' ministry agree with the historical evidence given by the gospels and interpreted by current biblical scholarship? (Boff's work here predates the third quest of the historical Jesus.) It has been noted above that Boff does not fall into the trap of making Jesus a first-century politician. But the question remains—were Jesus aims and program, which led to his crucifixion, such as Boff represents? Or is he over selective in his interpretation of Jesus' mission? The danger is that he may fall into the familiar snare of constructing a new Jesus in his own image—"Jesus Christ liberator," in succession to the other images of Christ constructed by other writers of lives of Jesus. Schweitzer's criticism (of the liberal Lives of Jesus in the nineteenth century) potentially applies to all reconstructions of Jesus. In fact, just as the Christology Boff presents appears to be remarkably orthodox and traditional in its essence, so is his handling of the historical evidence. He seems to take the traditional Synoptic account of Jesus' ministry and use it as it stands (for example, in the ascription of responsibility for the crucifixion primarily to the Jewish authorities) and, as noted above, he seems to take care to describe Jesus' ministry as implicitly, rather than explicitly political. His interpretation rests on the fact that Jesus could have posed a deeper political threat without being explicitly political in his program, for example, in aiming to overthrow the Romans or to bring about an immediate transfer of political power from the Sadducees to other groups in society. The controlling theme in Jesus' teaching, as Boff consistently points out, is the kingdom of God, which combines a primarily theological meaning with enormous and far reaching political ramifications. The question of whether or not Boff's account of the reasons for the crucifixion are consonant with modern scholarship can be answered in the same way as previously in the case of Yoder, who to a great extent shares Boff's view of Jesus' ministry as having political relevance, but not readily or neatly fitting into the political categories of his day.

Sobrino emphasizes the hermeneutically privileged status of liberation theology in assessing the events surrounding the crucifixion, in that the setting of liberation theology among the poor and oppressed mirrors the social class most at risk of crucifixion, the *servile supplicium*, the punishment of slaves. He does not offer definitive answers to exegetical questions, but the *locus* from which he does his theology offers a sharply focused perspective, especially on the cross. The contemporary cross sheds light on the historical cross. This is a two way process, as Sobrino recognizes:

> The view of the victims helps us to read christological texts and to know Jesus Christ better. Furthermore, this Jesus Christ, known in this way, helps us to understand the victims better and, above all, to work to defend them.[49]

This double hermeneutic does not in itself provide a sure proof for Sobrino's reconstruction of Jesus' ministry, especially its culmination in Jerusalem. It is, however, significant that one of the increasingly used tools in studying ancient history and archaeology is the application of sociological, anthropological, and economic models derived from investigations of contemporary societies. One of the three criteria of historicity Sobrino describes as guiding Latin American liberation theology is "the consistency of Jesus' death with what is narrated of his life" (the others being the criterion of multiple attestation and the criterion of dissimilarity).

> There [in Latin America] the deaths of hundreds and thousands of persons is analogous to Jesus' death, and the causes of their death are historically similar to the causes of Jesus' death. That Jesus must have lived and acted in the way he is reported to have lived and acted is not only plausible, it goes without saying.[50]

This last comment is no doubt an exaggeration, but Sobrino points to an *isomorfismo* (equivalence or similarity in shape), between the experience of the first followers of Jesus and present day Latin American Christians, which enables the latter to, as it were, read the gospels from the inside. The dangers of a circularity of argumentation are clear—it is quite possible that the Latin American (or any other) Christian can read his own situation into the gospels—but this approach, if used critically and in conjunction with other criteria, should not easily be dismissed.

C) CONCLUSION

A number of themes are shared between Yoder, Boff, and Sobrino. The cross must not be isolated, either historically or theologically, from the life of Jesus as a whole. The political nature of Jesus' ministry is stressed. For Yoder, Jesus' ministry is unashamedly political, but with a different kind of politics, involving a nonviolent refusal to take power. For Boff and Sobrino, Jesus' "historic project," the kingdom of God, has strong political connotations, and Jesus' death is a political execution caused by his faithfulness to that historic project. Boff and Sobrino, in their concern to defend liberation

---

49. Sobrino, *Christ the Liberator*, 8.
50. Sobrino, *Latin America*, 74.

theology from the charge of reducing Christianity to politics, are concerned not to overpoliticise Jesus in his historical ministry, but at the same time draw parallels between his faithfulness to his mission and the faithfulness expressed by those in Latin America who give their lives for a similar historic project. Yoder is attempting to establish Jesus as a subversive political figure against a background in North American Christianity which sees him as a spiritual teacher and his death as part of an atonement conceived primarily in transactional terms. The theological as well as the social contexts of these theologians are essential to an understanding of their work.

All three theologians display a remarkably similar methodology in their handling of the historical evidence underlying their theology. Yoder adopts what has come to be called a canonical approach, using the biblical text as it stands. He is not unaware of the possible historical reconstructions behind the text but is content that those reconstructions do not seriously damage his overall picture of the political nature of Jesus' ministry. Similarly, Boff and Sobrino work with the text as it stands, and do not rely on a political reconstruction of Jesus' ministry which goes significantly beyond (or contradicts) the texts. All three theologians face similar problems in justifying their portrait of Jesus in the light of the third quest. However, their reticence in ascribing an over-definite political status to Jesus gives them sufficient leeway for their representations of Jesus not to be overturned by recent research—with the exception of that research which might portray Jesus as a teacher of individual morality who was crucified by mistake.

Yoder's theological methodology makes him particularly vulnerable to the difficulty which Lessing referred to as the "ugly ditch"—that "the accidental truths of history can never become the proof of necessary truths of reason." Yoder's political theology rests overwhelmingly on the revelatory content of Jesus' reaction to the political circumstances of first-century Palestine which led to his crucifixion. How can those contingencies form a solid foundation for a twenty-first-century political theology? What, for example, would have ensued in the admittedly highly unlikely event of Jesus' political program being accepted by Romans, Sadduccees, and Pharisees? Behind this question lies a huge debate concerning revelation and contingency. But in defense of Yoder's cross-based political theology there is a sense in which the cross was inevitable, whatever the details of the historical contingencies. Given human sin, in particular the tendency for the powerful ruthlessly to preserve their power and to destroy those who seek to undermine it, any Christ-like threat to power would inevitably lead to crucifixion or the contemporary equivalent. In Jesus' passion predictions (e.g., Mark 8:31) the language of necessity also bears the meaning of inevitability. The necessity of Jesus' crucifixion lies not just in the salvific intention of God, but in the inevitability of the circumstances which faced Jesus in Jerusalem. Thus it makes no sense to posit the questions—what if the crucifixion had not occurred—where would that then leave Yoder's theology? Given the sinfulness of humanity, independent of the details of the contingent historical circumstances, the cross has a tragic inevitability.

Sobrino attempts to cross the "ugly ditch" by universalizing the suffering of Jesus through constantly juxtaposing it with the contemporary sufferings of the Latin American people. The idea of *isomorfismo* is central to this process, as is the constant pattern of power and oppression throughout history. Sobrino denies that Jesus' death was a historical accident—rather, it was "the culmination of a necessary historical process"[51] in that the groupings which opposed Jesus held various types of power, whether exercised militarily, economically, or religiously. These power structures have existed throughout human history. It is not necessary to hold to the totality of a Marxist doctrine of class struggle to see such power structures, with the concomitant relationships between oppressors and oppressed (varying in different historical manifestations) as a historical constant.

---

51. Sobrino, *Jesus the Liberator*, 199.

Summary 1

Towards a Political Theology of the Cross—Foundations

In the last two chapters I have attempted to lay the foundations for the subsequent study of Yoder, Boff, and Sobrino. Before moving on I outline some elements, chiefly methodological, arising from these opening chapters which I believe to be necessary for constructing a political theology of the cross.

THE IMPORTANCE OF CONTEXT

It has become widely recognized that any theology inevitably reflects its context, consciously or unconsciously. This recognition is essential both in terms of overcoming the blind spots occasioned by the theologian's context and also in ensuring that the theology speaks in a useful and accurate way to its context. In particular an attentiveness to context provides at least a partial safeguard against the Marxist critique of theology as an obfuscating ideology whose (unintentional) consequence is to mystify the human situation and hence serve the interests of the dominant class. The context of any political theology of the cross is the crucifixion of millions of people—in other words, systems of economic and political power which, while perhaps bringing many benefits, give rise to unnecessary and avoidable suffering on a huge scale. The context for a political theology of the cross, in European Christianity at least, is that of the church's increasing marginalization and weakness. We shall see that in many ways this is not a wholly negative situation, for at the root of a political theology of the cross is the realization that political theology should be exercised not merely, or even chiefly, from the perspective of the powerful. Its clearest perspective is from outside the gates of power, from among the vulnerable victims of the powerful and the recipients of the decisions of the powerful. In both of these contexts, a political theology of the cross cannot be dispassionate or disengaged, but must be a resource for liberative understanding and action as a result of the theological insights gained. Nor must a political theology of the cross begin from a neutral position, but from a prior pre-theological commitment to love, compassion, and justice, without which the cross is politically and theologically meaningless.

The relation between the contextual and the universal is one of interpenetration—on the one hand, a theology of the cross must be local and contextual as, for example, it speaks to the immediate victims and those who seek to bring them help and justice. But those contextual insights must be universalizable, in that a political theology of the cross must speak not just to the immediate context, but to victims, perpetrators, and those who are passive participants in a crucifying economic and political order.

THE CENTRALITY OF CHRIST IN REVELATION

If a political theology is to be Christian, it must begin with Jesus and explore his political and social exemplarity—in other words, the pattern of his interactions with the power structures of his time. In John's Gospel Jesus is described as the *logos*, the self communication of God, the consequence being that by studying his historical acts we gain insight into the eternal truth of God and of God's present mode of working. The saving exemplarity of the incarnation is central to a political theology of the cross, the cross being the radicalization of incarnation—more incarnate than the crucified Christ, God could not become. The cross, therefore, has a necessarily central function in theology as a whole and most particularly in political theology. The Lutheran saying, "every act of Christ is for our instruction" can be taken to extremes, but to ignore one of the most important trajectories within the life of Jesus, the way in which he reacted to the power structures of his day and the way in which they reacted to him, would be to omit something of enormous significance for political theology. In this study I adopt what might be described as a trinitarian christocentrism—my christocentrism is set in the context of the Trinity, but the other persons of Trinity cannot be in contradiction to the central exemplarity of Jesus and the cross. This centrality, or uniqueness, of Christ is inclusive rather than exclusive. On the one hand, Christ is the unique self expression of God and his death a definitive expression of God's salvific relationship with humankind. On the other hand, Christ's death is in solidarity with (and in historical circumstances little different from) the millions of crucifixions through the ages, thereby expressing God's co-suffering in all those crucifixions.

CHRISTOLOGICAL AND SOTERIOLOGICAL COHERENCE

The exemplarity of Jesus as outlined above gains fullest force when allied with a high Christology. If Jesus is not the definitive "human face of God" his exemplarity is much reduced. The methodology most profitable for a political theology of the cross is, in simple terms, not to set out a new Christianity, but to draw out fresh implications from the orthodox, traditional teachings of the church and the Bible. The same pattern as can be traced in other movements of renewal within the church—to draw on the old sources of Christian faith in the light of new contexts.

In systematic theology, at least since Barth, there has been a tendency to identify a unity between creation and atonement, incarnation and redemption, so that these are not seen as separate categories, but as intimately related. Similarly, political theology must not be seen as separate in any way from other doctrines, but as something intimately bound up with the rest. A political theology of the cross is hence most effective if it coheres with an overall theological pattern, especially in terms of soteriology. A cruciform political theology should not be tacked on as if it were a separate issue, or even as a deduction from a perceived central theme, but should be integral to soteriology as a whole. For example, a recognition that God's atoning act is nonviolent and that any violence in the cross is human, not flowing from a divine necessity for bloodshed, will radically affect both soteriological and political doctrines. Similarly, if a dominant symbol in atonement is peacemaking and restored relationships through self sacrificial solidarity, then both doctrine and politics will bear the stamp of that symbol. Political categories should be incorporated as components of an overall soteriology—for example, with regard to the relationship between corporate and individual sin and the role of the cross in the breaking of sin's power over both individuals and structures. Moreover, it is important to recognize that soteriology depends not solely on the moment of Christ's death, but on the factors which preceded and caused it. In the case of Jesus, that would include his self-chosen vulnerability, his resistance to the powerful, his refusal to use violence in response to evil; in the case of his crucifiers, their ruthless resistance to any threat to their power, their use of political and religious ideology to buttress that power, and their reliance on the power of the sword as the ultimate criterion. Without incorporating such factors into a holistic soteriology, sin and salvation become merely mechanical concepts untouched by human reality.

COHERENCE WITH HISTORICAL SCHOLARSHIP

A political theology of the cross as suggested above depends ultimately upon the historical exemplarity of Jesus and hence upon our knowledge of the nature of Jesus' ministry, as sufficiently established by historical scholarship. This, however, need not entail a very high level of detailed historical reconstruction of Jesus' ministry. For example, it is certainly not necessary to argue, in favor of a political theology of the cross, that Jesus was a zealot sympathizer. It is not enough, however, to ignore the importance of a careful historical reconstruction of Jesus' ministry, since there are certain reconstructions which militate against a political theology of the cross. The most damaging stumbling block would be to interpret Jesus as a Socratic individualist—in first-century terms, a Cynic-type figure—whose political interest was only tangential. Rather, a political theology of the cross relies on Jesus' choices and teaching being situated within, and not outside of politics, and adopting a politically relevant stance, albeit as a third way beyond the established political categories.

Underlying the shifting sands of historical research, though, is the fact that the historical incontestability of the crucifixion (even on a minimalist reading by the most radical critics) argues overwhelmingly for the political relevance of Jesus and thus for the possibility of a political theology of the cross. Within the context of first-century society, to make a crucified man the centre of proclamation would be subversive. To call such a man "Lord" would be doubly subversive and politically threatening. Any plausible historical reconstruction of the life and teachings of Jesus must make it possible, or even likely, that he would be crucified as "King of the Jews" by the Romans—in other words, as a political threat to those holding power. Horsley notes:

> The clear implication is that they [Jesus and his disciples] were engaged in activity that the authorities might consider so disruptive as to warrant execution. Nothing indicates that Jesus

or his followers' activity was violent in any way, but it was sufficiently oppositional or disruptive to evoke repressive action.[1]

Rivkin states:

> The titulus preserved in the gospels thus leaves us in no doubt as to why Jesus was crucified and by whom. And the fact that on either side of him was a revolutionary suffering the same fate [lestes in Josephus means revolutionary] evokes for us Rome's determination to eradicate anyone who challenged its rule, whether violent revolutionary or charismatic visionary.[2]

Within historical scholarship the cross is an almost universally agreed datum, but the historical causation of the crucifixion falls into three (very) rough categories of interpretation, of ascending political relevance. First, Jesus may have been crucified as a result of a mistake by the Jewish leadership and Pilate—he would still be an innocent victim of political power, but the political significance of the cross, on this interpretation, would be attenuated. Second, Jesus may have been crucified as a threat to the Jewish leadership, who therefore co-opted the power of the Romans to have him killed. This, the traditional explanation, points to Jesus being crucified as a threat to those holding religious and political power. Thirdly, Jesus may have been crucified as a threat to public order by the Romans, to whom he was an outsider who threatened their rule and therefore qualified for the *servile supplicium*. All three options interpret Jesus as the victim of the powerful, although only the last two make this the result of his deliberate political choices.

Can we go further? Crossan usefully sums up the political significance of Jesus' crucifixion:

> Pilate is the most important commentator on Jesus in the New Testament. By executing Jesus, officially, legally and publicly, he certified that Jesus was a lower-class subversive of Roman law and order. But by executing Jesus alone, that is, by not attempting to round up his companions, Pilate certified that Jesus and his companions represented nonviolent rather than violent resistance. Had Pilate considered them a violent threat, he would have acted as he did with Barabbas' group.[3]

In all these interpretations it is essential to remember the relevance of class to an analysis of the historical circumstances of Jesus' death. Jesus was, of

1. Horsley, *Jesus and the Politics*, 73.
2. Rivkin, *What Crucified Jesus?*, 66
3. Crossan, "Jesus," 132.

course, crucified on a Roman cross by Roman imperial power. But it is necessary to note the degree of co-operation and pragmatic unity between Roman imperialism and local political and economic aristocracies. Greg Woolf notes that:

> The early empire rested on a collusion of interests between the propertied classes of Rome and their counterparts in Italy and the provinces. Many of those elites were already installed within a world of city states, whether of Greek, Punic, Etruscan or other origin. Others were drawn into that mode of aristocracy and shaped in their image . . . The local property classes that ruled them [the cities] kept order and collected taxes, and in return the empire reserved and enhanced their power over other members of their societies.[4]

This practice, widespread throughout the empire, was mirrored in the British Empire by the policy of co-opting the local elites in maintaining imperial power. It is therefore not sufficient to state that Jesus was a victim of Roman imperialism—he was also a victim of the powerful classes in his society (for example, those who benefited from the temple system, or those who gained economic benefit from association with the Romans, such as the Herodians) who saw him as a political threat to their order—and, as Yoder observes, unless those classes and authorities were peculiarly obtuse, Jesus must at least have seemed a sufficient threat to their order for them to have brought about his crucifixion. It is not necessary to adopt a full Marxist analysis to recognize that the hallmark of crucifixion was the reinforcement of the dominance of one class over another, the public confirmation of the status of the crucifier and the crucified. In the very public nature of crucifixion the status of the dominated and of the dominating class was explicitly confirmed in the eyes of any who may have wished to question or challenge that structure of power.

CROSSING LESSING'S DITCH— CONTINGENCY AND NECESSITY

One of the most serious charges against a political theology of the cross is that Jesus' actions which led up to his crucifixion were contingent, restricted to his immediate context, not necessary (even irrelevant) to soteriology and therefore not binding in a revelatory sense for the construction of a political theology of the cross. There are two interrelated issues here—first, the

---

4. Woolf, *Rome*, 280.

argument used by traditional soteriology that the only aspect of the cross of any salvific importance was that Jesus was crucified by sinful humanity in a sinful rejection of God's Son, and second, Lessing's famous ditch between the contingent facts of history and the necessary truths of revelation.

I have argued above that a soteriology dependent simply on the moment of Jesus' death to the neglect of his preceding ministry is deficient, and risks restricting soteriology solely to an intra-trinitarian transaction which can seem dangerously disconnected from the concrete reality of actual human sinfulness. The sinful human nature which crucified Jesus also crucified, metaphorically and literally, the suffering people who were the main focus of Jesus' ministry. A holistic soteriology recognizes the crucifixion as an offence not solely against God but also against those to whom Jesus brought healing and salvation.

To cross Lessing's ditch it is important to recognize the continuing and unchanging patterns surrounding the crucifixion of Jesus which are evident in contemporary crucifixions. For example, the continuing existence of classes of dominated and dominating , of powerful and powerless, and the pattern of the cross-risking challenge to political power and the crucifying response of the powerful are the same in today's world as they were in Jesus' time. Similarly, a faithful and costly commitment to the kingdom of God and the values of justice, peace, and reconciliation invite from those who hold a different ideology the same potentially lethal response today as in first-century Palestine. There is a historical parallelism, or to use Sobrino's term, an *isomorfismo*, which enables the contingencies of Jesus' crucifixion to be transformed into the necessary truths of revelation. It is no shame to admit that Jesus was killed for the same historical reasons as a Camillo Torres or a peasant in El Salvador, since the fate of all three indicates a consistent and continuing pattern in human society.

Chapter 4

The Cross as a Definitive Source of Christian Political Ethics

In the previous chapters I have attempted to lay the foundations for a study of the cross in the political theology of Yoder, Boff, and Sobrino. I now turn to the ways in which these theologians interpret the cross in constructing their political theologies.

In this chapter I examine the role of the cross as a definitive source for Christian political ethics, and identify what the cross and cruciformity might mean as a controlling theme for the above theologians. What, for each of them, is the basic relationship between Jesus' cross and their political theology? In brief, for Yoder, the whole shape of Christian politics as vulnerable nonviolence is defined by the historical exemplarity of the crucified Jesus. For Boff and Sobrino, the cross is most of all a protest against suffering—the "cross against the crosses," based on a doctrine of the "crucified God."

A) YODER—THE CRUCIFORM NATURE OF CHRISTIAN POLITICS

Given the narrative and occasional nature of Yoder's writing, any schematization of his theology, such as is attempted here, is likely to have blurred and rough edges. The themes by which the theology of Yoder is analyzed are not in any way self contained or distinct, and should not be read as such.

Cruciformity as Normative

For Yoder, Christian social ethics are to be modeled on Jesus' incarnational exemplarity. The cross is the radicalization of the incarnation—the starkest and most critical point of Jesus' interaction with the powerful and identification with the powerless of his society. Therefore the crucifixion is bound to have a strong normative function in any social ethic with a firm christological base. Yoder's achievement is to take this definitive cruciformity seriously—more seriously than many other Christian social ethicists—and to see where it leads. Yoder, in attempting to construct a political theology out of the concrete politics of Jesus which led to his crucifixion, aims for a social ethic which is distinctively and authentically Christian. In such an ethic the key aspects of the faith, Jesus' preaching of the kingdom and especially his subsequent death and resurrection, are given full weight. It could be argued that Yoder does not necessarily read the cross and resurrection correctly at all points with regard to social ethics, but I would not wish to fault his cross-centered methodology.

The defenselessness of Christ on the cross is the lens, according to Yoder, through which we are to read God's intentions for human politics. Indeed, Yoder seems at times to regard this function of the crucifixion as primary, constituting "a new stance to be taken by repentant hearers in the midst of the world."[1] Hence Yoder interprets Jesus' rejection of Peter's efforts to defend him not in terms of "some metaphysically motivated doctrine of the atonement—it was because God's will for God's man in this world is that he should renounce legitimate defense."[2] This emphasis has occasioned the charge against Yoder of dissolving the gospel into politics—an unfair criticism, since, as we have seen above, Yoder's doctrine of atonement, with its insistence on a non-coercive and nonviolent Jesus, holds political categories firmly within the context of the soteriological. Politics and salvation are not identical, neither are they separate. God's eternal salvation is effected through a historical act (or series of actions) of Jesus which falls within the realm of the political.

The movement within Yoder's theology can be stated as follows: Jesus is the revealer of God's will for humanity; Jesus, in a series of political actions, instigates a new nonviolent and non-coercive way of living which challenges the powerful and leads inevitably to his crucifixion; the character of God himself is thus shown to be non-coercive and vulnerable; therefore

---

1. Yoder, *Politics*, 97.
2. Yoder, *Politics*, 98.

those who believe in that God are called to follow Jesus, individually and corporately, in a way of life that witnesses to that divine character.

Redefining the Nature of Christian Politics

The nature of the politics in which Christians are called to participate is radically changed by the political acts of Jesus and their consequence in the crucifixion—and yet Jesus' alternative to conventional politics is no less politically relevant. In fact, Jesus' alternative of "rejecting the sword and at the same time condemning those who wielded it"[3] is so radically politically relevant that his opponents, the Jewish and Roman political leaders, felt it necessary to kill him "in the name of both of their forms of political responsibility." Yoder argues that "Jesus' way is not less but more relevant to the question of how society moves than is the struggle for possession of the levers of command; to this Pilate and Caiaphas testify by their judgment on him."[4] Politics is radically redefined, but still remains politics. It is important to note that Yoder's Jesus does not withdraw from politics—rather he refuses to play by the usual rules, or to "concede that those in power represent an ideal, a logically proper, or even an empirically acceptable definition of what it means to be political."[5] In Jesus' ministry politics is redefined, and it is redefined for the Christian especially by Jesus' cross.

Some Criticisms

Before examining Yoder's political reading of the cross in more detail in the following chapters, some preliminary observations and criticisms may be made. First, Yoder's is an unambiguous ethic. Combining his logic of the radical exemplarity of the historical acts of Jesus with the starkness of the cross as the defining symbol of Christian politics it is almost inevitable that this should be so. Such a social ethic can be contrasted with Niebuhrian realism, which recognizes the inevitable ambiguity of most situations. This contrast, which will occur repeatedly in this analysis of Yoder's social ethics, is between an ethic which idealizes moral purity in the sense of consistency of witness and one which attempts to make the best of a situation where moral purity is not achievable. The Niebuhrian approach requires a degree of moral humility in decision making, and a willingness to put good at risk

---

3. Yoder, *Politics*, 106.
4. Yoder, *Politics*, 106.
5. Yoder, *Politics*, 224.

for the sake of a possibly greater good. Yoder's ethic is one of obedience and certainty, but its humility lies in a different direction—in its trust that God will honor the obedience given by the church and by Christians. Niebuhr's ethic is one of getting one's hands (and possibly one's conscience) dirty. Yoder's is one of a refusal to compromise a conscience formed by obedience. Both attempt to be faithful to the incarnation. The Niebuhrian might argue that the incarnation indicates a risk-taking compromise with the realities of history. Yoder argues that the incarnation does not baptize or ratify human sin but offers a different model of humanity.

Secondly, if Christ is the norm for social ethics, what kind of a norm does Yoder mean? Wright, a sympathetic critic, points out the difficulty in distinguishing "between that in Christ which is absolutely, presumptively, or suggestively binding."[6] Jesus' words and actions were directed towards a specific situation. How far, and by what process of interpretation, should those words and actions be seen as normative for different situations? Wright suggests that Yoder's emphasis on redemption needs to be complemented by a fuller doctrine of creation, if the "normative meaning of Jesus for necessary institutions" is to be made clear, and argues that "there remains obscurity about Jesus' mode of relevance and the building of the hermeneutical bridge from his situation to our own."[7] This significant criticism is partly answered by the fact that Yoder, with his emphasis on the eschatological nature of reality, does not differentiate sharply between redemption and creation or between ethics suitable for a crisis and the necessary institutional embodiment of Christian politics. Moreover, the process of interpretative transfer from the first century to the twenty-first does not of itself necessitate any weakening in the radicality of Jesus' ethic. Yoder's logic is that the crucifixion is where the incarnation, definitive of Christian political action, receives its full value. In whatever particular circumstance that incarnation might have occurred, the crucifixion is a necessary, in the sense of inevitable, concomitant. Therefore the pattern of the cross is definitive for every area of Christian social ethics and normative for Christian action in all circumstances—not just for first-century Palestine.

Does Yoder here arbitrarily overemphasize the cross? Again, we return to the necessity of the cross and its centrality to the incarnation. The cross is no chance concomitant, but the fullest and most inevitable expression of God's vulnerable incarnation. Yoder's methodology also argues against such an accusation. Yoder bases his doctrine of the centrality of the cross on the totality of the New Testament witness, involving both the gospel

---

6. Wright, *Disavowing*, 95.
7. Wright, *Disavowing*, 95.

accounts, where the history of the cross (and the choices which led to it) is described, and the Pauline corpus, where the impact of the cross on the social and personal practices of the early Christian community is explored theologically and ethically. This is far from plucking out in an arbitrary way an aspect of Christ's ministry and using it as an interpretative crux. The charge of arbitrariness in the selection of the cross as the defining centre for social ethics can be met by pointing to Yoder's care for the wholeness (at least as regards the New Testament) of the canonical context as evidenced by his seminal work, the *Politics of Jesus,* and his placing the cross within that whole context. This is especially significant given that the gospel Yoder chooses to study, Luke, is not one where the cross is most obviously the controlling feature, as it is more clearly in Mark. If his basic logic is followed, that Christian political ethics are, at root, an imitation of the pattern of Christ's political life and execution, Yoder is justified in regarding the cross as the definitive source of Christian imitation of Christ and, therefore, of Christian political ethics.

B) BOFF AND SOBRINO—THE "CROSS AGAINST THE CROSSES" AND THE "CRUCIFIED GOD"

Boff—The Cross as a Protest against Suffering

For Boff and Sobrino, and for liberation theology in general, the cross is a symbol both of suffering and of protest against that suffering. Boff sees the crucifixion as an evil and criminal act, as something to be resisted in itself and only to be accepted as a means of diminishing present and future crucifixions. He describes the cross, in chapter 10 of *Passion of Christ, Passion of the World,* as a symbol of hatred, imposed by the "creators of crosses"[8] on those who seek to remove the world's crosses. But when the cross thus imposed is accepted (in other words, suffering is risked as a necessary consequence of the task of removing crosses) a power is released: "To accept the cross is to be greater than the cross. To live thus is to be stronger than death."[9] The cross is not to be interpreted as "dolorism," or glorying in pain, but rather as the result of a positive commitment to following Jesus in making it "gradually impossible for human beings to crucify other human beings."[10]

---

8. Boff, *Passion,* 131.
9. Boff, *Passion,* 131.
10. Boff, *Passion,* 132.

Boff is greatly concerned to resist misuse of the cross, especially in Latin American Catholicism, in inculcating a fatalism, or even a glorification of suffering as something willed by God as spiritually beneficial in itself. Following the Marxist critique, he argues that the cross has been used by the powerful to demonstrate the inevitability, or even the value, of suffering as an integral part of life.[11] The cross is reduced to an individualist, fatalist and pietist necessity: individualist, in that there is no social consequence to bearing the cross beyond simply remaining within the class or social position in which one is placed; fatalist, in that there is no need or point in struggling against the situation, which simply has to be borne resignedly; and pietist, in that God blesses such an action. Crosses must be carried not as something unjustly imposed by the oppressive sin of others, but as a way of dealing with one's own sin, through a penitent submission, in the light of God's perfection.[12] *Passion of Christ, Passion of the World* is, to a great extent, a polemic against such a theology, the propagation of which is in the interests of those who hold, and are unwilling to relinquish, political power. Boff argues throughout his work that far from God having a preference for human suffering, God's will is for human well-being, and God's glory is expressed in and through human life and happiness. The cross should not be idolized as an end in itself or made an object of devotion for its own sake, as if there is something intrinsically good in suffering. Rather, it is an inevitable concomitant in the struggle for liberation and against suffering. In fact, the essence of *Passion of Christ, Passion of the World* could be summarized as "the cross against the crosses." The *telos* is not the cross but the resurrection, the two being in an inescapable "paschal" dialectic, worked out in active discipleship.[13] This tension, between combating and taking up the cross, between the cross as a hostile as well as a helpful symbol, is no merely theoretical technicality, but is central to a focused political spirituality.

Boff—Modern Theologies of the Cross Examined

With this anti-suffering criterion in mind, in chapters 8, 9, and 10 of *Passion of Christ, Passion of the World,* Boff spends much energy on reviewing contemporary interpretations of the cross. In chapter 8 he considers various theologies of the cross, using the criteria of how they relate to human suffering, how evil is interpreted and, more importantly, how it is overcome. It is worthwhile analyzing this chapter in detail, as it provides a good insight

11. Boff, *Passion*, 2.
12. Boff, *Passion*, 2.
13. Boff, *Passion*, 3–4.

into the criteria by which he judges theologies of the cross. Boff's overriding criterion is practical—a theology which legitimizes evil, and provides no way of overcoming suffering or evil, cannot be a legitimate theology. The task of the Christian is to overcome suffering, not to acquiesce in it or, even worse, to make it an integral and valued part of spirituality and theology.

He begins with Moltmann's *The Crucified God* which, following a Lutheran emphasis (although Moltmann is actually of the Reformed tradition) on the *theologia crucis*, puts the cross at the centre of the theological task as the distinguishing mark of Christianity. According to Moltmann, in Boff's interpretation, it is not enough to say that Christ died as a martyred prophet. The radical nature of the cross lies in the fact that Jesus was rejected by God, in addition to his rejection by his political and religious opponents. God's self revelation in impotence, rather than power, fundamentally changes our concept of God, transcending all human images which are nullified by the cross. This would, no doubt, be at least partially acceptable to Boff. But Moltmann moves beyond this to stress the profoundly intra-trinitarian nature of the cross—God the Father is instrumental in crucifying the Son, and suffers the death of the Son, in the pain of love. Crucifixion, death, is actualized in God's own self, and "God assumes the passion of the world. Human suffering is no longer exterior to God. It transpires within God."[14] Death is not thereby eternalized, made permanent, as a part of God—for God is in process through suffering love, and assumes full identity when evil and death are conquered and God will be all in all (an aspect of Moltmann's theology which Boff seems to downplay in subsequent criticisms). It is perhaps not difficult to see the problems Boff has with such a theology. The cross is seen (or can be portrayed as being seen) as part of the suprahistorical, intra-divine drama which may not only sideline the need for salvation to be worked out politically but also risks making suffering an integral part of the divine *modus operandi*. Although in the end, when God is all in all, evil is defeated, God is still responsible for imposing the death of his Son, as part of his plan of salvation. Again, this is a theme Boff is concerned to avoid, as a legitimization of human suffering. According to Boff, the necessity of Christ's death lies not in a divine plan, but in the inevitability of Jesus' suffering if he is to carry through his historical project. It is not something directly willed by God. Boff's God is crucified, not in any sense a crucifier.

Boff's basic criticism of Moltmann is that although suffering is to be eventually overcome, it is somehow internalized within God to the potential detriment of humanity. This, however, would not be a valid criticism. To conceive of a divine internalization of suffering is justified, if it is a way

---

14. Boff, *Passion*, 105.

of sympathy and solidarity with human suffering in order to overcome it. The danger, of which Boff is very much aware, occurs when suffering itself is deified or valued as something not wholly evil. Boff's critique, while pointing up certain inconsistencies in Moltmann's theology, would seem, in practice, to be extreme and unfair. One of the central aspects of Moltmann's *theologia crucis* is his insistence on the relevance of the crucified and risen Christ to political change and his sympathy with those who suffer, especially the disabled. Moltmann has himself protested against the caricature of his theology as represented by the phrase "God the crucifier." There is a wide difference between a sadistic deity who actively wills the crucifixion of his son and Moltmann's suffering God who "unwillingly wills" or painfully allows Jesus to be crucified for the sake of fulfilling his mission of solidarity and love. Boff and Moltmann are, in fact, much closer than Boff allows, and the differences are perhaps exaggerated through the wish of certain liberation theologians to distance themselves from European political theology.

Boff next turns to Hedinger's *Against God's reconciliation with misery: a critique of Christian theism and a-theism*. Hedinger's thesis, that suffering should be combated, rather than accepted, receives Boff's approval.[15] Hedinger refuses to attribute evil to God, or to sublimate evil and suffering. God cannot be responsible for the death of Jesus, which was a crime of political murder. Jesus did not have to die on the cross in order to manifest the love of God his Father—his whole life of faithfulness and commitment to God culminated in his death.[16] It is clear that Boff finds Hedinger's theology much more acceptable than Moltmann's. Hedinger argues that only a God without love would reject his Son. The relationship of God with Christ on the cross is not a rejection of the Son but a suffering alongside him. In a major passage which sums up much of Boff's theology of the cross, he argues thus:

> We may say that God suffers with us, and suffers in Jesus Christ, that God is in solidarity with Jesus' suffering and ours, that God is suffering too, to deliver us from suffering, introducing the universe to a kind of love that willingly assumes suffering and death, not because it perceives some value in it, but in order to render it impossible from within.[17]

A spirituality which glorifies suffering, inculcating a political passivity, is one of Boff's chief targets. Hence Boff concludes his survey with the contribution of liberation theology. He quotes Sobrino: "The cross is the outcome

---

15. Boff, *Passion*, 106.
16. Boff, *Passion*, 106.
17. Boff, *Passion*, 106.

of an incarnation situated in a world of sin that is revealed to be a power working against the God of Jesus."[18] Boff denies that the cross eternalized suffering—rather it is a sign of God's solidarity with human suffering in order to bring it to an end through love.[19] The only cross that can be projected within the being of God is the cross of love—not the cross of hate. Boff concludes, in a highly significant phrase, that the task of the Christian faith is "to render the hatred that generates the cross ever more impossible, not through violence, which simply forces whatever it wishes, but through love and reconciliation."[20] Here is a profound insight into the political role of the church. The cross is a symbol, not of resignation, but of protest against the continuing infliction of crosses. Boff notes also that such a political theology of the cross necessitates belief in a God who suffers (quoting the famous phrase of Bonhoeffer, that "only the suffering God can help"[21])—that almost seismic shift in much late twentieth-century theology, among theologians whom Boff criticizes as well as those whom he praises. However, it is not enough to speak in general terms of a suffering God or suffering in God. More accuracy is needed in the language used to describe such suffering. There is an ever present danger that a theology of the cross can be construed as suggesting that God is an active cause of pain, rather than a one who suffers in solidarity with that pain.[22]

In opposition to this Boff proposes a simple theology of an almost apophatic silence after the enunciation of the faith statement "Jesus is God." The cross is the "death of all systems." Speculative theology gives way to an ethic of discipleship of this Jesus who is also God. Faith seeks understanding not by speculation, but by discipleship; not by theodicy but by ethics. This way is, in fact, more true to the being, purpose, and suffering of God. God suffers in solidarity with the suffering of his creation, but with the aim not of glorifying, but of abolishing suffering. The meaning and the use of suffering is simply "to change and to transform the world."[23] The quest for a politically relevant meaning to suffering is a focal point of Boff's theology, his task being to provide spiritual resources for those of his contemporaries who suffer for the sake of justice. The deification of suffering, a view of the cross which produces fatalism and political apathy is, as noted above, his chief target, both in his criticisms of academic theologians and of grass-roots

---

18. Boff, *Passion*, 110.
19. Boff, *Passion*, 110.
20. Boff, *Passion*, 110.
21. Bonhoeffer, *Letters*, 361.
22. Boff, *Passion*, 111.
23. Boff, *Passion*, 114.

Catholic spirituality. As has been argued, Boff may be unfair in his criticism of Moltmann, but his general emphasis, "the cross against the crosses" is fully justified.

Sobrino—Jesus as the Revealer of the Crucified God

In his first major theological work, *Christology at the Crossroads,* Sobrino sets out fourteen theses on the death of Jesus. Number thirteen expounds what is possibly Sobrino's major contribution to liberation theology, the linkage between liberation and the crucified God in a Latin American context. At this point his theology closely follows and parallels that of Moltmann in a slightly earlier, European context.

> On the cross of Jesus Christ God himself is crucified. The Father suffers the death of the Son and takes upon himself all the pain and suffering of history. In this ultimate solidarity with humanity he reveals himself as the God of love, who opens up a hope and a future through the most negative side of history. Thus Christian existence is nothing else but a process of participating in this same process whereby God loves the world and hence in the very life of God.[24]

There are also notable parallels here with Bonhoeffer's idea of the Christian life as participating in the suffering of God vis-à-vis his creation.

Sobrino, in *Christology at the Crossroads,* describes various ways by which the radicality and the scandal of the cross are avoided: by concentrating on the resurrection; by burying the cross under the categories of noetic and salvific mystery; by holding a conception of God which does not begin from the cross; and by restricting the cross to the context of sacrificial cultic worship.[25] However, far from being the unchanged and unchanging God of Greek metaphysics, God suffers. And this suffering has a profound meaning for political theology, in pointing to a divine solidarity and a vulnerability which radically subverts a theology of power-as-force, of paternalism, or of withdrawal. In his last major christological work, *Christ the Liberator,* Sobrino returns to the "audacity and honesty" of the Fathers, who "upheld the divinity of Jesus Christ even without knowing where affirming the divinity of a crucified man was leading them."[26] An Arian Christ cannot reveal a

---

24. Sobrino, *Christology,* 224.
25. Sobrino, *Christology,* 185.
26. Sobrino, *Christ the Liberator,* 257.

God whose being is expressed above all in solidarity, vulnerability, and in suffering alongside and on behalf of creation.

Is suffering, then, intrinsic to God? How can Sobrino avoid the charge Boff lays against Moltmann, of deifying suffering? Sobrino avoids this pitfall by stressing that suffering is intrinsic to God *in his relationship to a suffering world*. Since God is love, suffering is an inevitable concomitant of God's response to a sinful and crucifying world. The cross is the inevitable result, given human sin, of incarnation. Sobrino describes God's choice to become consistently incarnate in history, with the result that God is radically affected by sin and death. The cross is not arbitrary, or a cruel divine punishment inflicted on Jesus, but is the inevitable result of God's choice to be unconditionally and lovingly incarnate within the historical process.[27] Since a large part of the sin which crucified Jesus and which crucifies contemporary sufferers is political in nature (in the sense of a misuse of power), this divine incarnation-suffering has profound political implications.

First, those who claim to follow Jesus are obliged to undergo a similar cross-risking incarnation. Sobrino quotes Romero in describing "a church incarnate in the problems of the people."[28] Second, the cross demonstrates the divine solidarity-in-suffering with the victims. Sobrino points out that the phrase "crucified God" is therefore no more than another term, provocative and shocking, with the same meaning as "God of solidarity." But why does solidarity have to be shown through crucifixion? Sobrino argues that solidarity without participating in the struggles and sufferings of those with whom one is in solidarity would be at best paternalist, and at worst despotic. "Solidarity in a world of victims that was not prepared to become a victim would in the end not be solidarity."[29] Suffering, therefore, is part of the divine, not intrinsically, but as a necessary consequence of God's choice to become incarnate in a suffering world. This suffering does not have value in itself, but only in relation to God's love reaching out to the world.

A sub-text in much liberation theology (and in much political theology as a whole) is the debate over the relationship between divine action and passivity, and the consequent relationship between the political responsibility and non-responsibility of the church (this tension is a major theme in Yoder's theology). This paradoxical tension comes to the fore most starkly in the cross. Sobrino boldly grasps the fact that on the cross God does not actively intervene but allows the tragedy of the crucifixion to unfold. Sobrino asks if this refusal to act actually reveals the purposes and nature of

---

27. Sobrino, *Jesus the Liberator*, 244.
28. Sobrino, *Christ the Liberator*, 273.
29. Sobrino, *Jesus the Liberator*, 245.

God, especially since this divine non-intervention is not confined to the cross of Jesus, but extends to the millions of deaths unjustly inflicted in human history, seemingly allowed by God.[30] Sobrino fully acknowledges the "scandal of God's silence in the crucifixion"[31] but sets it alongside the faith that God is somehow still present. This tension is the crux of any political theodicy, but it is a tension which can be resolved only by a mixture of contemplation of the suffering God and action to relieve suffering humanity through "taking responsibility for the crucified." This inevitably involves the Christian being open to the possibility of bearing suffering alongside the God who suffers in the crucified Christ.[32]

This does not, however, mean that there should be any acceptance of suffering as anything other than an evil. Sobrino, like Boff, insists that suffering is never to be justified or thought of as something essential to the being of God, with the crucial exception of God's relationship to a crucifying world. History can only be saved by "real incarnation in history" and this inevitably, given the world's sin, leads to the cross.[33] As we have seen with Boff, much of the theological backdrop to Sobrino's discussion is the trinitarian theology of Moltmann, which is interpreted as representing the Father being instrumental in the crucifixion of the Son, and thus being, ultimately, a crucifier, responsible for suffering. According to Boff and Sobrino, suffering is not eternalized in God's trinitarian being, and thus perpetuated. Rather, God resists suffering, even at the risk, in Jesus, of sharing victimhood with the victims. There is a necessary subtlety in the language used here. God neither abandoned Jesus nor intervened to stop him in his quest for faithfulness to his mission. God's prior decision for incarnation made the divine sufferings inevitable. Does this mean that God is silent (and non-interventionist) over contemporary crosses? Stalsett points to a dialectic in Sobrino's thought: God is absent, yet present, and that very presence-in-absence makes possible God's solidarity with contemporary crucifixions.[34] In other words, God is present on the cross in the person of Jesus, yet God the Father does not intervene in the crucifixion of the Son but abandons him to the necessity of incarnation in a crucifying world. A similar idea of the presence and the hiddenness of God is found also in Sobrino's recent theodicy following the Indian Ocean Tsunami. "God is hidden in the

30. Sobrino, *Jesus the Liberator*, 240.
31. Sobrino, *Jesus the Liberator*, 252.
32. Sobrino, *Jesus the Liberator*, 242.
33. Sobrino, *Jesus the Liberator*, 244.
34. Stalsett, *Crucified*, 465.

earthquake and suffers in silence with the victims. But hope does not die, and in hope God remains mysteriously present."[35]

The Crucified God and Political Salvation

"Only the suffering God can help."[36] Bonhoeffer's profound words pose as many questions as answers. How can a crucified and hence seemingly powerless God help? Love without power would seem to be ineffective, and power without love oppressive. Sobrino discusses this crucial question by describing the need of the poor for a rescuer from outside (alterity) and a rescuer from alongside (affinity).

The poor turn to God for saving power, and in that they see effective love. But they also turn to God who is alongside them in their suffering, and in that they see credible love.[37] This combination of vulnerability and intervention on behalf of the poor is, for Sobrino, exemplified in Archbishop Romero's rejection of personal protection whilst denouncing the forces which eventually killed him. Sobrino makes the enigmatic statement that sin must certainly be eradicated by fighting against it, but that "this fight means bearing sin . . . injustice cannot be eradicated unless it is borne."[38] What does this "bearing of sin and injustice" mean? This will be discussed at greater length in relation to the crucified people. Suffice it to say, here, that the fight against sin and injustice is not conducted, as it were, from a safe place, but in solidarity with the victims. The crucified Jesus demonstrates both alterity—a salvation from outside (an intervention)—and affinity—a salvation from alongside (a sharing of the suffering). The silence of God on the cross indicates a double solidarity, with Jesus and with those who have shared his cross throughout history. "History's victims look for an effective love, but also welcome a credible love."[39] Sobrino adduces this combination of alterity and affinity not merely as a theological formula, but as a guide to Christian pastoral and political practice. Power intervention from outside of the situation must be balanced by empathetic presence from within.

---

35. Sobrino, *Where Is God?*, 137.
36. Bonhoeffer, *Letters*, 361.
37. Sobrino, *Where Is God?*, 145.
38. Sobrino, *Jesus the Liberator*, 245–46.
39. Sobrino, *Jesus the Liberator*, 246.

C) CONCLUSION

Yoder's greatest contribution is to take seriously the normative nature of the crucifixion for Christian political ethics. Despite criticisms of Yoder for over-isolating the cross as a norm, I regard Yoder's overall methodology as fruitful and necessary. If a model of revelation is accepted in which Jesus is normative (and that is the basic assumption which Yoder makes, in my opinion, correctly), it is arbitrary to exclude either one highly significant aspect of Jesus' life—the crucifixion and its political causes—or one area of ethics—the political. Yoder seeks to redefine politics in obedience to the social exemplarity of Jesus, brought to sharp focus in the crucifixion, and to encourage the church to trust that God will honor that obedience.

The focus of Boff and Sobrino is different. For them, the cross is ultimately a protest against suffering and a necessary symbol of a campaign against such suffering. Both, but especially Sobrino, base this upon the fruit of the great paradigm shift in twentieth-century theology, the doctrine of a God who suffers in sympathy with the sufferings of humanity.

All three theologians find their focus primarily in response to the historical fact of the crucifixion but also in reaction to prevalent theologies and spiritualities—in the case of Yoder, the Christian realism of Reinhold Niebuhr and in the case of Boff and Sobrino the politically conservative dolorism of the Latin American church (and, to a lesser extent, an unease with certain aspects of Moltmann's theology of the cross). Their starting points are different in terms of the background of spirituality, geography, and politics against which they write, but their basic theologies of the cross are not contradictory.

Chapter 5

The Cross and Political Discipleship

For all three of our interlocutors, the cross is intimately associated with the practical demands of discipleship. In this chapter I explore their theologies to examine how a political discipleship can be exercised in the light of the cross.

A) YODER—THE CROSS AND NONCONFORMING POLITICAL DISCIPLESHIP

Discipleship as Bearing the Cross of Nonconformity

Yoder insists that crucifixion was a political event used by the Roman Empire in preserving the current system of power and acting as a visible deterrent to those who would oppose that power. Therefore the cross which the Christian disciple was called to bear in New Testament times and is called to bear in the present has inescapable and radical political connotations. Any other usage of the cross is inexplicable, given the widespread knowledge in the ancient world of the cross as the prime Roman method of dealing with challenges to their political and socio-economic hegemony. Yoder, first of all, is insistent in declaring what "bearing the cross," or "taking up the cross" (Mark 8: 34, NRSV) is not. Contrary to popular usage, where "bearing one's cross" refers to putting up with chance suffering due to sickness or other misfortune, Yoder states that the "believer's cross must be like his Lord's, the price of his social nonconformity."[1] Yoder differentiates carefully between this political

---

1. Yoder, *Politics*, 96.

interpretation of cross bearing and what he describes elsewhere as the cross in Protestant pastoral care. "It is not, like sickness or catastrophe, an inexplicable, unpredictable suffering; it is the end of a path freely chosen after counting the cost."[2] Nor is bearing the cross something inward or private, in the form of individual spiritual turmoil. Rather, it is "the social reality of representing in an unwilling world the Order to come."[3] Cross bearing is not something which simply happens to a Christian in the course of his or her *private* existence—it is the risk taken, the consequence incurred, by the *social* nonconformity inherent in following Jesus. Persecution and suffering for the Christian are inescapable consequences of "our social obedience to the Messianity of Jesus," and will parallel his suffering: "His people will encounter in ways analogous to his own the hostility of the old order."[4] Yoder gives a solemn warning to the contemporary church—discipleship involves a challenge to the established powers, and just as that challenge brought Jesus to crucifixion, so the Christian risks its contemporary equivalent.

Yoder stresses this point, since so much of both Protestant and Catholic spirituality has privatized the bearing of the cross and hence seriously restricted its nature. He sums up the conflictual and freely chosen nature of cross bearing: "To accept the cross as his destiny, to move toward it and even to provoke it, when he could well have done otherwise, was Jesus' constantly reiterated free choice."[5] And that choice led to predictable results—"The cross of Calvary . . . was the political, legally-to-be expected result of a moral clash with the powers ruling his society." As we have previously noted, suffering in itself is not a virtue in an ascetic sense. It only has value when it results from a nonconforming and nonviolent witness. The cross which the disciple bears is, therefore, the (potential) price of the social and political nonconformity which the disciple freely undertakes as a matter of deliberate choice in imitation of Jesus who likewise chose the path of such nonconformity.

This theme runs throughout the *Politics of Jesus*, but is also stressed in other writings of Yoder. For example, in *Royal Priesthood* in his discussion of the *Notae Missionis* of the church, Yoder writes, "The true missionary congregation is marked by suffering . . . not the result of misbehavior but of conformity with the path of Christ . . . the meaningful assumption of the cost of nonconformed obedience."[6] Similarly, in *For the Nations*, in his discussion of the cross-language of Martin Luther King, Yoder writes that cross

2. Yoder, *Politics*, 129.
3. Yoder, *Politics*, 96.
4. Yoder, *Politics*, 96.
5. Yoder, *Politics*, 129.
6. Yoder, *Royal Priesthood*, 86.

bearing is not about "psychic or moral weakness"—rather, it has to do with an ethical and strategic choice, consciously chosen suffering in response to injustice: "It signals the conscious choice of a path of vulnerable faithfulness, despite the knowledge that it will be costly."[7]

A criticism can perhaps be made at this point. Whilst Yoder's is a helpful corrective to the (pastorally valuable, but biblically unjustifiable) usages of cross-bearing language in terms of coping with unfortunate chance circumstances, he can justly be charged with neglecting the personal and psychological use of the cross in the Pauline terminology of dying and rising with Christ. Paul seems to go beyond Yoder's interpretation of a political imitation to one which at least includes the "inward experience of the self."[8] The cross as a political punishment for social nonconformity is, at least in part, used as a metaphor by Paul for an inward experience (which, of course, has social consequences). Yoder seems to posit an either/or rather than a both/and. The Pauline language of the cross, deriving as it did from the political event of the crucifixion, could well be used also in psychological or mystical terms.

Discipleship as an Imitation of the Crucified

Fundamental to Yoder's reading of the cross in this way is his insistence on discipleship as an imitation of Christ in the (often political) circumstances facing the Christian—"social obedience to the Messianity of Jesus."[9] Yoder's ethic in general is that of imitating the character of God as revealed in Christ. He is, however, at pains to make the proviso that this imitation of Jesus can only be justified, by scripture, at the sole and particular point of the cross. *Imitatio Christi* as a general pastoral, moral, or formational ideal (as in Franciscan spirituality or Islamic imitation of even the personal habits of Muhammad) is, according to Yoder, not justified by any appeal to the New Testament. It is only at the specific point of the cross (and the cross interpreted as the price of social nonconformity) that imitation is not merely allowed, but demanded.

This argument is made in two striking passages in the *Politics of Jesus*. First in the chapter "Trial Balance" which sums up the midpoint of his argument, Yoder discounts the "Franciscan and romantic" idea of imitating Christ in every particular of his life. Rather, "only at one point, only on one subject—but then consistently, universally—is Jesus our example: in

---

7. Yoder, *For the Nations*, 145–46.
8. Yoder, *Politics*, 129.
9. Yoder, *Politics*, 96.

his cross."[10] Second, at the end of his survey of discipleship-language in the New Testament he argues:

> There is no *general* concept of living like Jesus in the New Testament... There is but one realm in which the concept of imitation holds... This is at the point of the concrete social meaning of the cross in its relation to enmity and power. Servanthood replaces dominion, forgiveness absorbs hostility. Thus—and only thus—are we bound by New Testament thought to 'be like Jesus.'[11]

Here Yoder overstates his case. While correctly stating that a political *imitatio Christi* is demanded by the New Testament, he neglects wider forms of imitation. For example, in John 13:15 Jesus invites his disciples to imitate his love, humility, and service. Jesus' life of love certainly finds its culmination in the cross, but other aspects of Jesus life and character can justifiably be adduced as exemplary for the Christian. Even if this is not made absolutely explicit by the New Testament writers, Jesus' pre-crucifixion character and actions surely inform subsequent Christian ethics and spirituality. To argue otherwise would be to cut the connection between Jesus' social actions—for example, his radical extension of table fellowship—and subsequent church practice. Perhaps this is an instance of Yoder's potentially dangerous tendency towards a tunnel vision, which might lead to a neglect of some important aspects of Jesus' ministry, for example his loving humility or his respect for women.

Martyrdom and "Revolutionary Subordination"

Two aspects of a cruciform political discipleship identified by Yoder are martyrdom and "revolutionary subordination." The idea of the church as the community that witnesses through suffering will be discussed later, but here it may be sufficient to note the relevance of martyrdom for Yoder's doctrine of political discipleship. Yoder writes in *Royal Priesthood*, in the discussion mentioned above concerning the *Notae Missionis* of the church, that suffering due to obedient following of the nonconforming Christ is an inescapable mark of the church, and the church's witness is borne through the testimony of its innocent suffering. Nor is this merely a temporary phenomenon—it is "according to both Scripture and experience the continuing destiny of any faithful Christian community."[12] The traditional link of wit-

---

10. Yoder, *Politics*, 95.
11. Yoder, *Politics*, 130–31.
12. Yoder, *Royal Priesthood*, 86.

ness with suffering, and the increased value suffering gives to that witness, is a major theme in Yoder's theology of the church's political interaction with society. The outright collision of the values of the world and the gospel resulting in martyrdom should not be shunned by a community defined by messianic pacifism. Indeed, those who suffer publicly as a result of this collision should be regarded as truly representative of that community. Discipleship entails participation in a community whose nonviolent social and political nonconformity risks suffering which witnesses both to the character of God and to the community's faithfulness to Christ.

Thus far Yoder's reading of the cross and the place of suffering, although diverging from the traditional reading in ascribing greater political content to martyrdom, is relatively uncontroversial. His doctrine of revolutionary subordination (chapter 9 of *Politics of Jesus*) has attracted more serious criticism, with good reason. Yoder seeks to answer the question of how far the cross-ethic of Jesus persists in the early church. He adduces the example of the *haustafeln*, the "home and family ethics" in the Pauline epistles, which, he argues, can be traced to the teaching and example of Jesus, especially his cruciform non-resistance. In brief, his argument is as follows: Slaves, women, and other people in "subordinate" roles have received the news of freedom and worth in Christ. How should they use this freedom? By living out voluntarily Christ's self-giving, exemplified by the cross. "Subordination means the acceptance of an order, as it exists, but with the new meaning given to it by the fact that one's acceptance of it is willing and meaningfully motivated."[13] The clear weakness here is that while such subordination may conceivably, in some limited circumstances, be good for the soul of the individual (not a very Yoderian argument!) it is, in fact, a damaging collusion with an unjust social order; one is to realize one's freedom but immediately relinquish it by locating oneself again in exactly the same subordinate position in that social order. If a social order is unjust, it is surely dangerous to recommend collusion with it for the sake of supposed spiritual benefits, whether on earth or in the hereafter—the precise charge of Marx in his opiate accusation. It is difficult to see how there can be any motive for change either from below or from above if the existing order is upheld as a legitimate and inviolate framework for the exercise of the Christian's discipleship. Yoder argues that the *haustafeln* indicate a new and unprecedented reciprocity in social relationships, but still the underlying social structure is maintained. "Freedom can already be realized within his present status by voluntarily accepting subordination, in view of the relative unimportance of such social distinctions when seen

---

13. Yoder, *Politics*, 172.

in the light of the coming fulfillment of God's purposes."[14] Again, Yoder's insistence on the "relative unimportance" of the present corroborates Marx's criticism. Yoder's social ethics are radically eschatological, but it is highly dangerous to downplay the importance of the present in the light of a promised better future. Yoder denies that subordination is simply a religiously sanctioned confirmation of the existing power structures of society. Rather, "the subordinate person becomes a free ethical agent when he voluntarily accedes to his subordination in the power of Christ instead of bowing to it fatalistically or resentfully."[15] However, the hard fact is that the "free ethical agent" is still a slave in that stratified society, with the stratification essentially unchallenged and with all the injustices that entails both for himself and for others. Yoder is seeking to discover " . . . how in each role the servanthood of Christ, the voluntary subordination of one who knows that another regime is normative, could be made concrete"[16] but seems to omit the wider social significance of such subordination.

Perhaps this is an instance of a recurring weakness in Yoder's thought, in isolating a theme drawn from the example of the crucified Christ (in this case submission/subordination) and overemphasizing it in contexts where such an overemphasis is potentially misleading or even destructive. Yoder, while drawing this theme from the example of Christ, crucified through a certain combination of political circumstances, does not explain why it is intrinsically good in circumstances which may differ radically. We see here the form of action drawn from the crucified Christ—submission and subordination—overriding other equally valid aims.

B) BOFF AND SOBRINO—CRUCIFORM SPIRITUALITY AND MARTYRDOM

Boff—A Cruciform Spirituality for Political Discipleship

In chapter 10 of *Passion of Christ, Passion of the World*, "How to preach the cross of Jesus Christ today"[17] Boff sets out the practical conclusions of his study of the political relevance of the crucifixion. He begins his summary by pointing to the present meaning of discipleship in Latin America. Preaching the cross means commitment to the kingdom values of love, peace, community, justice, and denouncing whatever opposes those values. The result

---

14. Yoder, *Politics*, 182.
15. Yoder, *Politics*, 186.
16. Yoder, *Politics*, 187.
17. Boff, *Passion*, 129–30.

will be conflict, with the inevitable suffering that ensues.[18] In other words, the Christian is to take up Jesus' historic project and to expect the same order of opposition, with the same potential result. This provides the self-declared subtext of Boff's work—providing theological and spiritual resources for those involved in creating a more just society and attempting to find a meaning in the suffering incurred by such a task. Boff's aim is to provide help to those who, in their own suffering discipleship, attempt to find some meaning in the world's suffering. By meditating on Christ's passion, he enables them to find "some unsuspected source of strength for resistance and resurrection."[19]

For example, in chapter 5 of *Passion of Christ, Passion of the World* Boff offers encouragement to those whose self-surrender in the liberative political struggles of Latin America leads them to "the abyss of humiliation." A spirituality emphasizing total commitment is common in liberation theology, with the ever present reminder of, on the one hand, the risks of martyrdom from oppressive governments and, on the other, the example of Marxist inspired total commitment among the guerrillas of the left. The Christian has the example of the total commitment of Jesus which led to the cross, an apparent dead end were it not for the resurrection. The Pauline theme of dying to self, a dying paralleled and exemplified by the crucified Christ, is translated into a spirituality of political discipleship.

Boff ends *Passion of Christ, Passion of the World* (Chapter 11, "Conclusion—the Cross: Mystery and Mysticism") with a short meditation on the dual nature of the cross. On the one hand, it signifies something criminal, humans in their freedom rebelling against God. On the other, it points to the possibility of overcoming the crosses that bedevil humanity, and to the new life that comes through that struggle.[20] The cross of hate, unjustly imposed, can become a symbol of love when resisted, even if that resistance leads to crucifixion. This paradoxical ambiguity of the cross has to be kept in tension, otherwise it loses its power as the *logos tou staurou* (the word of the cross). This, however, can only be resolved through the praxis of taking up and combating the cross, a praxis which reveals meaning and engenders life. Evil is overcome not by reflecting on it from a safe distance, but by resisting it in its historical reality, following the example of Jesus whose historic project inevitably led to the cross.

---

18. Boff, *Passion*, 130.
19. Boff, *Passion*, xiii.
20. Boff, *Passion*, 134.

Boff—The Power of Martyrdom

This leads to another prominent theme in Boff's theology and spirituality, that preaching the cross involves martyrdom, both explicitly for God and implicitly for God's kingdom of justice and peace.[21] This martyrdom for justice opens up the future, in the sense of being a protest against the fatalism which can leave closed systems as they are. Martyrdom has a subversive effect in questioning the persistence of how things are and in drawing attention to the disordered, inverted standards prevalent in an oppressive society. The cross radically questions the commonly held values of such a society. "The martyr rips the mask from the face of the system"[22] by embodying, and being willing to suffer for, another order. This seemingly paradoxical willingness to bear the cross through a love that is willing to suffer is a prophetic sign of a reversal of values.[23]

The theme of the crucified people will be discussed in Chapter 8 with reference chiefly to Sobrino. But Boff also stresses the continuity between the cross of Jesus and the crucified people of today:

> Jesus' passion goes on in the passion of our suffering people.[24] Jesus continues to be crucified in all those who are crucified in history . . . there are not enough Stations of the Cross to depict all the ways in which the Lord continues to be persecuted, imprisoned, condemned to death, and crucified today in the ongoing passion of human life.[25]

The history of the crucifixion did not end with the deposition of the body of Jesus—Boff sees it continuing in the present experience of those seeking liberation. "Christ's passion is being completed by each succeeding generation and its martyrs."[26] There is a definite identity, continuity and similarity:

> Today the passion of the mystical Christ, embodied in the lives of those who are sacrificed for the cause of justice, preserves the same structure as the passion of the historical Jesus. Like Jesus, many people today are being persecuted and killed for defending the rights of the lowly and the just claims of the poor.[27]

---

21. Boff, *Passion*, 130.
22. Boff, *Passion*, 130.
23. Boff, *Passion*, 131.
24. Boff, *Way*, 7.
25. Boff, *Way*, 92–93.
26. Boff, *Way*, 108.
27. Boff, *Way*, ix.

Martyrdom, and the parallels (traditional in Christian spirituality and theology since the early days of the church) between those martyred and the crucified Jesus Christ, play a central role in Boff's theology of the cross. This is true for Latin American liberation theology as a whole, with Archbishop Romero the most famous (but by no means the only) example. In chapter 9 of *Passion of Christ, Passion of the World*, Boff adduces a practical example of "suffering born of the struggle against suffering" in the *passio vitae* of Fr. Carlos Alberto, which symbolizes the priests of the Latin American church who take up the liberation struggle and suffer through their commitment, those who sacrifice themselves for others.[28] As we have previously noted, Boff's choice of examples reveals the focus of his work. He is attempting to offer spiritual resources to those who take up the defense of the oppressed, rather than primarily to the oppressed themselves. Boff draws an explicit parallel with the *Acta Martyrum* of the early church, and the catalogue of martyrs in Hebrews 11. The martyrs of the Latin American church, who go back to the very early days of the Spanish and Portuguese conquest, are to be seen in precisely the same category as the more traditional martyrs of the church, in witnessing to the truth of the gospel through their suffering and, in many cases, death. The truth of the gospel, "integral salvation," is indivisible and so, Boff implies, there can be no distinction between martyrdom for purely spiritual reasons and martyrdom for political commitment impelled by the gospel. In different circumstances this distinction (or lack of distinction) was exemplified in the debate in the post war German church over the nature of the martyrdoms of the political Dietrich Bonhoeffer and the non-political Paul Schneider.[29] Unease was expressed at extending martyr status both to Bonhoeffer, executed for political reasons, as a result of his taking part in the conspiracy against Hitler, and Schneider, who met his death in Buchenwald for (supposedly) primarily religious reasons (although his opposition to the Nazis was strong and consistent, if expressed in religious, rather than political terms). Boff describes the Latin American martyrs as having a profoundly subversive effect, in leaving behind a memory which both disturbs and gives hope (as in the *memoria passionis* in the theology of Metz). Through their commitment to the gospel and their resistance to oppression, suffering is given a meaning. They follow in the steps of Jesus himself, of Isaiah's suffering servant, and of the prophets who suffered because of their message. Again, Boff emphasizes that suffering is not to be sought in itself, but only as an inevitable concomitant of resistance to those structures of oppression which contradict the gospel. Such a resistance inevitably involves conflict and suffering, but that suffering is not meaningless

---

28. Boff, *Passion*, 120.
29. See Slane, *Bonhoeffer*, and Foster, *Paul Schneider*.

or hopeless, because it is undertaken with a positive end in view, a just cause.[30] And, for the Christian, there is the hope given by Christ's resurrection in overcoming the historical manifestations of human sin which caused the crucifixion and which, through contemporary structures of sin continues to crucify.

Sobrino—A Spirituality of Martyrdom

Sobrino's theology took shape in a context of political violence in El Salvador, in particular the widespread murders by right-wing death squads. These most famously include Archbishop Romero, to whom Sobrino acted as theological consultant and, even more personally, the Jesuit colleagues of Sobrino who were killed together with their housekeeper and her daughter. These, whom Sobrino describes as martyrs, are only the most widely known of the thousands of Salvadoreans killed in the civil war, predominantly by the army and paramilitary forces. Any reading of Sobrino's theology must take into account this involvement with the political struggle and its personal consequences for Sobrino, in the tragic loss of colleagues and friends. It is perhaps no surprise that a cruciform spirituality of martyrdom is so prominent in his writing. Sobrino describes this most comprehensively in *Witnesses to the kingdom: the Martyrs of El Salvador and the Crucified Peoples* in which he links the themes of liberation and martyrdom as basic to liberation theology.[31] The combination of the two, in the light of a suffering God and a crucified people, constitute, alongside his Christology, Sobrino's chief contribution to liberation theology. Sobrino stresses the close interrelationship: "Liberation and martyrdom recover and maintain two essential and foundational realities of the New Testament, the kingdom of God and the cross of Jesus; the relationship between them strengthens them both."[32] Without a willingness to witness to it through the possibility of suffering, the kingdom of God risks becoming a superficial concept, divorced from the reality of a suffering world. Jesus, in the great prophetic tradition, witnessed to and proclaimed the kingdom of God in words and deeds, persisting in proclaiming it even when this brought him to crucifixion. The existence of martyrs in the contemporary church is the closest possible link with the ministry of Jesus. From one angle it provides the greatest hermeneutical aid in understanding the reasons for the death of Jesus, which are plain to any Salvadorean whose expertise lies not so much in historical learning as in the

---

30. Boff, *Passion*, 122.
31. Sobrino, *Witnesses*, 101.
32. Sobrino, *Witnesses*, 107.

experience of oppression—"they killed him for the same reason that they killed Archbishop Romero and many others."[33]

There is, as we have noted previously, a parallel historical causation, in that the powerful necessarily eliminate those who threaten their power. From another angle, the martyrs provide the most penetrating theological perspective in relating the crucified people to the crucifixion of Jesus. There is a parallel theological meaning, in that God, in Christ, suffers within and alongside the powerless at the hands of the powerful. The stark and physical fact of martyrdom brings those historical and theological parallels into the sharpest focus. Sobrino writes of the martyrs being a sign of the times in a suffering world; they bring realities to our attention and through their suffering the purposes of God are seen in sharper focus.[34]

Sobrino, like Boff, continually shifts the concept of martyrdom into another (less traditional) key, by referring to "Jesuanic martyrs" who "die in the same way Jesus died and for the same reasons."[35] These martyrs are "those who follow Jesus in the things that matter, live in dedication to the cause of Jesus, and die for the same reason that Jesus died"[36] as a result of their stand on behalf of and by the side of the poor. *Odium fidei* (hatred of the faith) is transposed to *odium iustitiae* (hatred of justice)[37] (Also see Sobrino's discussion of Rahner's defense of a wider concept of martyrdom[38]). Here Sobrino decisively crosses the line dividing "Paul Schneider religious martyr" from "Bonhoeffer political martyr," as in the post-war German debate. Sobrino takes up this debate in detail in *Jesus the liberator* in an extended discussion of the dispute over the status of the modern Latin American martyrs. He points to the anomaly that the church's canonical conditions for martyrdom in effect exclude "those who today are killed in a way that most resembles Jesus' death."[39] Sobrino asks if, on the traditional criteria, Jesus himself was a martyr, and concludes that he was a "martyr for the kingdom of God."[40] This is a significant use, since the term "kingdom of God" transcends matters solely of faith, and extends infinitely further. This extended idea of martyrdom, claims Sobrino, is "death for the sake of love."[41] In other words, those

33. Sobrino, *Witnesses*, 109.
34. Sobrino, *Witnesses*, 126–27.
35. Sobrino, *Witnesses*, 120.
36. Sobrino, *Witnesses*, 122.
37. Sobrino, *Witnesses*, 123.
38. Sobrino, *Jesus the Liberator*, 266.
39. Sobrino, *Jesus the Liberator*, 265.
40. Sobrino, *Jesus the Liberator*, 268.
41. Sobrino, *Jesus the Liberator*, 269.

whom Sobrino includes in the category of martyr lay down their lives not for the verbal confession of faith but through the consequences of their faith. The faith witnessed to in martyrdom is not a form of belief, but the social, ethical and political actions which flow from that belief, exemplified by the canonization of Maria Goretti (murdered as a result of resisting a sexual assault) whom Sobrino adduces as an example of witness borne through moral conduct being added to more traditional criteria for the status of martyr.[42]

Martyrdom, the Crucified People and the Church

So far we have seen Sobrino extending the concept of martyrdom to the social witness borne explicitly by Christians as a result of their faith. He extends the concept still further by including what may be called implicit or anonymous martyrdom (in a way analogous to his fellow Jesuit Rahner's concept of anonymous Christians). Sobrino seems to elide the term "Jesuanic martyrs" with the crucified people. It is possible, perhaps, to trace a hesitation in his thinking on this point. In *Jesus the Liberator* he seems reluctant to ascribe the status of martyr to those who do not consciously and deliberately suffer as Christians for the sake of justice. What about those who are killed after having espoused violence for the sake of love? "They share in martyrdom by analogy."[43] What about those masses innocently and anonymously murdered? Sobrino suggests that there is no exact word to describe them—they are not martyrs, because they do not give their lives freely, since the poor do not have that freedom. Rather, they illustrate innocence and vulnerability. Whatever their precise martyrological status those who die through poverty or oppression "are the ones who illustrate best the vast suffering of the world."[44] Does the exact terminology matter? In his later work, Sobrino insists that such martyrs for the poor are, at least, "martyrs in the church, but not of the church."[45] The distinction is made less sharp by the fact that the vast majority of the poor in Latin America are in fact members of the church.

Sobrino, in his later work, makes three important observations on martyrdom undertaken on behalf of the oppressed.[46] First, there can be an analogous understanding of martyrdom—the active martyrs, struggling against oppression, and the anonymous martyrs, the immense majority of the poor. Second, there must be a re-evaluation of sainthood—the active

---

42. Sobrino, *Jesus the Liberator*, 266.
43. Sobrino, *Jesus the Liberator*, 270.
44. Sobrino, *Jesus the Liberator*, 271.
45. Sobrino, *Witnesses*, 109.
46. Sobrino, *Witnesses*, 109.

martyrs are saints through showing great love. Third, Sobrino stresses the importance of anonymous and passive martyrs "who have neither the freedom nor the heroic virtues that would enable them to become martyrs or saints." Martyrdom, then, is a concept primarily and explicitly for those who are consciously acting and dying in the cause of (if not for the sake of) Christ. These bear witness to God's desire for justice. This concept, however, is extendable by analogy to others who are simply the victims of violence. These bear witness to the need for God's justice.

Sobrino's is, above all, a political spirituality of the cross. In *Christology at the Crossroads*, where he is working out the implications of a theology of the cross, thesis nine states: "The cross is the outcome of Jesus' historical path: hence Christian spirituality cannot be reduced to a *mystique* [my italics] of the cross. Christian spirituality must consist in following the path of Jesus."[47] The martyrs within the Latin American church are those who have followed that path as far as death. Sobrino, in his discussion of martyrdom, reminds his readers that the cross does not merely denote a personal suffering for private reasons—rather, the cross signifies "the death that comes from defending the oppressed and struggling against the oppressor."[48] The martyr church in Latin America participates in that struggle, and in the same way in which the early church prized those who remained faithful in the face of persecution, it similarly prizes those who have remained faithful to the present calling to seek justice. Sobrino enumerates the benefits such martyrs bring to the church: the martyrs challenge the church not to fall back; the martyrs make the church an incarnate, real church—not docetic; the martyrs point to the church's end being the salvation of the crucified people, rather than its own good; the martyrs inspire the church to take up the cross of reality against the "anti-kingdom" ; the martyrs inspire the church to live in freedom, joy, and hope, as a resurrected church (as triumph over self-centeredness, as triumph over sadness, hope against resignation).[49] More specifically, he asks how his colleagues, the Jesuit martyrs, will live on. What benefits have they brought to Salvadoreans? These martyrs are

> witnesses to the truth, so that they go on believing that truth is possible in their country . . . Witnesses to justice—structural justice, to put it coldly, or more expressively, love for the people . . . Witnesses to the God of life, so that Salvadoreans go on seeing God as their defender.[50]

47. Sobrino, *Christology*, 215.
48. Sobrino, *Witnesses*, 146.
49. Sobrino, *Witnesses*, 134.
50. Sobrino, *Witnesses*, 95.

C) CONCLUSION

Yoder, Boff, and Sobrino are deeply concerned to explore how the fact of Jesus' cross affects contemporary discipleship. For all three, taking up the cross involves a radical and sacrificial commitment to living out the kingdom of God. Again, the differences in their interpretations of taking up the cross are in many cases due to background as much as to theology. For Yoder, in a North American context, taking up the cross denotes social nonconformity; for Boff and Sobrino taking up the cross can mean, literally, death. To take up the cross means to share the sufferings of Christ, whose social nonconformity cost him his life. For all three theologians, the cross is not to be sought in itself, but is the price of faithful and obedient praxis. Above all, taking up the cross is not merely a private, inward movement. Rather, it is public and political, hence the emphasis on martyrdom and witness. Where Yoder and (particularly) Sobrino differ significantly is in the identity of those who bear the cross. Sobrino extends the martyrdom of cross bearing beyond the boundaries of church and explicit belief; for Yoder, witness is the task of the committed and faithful church. This difference is one which will be further explored in chapters 7 and 8.

Chapter 6

The Cross and a Response to Violence

For Yoder, the cross is a mark of social nonconformity, as the faithful Christian finds the values of the gospel running counter to the accepted values of the world. For Boff and Sobrino the cross, in the form of persecution and death, is the risk run by those who protest against an unjust social order. All three theologians are therefore faced with the possibility of conflict. How should that conflict be handled? How should the Christian respond to those who wage that conflict violently? How does the cross inform such a response? These questions are the subject of this chapter.

A) YODER—THE CROSS AND NONVIOLENCE

Christological Pacifism

It is generally acknowledged that the most lasting contribution of Yoder to Christian social ethics has been to strengthen the pacifist tradition by providing a firm christological foundation. Yoder sums up his central thesis in the *Politics of Jesus* as the pre-eminence in the New Testament of "a social style characterized by the creation of a new community and the rejection of violence of any kind." This is firmly based on the cross, which is the "model of Christian social efficacy, the power of God for those who believe. Vicit agnus noster; eum sequamur."*(Our lamb conquers; let us follow him)*[1] The message Yoder draws most of all from the crucifixion is a total rejection

---

1. Yoder, *Politics*, 242.

of violence and an absolute refusal to countenance its use. For example, in the agony in the garden, faced with the possibility of armed insurrection and the eschatological temptation of apocalyptic war with the support of legions of angels, Jesus deliberately chose the way of absolute, non-negotiable nonviolence and allowed himself to be crucified—or, more strictly, took the path whose inevitable end was crucifixion.

Yoder locates Jesus' way of the cross against the background of the political choices before him. He rejected the shortcut of violence, the zealot option of revolutionary armed struggle, even if that violence was to be exercised in what seemed an overwhelmingly righteous cause. Two other alternatives were also discounted: social and political withdrawal into a privatized spirituality (e.g., the monasticism of the Essenes or the pietism of the Pharisees) or an alliance with the Sadducean establishment "in the exercise of conservative social responsibility."[2] Yoder is here referring obliquely to current political options for Christians: the violence in a righteous cause espoused, to a degree, by liberation theologians; the privatized spirituality of much evangelicalism and traditional Catholicism; and the Constantinian alliance with the political establishment on the Christendom model. Yoder sums up Jesus' threefold rejection, which is to be paralleled by contemporary Christians, of "quietism . . . establishment responsibility, and the difficult, constantly reopened, genuinely attractive option of the crusade."[3] Against the liberation theologians (or, more accurately at the time of writing of the first edition of *Politics of Jesus*, the theologies of revolution popular in ecumenical circles) Yoder sets Jesus' rejection of "the temptation to exercise social responsibility, in the interest of justified revolution, through the use of available violent methods."[4]

As we have seen, Jesus as interpreted by Yoder is in many ways close to the zealots (or their forerunners). There is a significant overlap in social stance on behalf of the poor, creation of a tight-knit community of committed disciples, and even in the language used. Where Jesus and the zealots differed was in the justification of violence in a seemingly righteous cause. For Jesus, in Yoder's interpretation, the zealot option was not radical enough, since ultimately it rested on the same foundation as that of their opponents: the violence symbolized by the sword, the sacrifice of human lives to political ideology, the continuation of structures of oppressive power rather than divinely ordained suffering service. This interpretation closely

2. Yoder, *Politics*, 97.
3. Yoder, *Politics*, 97.
4. Yoder, *Politics*, 96.

echoes criticisms of liberation theology for not being thorough enough in its critique of the nature of power.

Yoder's pacifism, in line with his overall christocentric method, is radically christological. In his survey of varieties of religious pacifism, *Nevertheless*, he is careful to differentiate this christological pacifism from other forms of pacifism—that, for example of "utopian purism, the virtuous minority, the categorical imperative, absolute conscience," etc. Christological or messianic pacifism is the heart of Yoder's social ethic. It relies for its justification not on a broader ethical basis (for example consequentialism) but solely on the person of Jesus and the pattern of his political engagement, which inevitably led to the cross. Yoder's pacifism is rooted in his Christology. It rests not on isolated individual teachings of Jesus (the traditional criticism of both Anabaptist social ethics and much liberal pacifism) but on the historical actions of Jesus culminating in the cross, where Jesus' non-retaliatory self-giving comes to its sharpest focus. Since Yoder's Christology is a high Christology, whereby Jesus definitively reveals the divine purposes, messianic pacifism indicates, though the exemplarity of Jesus, the will of God for the pattern of human political action.

This pacifism could additionally be entitled "pacifism of community witness to the nonviolent Messiah." Such a pacifism, although potentially attractive in some ways to the non-Christian, makes sense primarily as an outworking of the Christian's profession of the lordship of Jesus, and can be properly exercised by those who voluntarily acknowledge that lordship. The validation of such pacifism is not by its immediate results, but by its faithfulness to the controlling pattern of Jesus' nonviolence as demonstrated by the cross. This cruciform pacifism is in sharp contrast to any pacifism of immediate ends, or calculating pacifism. Yoder insists that nonviolence is an absolute, not a mere tactic. Jesus' crucifixion is grossly misunderstood "if we think of the cross as a peculiarly efficacious technique (probably effective only in certain circumstances) for getting one's own way."[5] The accent is not on any calculation of effectiveness, but on an obedience which reflects the character of God. Suffering is not a tactical tool, but a sign of faithfulness to that divine character. Yoder continues: "The kind of faithfulness that is willing to accept evident defeat rather than complicity with evil is, by virtue of its *conformity with what happens to God when he works among us*, aligned with the ultimate triumph of the Lamb."[6] The italicized clause is key to Yoder's understanding of pacifism as a cruciform imitation of the crucified God.

---

5. Yoder, *Politics*, 237.
6. Yoder, *Politics*, 237.

Some Questions

Yoder argues that Jesus' third way led inexorably to the cross. Is this a legitimate argument from the historical evidence? Did the choice of this particular strategy, of nonviolent challenge, necessarily lead to crucifixion? Or, conversely, could Jesus have been crucified through following other political choices? The first is readily answered. The Romans were inordinately suspicious of any possible challenge to their hegemony. For example, in Trajan's letter to Pliny (the then Governor of Bithynia), the emperor expresses disquiet about the possible dangers of people combining even to form a fire brigade! If, as Yoder claims, Jesus' gospel and practice involved a challenge, albeit nonviolent, to the power structures of his time, he risked the accusation of subversion and therefore a subversive's death by crucifixion. The second question is not so easily answered. The mere fact that Jesus died on a cross does not necessarily indicate his preceding strategy. As we have seen, Jesus could, just possibly, have advocated a spirituality of withdrawal, and been grievously and fatally misunderstood. He could have attempted some symbolic act intended to precipitate an apocalyptic conflict and been labeled a subversive in consequence. He could, although the evidence is very much against this, have been an early first-century zealot, with the inevitable crucifixion if apprehended. The cross of itself does not necessarily identify Jesus with any one strategy (apart, perhaps, from ruling out Saducean collaborationism). It has to be seen in conjunction with Jesus' general teaching and actions. This Yoder attempts to do by setting the crucifixion in the context of Jesus' ministry whose credible, and inevitable, outcome is crucifixion. It is one of the triumphs of *Politics of Jesus* that Yoder reconstructs, from the survey of a whole gospel (and particularly episodes such as the temptations and the cleansing of the temple), a credible account of Jesus' ministry which led inexorably to his death as a subversive who adopted a radically different method of nonviolent politics.

Some Criticisms

Apart from the above historical question and criticisms of pacifism in general (which will be discussed later), two specific criticisms can be made of the methodology of Yoder's messianic pacifism. The first is that Christianity is somehow dissolved into pacifism, and Christian politics made co-terminous with pacifism. However, any reading of Yoder's work would indicate that there is much more to Christianity than pacifism. Yoder certainly sets pacifism firmly within the context of Christianity, and his christological pacifism makes sense only on the basis of a strong Christology. But that does not mean that Christianity and pacifism are identical or co-terminous. It is true to assert that the pacifist, nonviolent and non-coercive social ethic taught by Yoder rests upon a doctrine of God as peacemaking, nonviolent, and non-coercive, which colors Yoder's whole theology. From that perspective, non-coercive pacifism and the overall action of God in Christ can be seen to mesh closely. This, however, should not be seen as a fault, but as a strength. If this objection can thus be overcome theoretically, it is perhaps not so easily overcome in practice. The distinctiveness of Yoder's theology, and of the Mennonite community as a whole, rests largely (although not exclusively) on its pacifism. In practice (though no doubt unfairly) their faith could be interpreted as focusing on pacifism rather than, as Yoder would insist, on Christ.

A second criticism is perhaps more serious. Mott argues that Jesus' cross does not represent one definitive social-political-ethical option which is binding on subsequent Christian action.[7] He argues that the cross is unique, and therefore Jesus' actions which led to the cross are not normative for all time. "His powerlessness was a matter of timing rather than of ethical choice, not a principle of nonviolence but the unique enactment of sacrifice." In other words, the crucifixion was a one-off event for a particular salvific purpose and cannot be used as a pattern for Christian politics. What the Niebuhrian realist supports and the Yoderian pacifist refuses—armed defense on behalf of one's neighbor—was not, suggests Mott, within the possible options presented to Jesus, and therefore his actions (and his crucifixion) cannot be a guide to Christian conduct in this area of social ethics. Similarly, Biggar argues that Yoder "generalises beyond the data"[8] and claims that Yoder fails to justify his universalizing of Jesus' reactions to particular circumstances in his ministry.

This argument can be answered on a number of levels. On the question of how Jesus' non violent actions can be paradigmatic beyond the immediate context, it is difficult to see how Jesus could choose to be paradigmatic in any political circumstances other than those he was actually in. For example, Jesus was not faced with decisions concerning nuclear war. We have no other choice but to interpret his actions from his particular circumstances. Just because the form of violence he rejected was of a specific and circumstantially conditioned type, that certainly does not rule out a refusal of all violence, especially when the tenor of his teaching tended towards a universal command to love one's enemies. The historical particularity of

---

7. Wright, *Disavowing*, 92.
8. Biggar, *In Defence*, 23.

the incarnation does not mean, for example, that Jesus' acceptance of tax collectors and sinners should be restricted in the modern world to actual tax collectors and breakers of the Jewish law. Extensions of the exemplarity of certain aspects of Jesus' ministry are legitimate if they follow the overall trajectory of his ministry. Jesus was in fact faced with a genuine political choice. He could well have taken the zealot option of violence in a righteous cause, taking up arms to defend one's neighbor against a tyrannical aggressor. That option was open to him, but was refused, not just in the events which immediately preceded the cross but throughout his whole ministry.

Was Jesus' nonviolent choice theological rather than socio-ethical? If the cross is primarily salvific, it is necessary (if God's consistency is to be maintained) to assume that the mode of salvation and the method by which it is attained is consonant with both divine character and also the more general divine intentions for humanity. Yoder has demonstrated that nonviolent non-resistance, exemplified in the crucifixion, is integral to the character of God and is not merely an arbitrary addition. Jesus' non-resistance on the cross and God's non-coerciveness are one, and are therefore normative for the Christian. The atonement, although unique, should not be seen in isolation from (or indeed in contradiction to) other aspects of discipleship; salvation and sharing practically in the nonviolent nature of God are inextricably entwined.

Excursus—Pacifism in Interwar Britain and America

It is, perhaps, instructive and illustrative of Yoder's method to compare his christological and cruciform pacifism with the British and American liberal pacifism of the 1930s, the particular period of history when pacifism was a widely adopted political and religious option (the more restricted nuclear pacifism of the 1950s and 1980s is perhaps of a different order). Chatfield, in his history of mid twentieth- century American pacifism, described the Emergency Peace Campaign of 1936–7 as "the greatest unified effort made by peace advocates until at least the Vietnamese war."[9] He sums up the strength of pacifist influence as follows:

> Pacifists concluded that it is the responsibility of Christians to choose the kingdom of God, an ideal which was antithetical to the existing economic and international order. In a sense, Christianity implies pacifism . . . To a remarkable degree they made that view respectable among churchmen, and John C. Bennett, president of Union Theological Seminary, has said even that in

9. Chatfield, *Peace and Justice*, 256.

many Christian circles between the wars "the burden of proof" shifted to the non-pacifist.[10]

How does such pacifism's use of the cross differ from Yoder's? This is an especially relevant question for a time when the cross was used in popular culture as a symbol of military self-sacrifice, both in general discourse and in the public statuary of war memorials.

The 1930s were the high water mark of traditional liberal theology in both Britain and America. Although a Barthian theology of crisis was promulgated by theologians such as Hoskyns, it had not penetrated far into the general British ecclesiastical consciousness. The leading British pacifist theologian was Charles Raven, a vehement opponent of Barthianism, who combined an optimistic evolutionary liberalism with a christocentric emphasis which saw the centre of Christianity as a personal relationship between Christ and the individual. Raven, like Yoder, insisted on the exemplarity of the crucified Christ. Wilkinson comments, "Raven defines pacifism as the new way of defeating evil opened up by Christ on the cross."[11] He saw the cross as the supreme example of pacifist non-resistance, and regarded martyrdom as the Christian's ultimate obligation. Where he differed most markedly from the later Yoderian ethic was in his political optimism, shared by many at the time, that pacifism had the spiritual force to defeat the Nazi and Fascist dictators. This reflected the liberal evolutionary progressivism which somehow survived the First World War but faded after the Second. Yoder's hope is more humanly pessimistic and starkly eschatological, without necessarily abandoning the (admittedly not sufficiently worked out) theme that "God will fight for us" (chapter 4 in *Politics of Jesus*). Also, despite his membership of the Fellowship of Reconciliation, Raven's pacifism was primarily an act of individual or para-church discipleship. Yoder's stress is much more on the corporate nature of the pacifist witness, the pacifism of the Messianic community. The great popularizer of pacifism in inter-war Britain was Dick Sheppard, whose catchphrase was "not peace at any price, but love at all costs." It is difficult to see Yoder disagreeing with this.

American pacifism in the interwar years shared many features with the British, but certain differences may be noted. American pacifists drew upon a longstanding idealist tradition in the nineteenth and early twentieth century, where war, if it was to be fought at all, should be fought for internationalist and progressive reasons, in order to build a new world order for the good of humanity (the so-called Wilsonian crusade). This tradition, of course, was not followed consistently (as exemplified by the First Nation

10. Chatfield, *Peace and Justice*, 330.
11. Wilkinson, *Dissent*, 108.

wars and the conquest of the Philippines) but contrasts with the primary British motivation for war as an imperial venture or to protect the balance of power in Europe. Compared with British pacifists, the American peace movement had a more coherent and achievable political policy, in promulgating neutrality and noninterventionism. Not that American pacifists were necessarily isolationist—their aim, like that of the British pacifists, was a more just and peaceful international order.

Both British and American pacifism drew on the widespread disillusionment which set in after 1918, and both were closely aligned with religious liberalism. Chatfield notes that American "pacifism has its deepest roots in liberal Protestantism and its best organized constituency in the Protestant ministry."[12] He sums up the liberal Protestant pacifist ethos as follows:

> These men viewed God as active in history, but bound by the very moral laws he created. They rejected violence on the grounds that it is absolutely inconsistent with love and the moral order of the universe, with the Fatherhood and kingdom of God, the authority of Jesus' experience, and the historic and social role of the church.[13]

Chatfield describes the view of the cross held by one of the leading pacifist organizations, the Fellowship of Reconciliation, as follows: "The cross of Jesus was an important image throughout their literature precisely because it seemed to sanction sacrifice for the kingdom, suffering for others, universal love, and nonviolence."[14]

Paradoxically, the "theology of crisis" used the cross as an argument against pacifism. The proto-Barthian P.T. Forsyth wrote in *The Christian Ethic of War* of liberal pacifism, "It is the climax of a genial and gentle religion with the nerve of the cross cut."[15] The cross stands for a realism about sin which was absent from liberal optimism. The leading prophet of such realism, and the fierce antagonist of liberal pacifism, was Reinhold Niebuhr. Deeply influenced by both the theology of crisis and his own experiences defending workers in Detroit, Niebuhr came to believe that in a universally sinful world

> it was sometimes necessary to use coercive means to achieve a just end. Christian ethics remained central to politics because

---

12. Chatfield, *Peace and Justice*, 340.
13. Chatfield, *Peace and Justice*, 329.
14. Chatfield, *Peace and Justice*, 33.
15. Forsyth, *Christian Ethic*, 39.

they would help determine the acceptable limits of coercion and distinguish between just and unjust causes.[16]

It might be possible for society to constrain sin to a certain extent, but it was impossible to create a world free from sin, even through the most self sacrificial peace and justice-making. Preston notes the contrast with the liberal social gospel, many of whose adherents championed pacifism: "To Social Gospelers, sin was a product of human activity that could be ended by human activity. Sin was historical; love was eternal, and the cure for sin."[17] Such liberal optimism contrasts starkly with Niebuhrian pessimism. Yoder, in effect, sidesteps both. One of Yoder's greatest contributions to Christian social ethics was that he differentiated pacifism from such liberal optimism, took fully into account the pervasiveness and power of sin, and constructed a pacifism which rests precisely and definitively upon the stark foundation of the cross.

Wilkinson identifies five characteristics of British pacifism of the inter-war period which it is useful to compare with the pacifism of Yoder.[18] First, it rested on an optimism about human nature, a legacy of nineteenth-century liberalism (with the cross being a more general symbol of tragedy) which both Yoder and Niebuhr criticize for its weak and unrealistic view of human sinfulness. Second, British pacifism was largely an act of individual dissent, rather than an expression of corporate witness. Britain has never had a consistent peace church tradition. The nonconformist denominations, despite their opposition to the Boer War and its campaign of passive resistance to the Education Act of 1902, joined vigorously in the jingoism of 1914. Even among the Society of Friends a third of male adherents enlisted in the First World War.[19] For Yoder, pacifism is not merely a personal, but a corporate witness, exercised not just by individuals who bear the cross, but by a cruciform church. The pacifism of individual witness was granted legitimacy by such as Niebuhr and Temple, but the pacifism of a defined and disciplined church (i.e., a Yoderian church) was certainly not. Third, there was no agreed political program or set of objectives. Yoder deliberately eschews such thinking, but in the 1930's there was much confusion about what practical steps a pacifist could take. Fourth, there was much discussion about the spiritual power of nonviolence, especially influenced by Gandhi's campaigns. For Yoder, although he recognizes the spiritual strength of pacifism, messianic pacifism should not be turned into a technique for political

16. Preston, *Sword*, 305.
17. Preston, *Sword*, 307.
18. Wilkinson, *Dissent*, 125.
19. Wilkinson, *Dissent*, 53.

achievement. Fifthly, pacifism and appeasement largely overlapped, and the difference between the more pragmatic pacifiers and the more dogmatic pacifists was blurred. Yoder's pacifism can hardly be described as pragmatic.

The Cross and Non-resistance

The cross is a sign of nonviolence, but Yoder goes a step further in treating it as a sign of non-resistance. Whether Jesus actively offered himself as a willing sacrifice, or whether the cross was the unsought but inevitable consequence of his strategy, the Jesus of Yoder (and of the gospels) does not resist his assailants. Therefore, according to Yoder, the Christian and the church must espouse a similar non-resistance. It is, however, not always clear what this non-resistance entails. The traditional Mennonite insistence on non-participation in political life and their rejection of even nonviolent resistance is certainly bypassed by Yoder, as shown by his admiration for Martin Luther King and Gandhi in their active opposition to evil. Also, acts of Jesus such as the cleansing of the temple can hardly be described as passive. However, as will be noted, Yoder distances himself from the Gandhian use of nonviolence as a political tactic. This ambivalence is shown in Zimbelman's survey of the Yoderian "axioms of love" which motivate Christian political activity.[20] These, Zimbelman suggests, include such actions as non-retaliation in conformity to the mind of Christ. Thus far Yoder would be within the mainstream Gandhian pacifist tradition. Zimbelman, however, goes on to include commitments which are certainly not in the Gandhian tradition: for example "to avoid resistance of any kind if it jeopardizes the existence or proper functioning of duly appointed political authorities." While holding to a certain degree of non-resistance, Yoder seems to be situated between an absolutist (traditional) Mennonite stance of non-resistance and a more Gandhian position.

Another example of this attitude can be found in chapter 10 of *Politics of Jesus* "Let every soul be subject," where Yoder discusses the Christian's relationship to the state in the light of Romans 13. Yoder opposes the Calvinist doctrine of the legitimacy of rebellion against an unjust state, but does not thereby uncritically ratify such a state. Relationships with the state are another area in which subjection should be exercised. "The call is to a non-resistant attitude towards a tyrannical government."[21] However, Yoder qualifies non-resistance in a footnote, as not meaning "compliance or acquiescence in evil, but . . . the suffering renunciation of retaliation in kind.

20. Zimbelman, "Contribution," 389.
21. Yoder, *Politics*, 202.

It does not exclude other kinds of opposition to evil." Such "other kinds of opposition to evil" would presumably mean some form of nonviolent civil disobedience, the setting up of alternative networks of doing politics, etc. The Christian is simultaneously to "rebel against all and be subordinate to all; for subordination is itself the Christian form of rebellion. In this way we share in God's patience with a system we basically reject."[22] For reasons discussed above, it is difficult to accept Yoder's view of subordination as "the Christian form of rebellion." However, his basic point is clear; the Christian is in an ambivalent (or perhaps dialectical) relationship with the state, being subject and yet creating cruciform (and therefore nonviolent and non-resistant) alternative ways of doing politics.

The Cross and Non-coercion

Yoder's doctrine of the cross entails, first, nonviolence and a certain form of non-resistance. In this he has much in common with a strong minority stream in Christian ethical thought. But he goes far beyond this in his insistence that the nonviolent and non-resistant cross implies also non-coercion. Yoder here reads the cross in the light of his Mennonite allegiance (Anabaptism was in the forefront of the struggle within Christendom against coercion in religion). His championing of political non-coercion is consonant with his overall theology; we have seen how non-coercion is at the centre of his theology of the atonement, and later we will examine how non-coercion is traced by Yoder from the character and shape of a non-coercive providence. The problem arises when Yoder, at least in his earlier work, seems to make the assumption that coercion is impossible without violence, or at least the threat of violence. He perhaps neglects the fact that, for example, governmental coercion is maintained usually through nonviolent means (through consent and custom, backed up by police and fiscal powers) and that there is an important distinction between violence and force, a distinction which Yoder himself later recognized.[23]

Non-coercion entails a radically different form of Christian responsibility. Yoder's central and repeated claim is that it is not the responsibility of the church or the individual Christian to "move history in the right direction" through coercive means. Even pacifism is not a technique, as such, to coerce others. This is not the task given by God to the church, which must see its role in different terms. It is necessary to note that Yoder's position has subtly changed in emphasis over time. Zimbelman describes how in his later

22. Yoder, *Politics*, 200.
23. See Zimbelman, "Contribution," 388.

works (after 1974) Yoder often uses the phrase "nonviolent resistance" rather than "non-resistance." This usage reflects a change in how, as Zimbelman puts it, Christians might "expansively express a life of redemptive engagement and witness."[24] This is a real shift in Yoder's thinking, in acknowledging that a certain amount of nonviolent coercion is indeed an option for the Christian. Yoder makes the all-important distinction between violent force and a coercion which is not necessarily violent and may be morally neutral. This has significant implications for the life of the Christian community, since a recognition of the necessary coercive role of government opens up opportunities for Christian political involvement which would previously have been considered impossible.

Excursus—Yoder, Gandhi, and King

In an earlier excursus Yoder's cruciform pacifism was compared with British liberal pacifism in the 1930s. Another form of pacifism, or near pacifism, which became a political option at this time was that of Gandhi (later adapted by Martin Luther King.)[25] Gandhian peacemaking, despite significant differences, shares much with a Yoderian approach. The word Gandhi invented to describe his political campaigns was *satyagraha*, literally meaning "holding on to truth," or "truth force," encompassing *ahimsa*—nonviolence (or more strictly, non-harm), *sat* (truthfulness), and a self-sacrificial commitment to social change.

It would be foolish to deny the significant differences between Gandhi's *satyagraha* and Yoder's cruciform and christological pacifism. Most importantly, *satyagraha* does not denote an absolutist pacifism. Gandhi actively recruited for the British army in the First World War and continued to regard violence as an option in extreme circumstances. *Satyagraha*, for Gandhi, was a technique conditioned by and fitted to circumstances, and was intended to have a direct political effectiveness, in contrast to Yoder's rejection of the criterion of effectiveness. Yoder's pacifism rests on an orthodox reading of Christology and of Christian doctrine and an attempt to be faithful to and controlled by biblical revelation. Gandhi's *satyagraha* is pragmatically eclectic in the extreme. *Satyagraha*, in Gandhi's thought, is associated with strict asceticism. This aspect of spirituality is absent from Yoder's pacifism. Finally, Yoder's political theology has its focus in the church, an ideologically defined community with strong shared beliefs, rather than

---

24. Zimbelman, "Contribution," 388.
25. See Bishop, *Technique*.

primarily in society as a whole. Gandhi's *satyagraha* was intended to be much more of a mass movement.

Given these significant differences, it is tempting to conclude that there is little in common between the two approaches. There are, however, striking similarities both in form and content, to which Yoder himself occasionally alludes. The practical parallels between Yoder's nonviolence and Gandhi's *ahimsa* (refusal to harm) are plain, even if their theological source is different. The use of the Gandhian practice of *ahimsa* by Martin Luther King demonstrates the practical similarities and transferability between Gandhi's work and a Christian pacifism. Such practice, moreover, in both Gandhian and Yoderian thought, is not merely the passive non-resistance of the weak, but the confident and creative nonviolence of the spiritually strong. For both Gandhi and Yoder nonviolence involves the voluntary acceptance of suffering, and hence demands a courageous and trained discipleship, adopting communal spiritual disciplines. Being a member of the church, for Yoder, involves a spiritual discipline analogous to that of the *satyagrahi*. The Gandhian ideal of renunciation can be paralleled by a Christian kenotic self denying discipleship. In both Gandhi and Yoder there is a refusal to separate ends from means, and an insistence on the corrupting nature of attaining good ends by evil means. Gandhi's emphasis on *nishkama karma*, or disinterested service, doing the right thing because of its intrinsic value, without regard for consequences, has direct parallels in Yoder's dismissal of a consequentialist defense of Christian pacifism. One difference of approach lies in the seeking and use of political power. Gandhi was a skilled and experienced politician who unashamedly sought and used political power to bring about large scale social change. Yoder's views changed from a deep suspicion of power and an emphasis on servanthood to a more nuanced view of power, if exercised as servanthood, praising the work of Gandhi and King as examples of the potential for a minority ethic to accomplish political change. Finally, the word *satyagraha*, which Gandhi uses to describe his peacemaking, associates force or power with truth. Yoder's pacifism is based on the revealed truth of the nature of God, and of the necessity for Christians to base their actions on the closest possible approximation to that nature as revealed in Jesus without deviating from the uncompromising truth of the gospel. There is an openness and directness about Yoder's ethic which parallels Gandhi's adherence to truth-force.

Whilst the prime Christian influence on Gandhi's *satyagraha* was the teaching of Jesus, the cross certainly played an important part—his favorite Christian hymn was "When I survey the wondrous cross," and the only icon he allowed in his ashram was that of the crucified Jesus. Whereas the chief meaning of the cross for Gandhi seems to have been a symbol of personal self renunciation, without the explicit connotations of political nonconformity ascribed to it by Yoder, the cross also had an implicit meaning as demonstrating the redemptive and transformative power of suffering love, which would certainly not be alien to a Yoderian interpretation.

B) BOFF AND SOBRINO—A CRUCIFORM RESPONSE TO OPPRESSION

Boff—Violence and the Cross

In his emphasis on Jesus' commitment, courage, and self-surrender which culminated in the cross, Boff has in mind the similar qualities required of those struggling with poverty and oppression in Latin America. But Jesus' death is more than an example of courage in the face of a cruel death; Boff touches tangentially (although, as noted below, he does not develop the theme) on Jesus' death as a model for Christian resistance to evil. In this section we explore elements from Boff's writing which indicate a cross-informed nonviolent and non-retaliatory approach to resistance. Such elements in Boff's writings go some way towards countering the accusation that liberation theology operates with the same categories of power, violence, and retaliation as its opponents.

For example, Boff insists that Jesus did not play by the rules of his enemies by retaliating with violence and oppression. As son of God, he could have drawn upon divine power to triumph forcefully, but he deliberately refrained.[26] Here Boff touches on a very fertile theme indeed—that of the relationship between the divine refusal (or redefinition) of power as expressed in the death of Christ and "power as domination." The power of domination is diabolical in that it "generates oppression and obstacles to communion." God's power is the power of love which does the opposite, in generating liberation and solidarity and opening up new possibilities for the future. This liberating love is described in terms strikingly similar to those of Yoder; it excludes "all violence and oppression, *even for the sake of imposing itself.*"[27] The effectiveness of love is in a different category to the effectiveness of violence, since violence brings about a change, but at the cost of human lives, and "fails to free itself from the spirit of oppression." The effectiveness of love is more long term and enduring, since it rests on the hope that the future is not necessarily constituted by oppression, but by

---

26. Boff, *Passion*, 64.
27. Boff, *Passion*, 64. My italics.

justice and love.[28] It is interesting that Boff begins this theme, which is more fully taken up by such theologians as Yoder and Hauerwas, but does not follow up its implications—a regrettable omission, since it has great relevance to the debate in liberation theology over the ethics of revolutionary violence and the nature of political power. Later, Boff writes of the revelation of God's power and salvation in weakness and powerlessness. Such vulnerability demonstrates the true and revolutionary power of love which embodies God's saving purposes.[29] Again, the power/weakness motif is touched upon, but not fully developed.

We have noted Boff's purpose of providing a spirituality for those engaged in the struggle for justice. But, no less significantly, he gives a pointer to the practical conduct of that struggle. The Christian is not merely committed to the struggle, but to a particular way of conducting that struggle. Boff writes of the efficacy of the "just in apparent defeat," and contrasts this with the illusory effectiveness of violence, which ultimately fails because it locks the participants into the spiral of violence. By contrast, suffering as a result of participating in a just cause has a more indirect, but longer lasting effectiveness, in witnessing to genuine human values rather than a reliance on violence and raw power.[30] Here again are resonances of a Christian pacifist theology of suffering and the cross, as found in theologians such as Yoder and others in the Mennonite tradition. That this theology is not more fully developed is probably due to Boff's sense of solidarity with those who feel compelled to adopt (defensive) violence in response to the violence of the state. However, it is significant to discover in Boff's political theology seeds similar to those which in Yoder grow into a fully fledged pacifist ethic.

Sobrino—The Question of Violence

One of the major elements in Sobrino's political Christology is that of the victimhood of Jesus, and the fact that any victory of Jesus is that of the "victorious victim," from a position of affinity rather than alterity. This radically affects both the nature of the victory and the methods by which the victory is won. Sobrino is fully aware of the debate over the use of violence in resisting oppression, and over the possible overlap between Jesus and the violent freedom fighters of his day, the zealots. For the Latin American church the dilemma over the use of violence to resist evil is an ongoing ethical, theological, and pastoral problem. Sobrino adduces as an example Bishop

28. Boff, *Passion*, 64–65.
29. Boff, *Passion*, 82.
30. Boff, *Passion*, 125.

Casaldaliga, of the Brazilian diocese of São Félix do Araguaia, who took the side of the indigenous people against the developers of the rain forest and whose assistant was murdered by the police. Casaldaliga taught that he would rather be killed than kill, but declared that he did not have the right to condemn anyone using violence against their violent oppressors in defence of the victims or in order to break down the structures of oppression.[31]

Sobrino argues that there is no recorded attack by Jesus on the zealots, and that Jesus shared certain zealot attitudes.[32] However, Jesus' followers included not only Simon the Zealot but also Matthew, a publican collaborator, and the Sermon on the Mount in many places runs directly counter to zealot violence. Jesus himself was certainly not a zealot, even though there was some contact and proximity between Jesus and those who attempted to drive out the Romans by force.[33] Rather, Jesus' attitude to power is more nuanced. Sobrino's recognition of this goes some way, as we have seen in our discussion of Boff, towards countering the attack on liberation theology for advocating a doctrine of power not significantly different from that of the oppressors. Sobrino suggests that the kingdom of God does not consist in an apolitical stance or a pacifism interpreted as an "absence of struggle" (a rather weak and unsatisfactory definition of pacifism, by either Gandhian or Yoderian standards), but is rather to be established by the human values of "truth, justice, and love" but most of all by grace, which, above all, makes the kingdom distinctive.[34]

It is perhaps worth noting that Sobrino, like Boff, does not link this view of power and violence explicitly to the cross. For Yoder, the definitiveness of the crucified Jesus refusing a violent response necessitates a rigorous and uncompromising pacifism. Sobrino is more doubtful as to how definitive a stance on violence can be ascribed to the words or actions of Jesus, and suggests an agnosticism over what can be known about his attitude to violence or to the kind of armed guerrilla struggle common in Latin America, given the complexity of that violence. "There does not seem to be a single response that is adequate and embraces the innumerable problems it poses, even in terms of the gospel of Jesus."[35] In any case, to apply the historical evidence of the gospels, where apocalyptic expectation was an ever present

---

31. Sobrino, *Jesus the Liberator*, 216.
32. Sobrino, *Jesus the Liberator*, 214.
33. Sobrino, *Jesus the Liberator*, 215.
34. Sobrino, *Jesus the Liberator*, 215.
35. Sobrino, *Jesus the Liberator*, 216.

reality, to the question of using violence as a political method today would be to commit the folly of anachronism.[36]

Sobrino does, however, set down four principles: first, the necessity of unmasking structural injustice as institutionalized violence; second, the fact that violence, even if legitimate, is potentially dehumanizing; third, that Jesus offers as an alternative to violence the utopia of peace as a goal to aim for and as a means to achieve it, through what Sobrino describes as "utopian gestures," i.e., vulnerability and forgiveness, which break the spiral of violence; fourth, that all violence needs redemption.[37]

Is the cross, then, a form of "utopian gesture"? It is here, perhaps, that Sobrino comes closest to Yoder in ascribing to the cross a power to overcome violence itself. In a meditation on the fact that violence always needs redemption, Sobrino describes the necessity of both "fighting against the roots of violence, *but also bearing it*."[38] Injustice has to be born in solidarity with the victims of violence in order for redemption to take place. Here, in embryo, is a more Yoderian theology of the cross, where suffering the consequences of violence is a way (although Yoder would say the only way) of overcoming that violence.

Sobrino ends his excursus on "Jesus and Violence" in *Jesus the Liberator* by quoting words of his colleague and mentor Ellacuria on the violent situation of El Salvador.[39] It is worth examining this passage in detail, as it provides another useful answer to those who accuse liberation theology of a too ready advocacy of violence. Violence is an evil, even if a Christian has inevitably to accept a degree of "non-terrorist liberating violence" in the light of the deadly oppression in the form of structural violence faced by so many. Ellacuria, however, makes the striking statement that from the point of view of the "perfection of the discipleship of the historical Jesus" violence should not be used by those who are "doubly Christian." Using language which resonates (unconsciously) with that of Yoder, Ellacuria suggests that the "specific witness" given by Christians is not normally made through violence—rather, Christians should witness most of all to the primacy of love over hate. This, however, will only be effective if Christians, in the Yoderian sense, take up the cross, in being willing to "risk even martyrdom." A refusal to use violence is justified if Christians are willing to sacrifice themselves in (peaceful) defense of those at risk. "The Christian vocation calls for the use of peaceful means, which does not mean less effort, to solve the problems

---

36. Sobrino, *Jesus the Liberator*, 215.
37. Sobrino, *Jesus the Liberator*, 215–16.
38. Sobrino, *Jesus the Liberator*, 216. My italics.
39. Sobrino, *Jesus the Liberator*, 218.

of injustice and violence in the world, rather than violent means, however much these may sometimes be justified." Jesus' eschewing of violence even in a righteous cause is at the centre of Yoder's theology, and it is significant that Ellacuria (quoted with approval by Sobrino) uses a similar argument.

C) CONCLUSION

Yoder's vision of a christological pacifism is firmly based on a theological foundation where nonviolence is integral to the being and actions of God and is therefore obligatory for his people. It does not stand as an adjunct to Yoder's theology—it forms the basis for that theology. Where Boff and Sobrino lean towards nonviolence, it appears to be much less soundly based on a coherent theological framework, especially with regard to the cross. Differences in ecclesiastical background should not be underestimated. Yoder writes from a tradition of uncompromising pacifism, which he integrates into a coherent theological framework. Boff and Sobrino write from a tradition where pacifism is exceptionally rare, and the just war theory dominant, and both would gain from a more systematic approach to the nonviolence which Yoder sees inherent in the cross. However, faced with the structural violence of Latin America and the crosses which that violence inflicts, Boff and Sobrino appear to believe that a certain degree of violence is justified if the crucified are to be "taken down from their crosses." The option of using violence is limited by the demands of the gospel, but both Boff and Sobrino are aware of the dangers of a doctrine of passive suffering which totally rules out active (and sometimes, as a last resort, violent) resistance. Such a doctrine would risk inculcating a fatalism which inevitably plays into the hands of the powerful. Both Boff and Sobrino could perhaps gain from Yoder's interpretation of a cruciform pacifism which is soundly based upon Christology, exercised by community, and motivated by the divine demand for justice. Yoderian pacifism could perhaps benefit from the realism and immediacy with which Boff and Sobrino treat the crucifixion of the poor and oppressed, and their attempts to "take the crucified from their crosses," which may *in extremis* involve the reluctant use of limited violent means.

Summary 2

Towards a Political Theology of the Cross—Discipleship and Peacemaking

In the last three chapters I have attempted to explore how the theologies of the cross in Yoder, Boff, and Sobrino can shed light on political discipleship in a world of poverty, suffering, and oppression. Before moving to a consideration of the cruciform and crucified people, I will again outline elements arising from these chapters which I believe should be incorporated in a political theology of the cross.

A CRUCIFORM IMITATION OF THE CRUCIFIED GOD IN A CRUCIFIED WORLD

A political ethic which bears the name Christian must, at the very least, attempt to approximate to the pattern of Jesus' incarnational social exemplarity. Since the crucifixion is the place where the incarnation is at its most radical, a Christian political ethic must be shaped by the cross—that is, it must be cruciform. This definitive cruciformity is an essential element (perhaps *the* essential distinguishing element) in any political ethic which calls itself Christian. This can be summed up by the following formula: a cruciform imitation of the crucified God in the context of a crucified world. At the heart of Jesus' ethical teaching is the command "be as your Father." Followers of Jesus are called, in all their actions, to act in conformity to the character of God as seen in the words and actions of Jesus: an *imitatio dei* through an *imitatio Christi*. Burridge describes the "entire story of Jesus" as a "moral paradigm that offers normative guidance."[1] It is obvious that the above formula does not say all that needs to be said about Christian political involvement, but it can perhaps set a useful framework. A cruciform politics will attempt to imitate the character of God as seen in the historical acts of Jesus (and their consequence, the crucifixion), will bear witness to the character of God by its political actions, and will have the faith that God will honor that imitation and witness.

This has relevance both to the content of the political ethic and to the location of its practitioners. The content of a cruciform politics, to give a very over-simplified outline, is that of a nonviolent, non-retaliatory form of political action which seeks justice and compassion, and which has the ever-present potential to threaten the powerful. The location of a cruciform politics is no less significant. Just as the crucified God is pushed to the margins of power, so the place where a Christian political ethic comes into sharpest focus is likewise on the margins, among the crucified people, or at least in contact with them, and with their interests at the forefront. It must therefore be recognized that the cruciform nature of this political ethic means that a significant process of interpretative transfer must take place before it can be used by those holding positions of power. This is certainly not to argue that Christian political ethics are irrelevant to the Christian politician—that would be to take the Lutheran two kingdom doctrine to ridiculous lengths. It is, however, essential to recognize that the focal point of Christian political ethics is not Pilate's palace or the offices of the Sanhedrin but the cross outside the gates of power.

A DIFFERENT CRITERION FOR POLITICAL SUCCESS

One of the most important tasks for a political theology of the cross is to investigate how the cross can be liberative, and not oppressive. Theologically, the cross entailed a reversal of values for the first Christians; politically, the cross entails a similar questioning of values. In Mark's account, on the journey to the dénouement at Jerusalem, after warning his disciples about the forthcoming crucifixion, Jesus makes one of his most significant political statements: "You know that among the Gentiles those whom they recognize as their rulers lord it over them, and their great ones are tyrants over them. *But it is not so among you.*" (Mark 10:42–43, NRSV; my italics) The cross likewise radically redefines both the aims and conduct of politics, calling into question established political values such as power or victory.

---

1. Burridge, *Imitating*, 75.

For example, the cross subverts power as violent force, by its demonstration of the alternative power of suffering love; paternalism, by its demonstration of involved affinity rather than detached alterity; and non-political withdrawal, by its demonstration of costly compassion. Most of all, the overriding aim of politics is redefined not as the quest for power *per se*, which is undercut by a cruciform hermeneutic of suspicion of power, but as the relief of human suffering—taking the crucified from their crosses—and its converse, the promotion of human flourishing.

This view of Christian politics should be undergirded by a careful analysis of the relationship between God and suffering, especially with regard to the cross. God must not be represented as inflicting suffering, or in any way privileging it, in theologies either of providence or atonement. The only part God plays in the violence of the cross is to endure it, both physically in the suffering of Jesus, and psychologically in an agonized and reluctant willingness to allow Jesus to endure crucifixion in fulfillment of his mission. Suffering is intrinsic to God only vis-à-vis the suffering of creation, as God seeks to diminish that suffering. Here we see the ambiguity in the symbol of the cross; the cross of Jesus is only valid theologically as a way to remove the crosses of humanity, both the cross of physical suffering and the cross of alienation from God.

A SPIRITUALITY OF COSTLY COMMITMENT

The cross is the starting point for a spirituality of costly commitment involving those working to bring about political change in the direction of the kingdom values of love, peace, justice, and community, and opposing whatever contradicts those values. Jesus' commitment to his historic project, which led to the cross, must be mirrored by those who continue that historic project against sometimes lethal opposition. Their suffering is given meaning by the cross; in other words, their suffering is seen not just as individual suffering, but as part of a grand narrative in which they share. Again, the ambiguity of the cross is manifest; cruciform suffering is certainly not sought, but is the inevitable by-product of engaging in the struggle to remove the crucified from their crosses. As Biggar necessarily points out, the Christian's vocation is not to "suffer in general."[2] This was not the definitive aspect of Jesus' ministry, and it is better to speak of Jesus' suffering as correlative with certain aspects of his ministry, rather than it being uniquely privileged.

2. Biggar, *In Defence*, 50.

This political spirituality is further resourced by the "justification by grace through faith" which finds its focus, in Pauline theology, in the cross. The gratuitousness of salvation and the consequent redirection of energy away from an agonized concern for one's standing with God energized, for example, John Wesley and led to an amazing revival. A similar personal decentering and recentering on others frees the Christian for political action. A cruciform spirituality is based on decentered solidarity—solidarity with God in the divine suffering and solidarity with the suffering peoples of the world. Bonhoeffer wrote of "sharing in God's sufferings at the hands of a godless world," and that "it is not the religious act that makes the Christian, but participation in the sufferings of God in the secular life."[3] A cruciform spirituality is conscious of this participation in the divine suffering, and also of solidarity in bearing the cross with others across national, ecclesiastical, and socio-economic boundaries. This consciousness and this solidarity mean that Christian political involvement is based on affinity, rather than alterity—salvation from inside (compassionate and empathetic solidarity) rather than merely from outside (intervention *de haut en bas*).

Lastly, to discover the meaning of the cross it is necessary to have a spirituality of the cross. An intellectual grasp of the various theories of the cross can only take us so far. The cross only begins to be properly understood when we immerse ourselves in a potentially costly discipleship expressed through engagement with a suffering world.

MARTYRDOM AND RESISTANCE TO PRIVATIZING THE CROSS

Taking up the cross, for the Christian, is not something private or primarily individual, but public and corporate. Cross bearing is the price of social nonconformity in imitation of the social nonconformity of Jesus which brought him to the cross. This is to be exercised both individually and corporately, in terms both of personal discipleship and of the church publicly seeking the kingdom of God and publicly paying the price for that commitment. A rediscovery of the concept of martyrdom is needed; the cross was a public political event, and is paralleled by the public political event of martyrdom, in the sense of a potentially suffering witness to the kingdom of God. Rodney Stark, a sociologist of religion who has applied sociological insights into the early growth of Christianity, writes:

---

3. Bonhoeffer, *Letters*, 361.

> Martyrs are the most credible exponents of the value of a religion, and this is especially true if there is a voluntary aspect to their martyrdom. By voluntarily accepting torture and death rather than defecting, a person sets the highest imaginable value upon a religion and communicates that value to others.[4]

This witness can come about in the present day through straightforward religious persecution, compassionate action involving risk, conscientious withdrawal, and public payment of the penalty when that stance is rejected by an unbelieving society. The traditional concept of martyrdom can also be usefully expanded. Primarily, martyrdom is "Christian"—the traditional form, suffering and death for explicit faith in Jesus; secondarily "Jesuanic"—suffering and death for taking up Jesus' historic project, the justice, peace and wholeness of the Kingdom of God; and thirdly "anonymous"— the unwilling and often unconscious witness made by the victims of the world's crosses, who are martyrs by analogy, who suffer, not consciously in the cause of Christ, but in the same way and for similar historical reasons as Christ. Such martyrs are signs of the times, prophetic indicators of different and often subversive values. The effectiveness of such martyrdom cannot be precisely calculated or deliberately used as part of a political strategy.[5] However, the political power of martyrdom should not be underestimated as it demonstrates in human history the divine willingness to suffer without retaliation, and hence puts a brake on the spiral of retaliatory violence.

It is salutary, however, to recognize the possible pitfalls in the use of the concept of martyrdom. Candida Moss has given a timely warning about the possible abuses in the contemporary church.[6] Martyrdom can be misinterpreted, for example, by Christian social conservatives who object to the liberalization of laws concerning gay relationships; to regard one's community as inevitably under attack can be harmful; a purely victimological approach can lead to a competition in suffering; an overemphasis on martyrdom can even generate counter violence through an unnecessarily polarized view of the world. Moss tends to downplay the very real persecution in the early church (men and women were executed by the otherwise humane governor Pliny simply as a consequence of their persistence in their Christian faith) and even to blame the early Christians for their own persecution. This, however, should not cloud the potential danger she uncovers. Martyrdom is too important a concept to be misused by those who feel themselves marginalized through a loss of former social and political power.

4. Stark, *Rise*, 174.
5. A point usefully made in Hovey, *To Share*.
6. See Moss, *Myth*.

THE INEVITABILITY OF CONFLICT AND THE NECESSITY FOR ENGAGEMENT

There is a profound paradox in that a political theology of the cross indicates nonviolence, but also presupposes the inevitability of conflict. The cross is the conflictual meeting place of the powerful, ruthlessly seeking to defend their power, and the powerless, attempting to subvert (or escape from) that power. Any pacifism arising from a theology of the cross cannot expect an absence of struggle. Pacifism, in both its etymology and its fullest political meaning, is not withdrawal into neutrality, but active peacemaking; living, in the Quaker phrase, in the "life and power that takes away the occasion for war." Christological and cruciform pacifism, in contrast to much optimistic liberal pacifism, seeks to be a realistic ethic, taking seriously the power of sin and conflict.

Such a recognition of the inevitability of conflict cuts against the grain of much of the social ethics practiced by the mainstream churches. The predominant model has been to seek common ground from a basic assumption that participants in the political process are invariably working towards the good of society but through different means. Anglican social theology has often sought middle axioms, drawing on the views of experts, and aiming for a consensus based on a general goodwill. John Hughes comments on the middle axiom approach:

> This approach often presents itself as embodying a certain form of broad inclusive 'Anglican' national consensus, against what is seen as the pietism and absolutism of more extreme 'partisan' integralist alternatives such as Catholic liberation theology or evangelical communitarian thought.[7]

Such a political theology reflected the post war Butskillite consensus in Britain, where it could be argued that there was a basic agreement on the common good. It is doubtful how useful this approach continued to be in more polarized political circumstances, for example, after the neo-liberal (and, in Britain, Thatcherite) revolution, where such an agreement on the nature of the common good could no longer be taken for granted. Filby notes that "centrism, inclusivity and paternalism, rather than revolution or class conflict always characterised the Anglican approach to social and economic issues right up to the 1980's."[8] Her description of the Church of England's role in the miners' strike of 1984 indicates a similar even handed centrism—"a classic and instinctive Anglican reassertion of the centre ground, much

---

7. Hughes, "After Temple?," 79.
8. Filby, *Mrs. Thatcher*, 55.

like Archbishop Randall Davidson's botched intervention in 1926."[9] Such innate centrism may be a good instinct, with the aim of healing divisions, but stands in danger of minimizing the actual reality of conflict of interest. It is not necessary to adopt a Marxist analysis—Maurice Cowling, a founder of the influential right wing Salisbury group, wrote provocatively:

> If there *is* a class war—and there is—it is important that it should be handled with subtlety and skill . . . it is not freedom that Conservatives want; what they want is the sort of freedom that will maintain existing inequalities or restore lost ones.[10]

Cowling may have been on an extreme of British neo-conservatism, but his remarks indicate the folly of assuming a social vision shared by virtually all people of goodwill.

Lloyd George is said to have summed up the career of one of his opponents, John Simon, with the words "he has sat on the fence so long that the iron has entered his soul." A similar ecclesiastical reluctance to confront the reality of dangerously conflicting visions of society may have seriously vitiated political theology. The cross illustrates the unhappy fact that politics is often about oppression and oppressors, winners and losers, the choice to inflict or to relieve suffering. Sometimes the church, in following a cruciform theology, must have the courage to take sides.

NONVIOLENCE THE DEFAULT OPTION FOR THE CHRISTIAN

The defenselessness of Jesus on the cross radically challenges a Christian's right to adopt premeditatedly lethal means of self defense and indicates what can be described as a christological pacifism. Such a pacifism, exercised by the Christian community as a whole, is based on imitation of God's action in Christ. It witnesses to God's character as revealed in Christ's reaction to violence, and rests on faith in God who raised the nonviolent Christ from the dead.

It is important to emphasize that this is not necessarily an absolute ethic since there are (as we will explore in subsequent chapters) ethics of conflicting duty to be brought into the equation. Alan Billings gives a warning:

---

9. Filby, *Mrs. Thatcher*, 191.
10. Cowling, *Conservative Essays*, 1, 9.

> The principal difficulty with pacifism was its absolutism. If the use of force was wrong in any circumstances, it did not allow distinctions to be made between types of violence. Taking up arms to defend oneself and one's neighbour from attack was just as reprehensible as taking up arms for one's own aggrandizement. Yet most people would see a moral difference between the two. In other words, pacifism in the end blunts our normal moral sensitivities because it will not allow us to make these distinctions and then act (differently) on the basis of them.[11]

Short term and limited defensive violence in protection of the vulnerable may be a possibility, as Christology cannot totally trump consequentialism in ethical judgment. If Christians do not have the right to defend themselves, they may have the duty to defend others. A cruciform ethic may well be an ethic of vulnerability, but it may not be legitimate to sacrifice actual vulnerable people to theological consistency. This will be explored in more detail later, but is a potential Achilles' heel of absolutist pacifism. To paraphrase Berdyaev's famous saying about bread for myself and my neighbor, defense of myself may be a material question, but defense of my neighbor is a spiritual question. There is also the complicating factor of the complexity of violence, in the form of structural injustice and institutional violence, which means that to restrict pacifism simply to questions of war and peace is potentially misleading, in that it fails to come to terms with underlying violence which is often more pernicious than outright warfare. Kenneth Kaunda, significantly, taught that "violence can only be justified, and that only as a last resort, when it is directed against an order in which violence itself is implicit."[12]

EXCURSUS—CAN PACIFISM (OR SOMETHING LIKE IT) BECOME A POLICY?

One of Biggar's most damaging allegations against a Yoderian pacifism is that it prioritizes witness over responsibility. He accuses Yoder and Hauerwas of "nonchalance" in that they "give the impression that they care not one way of another whether their testimony is effective."[13] Such indifference to effectiveness is harmful. "While not every witness need care about the outcome of what he says, a Christian witness must . . . one cannot reflect God without loving the world God loves."

11. Billings, *Dove*, 37.
12. Mayhew, *Theology*, 14.
13. Biggar, *In Defence*, 329.

Similarly, Billings describes pacifists as belonging to a sect—"a religious group that does not believe it has any particular obligation towards society or the state, a group that to this extent is world-rejecting."[14] This, of course, ignores the fact that a pacifist church can seek the welfare of the community precisely through peace making and through a selective (not total) withdrawal from certain aspects of society. By refusing to take part in war, one can be fulfilling one's obligation not solely to the society of which one is a part, but to the wider society of humanity to which the church has its broader obligations. However, the question must be faced—can pacifism become a responsible policy, rather than (or as well as) a witness?

I would respond, yes; an absolutist pacifism can be responsible, for the reasons given above. And yes, in terms of a practical, if non-absolutist, pacifism—perhaps on the lines of Barth's "a Christian should almost be a pacifist."[15] It might be argued that such a semi-pacifism, which makes room for a degree of violent coercion, is not pacifism at all, but a weak variant on just war doctrine. Be that as it may, the basis for my argument is that a cruciform social ethic entails a strong predisposition towards nonviolence, with only exceptional factors overcoming an otherwise radical eschewal of violence. Just as Jesus shared many similarities with the zealots, but with the literally crucial difference of adopting non-retaliation and nonviolence, so a cruciform ethic indicates an analogous role for the church, in going beyond categories of power and violence to conduct a different kind of pacifist (peacemaking) politics. What might that mean in practice? To conclude this chapter I shall outline six elements in such a policy—a deep suspicion of violence itself; a deep suspicion of our own (sometimes violent) motives; an unwillingness to turn to lethal violence as a normal option; a refusal to use violence except as a police action; a refusal to allow such police actions to turn to militarism; an unwillingness to embark upon crusades; and a determined effort to work to remove the occasions of war.

First, violence must be radically questioned, since it is both dehumanizing (in the sense of being destructive of human life) and "detheizing" (in the sense of being contrary to the character of God and involving a defacement of God's image in humanity). The futility of violence and its self replicating nature must be recognized, with a deep cynicism towards human motives in choosing violence, especially in military adventurism.

This leads to a deep suspicion of our own violent motives, a suspicion shared by both pacifists and Augustinian just warriors. Niebuhr, for example, was insistent on the sinfulness of the USA, even when supporting its

---

14. Billings, *Dove*, 9.
15. Barth, *Church Dogmatics III/4*, 455.

war-making in both the Second Word War and the Cold War. Biggar rules out "religious nationalism, which sees the enemy as infidels to be ruthlessly destroyed by the righteous, rather than as one set of fellow sinners whose evil actions must, alas, be curtailed by another set."[16] There is a law of unintended consequences in the use of violence and, often, hidden motivations towards violence which are not obvious even to the perpetrator. One of the roles of a semi-pacifism is to put a continual check on the use of violence, so that it does not run away with itself, and also to inculcate a true realism both about the nature of violence and the ambivalence of one's own motives,

Next, such a policy involves an unwillingness to turn to lethal violence as a normal option, and an intention to relegate the use of violence to extreme situations, Barth's and Bonhoeffer's *grenzfalle*. Violence can too often be seen not just as a last ditch alternative to peace, but as an all too viable option. If the bar to just war is set too low—which national self justification tends to do—this can cut the nerve of any creativity in seeking peaceful solutions. A cruciform church can be a brake on the ever present tendency to use the short cut of violence, and an encouragement, wherever possible, to seek means of de-escalation. Perhaps the difference in policing between the USA and Britain illustrates what can be dangerously diverging presuppositions concerning the use of violence—in the former, lethal violence seems to be a much readier option than in the latter, with the inevitable tragic results.

If violence has to be used, it should, in addition to being an absolute last resort, be seen as an extended police action, as in international law enforcement. *Pace* the early Yoder, and certain Mennonites, coercion, which in the long run is backed by violence, is permissible in domestic law enforcement. Given the lack of a global state, and the regrettable lack of respect for the United Nations, violence as police action cannot be totally analogous with domestic policing, but the analogy can still be powerful. Kofi Annan asks, "Why was the United Nations established, if not to act as a benign policeman or doctor?"[17] Absolute pacifism insists on "a morally relevant difference between a state's use of police force within own boundaries and military force against other nations"[18] but that difference can become blurred in the case of wars of humanitarian intervention.

Vaclav Havel states the case for humanitarian intervention vigorously with regard to the intervention of NATO in Kosovo to prevent further ethnic cleansing. "Decent people cannot simply tolerate this, and they cannot fail to

---

16. Biggar, *In Defence*, 59.
17. Clough and Stiltner, *Faith and Force*, 81.
18. Clough and Stiltner, *Faith and Force*, 47.

come to the rescue if a rescue action is within their power."[19] In such a situation, if the violence is strictly controlled and exercised not as an expression of national power seeking but under the auspices of an international body such as the United Nations, then a pacifist may conclude that the violence falls into the permissible character of police action rather than outright war. The fact, however, that the NATO intervention in the Kosovo war was not under the auspices of the United Nations, was hotly contested diplomatically, and involved accusations by Amnesty International of war crimes, might induce caution in applying the category of police action too readily.

Even if violence is exercised as a police action in humanitarian intervention, it still requires men and women to be trained to kill and for military resources to be held in order that the intervention be effective. How can armed forces be maintained without police action becoming militarism? And how can we avoid militarism—the distortion of political values by the assumption that violent force is an option to be used in situations other than the *grenzfall*? Andrew Bacevich, a retired US army Colonel and a conservative Catholic, echoes Eisenhower's critique of the military-industrial complex in *The New American Militarism: How Americans are seduced by war*. He describes

> a phenomenon that C Wright Mills in the early days of the Cold War described as a "military metaphysics"—a tendency to see international problems as military problems and to discount likelihood of finding a solution except through military means . . . Americans in our own time have fallen prey to militarism, manifesting itself in a romanticized view of soldiers, a tendency to see military power as the truest measure of national greatness, and outsized expectations regarding the efficacy of force.[20]

Even more disturbingly, such an attitude has been bolstered by religious ideology. While showing proper respect to those who risk their lives in military service, a more pacifist mindset is urgently needed to counter this tendency.

This means, in practice, no crusades, in the sense of violence in a righteous cause, either from the right, as part of the military establishment, or from the left, in revolutionary violence. Just as governmental use of force is limited to police action or humanitarian intervention, and weapons of mass destruction, whether nuclear or chemical, ruled out, so revolutionary violence must be restricted simply to a last resort defense of victims.

Finally, a semi pacifist policy means taking seriously (and giving sufficient resources to) understanding and removing, in the Quaker phrase, the

---

19. Clough and Stiltner, *Faith and Force*, 93.
20. Bacevich, *Militarism*, 2.

"occasions of war." To turn Vegetius on his head—if you wish for peace, prepare for peace. It must be recognized, however, that such a stance on behalf of the church that prioritizes nonviolence is only possible if Christians are willing to take up the cross which is the price of such nonviolence. A cruciform response to violence involves not inflicting more violence, but rather, potentially suffering the violence on behalf of others. As Gandhi observed, "Just as one may learn the art of killing in the training for violence, so one must learn the art of dying in the training for nonviolence."[21] Similarly, David Clough writes, "Part of what will make Christian life distinctive in a violent world is that Christians refuse to participate in its violence, *instead making themselves subject to it*" (my italics).[22]

---

21. Wink, *Engaging*, 163.
22. Clough and Stiltner, *Faith and Force*, 36.

Chapter 7

The Cruciform People—The Church and Political Responsibility

One of the leading themes of the Bible is the way in which God is represented as working through sociological groupings: the family of Abraham, the people of Israel, and the Christian community. The way the people of God organizes and expresses itself politically is central to its task of bearing witness to God and acting as a channel through which God can work in the world. What does it mean, in this context, for the church to be cruciform—in other words, to correspond to the crucified Jesus whose present body it is? How might that affect its political responsibility? In this chapter we examine the differing ways in which Yoder, Boff and Sobrino answer these questions.

A) YODER—THE CHURCH, THE CROSS AND THE QUESTION OF RESPONSIBILITY

The Question of Social Responsibility

Yoder's aim is to enunciate a cruciform political ethic, and to guide the church to be cruciform in its political activities. We have noted how this leads him to conceive of the church's political task in terms which differ significantly from the dominant realist paradigm. The most severe criticism leveled at Yoder's cruciform political ethic is in the area of political responsibility. Does the cross imply (and necessitate) a radically different form of responsibility, so different that the charge of irresponsibility (from a

Niebuhrian perspective) can be maintained? Does Yoder react against what he terms Constantinianism so much that his theology becomes unbalanced at this point? Is his reading of the cross definitive, or is his emphasis on non-coercion in fact drawn from other sources? Does Yoder take one aspect of the cross and over-emphasize it to the detriment of other aspects of Christian politics (a recurring criticism of Yoder's theology)? These questions underlie the following discussion of Yoder's doctrine of, if not non-responsibility, at least a radically different form of responsibility. Yoder is insistent that he is misrepresented as encouraging an ethic of political withdrawal—but do his teachings in fact point that way?

An important statement on the aims of Jesus vis-à-vis social responsibility is found in Yoder's discussion in *Politics of Jesus* of the temptations in the wilderness and Gethsemane. These passages are especially significant since they delineate the range of possible options open to Jesus and the choice he makes—a choice which, in the one case, determines the nature of his ministry from the outset, and, in the other, confirms his political choices at the climax of that ministry. Yoder writes, in a passage quoted previously: "The one temptation Jesus faced—and faced again and again—as a constitutive element in his public ministry, was the temptation to exercise social responsibility, in the interest of justified revolution, through the use of available violent methods."[1] This is a central passage in understanding Yoder's interpretation of the social and political role of Jesus. Yoder's Jesus refuses to exercise social responsibility, even if in a good cause (i.e., for the sake of liberating his country from oppression) by adopting the politics of violence.

Is Yoder's Jesus interested in exercising social responsibility at all? Yes, but in such a different way that the meaning of social responsibility is radically altered. Jesus' temptations are interpreted by Yoder as revealing Jesus "facing, and rejecting, the claim that the exercise of social responsibility through the use of self-evidently necessary means is a moral duty."[2] Jesus does not refuse social responsibility (i.e., kingship as such), but by refusing to play the game of using the obvious and traditional methods (violent and coercive) he transposes social responsibility into another, more distant key.

What is the relationship of the cross to such a strategy? Yoder argues that Jesus' nonviolent and non-coercive yet politically subversive actions led to the cross. It is, however, probable that Jesus would have risked the cross equally (if not more) if he had set himself up as a violent and coercive rebel against the Romans. Yoder's "different social responsibility" seems therefore to be based not so much on the acts of Jesus which led to his crucifixion,

---

1. Yoder, *Politics*, 96.
2. Yoder, *Politics*, 98.

as on the non-coercive character of God, who allows Jesus to be crucified rather than sending the twelve legions of angels to defend him.

Moving History in the Right Direction

Yoder's chief target for criticism is the view that the goal of Christian social ethics is to move history in the right direction, if necessary by coercive means and through the church's use of the political structures of power. The place of Reinhold Niebuhr as the trusted adviser to American presidents is a prime example of this chaplaincy to power approach to social ethics—it is, in fact, difficult to understand Yoder without acknowledging the presence and power of Niebuhr in American political theology. There is, according to Yoder, an obsession with ends in such social ethics, the predominant Christian social ethic being overwhelmingly teleological or consequentialist:

> Christians in our age are obsessed with the meaning and direction of history. Social ethical concern is moved by a deep desire to make things move in the right direction. Whether a given action is right or not seems to be inseparable from the question of what effects it will cause.[3]

Therefore part, if not all, of social concern has to do with looking for the right handle by which one can "get a hold on" the course of history and move it in the right direction. Once this handle is identified, "it is justified to sacrifice to this one cause other subordinate values." Yoder adduces as examples Luther's alliance with the German Princes at the time of the Reformation and, from a Marxist angle, the compromises of Communist Russia with small scale capitalism. Yoder criticizes this theory on two grounds—he questions first whether it is possible to manage cause and effect with (inevitably) inadequate information to guide such management, and second whether the "overriding moral yardstick"[4] is effectiveness in achieving these goals. Once the right cause is identified, "it is assumed that we should be willing to sacrifice for it—not only our own values but also those of the neighbor and especially the enemy . . . This creates a new autonomous ethical value 'relevance,' itself a good in the name of which evil may be done."[5]

Yoder's intention throughout is to establish a political ethic concerned with faithfulness, and not with a calculation (if this were possible) of the consequences. This intention is christologically grounded, in particular in

---

3. Yoder, *Politics*, 228.
4. Yoder, *Politics*, 230.
5. Yoder, *Politics*, 248.

The Cruciform People—The Church and Political Responsibility

the kenotic hymn in Philippians 2 where equality with God is interpreted by Yoder as not some metaphysical attribute, but control over the universe. What was rejected by Christ was the "element of providential control over events, the alternative being the acceptance of impotence"[6]—an impotence graphically and definitively demonstrated by the cross. Jesus, according to Yoder, did not simply renounce "the metaphysical nature of sonship, but rather the untrammeled sovereign exercise of power in the affairs of that humanity amid which he came to dwell." The kenosis Paul describes, the servant nature and obedience to the death of the cross, is read as "his renunciation of lordship, his apparent abandonment of any obligation to be effective in making history move down the right track."[7] This kenosis is honored by God, the designation "Lord" being an "affirmation of his victorious relation to the powers of the cosmos." A kenotic strategy is extended to the cross bearing of Jesus' followers, being "the inevitable suffering of those whose only goal is to be faithful to that love which puts one at the mercy of one's neighbor."[8]

Cross-bearing is interpreted as something positive—not an aloof withdrawal, but active peacemaking and reconciliation. This, it seems, is moving history in the right direction, but in a more oblique way:

> What Jesus renounced is not first of all violence, but rather the compulsiveness of purpose that leads the strong to violate the dignity of others. The point is not that one can attain all of one's legitimate ends without using violent means. It is rather that our readiness to renounce our legitimate ends whenever they cannot be attained by legitimate means itself constitutes our participation in the triumphant suffering of the Lamb.[9]

There seems to be a significant shift here (or possibly confusion). We are, after all, to move history in the right way, since there are legitimate ends—but only by using legitimate, i.e., cruciform, nonviolent means, following the divine pattern exemplified by the historical acts of Jesus which culminated in his crucifixion.

Yoder recognizes that modern social ethics are primarily (and almost inevitably) consequentialist and based on the use of immediately available power, rather than on a more long term faithfulness, which is only seen to be correct in the light of the resurrection and the eternal glory of the Lamb. Christian politics, suggests Yoder, is not a question of "determining

---

6. Yoder, *Politics*, 34.
7. Yoder, *Politics*, 235.
8. Yoder, *Politics*, 236.
9. Yoder, *Politics*, 237.

which aristocrats are morally justified, by virtue of their better ideology, to use the power of society from the top so as to lead the whole system in their direction."[10] It is easy to identify Yoder's targets here—Christian realist social ethics, which operate from a position of chaplaincy to power. The question must be asked, however, whether Yoder fails to recognize a difference between a Constantinian seizure of power in order to move history and action taken in response to particular situations in obedience to the love command of Jesus. In that particular, is the Christian to refrain from moving history in the right direction? Yoder could justly be accused of setting up a straw man to demolish. From the point of view of liberation theology, the refusal to manage history is highly dangerous, because of the dire social consequences of leaving such management to a powerful and selfish elite. As we shall see, Yoder has a potentially dangerous suspicion of the use of power itself. Yoder's major adversary is that outworking of the alliance of Christianity and worldly power, Constantinianism.

The Cross against Constantinianism

Yoder interprets the cross as indicating a Christianity "the right way up." Whereas the sixteenth-century magisterial reformers identified the fall of the church in the corruption of the medieval papacy, the radical reformers saw this fall occurring a thousand year previously. Constantine, or the socio-religious changes associated with him, turned Christianity upside down by systematically reversing Jesus' emphases, with the result that Jesus was crucified by the same empire and the same values which Constantine embodied (whatever the exact nature and timing of the changes, and whatever Constantine's own role in them—it is at least arguable that some of what Yoder identifies as Constantinianism can be ascribed more fairly to Theodosius and his successors). What we will refer to as Constantinianism stands as an important symbol of Yoder's diagnosis of a wrong turn in Christian social ethics which still has immense influence across the political/religious spectrum. Constantinianism describes the church imposing what it sees as the values of Christianity from a position of political power and social privilege, and using that power to forward the church's interpretation of God's will and kingdom. This Constantinian postulate assumes a state church and Christian control, or at least very strong influence, on the levers of power, so that ideally there is a unity of ideology and intent between the church and the ruling powers. Hence the task of the Christian (and the church) in politics is to stand in solidarity and alliance with those who hold power in order

10. Yoder, *Politics*, 238.

to determine the course of society in a way which approximates as closely as possible to the kingdom of God. The prophetic role (whether interpreted as that of the Old Testament prophets, Jesus himself, or the church) takes second place to a royal interpretation of holding power. This view, which is close to the Christendom tradition, takes seriously the necessity for power to achieve (at least short term) aims in politics—and such short term aims in politics are the practical norm. Beyond that, Constantinianism aims for Christianization of society as a whole, with the church the religious expression of the community in general—the Christendom model.

Christendom has been defended on the grounds of both its inevitability and its usefulness in spreading and preserving the gospel. O'Donovan (a severe critic of Yoder, who does not, however, advocate a return to Christendom) writes that Christendom is "simply what happens when the rulers of the world submit (with varying degrees of sincerity) to Christ, rather than a sinister alliance with corrupting power."[11] After centuries of persecution and state hostility, the new political and religious situation inaugurated under Constantine offered a new beginning. Newbiggin asks,

> Could any other choice have been made? When the ancient classical world ran out of spiritual fuel and turned to the church as the one society that could hold a disintegrating world together, should the church have refused the appeal and washed its hands of responsibility for the political order?[12]

Constantinianism (and the ensuing Christendom) can thus be seen as a contextualising of the gospel in the contemporary culture and an inevitable consequence of the success of the church's mission.

However, for all the inevitability of Christendom, it is difficult to deny the corruption that resulted, both theologically and ecclesiologically. The church became an integral part of the structures of power, with long lasting consequences—one of the achievements of liberation theology has been to detach the church from an almost unquestioned alliance with Latin American elites. Theologically, too, the results have been disastrous. Roger Haydon Mitchell writes of the "acceptance of imperial power as the means to the temporal fulfillment of eschatological peace"[13] and" the loss of the humble, human Jesus of Nazareth in the search for Christ the territorial king."[14] Donald MacKinnon observes that "by the

---

11. Hughes, "After Temple?," 86.
12. Newbiggin, *Foolishness*, 100–101.
13. Mitchell, *Church*, 8.
14. Mitchell, *Church*, 84.

most damaging anthropomorphism of all Christian intellectual history, the creator and governor of the world had been invested with the quality of an absolute, human ruler."[15]

It is not difficult to see how such a vision is antithetical to Yoder's cruciform Christology and ecclesiology. Jesus was crucified precisely by such an alliance of religious and political power, by those who sought to keep intact their handle on moving history in what they saw as the right direction, and were willing to sacrifice an innocent man for that worthy cause. As a Mennonite, Yoder's ecclesiology is that of a markedly separate, distinctive and voluntary church, whose task is not to handle the levers of power, but to renounce all semblance of control. The church's responsibility is to be the church, to fulfill the its prime function of vulnerable witness, prophetic worship, and reconciling fellowship, and not to assume an unrealistic responsibility for everything that happens. By contrast, Constantinianism rests on the responsibility of those who hold power, of the individual Christian and of the church, to exercise their power as far as possible to achieve righteous ends. This emphasis on responsibility implies accountability; both church and government are accountable to God for exercising or neglecting to exercise (if necessary by coercion) their power for good. The contrast with Yoder's voluntary, subordinate, and non-coercive model, which sees responsibility in radically different terms, is stark; Constantinianism is centered not christologically, but on the (presumably God given, but fatally sinful) capabilities of humanity.

Yoder sees such Constantinianism as shared by political theologies both of the right (the traditional conservative alliance between church and state) and of the left (theologies of revolution and liberation). In the chapter "Christ, the hope of the world" in *The Original Revolution* Yoder indicts liberation theology as "neo-neo-neo-neo Constantinianism"![16] The ideology of those in power is not so great a problem as the church's attempts to associate with those in power. Echoing the criticism that liberation theology is not radical enough in its critique of power, Yoder finds fault with liberation theology not so much in its goals as in its Constantinian methodology, in overemphasizing the need for seizing political power. In brief, Yoder's quarrel with Constantinianism seems, first of all, to be over its use of coercive and often violent power even for justifiable ends. God's love, as expressed in the crucified Jesus, is radically non-coercive—the cruciform church, therefore, must eschew coercion as incompatible with the gospel. Still more deeply, Yoder is concerned about the possible consequences of a

15. MacKinnon, *Stripping*, 8.
16. Yoder, *Original Revolution*, 145.

Constantinian view of history, especially as interpreted by an apologist like Eusebius. As Doerksen observes, quoting Yoder,

> The ultimate meaning of history is to be found in the work of the church. Thus when people look for the meaning of history in the secular powers, a fundamental confusion has taken place, wherein the providential purpose of the state has been confused with the redemptive purpose of God, or put another way, the kingdom of this world has become the kingdom of God.[17]

This is not to deny that God works beyond the church—to do so would be to deny the work of the Holy Spirit beyond the (sometimes ill defined) ecclesial body. But the sharper focus of God's work, for Yoder, is most definitely the church.

An Unwarranted Suspicion of Power?

Any theology focused upon the powerless figure on the cross is likely to exercise at least a hermeneutic of suspicion of the exercise of power. But Yoder's reading of God's crucified and uncoercive love necessitating a distancing of the church from political power leaves him open to the charge of a dangerous suspicion (and avoidance) of power itself as expressed necessarily in government. The liberation theologian Jose Miguez Bonino, for example, in his sympathetic discussion of Yoder's work, comments that "it is difficult to see how the church can avoid coming to grips with the concrete issues and options of the outside world—and even if it could, it would still have to face questions of power and injustice within the community itself."[18] He agrees that Yoder is well aware of such questions, but argues that "the very radicalness of his hermeneutical choice seems practically to foreclose such discussion from the outset."

This suspicion of Christian involvement in structures of power and government manifests itself at certain points in *Politics of Jesus*. Yoder is discussing the absence in the New Testament of an invitation to "the king to conceive of himself as a public servant." Yoder asks whether this was due to the social composition of the early Christian congregations or to a more profound reason—"Was it that . . . Jesus has instructed his disciples specifically to reject governmental domination over others as unworthy of the disciple's calling of servanthood?"[19] Yoder here comes perilously close to

---

17. Yoder, *Anabaptism*, 258, and Doerksen, *Beyond Suspicion*, 158.
18. Bonino, *Towards*, 36.
19. Yoder, *Politics*, 183.

prohibiting Christians from taking part in government, by making servanthood the exclusive and solely determinant Christian social position vis-à-vis power. On this reading, Christians should be as servants, (to take the New Testament context seriously, as slaves) always on the receiving end of power, not its wielders. Good government is necessary—but Christians are excluded from the role of governors. This dangerous tendency in Yoder's thought plays down the necessary servant aspect within government—as in the British civil service. He writes in a similar manner:

> Is there not in Christ's teaching on meekness, or in the attitude of Jesus towards power and servanthood, a deeper question being raised about whether it is our business at all to guide our action by the course we wish history to take?[20]

Here Yoder is in danger of a simple withdrawal from anything resembling the exercise of power through his misreading of the example of Jesus, and especially the powerlessness of Jesus on the cross. His concentration on the target of Constantinianism can lead to a seemingly over rigorous prohibition of Christians exercising political power at all. Perhaps an emphasis on politics as service rather than domination could be a useful corrective here.

At the centre of Yoder's argument is his strict differentiation between church and state, especially with regard to their use of power, the church being a community of servanthood using nonviolence and non-coercion, the state resting ultimately on coercion and at least the threat of violence. Problems with this argument arise when church and state are seen as hermetically sealed categories, with no interpenetration; where participation in one power structure excludes participation in the other. The church and state are, indeed, correctly identified by Yoder as separate entities—but the relationship is a dialectical one, and individual Christians should not be barred from participation as servants in the (God-given, as Yoder would agree) state structures.

Yoder rightly observes that it is highly dangerous and contrary to the gospel for the church to exercise the function of state. But it is not legitimate to argue, by extension, that Christians are to remain wholly outside the power structures of the state. This would rest on an unstated presupposition that Christians have a minority status in the extreme. Otherwise who would staff the necessary police or law enforcement? Is all this to be left to non-Christians? This argument applies not merely to the area of justice, but also of welfare and taxation, which rest not on voluntary participation, but on some form of coercion (even if this coercion is usually nonviolent). It is

---

20. Yoder, *Politics*, 230.

difficult to identify any significant areas of the state in which the Christian can participate as a wielder of power. Are Christians, then, limited solely to free enterprise? One is bound to ask, with Hauerwas, if Yoder is too Hobbesian in his understanding of the state.[21] Coercion need not be violent, and laws within a community can be—and, in practice, usually are—based on common consent. It is only in extreme situations that the essence of the state is violence, and Yoder errs in neglecting the state's constructive aspect, its reflection of the human capacity for co-operation for the common good. In modern Britain the state is symbolized not so much by the sword (i.e., violent coercion) as by the National Health Service and social services.

Yoder's definitive christocentrism and concentration on the powerlessness of Christ crucified by an oppressive state risks neglecting a necessary Lutheran corrective, God's "strange work" which conceives of a divinely sanctioned use of power by government to limit human sin. Power is not necessarily an evil, and an overemphasis on Christ's powerlessness as a necessary model for the Christian leads to a dangerous imbalance. A useful distinction in emphasis can be made between political theologies (such as Christian realism) which emphasize the constructive use of power in the long haul of human history, without much eschatological emphasis save in a far off final judgment, and theologies such as Yoder's, which rest on a more immediate eschatological consciousness.

Zimbelman discovers a more dialectical and nuanced relationship with the state in Yoder's doctrine of subordination. Christians are to be subject, but, in the face of injustice, can exercise "conscientious objection and resistance aimed at altering specific attitudes, actions and policies of the state."[22] There is a fine line—but a crucial difference—between critical solidarity, where Christians see themselves within the power structure and critical subordination, where Christians set themselves deliberately outside (or on the bottom rung of) such a structure, seeing participation in the power structure as not being a Christian responsibility. In practice, Yoder allows a degree of the former, whereas his logic would probably necessitate the latter.

Ethics of Conflicting Duty

Another aspect of Yoder's doctrine of responsibility and non-responsibility which can justly incur criticism is in the area of "ethics of conflicting duty."[23]

21. Hauerwas, *Vision*, 218.
22. Zimbelman, "Contribution," 398.
23. Wright, *Disavowing*, 92.

Such a criticism can be directed at pacifism as a whole, and is certainly not confined to Yoder's interpretation, but in his doctrine of messianic pacifism his disavowal of direct responsibility for preventing evil consequences lays him open to a sharper criticism. Yoder draws an absolute ethic of non-resistance from the non-resistance of the crucified Christ, and prescribes such non-resistance for the Messianic community which follows his example and witnesses to him. It might be argued that Yoder chooses the wrong absolute—he emphasizes non-resistance as an absolute, but the true absolute is love (which includes, as a subset, justice, and thus can sometimes mean coercion). Which takes priority—non-resistance or the welfare of my neighbor?

It is not simply a question of either/or. Justice and peace are deeply interconnected, and the one cannot be treated in isolation from the other. But the question of priority, and of ruling out absolutely one form of action—a coercion which rests on violence as its ultimate sanction—is settled by Yoder firmly on the side of absolute nonviolence. Neighbor-love, in the sense of intervening (with the possibility or probability of violence) on behalf of a neighbor in need of protection, or on behalf of a neighbor suffering injustice, takes second place to the priority of nonviolence as a witness to the gospel.

Yoder thus lays himself open to the Christian realist criticism that by aiming for the ideal he refuses to intervene in a situation which it is within his power to ameliorate. Paul Ramsey, for example, asks the question, "What would Jesus have the Samaritan do if he came across the robbers still at their fell work?"[24] Yoder argues that there are hard choices, but insists that it is false to posit only two options and to ignore the possibility of nonviolent resistance. He is reluctant to accept the necessity of ambiguous choice through fear of undercutting the maxim that Christian ethics should not be determined by hard cases or exceptional circumstances. An exception cannot be predicted—once prepared for it becomes the determining norm.[25] It is true that borderline situations should not determine the overall thrust of ethics, yet war and violence are in themselves *grenzfallen* or exceptional circumstances. Barth's doctrine of borderline situations and Bonhoeffer's example of a heroic individual taking responsibility for violence as *simul justus et peccator* can usefully be set alongside Yoder's normative pacifism. Yoder runs the risk of neglecting this by his insistence on the absolute priority of witness over responsibility. This tension is particularly acute in situations where to refuse to use force would allow greater evil to ensue, at least in the immediate context. The demands of love and justice, on the one hand, and nonviolence on the other may well come into irresolvable conflict, and the

---

24. Clough and Stiltner, *Faith and Force*, 82.
25. As argued by Wright, *Disavowing*, 91–92.

criterion of immediate effectiveness cannot totally be discounted. Yoder's emphasis on the crucial importance of the unalloyed witness of the church to nonviolence and its long term value will be discussed in the next section. Here it may suffice to note the dilemma for all pacifist systems occasioned by the ethics of conflicting duty, which is particularly acute in the case of Yoder's pacifism with its radical dependence on the example of Christ crucified transmitted through the church.

The Social Responsibility of the Church

What, then, is this social responsibility of the cruciform church? Does Yoder shrug off the question of responsibility—or is the difference merely between two varieties of social responsibility (which is probably a more accurate analysis of his position)? One approach could be described as proactive and direct, seeking to influence (if not control) policy from inside the walls of power. The other could be described as a reactive and indirect approach, prophesying and witnessing from outside those walls. Neither approach can justly incur the reproach of opting out. The primary question for Yoder is which approach is most congruent with the one who was crucified outside the gates of power by the powerful. Yoder insists that he is moving the goalposts concerning responsibility, and that one can be both faithful and responsible. If the common view of responsibility is accepted, then Yoder might be thought to be irresponsible. But the parameters of the discussion on responsibility, set by Troeltsch and the Niebuhrs, are precisely what Yoder questions, in the name of that alternative social construct which is the church. The church's primary ethical task is to be the church, and to live out a faithful and consistent witness. This is stressed by Yoder, whose theological and ethical strategy is shared by Hauerwas, who argues on the grounds of actual effectiveness as witnessed to by history: "The church does not fulfill her social responsibility by attacking directly the social structures of society, but by being itself it indirectly has a tremendous significance for the ethical form of society."[26] The issue is, according to Yoder "not whether the Christian is to be responsible or not, but rather what form that responsibility is to take in the light of God's action in Jesus Christ."[27]

Responsibility, in the Constantinian sense is, as we have noted, a temptation both for political left and right. The liberation theologian, however, might well argue—*cui bono* Yoder's idea of responsibility? The damaging structures of power remain the same, and all the church does is nibble at

26. Hauerwas, *Vision*, 212.
27. Hauerwas, *Vision*, 214.

the edges. Yet Hauerwas continues with the suggestion that one of Yoder's strengths is that the "interest of the poor and disadvantaged" is not the sole determining factor in Christian social ethics. Certainly, "the Church has a special relation to the poor as it is obedient to the call of its Lord, but this does not mean that it is its job to simply identify with the self interest of the poor in terms of the power strategies necessary to achieve a more relative justice." The conflict with liberation theology is clear. The church must be aware that "the political tactics used by the poor, while perhaps achieving a greater justice according to the world, only makes them as men more subject to the powers of this world."[28] This, as has been previously observed, echoes criticisms of liberation theology that its analysis of human sinfulness vis-à-vis power is not deep enough, if its aim is merely to change one power structure for another. Rather, a more radical critique of power itself is required. This may well be true (and will be explored in depth later) but risks the obvious criticism, that a government which uses its power justly is clearly preferable to one which uses its power oppressively. For the poor on the receiving end of governmental power, proximate justice is preferable to safeguarding what may seem to be an abstract theological principle. Hauerwas stresses that this must not be misused in a conservative way, but claims that "true justice cannot be achieved by engaging in action that forces us to join hands with the devil as we work for good ends."[29] This means that "the Christian cannot participate in every form of life he finds present in his societal context." Any participation is secondary to this: "The first question of significance for Christian social ethics cannot be which social cause should the church support, but rather what form the church must assume in order to be true to the Lord of all society."[30] That shape is cruciform, which means, according to Hauerwas and Yoder, a radically different doctrine of responsibility.

A Salutary Example—The Confessing Church

The most obvious example of such a church, whose prime theological concern is to be the church, is the Confessing Church in Nazi Germany. It is instructive and perhaps disturbing to assess the political consequences of such a church. (It is no accident that Yoder's theological mentor Karl Barth was one of the main theological influences on the Confessing Church.) The Confessing Church steadfastly resisted Hitler's attempt to co-opt the

---

28. Hauerwas, *Vision*, 214.
29. Hauerwas, *Vision*, 215.
30. Hauerwas, *Vision*, 216.

church, and therefore separated itself from the "German Christian" movement who succumbed, thus maintaining its witness uncorrupted. The Barmen Declaration, the foundation document for the Confessing Church, provided a strongly christological basis for such resistance. The resistance element must not be underestimated, as the Confessing Church rejected the absolute demands of Nazism, including the Fuhrer principle and the process of *gleichshaltung*, or coordination, whereby all elements of German life were brought under the control of the Nazi party.

However, Charles Marsh, in his biography of Dietrich Bonhoeffer, comments on Barmen—"it never amounted to more than a statement for *potential* political resistance."[31] Marsh notes that

> Bonhoeffer had worried since 1933 that the Confessing Church was more concerned with ecclesial purity—which is to say, its own organizational autonomy—than with Hitler's world-scale epochal ambitions. On Jewish suffering and persecution it would remain hopelessly, infuriatingly silent, if not indifferent.[32]

It is all too easy to criticize the behavior of a threatened minority faced with an overwhelming tyranny, but the Confessing Church's record of political resistance to Nazism and protest on behalf of the Jews (with the exception of Jewish Christians) was not good, despite the urgings of Bonhoeffer and his colleagues. A negative witness, however pure, is not enough for a church which seeks to be cruciform. (A similar parallel from the German resistance might be between the Yoderian nonviolent approach of von Moltke of the Kreisau circle and the realist assassination conspiracies of von Stauffenberg and other army officers.)

The Confessing Church cannot be equated with a Yoderian church in its entirety—its doctrine was not self consciously non-resistant and its witness not nonviolent, since few of the members took a pacifist stance—but its concern for preserving an uncorrupted witness and its limited sense of wider political responsibility (caused, to some extent by the totalitarian society in which it was set, but also partly by its Lutheran social ethic) show both the strength and the potential weakness of Yoder's cruciform church. In the next section we will explore how Yoder's political theology of the cross utilizes a different and more positive view of historical causation and the church's role in that causation.

---

31. Marsh, *Strange Glory*, 224–25.
32. Marsh, *Strange Glory*, 271.

A New Way of Doing Politics—Through a Cruciform Church

The criticisms of aspects of Yoder's theology as outlined above are serious, but need not be fatal to his central claim that the Christian (and the church) is called to share in the pattern of the divine love as revealed definitively in the cross of Jesus. The manner in which God deals with evil through the patient nonviolence and non-resistance of the cross might not supply an all-inclusive ethic, but certainly points towards a stance which has far reaching social and political implications. Whilst the correspondence between divine providential action and human political action need not be absolute, it would be paradoxical and even ridiculous if the two were unrelated. The fact that God's way in Christ of encountering evil (in its starkest political form) involved self-giving, nonviolent, and non-resistant love cannot be irrelevant to any strategy which can bear the name Christian. This necessitates, for the corporate church and for the individual Christian, an alternative approach to politics. Yoder's concern is to redefine what it means to do politics:

> He [Jesus] refused to concede that those in power represent an ideal, a logically proper, or even an empirically acceptable definition of what it means to be political. He did not say (as some sectarian pacifists or some pietists might) 'You can have your politics and I shall do something more important'; he said, 'Your definition of polis, of the social, of the wholeness of being human socially is perverted.'[33]

In attempting to formulate a Christian politics which conforms to God's action in the cross, Yoder emphasizes the role of the church as the cruciform community, patiently suffering and witnessing, as the supreme agent of God's purposes. The argument can be summarized as follows: the distinction between the church and the world is central to social ethics; the pattern of social ethics must be christocentric and hence cruciform; this pattern can, indeed must, be required of the church, but is not expected of the world. An obedient church bearing a consistent, Christlike and cruciform witness to God's kingdom in an unbelieving world through its deviant values is at the heart of Yoder's thinking.

The church itself is a social ethic, and the most valuable contribution the church can make to society is to be itself, uncorrupted and consistent. The cruciform church is to be a community of creative dissent, and is to be wary of the temptation, in Martin Luther King's analogy, of merely being a thermometer reflecting the temperature of society[34] (although perhaps

---

33. Yoder, *Politics*, 94–95.
34. King, *Testament*, 300.

Yoder would regard King's rhetorical alternative, the church as thermostat controlling that temperature, as assuming too much direct responsibility). The principal community for the exercise of Christian politics is not the state and its exercise of coercive power, as in realist thought, nor the nation, as in conservative thought, but the church. Whereas the realist seeks to forward a Christian politics through close interaction with those who hold power, the Yoderian strategy is to concentrate on the church: first by the positive steps of building a Christlike community and second by the negative steps of refusing to participate in actions which violate the cruciform, nonviolent essence of the gospel. Hence the church, not the state, is the first target of prophetic criticism. Judgment begins within the house of God and the church's contribution to the mentality in which nations wage war: "The polemic of a valid Christian pacifist witness must be theological and first of all directed to the church."[35] "The audience to whom it needs to be directed is the circle of those who have affirmed knowledge of and commitment to an overarching divine purposefulness active in history."

This is especially relevant in twenty-first-century Europe with the demise of Christendom and no reasonable pretension to Constantinianism possible, either in its conservative or liberal variety, due to Christianity's minority status. As will be explored more fully, the church's witness is paradoxically more valid in a post Constantinian situation since it has been forced to relinquish Constantinian pretensions and to bear witness from a position of relative powerlessness (a painful exception to this being the influence of the radical Christian right on American government policies). Yoder acknowledges this new (at least post-Constantinian) situation for Christian social ethics, where Christians live as a minority in a pluralist world, and any possibility of managing society is excluded. The church exists through its solidarity-relationship to and unity with Christ, not through any parasitic relationship with the state. The church is theologically prior to the state, as a foretaste and catalyst of the reconciliation of humanity to God through evangelization and through preserving the purity of its essence and witness.

Church, Kingdom, and World

The church's relationship to the kingdom of God is that of a foretaste, a model, and a herald of what is to be. Yoder describes the relationship as follows:

---

35. Yoder, *Politics*, 240.

> The people of God are not a substitute or an escape from the whole world's being brought to the effective knowledge of divine righteousness; the believing community is the beginning, the pilot run, the bridgehead of the new world on the way.[36]

The church itself is not the kingdom, but the reality of the kingdom must be distinctively visible in the church, in its conformity to the character of Jesus and in its solidarity with him. The church is a visible sign in time of the eternal realization of God's kingdom—which means that salvation should not be over-identified in the liberative political movements which liberation theology regards as at least a part of the process of salvation. Not only, Yoder argues, is this neo-Constantinian, but also it is dangerous to read political victories as signs of God's providence, as in Eusebius' triumphalist interpretation of Constantine's success.

If there is a continuity in the relationship between church and kingdom, there is much less in that between church and world, due to the church's cruciform distinctiveness. Yoder's non-resisting pacifist witness is, as we have seen, firmly christological and cruciform—but such cruciformity cannot be expected of society as a whole, certainly not the voluntary cruciformity assumed by the church. We shall examine later how liberation theologians treat involuntary cruciformity. The believing, voluntary church is separate in its ethical norms from unbelieving society. Yoder asks, rhetorically, if it makes sense to expect the enforcement by public authorities of "standards of fraternity and equity which Christians can seek after in the church on the basis of the free assent of those who claim to be committed to Christian obedience."[37]

The Christian is not to be indifferent to the politics of the world, since the relationship of the church to the world is parallel to that of God to the world—sacrificial and loving concern but without an attempt to manage or control. This delicate balance of concerned engagement from a position of service rather than of power is difficult to maintain. It is, however, essential in liberating the church from a compulsion to control in order to exercise its proper role vis-à-vis society, primarily to be formed into a body which shares in the love of God as revealed in Christ and seeks to witness to that love by word and deed. Yoder suggests that "a church once freed from compulsiveness and from the urge to manage the world might then find ways and words to suggest as well to those outside her bounds the invitation to a servant stance in society."[38]

36. Yoder, *For the Nations*, 216.
37. Yoder, *Politics*, 239.
38. Yoder, *Politics*, 240.

In *The Priestly Kingdom* Yoder writes of the church's "servant strength."[39] This servant strength, itself derived from the self giving of the crucified Christ, both requires and empowers patience, in its dual etymological meaning of persistence and suffering. Just as God (and, in his earthly ministry, Jesus) accepts and suffers the consequences of the world's spurning of God's saving initiative, so must the church do also. This does not mean that the church writes off the world and lives hermetically sealed from it. Rather, the church continues to serve the world even as the world rejects the gospel and, in that rejection inflicts suffering on the church. This is not a denial of responsibility, or a form of opting out. By its patience and its distinctiveness the Yoderian church preserves its capacity to be a channel for the divine movement of history which a more obviously responsible but compromised church would lose. The danger of a social ethic of responsibility is an over-identification of the church with the world, so that the social message of the gospel and the ethical nature of the church are watered down into a pragmatism unsatisfying, ultimately, to both church and world. It results in the church attempting to formulate an ethic which is a weak compromise between the radical demands of faith and policies acceptable to the non-Christian.

Moreover, a conscious withdrawal from responsibility is, paradoxically, a strategy supported by a strictly realist view of social ethics, given the minority situation and social weakness of the church (a position much more marked in Britain than the USA). The church simply does not have the power to exercise responsibility, since there are huge areas of life which cannot possibly be under its control, even if it believed itself justified in making the attempt at such control. It must therefore, according to Yoder, free itself from fruitless concerns over responsibility, in order to concentrate on its true mission—its identity as a body bearing a consistent witness to the revelation of God in Jesus and its prophetic ministry, which seeks to speak to particular acts of injustice or abuse rather than to assume responsibility for the whole picture.

Criticisms of Yoder's Doctrine of the Cruciform Church

Yoder's doctrine of a "non-responsible" social ethic of a cruciform church witnessing within a majority unbelieving society can be criticized at various points, both empirically and with regard to the doctrines of the Spirit and the Trinity.

---

39. Yoder, *Priestly Kingdom*, 96.

The first and major empirical criticism is that Yoder idealizes (and idolizes?) the church. The church is the Messianic community—but regarded empirically, it falls far short of its calling as a body which witnesses to Christ by its ethical consistency and solidarity with its founder. It can appear to many, both within the church and outside, that non-Christians often have higher ethical standards, at least in the realm of social ethics (for example, the destructive alliance between certain forms of evangelicalism in the USA and the political right). Moreover, even churches with a strong form of *magisterium*, whether ecclesiastical or biblical, differ widely in their political ethics. A political ecclesiology such as Yoder's has to be based on how the church actually is, and not merely on an idealized church. In addition to the discrepancy caused by human sin between the church's ideal nature and actual performance, the church is always in a dialectical relationship with the community in which it is set. There is, perhaps, much more interpenetration, for good or ill, than Yoder recognizes, and his rigid church-world dichotomy is probably overdrawn. This is certainly the case in Britain, where the established church has relatively weak boundaries. Yoder counters this empirical view of the actual performance of the church by asserting that although the church falls short of its vocation, it is in a process of continual self-examination, self-criticism, and self-correction. Yoder writes in his introduction to *The Priestly Kingdom*: "Any existing church is not only fallible but in fact peccable. That is why there needs to be a constant potential for reformation and in the more dramatic situations a readiness for the reformation even to be radical."[40] Yoder has in mind a disciplined body with a shared and accepted ethical strategy, a situation not possible for the traditional Christendom churches. Perhaps as the churches are forced beyond Christendom to a position of minority status this distinctiveness might be easier to attain.

Next, it is possible to criticize Yoder's distinction (highlighted by Hauerwas) between the "norm of Christ and the form of the world. The kind of life assumed by the faithful Christian is not the same as the secular man of good will."[41] It must be questioned how far this is empirically correct. Without accepting Rahner's anonymous Christian hypothesis in its entirety, there is surely a sense in which God's Spirit can inspire, even if unconsciously, those of good will. For example, in participating in the attempted rescue of Jews in the Nazi occupied Netherlands, the ethical value of the actions of the devout Christian Corrie ten Boom was precisely equivalent to those of a secular Dutchman. A Christian may have (and does have) an added

---

40. Yoder, *Priestly Kingdom*, 5.
41. Hauerwas, *Vision*, 205–6.

motivation, but the "form of the world" in a particular instance may often be identical to the "norm of Christ." It is true that an ethically mixed body of people cannot have the same ethical discipline as a smaller, more homogeneous group, and cannot draw on the same resources as a faith community, but Yoder runs the risk of underestimating both the inescapable sinfulness of the church (which in effect may resemble the world much more closely than he would perhaps care to admit) and also the role of the Spirit in working beyond the church.

This aspect of the work of the Spirit is seriously downplayed in Yoder's theology. Reinhold Niebuhr provides a necessary corrective, in criticizing a doctrine of an over wide disparity in the actual performance of church and world: "The church must recognize that there are sensitive secular elements within modern nations, who though they deny the reality of divine judgment, are nevertheless more aware of the perils of national pride than many members of the church."[42] Similarly, Daniel Day Williams suggests a broader perspective: "A hidden Christ operates in history. Therefore there is always the possibility that those who do not know the historical revelation may be more repentant than those who do."[43] A more trinitarian theology, with an increased emphasis on God the creator and sustainer, and on the Holy Spirit working beyond the boundaries of the church, would greatly enhance (and would certainly not weaken the impact of) Yoder's analysis. It is possible to assert the necessary distinctive and voluntary cruciformity of the church whilst acknowledging that the Spirit may work beyond the church, even (as will be investigated later) in an involuntary cruciformity in civil society.

Cruciformity as Suffering Non-resistance

To sum up: Yoder argues that the church's cruciformity is exhibited in its non-resistance (and therefore non-participation in certain aspects of society) and in its readiness to suffer as a part of its witness. Non-resistance and non-participation, moreover, should not be seen as opting out in an irresponsible way, but as a contribution to social good. Yoder comments in a key passage in *Politics of Jesus*, that the Christian

> chooses not to exercise certain types of power because, in a given context, the rebellion of the structure of a given particular power is so incorrigible that at the time the most effective way to

---

42. Niebuhr, *Discerning*, 33.
43. Williams, *Spirit*, chapter 12.

> take responsibility is to refuse to collaborate, and by that refusal to take sides in favor of the victims whom that power is oppressing. This refusal is not a withdrawal from society. It is rather a major negative intervention within the process of social change, a refusal to use unworthy means even for what seems to be a worthy end.[44]

Sociologically, a minority community which chooses carefully the areas of its participation and non-participation in society can have a great impact through its promulgation of an alternative way of living. Its smallness can, paradoxically, be an advantage, in removing both the temptation to control and the threat to others whom the church might in other circumstances wish to control, and in allowing a consistency and a discipline impossible in a more disparate community.

The church, as an alternative society, must be prepared for suffering inflicted by the society to which it refuses to conform. This may not necessarily be for religious reasons. Just as Jesus was crucified, not for his specifically religious reasons but for his social nonconformity, so the church will suffer for its social nonconformity. Persecution is usually a response by the powerful to a challenge to their power. If the church's message was merely vertical there would be no need for persecution—it is when the vertical aspects of faith impinge on the horizontal that persecution is incurred (for example, again, the debate in post-war Germany over whether Bonhoeffer should be accounted a martyr, because his execution was for political resistance). Yoder comments:

> Such a dichotomy between the religious and the social must be imported into the [biblical] texts; it cannot be found there. The 'cross' of Jesus was a political punishment; and when Christians are made to suffer by government it is usually because of the practical import of their faith, and the doubt they cast upon the rulers' claim to be 'benefactor.'[45]

Suffering is not a good in itself, nor should nonconformity be courted for its own sake; it is only required because the values of the church run counter to the values of the world (although, as we have seen, the division is not always necessarily clear cut). This suffering has an added significance as a sign of participation in the divine presence and purpose. Yoder describes such suffering as "a participation in the character of God's

---

44. Yoder, *Politics*, 154.
45. Yoder, *Politics*, 125.

victorious patience with the rebellious powers of his creation."[46] By the suffering of the Christian church, "the suffering of the cross is perfected in history."[47] The suffering of God, and hence his power to move history, is represented within that continuing history by the suffering of the church. The importance of this concept of correspondence between the cruciform church, which takes up the cross of suffering, and God's action in the crucified Christ is central in Yoder's thinking. The church's power and purpose derives from the witness it gives through that correspondence. It is through this witness that the church fulfils its chief role in politics. Zimbelman contrasts the Constantinian rationale of direct, humanistic causation with Yoder's theology of a providential vision of history where causation is more oblique. He describes this redefinition of the role of the church in politics in terms of an "expressive" rationality, whereby deeds must be measured not only by whether they fit certain rules, nor by expected results we hope to achieve, but by what they "say."[48]

The church, then, eschews a proactive role, so as to adopt a witness uncorrupted by compromise. In this, a cross-bearing pacifism is not an optional extra or a mere tactic; it is intrinsic to the church's distinctive being as "participants in the loving nature of God as revealed in Christ."[49] Any other stance would, according to Yoder, be self contradictory. This is not an ethic of withdrawal, for the essential otherness of the church provides a base for a reactive political activity wherever the church discerns, first, that there is a need and, second, that it can act without going against its essential nonviolent ethic. In Archimedean terms, Yoder seeks a *dos moi pou sto* (give me somewhere where I might stand and I will move the world) outside of (or at least on the fringes of) the compromises of politics, in contrast to the Niebuhrian who seeks to move politics from the inside. This nonconformist stance will bring suffering which, as martyrdom, is itself a witness to God's essential nonviolence, suffering and patient love. As Yoder states in his conclusion to *Politics of Jesus*:

> The kind of faithfulness that is willing to accept evident defeat rather than complicity with evil is, by virtue of its conformity with what happens to God when he works among us, aligned with the ultimate triumph of the Lamb.[50]

---

46. Yoder, *Politics*, 209.
47. Yoder, *Preface*, 237.
48. Zimbelman, "Contribution," 383.
49. Yoder, *Politics*, 240.
50. Yoder, *Politics*, 238.

B) BOFF AND SOBRINO—POLITICS AND A CRUCIFORM CHURCH

We now move to a discussion of what it means in the theology of Boff and Sobrino to be a cruciform church, and how the cross might inform the church in its political involvement. This will be discussed under three headings: cruciformity as sociological re-positioning, as persecution and martyrdom, and as a redefinition of accessing power. The three ecclesiological works discussed are Boff's *Church, Charism and Power* and *Ecclesiogenesis* and Sobrino's *The True Church and the Poor*.

Cruciformity as Sociological Repositioning

For liberation theology in general, the cruciformity of the church can be seen in its sociological location among the poor and powerless, rather than, as in Yoder, a policy of nonconforming self-restraint towards the use of power, and of suffering as a result of that nonconformity. The aim of liberation theology has been to become a church of the poor, and the base ecclesiastical communities have become a significant component of the Latin American Catholic Church, even if their growth and development has not matched the high hopes of the nineteen sixties and nineteen seventies—it could be argued that the true church of the poor in Latin America is now Pentecostalism. For Boff, this aim to be the church of the poor is rooted in a Franciscan spirituality which seeks an authentic following of Christ in a committed community marked by poverty, equality, and a concern for the disadvantaged. For liberation theology in general, this was encouraged by the ecclesiology of Vatican II, with its emphasis on collegiality, subsidiarity, and the church as the people of God, and by the teaching by the CELAM Medellin conference on the necessity of taking the option for the poor.

As a Brazilian, Boff's ecclesiological work is radically influenced by the base communities, which began to be founded by the Catholic Church in Brazil and Nicaragua in the mid nineteen sixties and hence form the backdrop to much of his work. The base communities can be described as liberation theology in practice—groups of lay led Christians, usually in rural or slum areas, meeting regularly to read the scriptures, pray, worship, and discuss community problems and how to react to them. They function as a popular rather than institutional church, but usually with a link to parish churches for liturgical services. It is perhaps significant that the base communities do not usually seem to include the poorest of the poor, but are drawn from the more articulate, aware, and (potentially) politically active strata of society. There is a differentiation in Sobrino's theology (which will be explored in more detail in the next chapter) between the active crucified people and the passive crucified people—those who are organized for political change, and those who are simply the passive recipients of disadvantage and injustice. It is arguable that the former are further to the forefront of Sobrino's thought in his teaching concerning the salvific role of the crucified people. Boff champions such groups and sees in them a "reinvention"[51] of the church. His trenchant criticism of the institutional church caused him to be silenced for a year in 1985 by the Congregation for the Doctrine of the Faith. He sees, however, a role for both institutional and base church, while stressing the importance of the style in which the institutional church lives, "whether the functionaries are over the communities . . . or within them."[52] *Church, Charism and Power* is specifically concerned with issues of power within the church, emphasizing power from below, lay leadership rather than clerical hegemony, but Boff's analysis of power has political implications beyond the church.

The base communities are not universal in Latin America. In Central America, the Solentiname community in Nicaragua became famous through the work of Ernesto Cardenal, but in El Salvador the emphasis in liberation theology has rather been on a more general church of the poor. Sobrino differentiates between a church "of" the poor and a church "for" the poor;[53] the church must not just be concerned for the poor, since such a church "assists the poor but ignores the poverty." The privileged theological position of the poor means that the poor must constitute the essence of the church. The church of the poor "does not seek to organize itself on the basis of what the world calls power, wisdom, or beauty, but rather on the basis of the poor, the persecuted and all those crucified by history."[54] It accepts the "scandal of history" and uses it as a basis for its own structure. In this way it expresses authentic Christianity, deriving from Jesus himself and expressing his presence. Sobrino stresses that "the risen Lord who brings a community into existence is not just any human being or any Christ but the crucified Jesus of Nazareth."[55] A church which expresses Jesus must reflect his crucifixion. This is achieved by making the crucified people the sociological, as well as the theological, essence of the church.

51. Boff, *Ecclesiogenesis*, 23–24.
52. Boff, *Ecclesiogenesis*, 60.
53. Sobrino, *True Church*, 92.
54. Sobrino, *True Church*, 154.
55. Sobrino, *True Church*, 89.

Cruciformity as Risking Persecution and Martyrdom

Such a repositioning puts the church in a situation of extreme vulnerability. Sobrino quotes Archbishop Romero's words concerning the persecution of the church in El Salvador:

> I rejoice, my brothers, that priests have been murdered in our country. It would be a sad thing if, when so many Salvadoreans have been murdered, no priests would be murdered. They show that the church has taken flesh in poverty.[56]

Sobrino is writing against a background of persecution, most dramatically illustrated by the murders of Fr. Rutilio Grande, Archbishop Romero,[57] and, later, Sobrino's Jesuit colleagues. The centrality of martyrdom has been discussed previously and need not be revisited at great length here. Sobrino links the persecution of the contemporary church closely with the persecution of Jesus and the cross which ensued. The church, in following Jesus' praxis, will be subject to the same persecution. This, however, is not foreign to the mission of the church, but congruent with its early experience, uncorrupted by subsequent Constantinian compromises. Boff contrasts the primitive martyr church with the later Constantinian (and by extension, compromised contemporary) church. The primitive church

> did not care about survival because it believed in the Lord's promise that guaranteed it would not fail . . . The later church was opportunistic; that it would not fail was a question of prudence and compromise that allowed it to survive in the midst of totalitarian regimes, at the expense of gospel demands.[58]

Here, the idea of the consistency of the church, relying on the providence of God rather than prudence, leading to a possible crucifixion, is strikingly similar to Yoder's insistence that the church should never compromise the values of the gospel simply in order to maintain a position alongside the powerful.

Cruciformity as a Redefinition of Accessing Power

At the heart of liberation theology is the conviction that the church is inescapably political. This, of course, is nothing new. The church has always

---

56. Ellacuria and Sobrino, *Mysterium*, 695.
57. Berryman, *Religious Roots*, esp. chapter 5 concerning El Salvador.
58. Boff, *Church*, 54–55.

acted politically in condoning or blessing certain governments, institutions, armies, or even weapons. A refusal to speak out, for example, against the widespread torture in Argentina under the military junta, was as political as denouncing such actions. It is, moreover, ironic that liberation theology should be accused of politicizing the gospel when, in the twentieth century, the Roman Catholic church has encouraged major party political involvement in the shape of, for example, the Catholic Centre Party in Weimar Germany and the Christian Democrats in post-war Europe. By contrast, liberation theology has exercised a remarkable reserve in refusing to endorse, or, as Gutiérrez puts it, "baptize" specific political programs (Christians for Socialism in Chile and the Cardenals' participation in the Sandinista government in Nicaragua being relatively minor exceptions to the rule). Nevertheless, it is clear that liberation theology insists on the church becoming politically involved with the poor in their struggle for change and liberation. In what might be described as the seminal text of liberation theology, *A Theology of Liberation*, Gutiérrez writes that the church has an inescapable political dimension and must both denounce unjust and dehumanizing situations and announce the need for transformation.[59]

Catholic social teaching (for example *Sollicitudo rei socialis*) emphasizes the need to transform sinful social structures. The contribution of liberation theology in this area has been to stress the need for change from the bottom up rather than by conversion of the power-holding elites. Liberation theology looks to Christ crucified outside the gates of power, rather than to the residents of Pilate's palace. To be located in such a palace, among the elites, is inevitably to adopt their perspective. The stark image of Jesus the powerless, crucified by the powerful, provokes a radical suspicion of power, of the motives of those who hold the power, and of the lengths to which they will go to maintain that power. Hence power must be sought in different ways, not by associating with and attempting to influence the powerholders, but by looking to power from below. In *Ecclesiogenesis* (where his focus is primarily power within the church, but his analysis can be translated to a wider critique of power) Boff contrasts the top down institution with from below community. He sees the institutional church as centered in "society's affluent sectors, where it enjoys social power and constitutes the church's exclusive interlocutor with the powers of society."[60] The church is therefore faced with a choice: either to "continue good relations with the state and wealthy classes represented by the state or take the network of basic communities seriously, with the call for justice and social transformation this will imply." This is a

59. Gutiérrez, *Power*, 114–15.
60. Boff, *Ecclesiogenesis*, 8.

cross-risking path—for with this second course of action comes "insecurity, official displeasure, and the fate of the disciples of Jesus."

C) CONCLUSION

In contrast to the next chapter, where the focus is upon the crucified people as interpreted by Boff and Sobrino, this chapter has concentrated upon Yoder's cruciform ecclesiology. Yoder's teaching on the relationship between church and politics is a direct challenge to the Christian realist school, and envisages an alternative approach which might well be especially fruitful given the church's increasing marginalization from traditional political power. However, serious criticisms can be made. The social and political nonconformity indicated and empowered by the cross is arguably strong on form, but weak on content. Nonconformity of itself is morally neutral, and Yoder runs the risk of deifying nonconformity as such, without necessarily examining the destination to which that nonconformity leads. The ends of political nonconformity (e.g., justice, freedom, and shalom) are as important as the method by which those ends are attained, and both are intertwined. Yoder's ethic here faces the objection that it provides an essential negative function—a way of criticizing certain violent responses to evil and oppressive power and exploring how suffering can be used in a Christian response, in non-retaliation and nonviolence. But *in itself* it does not provide a wide enough framework for a Christian politics. Yoder's Jesus rejects certain kinds of kingship, but how should a king use the royal power? Yoder goes half way—a crucial half way—but not the full journey. For example, Yoder's remark that "the cross is the kingdom come" could be seen to confuse means with ends. Yoder's deliberate neglect of how to handle power could condemn the Christian to a state of mind where permanent opposition is preferable to government (as in certain sections of the British Labour party in the 1980's) or, paradoxically, to an attitude which serves the conservative purpose of keeping existing powers undisturbed. Of course, Yoder's general oeuvre provides many examples of a wider framework (the necessity of justice, for example) but it would perhaps strengthen his case if the doctrine of the exemplarity of Jesus included, alongside cross-bearing, other aspects of Jesus' life (for example his radical inclusiveness of sinners and outcasts).

Against this criticism, Hauerwas argues that Yoder's interpretation of cross bearing is in fact of the highest political significance, because it points to a radically different way of political interaction. Jesus "brought a definite form of politics by calling men to participate in the non-resistant community."[61] Christ's cross is not primarily for my personal justification, whether pietist or existential—it is "the first mark of the creation of a new social reality."[62] The defining characteristic of the imperial Roman order was that it ruled by violence—therefore a politics which did not attempt violence was in itself subversive of that ultimately destructive order. Nonresistance is not merely negative—it means being part of a community which "gives a new way to deal with a corrupt society; it builds a new order rather than smashing the old."[63] Form, according to this argument, can be as significant as content. In defense of Yoder, it must also be stressed that in his definitive work, *Politics of Jesus*, he is not attempting a systematic and comprehensive statement of Christian politics, where issues of justice, equality, inclusiveness, etc., might be further developed (although Yoder deals with such issues extensively in other more occasional articles). He is attempting to read off a definitive political method from the life, and particularly the death, of Jesus, which can be applied to contemporary politics. The Liberation theology of Boff and Sobrino does not start from the same theological basis as Yoder, but it is, ironically, in the base communities of Latin America that such a Yoderian politics has most vividly been put into practice. These Christian communities have taken a vulnerable position outside the gates of power and have exercised a powerful political witness.

---

61. Hauerwas, "John Howard Yoder," 252.
62. Hauerwas, "John Howard Yoder," 252.
63. Hauerwas, "John Howard Yoder," 253.

Chapter 8

The Crucified People—Solidarity between the Poor and the Crucified Christ

The last chapter concentrated on the political ecclesiology of Yoder, and his attempts to express the relationship between politics and a cruciform church. In this chapter I change the usual order and begin with the teaching of Sobrino on the crucified people. I then consider aspects of the theology of Boff and Yoder which might illuminate Sobrino's teaching.

A) SOBRINO—THE CRUCIFIED PEOPLE

Introduction—The Theme of the Crucified People

When discussing the theme of the crucified people in the theology of Sobrino, it is important to recognize its antecedents, especially the contribution of Ellacuria, Sobrino's martyred Jesuit colleague in El Salvador. The "scourged Christ of the Indies" has been a theme in Latin American theology since the time of De Las Casas. His famous saying, "In the Indies I leave Jesus Christ, our God, being whipped and afflicted, and buffeted and crucified, not once but a thousand times, as often as the Spaniards assault and destroy those people," forms the backdrop to Sobrino's (and Ellacuria's) theology of the cross. Ellacuria, in an article[1] written as a preliminary paper to the CELAM Puebla conference in 1979, linked this old, but often neglected,

---

1. Ellacuria and Sobrino, *Mysterium*, 580–603.

theme with soteriology in a new and radical way. In European theology, in his groundbreaking work *The Crucified God*, Moltmann had formulated a theology of crucifixion, but in this early work he restricted the metaphor of "taking up of the cross" to Christian believers without extending it more widely to those who do not choose to bear the cross, but have it thrust upon them.[2] It is significant that, possibly under the influence of Latin American theologies of the cross, Moltmann later extended cross bearing to sociological as well as religious categories.

Sobrino locates the rediscovery of this theme in the political circumstances of El Salvador. He relates how Ellacuria "saw the Salvadorean reality as poverty, injustice, oppression, repression and war. He saw the people bearing the burden of it all. He called them the crucified people." Ellacuria applied his reading of the situation in El Salvador more widely, and interpreted the reality of the world in terms of crucifixion. A large part of humanity has been and continues to be "crucified by the oppression of nature and, above all, by historical and personal oppression."[3] The crucified people are a constant factor in world history, although the mode of crucifixion might change. They become the historical successors to the biblical figure of the suffering servant.

Sobrino, following Ellacuria, links the present crucified people intimately with a fairly traditional and comprehensive Christology. He also integrates the theme of the crucified people with soteriology, and gives them an important soteriological role. This linking of the crucifixion of peoples, of Christology, and of soteriology, in the light of such biblical passages as the Servant Songs and Paul's enigmatic phrase about "in my flesh I am completing what is lacking in Christ's afflictions" (Col 1:24, NRSV) poses searching questions about the identity and salvific potential of Christ's suffering body in history, the relationship between the cross of Christ and the individual or collective crosses of Latin America, and the spirituality which responds to such crucifixion

In Sobrino's early works the theme is present only indirectly. In *Christology at the Crossroads* he links contemporary Latin American suffering with the cross, writing of "the cross of Jesus and the historical crosses" in tandem.[4] In *Jesus in Latin America* Sobrino includes a chapter entitled "The Risen One is the One who was Crucified: Jesus' resurrection from among the world's crucified" and describes the "crucified of history" as constituting not just the conscious and faithful followers of Jesus: "In the human race

2. Moltmann, *Crucified*, 64.
3. Sobrino, *Where Is God?*, 50.
4. Sobrino, *Christology*, 230.

today—and certainly where I am writing—many women and men, indeed entire peoples—are crucified."[5] He adds, "We must not forget that there are millions of persons in the world who do not simply die, but, in various ways, die as Jesus died."[6] Sobrino's collection of essays originally published in 1992 is significantly entitled, *The Principle of Mercy: Taking the Crucified People from the Cross* . The fullest outworking of this theme is found in his developed Christology, *Jesus the Liberator* and in his tribute to and theological reflection upon the Jesuit martyrs in *Witnesses to the Kingdom: the Martyrs of El Salvador and the Crucified Peoples*. In one of his later works, *Where Is God? Earthquake, Terrorism, Barbarity and Hope* Sobrino returns to this theme. The motif of the crucified people is "vigorous and rigorous"—it denotes people really dead, not merely hurt; killed, not dying "naturally"; dying a shameful and undeserved death; and dying a death connected to Jesus and his fate.[7] The crucifier is injustice: "Injustice crucifies; there are different forms of crucifixion according to the circumstances."[8] It is from these works that a description and a critique of the theme will mainly be drawn, in dialogue with the Norwegian theologian and social ethicist Sturla Stalsett whose study *The Crucified and the Crucified* is a comprehensive and penetrating examination of the theme from a Lutheran viewpoint.

What Is Meant by the Crucified People?

In discussing this question it is salutary to remember that the crucified people are, first of all, a tragic sociological reality and only secondarily a theological concept. Sobrino locates the theme of crucified people in the linkage between the historically crucified body of Jesus and a contemporary body of Christ. He asks of this contemporary body "whether this body is crucified, what element of this body is crucified, and if its crucifixion is the presence of the crucified Christ in history."[9] The cross is not confined to the time of Jesus, but is a present reality, especially in the tragedy of the poverty and political oppression of Latin America, where the cross continues to exist "not just individual crosses, but collective crosses of whole peoples." The only way to express the theological and sociological gravity of the situation is to use the term "crucified peoples."[10] This term crucified people denotes

5. Sobrino, *Latin America*, 148.
6. Sobrino, *Latin America*, 151.
7. Sobrino, *Where Is God?*, 51.
8. Sobrino, *Where Is God?*, 53.
9. Sobrino, *Jesus the Liberator*, 254.
10. Sobrino, *Jesus the Liberator*, 254.

not just any death, but primarily that actively inflicted by unjust structures, the institutionalized violence of poverty and oppression. There are not only victims but also executioners. On a religious level the cross represents the death that Jesus died, and therefore for the believer it can "evoke the fundamentals of the faith" and link, in Stalsett's term, the "crucified" with the "Crucified." The crucified people are the "actual presence of the crucified Christ in history."[11] The relation between Christ and the crucified people is reciprocal: "In this crucified people Christ acquires a body in history and . . . the crucified people embody Christ in history as crucified."[12]

Sobrino later amplifies this.[13] The language of contemporary crucifixion is metaphorical and conveys much better than other language "the historical enormity of the disaster and its meaning for faith." It denotes the "slow, but real death caused by the poverty generated by unjust structures." Such death is multifaceted and includes not just the obvious violence of war. "Swift, violent death, caused by repression and wars, when the poor threaten these unjust structures . . . Indirect but effective death when peoples are deprived even of their cultures in order to weaken their identities and make them more defenseless." It is a useful and necessary description of a conflictual reality "because cross expresses a type of death actively inflicted. To die crucified does not mean simply to die, but to be put to death; it means that there are victims and there are executioners." The Latin American people's cross has been inflicted upon them by various empires: Spanish and Portuguese yesterday, the US and its allies today, through military, cultural, religious or economic oppression. Such language is useful and necessary at the religious level also because the word cross, denoting the fact that Jesus suffered death on the cross and not any other death "evokes sin and grace, condemnation and salvation, human action and God's action." The cross is a symbol, but much more than a symbol; it is the presence of God himself on the cross that is an effectual sign to humanity. "From a Christian point of view, God himself makes himself present in these crosses, and the crucified people become the principal sign of the times. This sign [of God's presence in our world] is always the historically crucified people."

The language used is, of course, metaphorical; cases of actual contemporary torture and execution by crucifixion, in a manner physically identical to that of Jesus, are obviously not the point of Sobrino's work. The relationship between the cross of Jesus and the crosses of Latin America is analogical and as with any analogy it is essential to note there is not

11. Sobrino, *Jesus the Liberator*, 255.
12. Sobrino, *Jesus the Liberator*, 255.
13. Sobrino, *Witnesses*, 156.

necessarily complete correspondence. We explore later how Sobrino perhaps aims for a more complete correspondence in terms of salvation than is warranted. The language of crucifixion, however, has a meaning which it would be difficult to express in any other way, especially for a Christian theologian seeking to link religious truth with the contemporary situation of suffering. It describes a conflictual situation common to both the crucifixion of Jesus and the contemporary world. Most of all it links the crucified people with the person of the crucified Jesus in a reciprocal movement—the crucified people shed historical and sociological light on the crucified Jesus and the crucified Jesus sheds theological light on the crucified people. This is, perhaps, separating too sharply the theological and sociological; a liberation theologian would argue that the two are intimately linked.

Who Are the Crucified People?

We have already noted that one of the innovations of Ellacuria and Sobrino was to extend the bearing of the cross from those who specifically choose to do so as Christians to those who have crucifixion thrust upon them; those who, in Rahnerian terminology, are anonymous cross bearers rather than cross bearers by choice. Ellacuria defines the crucified people as follows:

> That collective body, which as the majority of humankind owes its situation of crucifixion to the way society is organized and maintained by a minority that exercises its dominion through a series of factors, which taken together and given their concrete impact within history, must be regarded as sin.[14]

Hence the term denotes those suffering from the consequences of a sinful ordering of society. This suffering is not due to the chance misfortunes of life, but to a situation of structural oppression, deliberate in that there are those who benefit from sinful structures and seek to keep them in place. Given the metaphorical nature of the language, there is some inevitable flexibility in its usage, and this lack of precision can lead to potential dangers, especially, as we shall see, when the crucified people are linked with soteriology. Perhaps Sobrino uses differing aspects of the crucified people imprecisely? Liberation theology is, above all a contextual theology, and it is important to recognize how changes in context broaden the scope of the theme of the crucified people. Analyses of Latin American poverty have increasingly encompassed issues of sexual and racial inequality and erosion of traditional culture, and globalization has (at least partially) changed the

14. Ellacuria and Sobrino, *Mysterium*, 590.

nature of economic poverty from oppression to exclusion. Does Sobrino have in mind the poor as politically organized (most specifically, the base communities) or, in Marxist terms, the lumpenproletariat poor whose death is unnoticed and unremarked?[15]

The theologically controversial leap undertaken by Ellacuria and Sobrino is, as suggested above, to extend cross bearing from those who bear the cross as a result of their following Jesus to a wider suffering community. Is it justifiable to make such an extension, from suffering explicitly for Jesus' sake to a more general suffering? If Rahner is at all correct in arguing for anonymous Christianity—i.e., that it is not necessary to name Christ explicitly to be sharing his way—then the corollary might be that it is not necessary to suffer explicitly for Christ in order to share in his suffering. It is necessary only to suffer in the way that Christ suffered—and for similar historical reasons—at the hands of those who hold power, and crucify those who threaten that power. Sobrino wrestles with this in his discussion of the relation between the "Jesuanic martyrs" and the crucified people:

> If martyrdom is the response of the anti-kingdom to those who struggle actively for the kingdom, then the analogatum princeps is being like Jesus, as exemplified in Archbishop Romero. If martyrdom is bearing the burden of the sin of the anti-kingdom, then these defenseless majorities—killed innocently, massively and passively, are the analogatum princeps.[16]

The crucified people "without intending it and without knowing it . . . fulfill in the flesh what was lacking in the passion of Christ." Sobrino will be aware that in using this verse (Col 1:24) in this way he is going far beyond the meaning of Paul, who refers in that passage to those engaged in apostolic labors for the sake of the church. Is this transposition justified? Or is Sobrino pushing the language too far in identifying the crucified people too closely with those in the New Testament who suffer with and for Christ? I would argue that such an identification is justified, so long as the metaphorical nature of the crucified people language is recognized, and no attempts are made to apply the metaphor indiscriminately to every point of comparison.

Interpreting the Role of the Crucified People

As before, it is important to recognize that the crucified people do not, primarily, have a role; they simply exist in their own right and are defined

15. Sobrino, *Witnesses*, 132.
16. Sobrino, *Witnesses*, 132.

as crucified people by their oppressed situation. Stalsett has attempted to describe three "axes"(or interpretative relationships) between Jesus and the crucified people in Sobrino's theology.[17] The first he names as "epistemological-hermeneutical," denoting the two-way hermeneutic we have already noted between Jesus and oppressed peoples today. Theological and sociological understanding of one aids similar understanding of the other. The second he describes as "historical-soteriological"—salvation is manifested and transmitted in history by the crucified people. The third of Stalsett's axes is "ethical-praxical"—Jesus' historical praxis and that of the crucified people "mediate a call from God to all human beings to participate in the mission to overcome all suffering—to 'take the crucified down from their cross.'"[18]

Although I would regard these axes as useful, I wish to analyze the theme of the crucified people in a slightly different way: first, in relation to a discipleship shaped by the reality of suffering interpreted through the prism of the cross of Jesus; and, secondly, in relation to solidarity and salvation. Since the second is the most theologically innovative, I will devote much of my discussion here to the soteriological aspects of the crucified people. This is not, however, to downplay the pastoral and ecclesiological aspects of the crucified people, which will be discussed in greater detail later.

The Crucified People and a Theology of Cruciform Discipleship

The reality in which Sobrino does his theology is a crucified reality—in other words, a reality of suffering—and this crucified reality forms the bedrock of his interpretation. It may be argued that to regard reality as fundamentally crucified is arbitrarily to pluck out one aspect of the human experience and to privilege it above all others. This criticism can be answered in two ways. First, liberation theologians work consciously from their context (liberation theology argues that other theologies likewise work from their context, but often do so unconsciously), and Sobrino's context in war torn and often desperately poor El Salvador is best described, theologically, as crucified. Secondly, a downplaying of suffering, when it is regarded as merely yet another aspect of the world, risks the accusation of theological and social complacency and an ignorance (unconscious or willful) of the mechanisms by which the powerful hold their power and the powerless are excluded. A theological and pastoral recognition of the crucified people makes possible

17. Stalsett, *Crucified*, 164–65.
18. Stalsett, *Crucified*, 165.

a true knowledge both of the crucified reality of the world and of the divine response to that crucified reality. What Gutiérrez described as the "underside of history"[19] is brought to the surface. This gaining of a true knowledge of reality through the prism both of the cross of Christ and of its historical concomitant, the crucified people, forms a concrete and transformative "epistemological hermeneutic."

The transformative potential of the hermeneutic provided by the crucified people is immense. At its simplest, for theology to recognize the existence (and centrality) of the crucified people is to shift the perspective in theology from the powerful to the victims. This is the prism through which theological truth is mediated in a privileged way. Theology and praxis are intertwined, so that the theological truth thus mediated is translated into compassionate discipleship, an encounter with the crucified people in a discipleship of the crucified Jesus. This encounter must not be from a position of neutrality or for a purpose of detached observation or philosophical theodicy. Sobrino, as we have seen, extends the first world's dilemma of how to do theology *after* Auschwitz to the yet more challenging question of how to do theology *within* Auschwitz. In such a situation, analysis of crucifixion without an attempt to abolish crucifixion is pointless. Sobrino recounts how Ellacuria admired Moltmann's *The Crucified God* (a bloodstained copy of which was found in Ellacuria's house following his murder by a paramilitary death squad) but he made a point of stressing a more urgent practical and theological idea—the crucified people, whose primary need is to be brought down from the cross.[20]

The Crucified People, Solidarity and Salvation

In exploring a parallelism between the crucified Christ and contemporary suffering, Ellacuria and Sobrino have followed a path which can be traced in more traditional theology. However, in ascribing salvific significance to the crucified people they consciously go beyond the traditional. It is important to preface an analysis of this by a consideration of what Ellacuria and Sobrino mean by salvation.

Salvation is not something divorced from the historical process of oppression and liberation. It is not simply an intra-trinitarian operation, nor something solely to be awaited in a far off unworldly future, but something to be experienced in the present history of the world. This is not totally to discount the more traditional views of salvation (although there is little

19. Gutiérrez, *Power*, 169.
20. Sobrino, *Witnesses*, 155.

doubt that in practice the traditionally heavenly aspects of salvation are downplayed in much liberation theology) but to emphasize its present reality in the particulars of history. In a similar way, Gunton argues that "the universal salvation must take concrete shape in particular parts of the creation."[21] It is the role of the Holy Spirit to "particularize the universal redemption in anticipations of the eschatological redemption." Salvation is seen by Boff and Sobrino in such terms as humanization and deification, the two not being contradictory. It is not simply brought about by a divine fiat of grace but is (at any rate in its historical manifestations, upon which liberation theology concentrates) accomplished by active human participation. It is important also to note the gap not only between traditional and liberation theologies, but between Protestant and Catholic understandings of salvation: the Protestant emphasizing the never to be repeated gracious action of God in Christ; the Catholic emphasizing the ongoing participation in that action by humanity. As a Roman Catholic liberation theologian, it is hardly surprising that Sobrino's view of salvation presupposes salvation as something to be worked out in the present. The correctness or otherwise of this presupposition deeply affects any judgment of the appropriateness of utilizing the theme of crucified people in soteriology.

Sobrino's doctrine of the crucified people rests on a solidarity between God in Christ and those who suffer. Sobrino argues, "The crucified people are the presence of Christ crucified in history . . . it is idle to say that Christ crucified has a body in history and not identify it in some way."[22] There is a parallelism which goes beyond mere similarity—Stalsett usefully describes a *communicatio idiomatum*, a mutual exchange of properties between the suffering Jesus and the suffering people.[23] If the historical cross of Jesus demonstrates the vulnerable presence of God in sharing human suffering, then it is analogically correct to ascribe God's vulnerable presence also to the crosses of the contemporary world. This divine sympathy is in itself a sign of salvation, in demonstrating God's solidarity with those who suffer. Sobrino takes this further by utilizing the Isaianic figure of the suffering servant (especially as portrayed in Isaiah 53). He finds significant similarities between the suffering servant and the crucified peoples of today: in their suffering, in their being "despised and rejected," and in their being killed for "establishing right and justice." This triple identification—of the suffering servant, of Jesus, and of the crucified peoples—is the starting point for Sobrino's new soteriological departure.

21. Gunton, *Actuality*, 170.
22. Sobrino, *Jesus the Liberator*, 264.
23. Stalsett, *Crucified*, 166.

It is interesting to note that Sobrino does not necessarily ascribe a greater salvific role to those who are active in political and economic change. He certainly likens this role to that of the servant, but identification with the suffering servant is not restricted to those who identify themselves as Christians or who are political activists. These are not actively involved—rather, they take on the servant role simply because of who they are, because of their passive existence in suffering. Even as silent witnesses, "they are the greatest proof of injustice and the greatest protest against it."[24] The relationship is a reciprocal one: "Without the active Servant, the passive Servant would have no voice, and unless the passive Servant existed, the active Servant would have no reason to exist."[25] The sin-bearing role of the Servant is interpreted thus: "The invisible wrong done to God becomes historical in the visible wrong done to the victims." What, then should be done about sin? It is necessary to "eradicate it, but with one essential condition—by bearing it." The theme of sin bearing is crucial for Sobrino: "Rather than taking on the guilt of sin, bearing the sin of others means bearing the sin's historical effects: being ground down, crushed, put to death." This is not merely negative, but has soteriological import: "The crucified people bear the sins of their oppressors on their shoulders . . . nevertheless, by really taking on the sin historically, the Servant can eradicate it." This is a remarkable statement by Sobrino. The crucified people become bearers of "historical soteriology" in a similar way to the suffering servant's role as bearer of salvation. In a significant later passage Sobrino writes, "The one chosen by God to bring salvation is the servant, which increases the scandal."[26] The scandal is salvation coming from below, from an unexpected place. The crucified people are not only those to whom God's salvation is primarily offered, but are also the key to the world's salvation (there is an interesting parallel in the privileged position of the proletariat in Marx's scheme of "salvation"). Sobrino downplays the vicarious expiation aspect of the Servant's role as not illuminating "what salvation the cross brings, far less what historical salvation the cross brings today."[27] And yet, to be true to the biblical model, salvation must somehow be found in the figure of the suffering servant. This is not "only or principally a matter of speculation and interpretation of texts. It is a matter of grasping the reality." Sobrino attempts to describe three ways in which the suffering servant/crucified people can be said to be bearers of

---

24. Sobrino, *Jesus the Liberator*, 258.
25. Sobrino, *Jesus the Liberator*, 259.
26. Sobrino, *Witnesses*, 160.
27. Sobrino, *Witnesses*, 160.

salvation—"as shedding light on the human situation; as offering humanizing values; and as bearing the sin of the world."

First, Sobrino describes the crucified people as giving light, bringing into sharp focus the injustices of the world. They demonstrate, as nothing else can, "that true progress cannot consist in what is offered now, but in bringing the crucified people down from the cross and sharing the resources and everybody's goods with all."[28] This light "shows the nations what they really are." It unmasks lies: "If the First World cannot see its own reality in this light, we do not know what can make it do so." It demonstrates the ethical unsustainability of the present situation: "The solution offered by the First World today is factually wrong, because it is unreal; it is not universalizable. And it is ethically wrong, for them and for the Third World."[29] The first step in salvation is the manifestation of the sin, what might be called in traditional evangelical language conviction of sin. The existence of crucified people means that economics and politics are revealed to be a matter not merely of figures on a balance sheet or games played by the powerful, but to involve actual crucifying effects on human beings. They show the reality of sin, its effects upon humanity, and what must be done with it.

Next, Sobrino turns to the positive and notes the salvific (in Sobrino's terms "humanizing") values which the crucified people bring. They offer unique values

> . . . evangelizing potential . . . the gospel values of solidarity, service, simplicity and readiness to receive God's gift; a humanizing potential, offering community against individualism, co-operation against selfishness, simplicity against opulence, openness to transcendence against blatant positivism.[30]

The crucified people offer hope, great love, forgiveness, a faith, a way of being church, as well as authentic, relevant and Jesus shaped holiness.[31] Sobrino is aware of this from personal and pastoral experience—there is the danger, though, that in other hands this doctrine could veer too closely toward a Rousseau-like idealization. The crucified people of the third world offer these gifts to the whole world in what could be a beneficial exchange: "Liberated and given grace by the crucified people, the first world could become grace and liberation for them."[32] Moreover, the crucified people

---

28. Sobrino, *Witnesses*, 161.
29. Sobrino, *Witnesses*, 160.
30. Sobrino, *Witnesses*, 161.
31. Sobrino, *Jesus the Liberator*, 263–64.
32. Sobrino, *Witnesses*, 162.

demonstrate some of the most striking features of Jesus' life in the world, and hence show what it means to share in Jesus' status as sons and daughters of God. In this sense, they mediate the life of Jesus to the world.

Third, the poor "bear the sin of the world." The crucified peoples, as the chief recipient of the harmful results of sinful economic and political structures, can be said to "bear the sin of the word" in that they bear its consequences. However, Ellacuria and Sobrino seem to go beyond this relatively simple concept in suggesting that the power of sin can only be overcome by bearing its consequences, by suffering under it. Stalsett interprets this to mean that "salvation in history can be achieved only through confronting sin in an active struggle against it, and bearing the consequences of the opposition which such a struggle always—by historical necessity—will meet."[33] This would in itself be an adequate and fruitful interpretation, but Ellacuria and Sobrino seem to go beyond this in ascribing to the crucified people a special salvific role with the phrase: "There is no liberation from sin without the bearing of sin." But does sin (in the liberation theologian's sense of injustice and dehumanization) have to be borne, in the sense of suffered, for salvation to take place? Can it not simply be halted, changed, brought to an end? This change may well involve suffering on behalf of those who attempt such a course, but Ellacuria and Sobrino seem to suggest that there is something not only ultimately beneficial but absolutely necessary in soaking up the sin by suffering injustice and oppression. This image (Christ nullifying the power of sin by soaking up all that could be directed at him) has been fruitful in providing a new model of atonement, but it is difficult to see how this can be used profitably with the crucified people, whose liberation lies not in receiving more injustice in order to soak it up but in being delivered from it.

Stalsett provides a useful summary of the salvific benefits of the crucified people and attempts to integrate Sobrino's teaching with more traditional doctrines of salvation: "Since God's presence with the crucified Jesus is a salvific presence, there are signs of God's salvific presence also in the crosses of history."[34] This happens in the following ways: "The crucified people share salvation with the world by testifying to God's salvific presence, and by transmitting and communicating signs and fruits of this salvation to others." Their role is that of an effectual witness: ". . . through hope, through promoting life, forgiving, they generate solidarity and mercy, and confess the God of life."[35] Stalsett is careful to distinguish between Jesus and the

33. Stalsett, *Crucified*, 141.
34. Stalsett, *Crucified*, 538–39.
35. Stalsett, *Crucified*, 538–39.

crucified people in the mediation of salvation: the crucified people mediate salvation in a derived sense; Jesus is the prime mediator, and calls others to follow him. Similarly, whereas the crucified people are indispensable for salvation, they do not, as it were, create salvation. They are not, in Stalsett's view, saviors, and do not play a salvific role in an ultimate sense. Jesus alone is the savior. They do not carry the sins of others away; this, according to Stalsett, would be a wrong extension of the suffering servant analogy. They may carry other people's sins as scapegoats, in a Girardian sense, but Christianity breaks the logic of scapegoating, since Jesus is on the side of the scapegoated people, enabling them to break free from their scapegoat role. Suffering in itself is not salvific—salvation lies in the love of God, present in the Crucified.

I would largely agree with Stalsett's sympathetic critique. This doctrine of the crucified people is a dramatic and vivid transposition of the historical cross of Jesus to present circumstances. By analogy with the presence of God in the suffering Jesus, it emphasizes God's solidarity with those who suffer today. Perhaps Sobrino would have been wise to restrict salvific value to that divine solidarity, and to have been more hesitant in over-applying the analogy with Christ. Sobrino risks appearing to suggest that the crucified people themselves take over the work of Christ, if not *in toto*, then to a substantial degree. There are two problems with this: first, that it derogates from the unique and definitive nature of Christ (although Sobrino is clear that the crucified people's mediation of salvation is a derived mediation, and in line with the traditional theology of the body of Christ perpetuating Christ's ministry); and second, that it portrays only a partial view of salvation—there is (quite rightly) nothing ascribed to the crucified people encompassing such soteriological models as atoning sacrifice, substitution, etc. which are found within the model of the suffering servant. Perhaps refuge can be taken in the argument that liberation theology only emphasizes that part of theology which is particularly relevant for its own situation—it does not deny the rest, but concentrates on certain aspects. For example, the crucified people undoubtedly illustrate certain aspects of salvation, in acting as an open wound of humanity thus bringing into sharp focus political and economic sin and the need for redemption.

There is, however, a further problem in directly ascribing salvific value to the crucified people's sufferings. True, their sufferings do bring to light an unjust situation, but that is, as we have seen, only a preliminary to salvation, not salvation itself. Sobrino himself suggests that salvation occurs when the crucified people are taken down from the cross. Their sufferings may well enable acts of remedial justice, kindness, compassion to take place, and hence have value, but that is similar to a pastoral situation where a seriously ill, or disabled person is informed that their life has value and purpose in being a focus of love, in being a recipient of care and an opportunity for others to demonstrate compassion. This may well be true, but it fundamentally transgresses the Kantian ethic of never treating humans as means to an end, but rather as an end in themselves. Sobrino's theology here risks instrumentalizing the crucified people, in addition to the ever present danger of legitimizing poverty. This danger can to some extent be countered by his insistence on the absolute primacy of taking the crucified from their crosses. Although God, in Sobrino's theology, chooses the poor as the principal means of salvation, this certainly does not mean that he intends them to remain poor or sacralizes their poverty.

Much of the above criticism is lessened if the salvific element of the crucified people is specifically identified as those (within the crucified people or acting on their behalf) who actively resist systems of poverty and political oppression, and suffer as a consequence. The obvious candidates, close to Sobrino's own experience, are those sections of the church which seek to "take down the suffering people from their crosses" most notably, the martyrs of El Salvador. Sobrino quotes Ellacuria's assertion that the "specifically Christian task is to fight to eradicate sin by bearing its burden."[36] This would describe very accurately those within the Latin American church who actively campaign against poverty and oppression, and bear the burden of suffering which this entails. Sobrino continues, "Although it is true that historical sin can only be eradicated by means of a power outside the sin, it also has to be done by someone willing to bear the burdensome reality of that sin which destroys and sows death."[37] In other words this means not merely attacking the system from the outside, but bearing the consequences of that system from within and being willing to accept the possible outcome. Suffering, in itself, does not bring salvation, but a willingness to suffer for a salvific cause is part of the salvific process, a distinction well made by Stalsett: "Life in service of the kingdom saves, with death a possible and likely consequence. Therefore the suffering people are salvific only insofar as there is a reproduction of Jesus' service for the kingdom in history."[38] That service, and therefore salvific action, can be unconscious or anonymous (in the Rahnerian sense) and Jesus does not need to be named for the service to be Christlike. Sobrino is well aware of the distinction between active salvific action and passive salvific action. Perhaps his unwillingness to dismiss passive salvific action is due to a justifiable reluctance to separate too radically

36. Sobrino, *Witnesses*, 96.
37. Sobrino, *Witnesses*, 103.
38. Stalsett, *Crucified*, 148–49.

the politically active from the masses they represent. It would probably be more accurate to identify different sections of the crucified people with different parts of the salvific process—the passive with the role of providing evidence for conviction of sin, the active bearing the weight of that sin in order to overcome it.

B) BOFF AND YODER—A THEOLOGY OF SOLIDARITY

Boff and Cruciform Solidarity

Sobrino's doctrine of the crucified people rests on the solidarity of God with those who suffer. This theme of solidarity, between the poor and the crucified Christ, and by extension, between the poor and the present body of Christ, is central to Boff's theology. In his summary chapter "How to preach the cross of Jesus Christ today" he expounds this theme in two ways. First, carrying the cross means acting in committed solidarity with those who are crucified in today's world, in the dangerous process of both defending the oppressed and denouncing their oppressors. Just as Jesus suffered crucifixion for such actions, so a similar commitment today risks an analogous fate.[39] Boff no doubt has in mind the option for the poor adopted by the Roman Catholic church in Latin America following Medellin. Second, the cross is the sign of God's actual, historical solidarity with the victims of history: "God's preferred mediation is the concrete, real-life suffering of the oppressed . . . To draw near to God is to draw near the oppressed . . . God loves sufferers so much that he suffers and dies along with them."[40] Boff finds a radical congruence between the perspective of the poor and that of the crucified Christ. A core biblical passage in Boff's interpretation of the cross is the parable of the Sheep and the Goats (Matt 25:31–46). He comments, "God really does lie hidden and unknown beneath every person in need."[41] The fact that God, or Jesus, continues to suffer in the poor and oppressed is integral to Boff's theology of the cross, and crucial to his methodology.

Hence, Boff insists on the link between the Jesus of history and the Christ of faith—there is a radical continuity between the crucified Jesus of Nazareth and the Christ whose crucifixion continues in present day victims.[42] This forms the basis for his spirituality of a present encounter with God. Where does that encounter occur? What are the ramifications of that

---

39. Boff, *Passion*, 130.
40. Boff, *Passion*, 132–33.
41. Boff, *Way*, 37–39.
42. Boff, *Way*, viii.

encounter? Boff stresses the mystical solidarity between Jesus (and God) on the cross and those crucified today: "Since God himself was crucified in Jesus Christ, no cross imposed unjustly is a matter of indifference to him. He is in solidarity with all who hang on crosses."[43] How does God wish to be encountered? "God wishes to be encountered and served in the face of this humiliated and outraged person, in the disfigured face of this man who was the victim of violence."[44] This divine choice is central to genuine spirituality: "God chose to concentrate his presence, to privilege certain situations. If we do not encounter him there, where he chose to be, then we simply do not encounter him at all, nor do we commune with the real God of Jesus Christ."[45] The *locus* chosen by God for the divine human encounter is first of all Jesus Christ, a "frail, powerless human being."[46] "Second, we encounter God in the lives and faces of the humiliated and the downtrodden." Boff combines Jesus as the human face of God, Jesus' teaching in the parable of the Sheep and the Goats, and the identification of God with Jesus on the cross to create a spirituality of encounter with the divine in the ongoing crucifixion of human beings.

To adopt Kitamori's phrase, Boff's is a theology of the "pain of God."[47] Boff stresses that God suffers as a result of being love, and takes up the cross as something very much *extra deum* as an expression of that love. Moreover, the chosen and free solidarity of God, in Christ, with the suffering of the oppressed must be paralleled by a similar chosen and free solidarity on behalf of the church. In this way the church truly incarnates the present body of Christ. A contemplation of God in such suffering, and of human suffering in the perspective of the divine, means that solidarity and identification with the crucified of today are indispensible in the struggle against today's crosses. The process of liberation depends on such solidarity, both human and divine, as demonstrated by Jesus himself.[48] Suffering is not to be sought, but accepted as a result of such identification. This follows the divine pattern— the cross and suffering are *extra deum*, and therefore not intrinsic to God, but God takes them up in freedom, and invites others to take up the cross in freedom and love as a means of accomplishing liberation from the crosses of oppression. This is the basis for Boff's cruciform spirituality of liberation: the cross is most of all the focus of God's love which destroys hatred as

43. Boff, *Way*, 16.
44. Boff, *Way*, 45.
45. Boff, *Way*, 46–47.
46. Boff, *Way*, 47.
47. Boff, *Passion*, 115–16.
48. Boff, *Passion*, 115–16.

God, and humanity, take up the cross in the process of that liberation.[49] This emphasis on solidarity is fundamental to Boff's Christology, and is a radical outworking of his doctrine of the "cosmic Christ." Through the resurrection, "Christ penetrated [the world] in a more profound manner and is now present in all reality in the same way God is present in all things."[50] Boff is indebted to Rahner in the extent to which he sees the "cosmic Christ" at work in all people.[51] This means that "each person is actually a brother or sister to Jesus and in some way participates in his reality."[52] Presumably the converse holds true, that the "cosmic Christ" participates, often incognito, in the reality of each person. Reality, in Teilhardian terms, has a "Christic structure."[53]

Yoder—Discipleship as Solidarity

Yoder's cruciform discipleship rests on a multifaceted solidarity with the crucified Christ. The disciple, in imitation of the character of God as revealed in Christ, shares radically in Christ's sufferings. Yoder uses such words as "participation" or "correspondence"[54] to describe this relationship and describes "suffering with Christ as the definition of apostolic existence."[55] The Christian thus shares in the "divine condescension," exemplified in the incarnation and especially the crucifixion of Jesus. Christ's free solidarity with suffering humankind through the cross is paralleled by the church's willingness to suffer in solidarity with him. Being in Christ necessitates and empowers an identity between Jesus and the disciple-church which gives the church both its political ethic and its vulnerability to suffering. This solidarity-in-suffering of the church with the crucified Christ is the practical and historical source and outcome of the political nonconformity undertaken by the church in obedience to Christ.

---

49. Boff, *Passion*, 116.
50. Boff, *Jesus Christ*, 207.
51. As demonstrated by Waltermire, *Liberation Christologies*, 40.
52. Boff, *Jesus Christ*, 218.
53. Waltermire, *Liberation Christologies*, 42.
54. Yoder, *Politics*, 113.
55. Yoder, *Politics*, 120.

3) CONCLUSION

Boff's stress on the solidarity of God through Christ with the world's suffering is a useful complement to Sobrino's doctrine of the crucified people. Both themes are christologically focused, through Boff's teaching on the "cosmic Christ" and Sobrino's linking of the crucified with the Crucified. Both rest, too, on a theology of a suffering God who in freedom suffers the pain of the creation, and both give rise to a political spirituality of commitment, encounter, and identification. Both (particularly Sobrino) are concerned not to restrict the crucified people to those claiming explicit Christian commitment or church membership. This is the critical point of divergence between Yoder's theology of Christ in solidarity with his suffering (Christian) people and Sobrino's theology of a crucified people whose only qualification for the title is their suffering. For Yoder, such solidarity is gained not through a more general suffering, but through suffering specifically as a member of a Christlike, persecuted church. As previously noted, it is important to recognize that the distinction may not in practice be as clear cut as it first appears. Sobrino and Boff write within a situation where the default position of most people is Christian, and where despite the decline in the practice of Catholicism in Latin America, most would regard themselves as Christians and members of the church. For Yoder, membership of the church is, both sociologically and theologically, more a matter of choice. There is, however, a significant difference between Sobrino's approach, much influenced by Rahner's anonymous Christianity, and Yoder's theology, which is based on a committed and disciplined church, consciously imitating Christ's suffering. I would argue, however, that the two approaches can be combined. Yoder's committed and suffering community is an explicit sign of Christ's cross—but that does not diminish the truth that a God of sympathy and solidarity does not restrict that sympathy and solidarity to those who bear the name of Christ.

Summary 3

Towards a Political Theology of the Cross—Community, Crucifixion and Responsibility

The last two chapters have discussed the cross in relation to two categories of people—the cruciform and the crucified people. I now attempt to outline elements arising from these chapters which I believe should be incorporated in a political theology of the cross.

THE CORPORATE CHRIST AND THE PEOPLE OF GOD

In Pauline theology, Christ has a corporate, as well as an individual, nature. This is especially significant in Paul's teaching about the body of Christ, referring not just to the physical body of Jesus of Nazareth but to his community of followers. From the human perspective, what is described as the body of Christ is a continuation in physical form, in the present, of the reality of the historical Jesus. From the divine perspective, it denotes that part/aspect/mode of the divine that was in Jesus, which takes shape in human reality today. Hence the body of Christ is intimately linked with the historical Jesus as well as being a present sociological reality. In that sense, the body of Christ is an extension of the incarnation. How can that present body act politically, as Jesus did? How far is that body bound to follow the same pattern of life which, for Jesus, led to crucifixion? How far does that body extend? Is it restricted to those who bear the name of Christ, or does it include those who have done to them what was done to Christ? In general terms, I have described the former as the "cruciform people" and the latter as the "crucified people." There is certainly an overlap, but the term cruciform people denotes those who actively choose to be members of a community seeking a political path which may lead to crucifixion; the crucified people denote those whose crucifixion is not necessarily chosen, but inflicted as a result of their unchosen sociological location. Both can claim to share in the corporate nature of Christ, the former through willing participation in his mission, the latter through unwillingly undergoing the same persecution he suffered at the hands of those whose power is threatened.

THE CROSS AND A MODIFIED RESPONSIBILITY

The church's political responsibility is enlarged, not diminished, by the cross. The fact that Jesus' political choices led him to a position of non-resistance, nonviolence, and non-coercion does not mean that Christian responsibility for the world is denied. While acknowledging that the Christendom approach may involve a tragic category mistake in conflating Christianity with civil power and that the Niebuhrian chaplaincy to power strategy runs the risk of complicity in evil, the Christian's loving responsibility for a suffering world cannot be escaped. William Temple stated that the church "cannot abandon the task of guiding society as far as society consents to be guided. It has a special illumination which it is called to bring to bear on the whole range of human relationships."[1] Biggar wisely comments that it is the role of the responsible person to be "providence ourselves . . . The issue is not whether we should be provident, but what the moral constraints are that should discipline our providence."[2]

The question is—how is that responsibility to be exercised? In the teaching of Jesus, sins of omission are as harmful as sins of commission, and a refusal to ameliorate a situation when it is within one's power to do so should not be countenanced unless for overwhelmingly good reasons. The ethics of conflicting duty—on the one hand to peace and nonviolence, on the other to justice and love of neighbor—mean that moral decisions cannot necessarily be clear cut, and the tension between witness and responsibility remains acute. Charles Marsh, in his biography of Bonhoeffer, describes the tension between Bonhoeffer's pacifism and his recognition of the need to stop Hitler. Bonhoeffer saw himself as a sinner whichever course he took. And so, following Luther's injunction to sin boldly, one could "at least sin for the sake of righteousness. Bonhoeffer did not try to resolve the paradox by

1. Temple, *Religious Experience*, 244.
2. Biggar, *In Defence*, 31.

assuming moral innocence but accepted the paradox by incurring the guilt born out of responsible action."[3] Marsh summarizes Bonhoeffer's dilemma:

> A peace ethic acknowledges that in historical existence certain extreme circumstances inevitably arise that require actions unacceptable in the pacifist's worldview—these are the so-called *Grenzfalle*, the extreme cases, the boundary situations. In such instances, the decision to use violence must be risked if the pure principles of peace block the way to responsible action and the relief of innocent suffering.[4]

In the midst of such dilemmas, the Christian should not be afraid of wishing to move history in the right direction; in the light of the eschatological hope of the coming kingdom, the Christian recognizes a *telos* and seeks to move towards it. This is not to argue in a totally consequentialist manner that the *telos* requires a strategy to which all else can and should be sacrificed. There are legitimate ends—but the means to those ends are as important as the ends themselves. Christian responsibility should only be exercised through legitimate (i.e., nonviolent and non-retaliatory) channels. Can the goodness of the legitimate ends ever outweigh the evil of illegitimate methods? A short term Niebuhrian realist would answer in the affirmative, the Yoderian (relying on the efficacy of long term witness) in the negative. For reasons outlined above, it is difficult totally to discount the short term approach—provided that one maintains a deep awareness of human sinfulness, a wise cynicism about the motivation for supposedly good actions, and an awareness of unforeseen and unintended consequences. The Second World War is, perhaps, a prime example: a war fought for overwhelmingly legitimate ends, in defense against a criminal, vicious, and racist expansionary dictatorship, but fought in alliance with a comparably evil totalitarian regime, and with increasingly barbaric methods (such as the escalation of bombing from purely military targets to civilian terrorization). Can responsibility and a faithful witness to the nonviolent nature of God be combined? This will be discussed more fully in the next section, but it is worth noting at this point that the truest witness to God reflects all possible aspects of the divine nature. A nonviolent church witnesses to the nonviolence of God, but also a responsible church witnesses to the loving responsibility of God. The church can never witness perfectly to the character of God—the best that can be hoped for is an ethic of approximation to the form of Christ.

It is a false dichotomy to posit the choice between being the church and taking on the responsibility of doing politics. Being the church in a

---

3. Marsh, *Strange Glory*, 346.
4. Marsh, *Strange Glory*, 347.

negative and defensive way is not enough, even if this preserves, in one sense, a purer witness to one aspect of God's character. Nor is it a question of Christian social ethics choosing between which cause should the church support and what form the church should take. The church supports causes because of what it is, and its actions—or, on occasion, abstention from action—witness to what kind of a body it is. Either way it can incur the risk of crucifixion. This risk of crucifixion is the hard alternative to fight or flight. Jesus, in the garden of Gethsemane, was confronted by the alternatives of fight (the legions of angels), flight (returning quietly to Galilee) or remaining and facing the inevitable crucifixion.[5] Similarly, the church can fight (attempt to integrate itself into a system of power), flee (into a withdrawn and supposedly pure state which contradicts the principle of the incarnation) or remain, as a vulnerable martyr/witness of the gospel.

THE POTENTIAL COST OF USING OR NOT USING FORCE

The just war theory is one way for Christians to assume responsibility, involving the potential use of lethal force. A sympathetic commentator argues that

> [the just war tradition] provides a path for Christians from their basic faith commitments to responsible participation in world affairs. The just war tradition is the attempt of Christians to come to terms with what it means to love their neighbor, protect the widow and orphan, and recognize God's providential ordering of human affairs through political authority.[6]

Just war theory rests its case on the presumption that a refusal to use lethal force can often lead to a worse situation. It calculates that by inflicting suffering on a limited scale suffering on a larger scale can be avoided or minimized. Biggar, for example, argues that pacifist inaction can have significant costs. Adducing the tragedies of Rwanda and Srebrenica he suggests that a refusal to intervene had terrible consequences: "If peace were always simple, then war could never be preferable. But peace is seldom simple."[7]

A pacifist must justify his or her refusal to intervene, no less than the just warrior must justify the intention to intervene with violence. The Yoderian pacifist would argue that if one is following the divine pattern of nonviolence one must be acting optimally in the long run, even if there

---

5. As suggested by Hovey, *To Share*, 86.
6. Clough and Stiltner, *Faith and Force*, 222.
7. Biggar, *In Defence*, 168.

is proximate suffering. The basis of the Yoderian argument is to prioritize witness over direct responsibility—but the Yoderian could still argue practically that violence is self perpetuating, and therefore in the long run is a dead end. Stiltner sums up the discussion:

> Just war thinkers might argue that pacifists do not give practical answers for dealing with evil in the real world, and pacifists charge that just warriors renounce the practices that Jesus commanded to make the reign of God more evident in our midst.[8]

It is perhaps significant that a leading historian of the First World War takes a nuanced view of the choice that faced Europe in 1914:

> Any decision for war must confront the historical evidence that it is a fearfully blunt instrument, the repercussions of whose use cannot reliably be predicted and which may make matters even worse. Intrinsic to all military undertakings, however legitimate their motives, is the risk that they will violate the principle of proportionality between ends and means, and that they too will lead to a bad war and a bad peace. The 1914–18 conflict and the settlement that followed it remain archetypes of both.[9]

It would be a mistake to suggest that the pacifist relies solely on a deontological ethic and the just warrior on consequentialism. Whereas it is true that Yoder's ethic is chiefly deontological, a significant difference between the Yoderian pacifist and the Niebuhrian just warrior (or the liberationist who turns, as a last resort, to violence) is that the consequential horizon of the former is in the (often far) future, whereas that of the latter is in the present. Both positions incur risks involving human suffering. A Yoderian pacifist faces a charge of immediate irresponsibility, which can only be avoided if he or she is involved in costly peacemaking. A just warrior faces the charge of ultimate irresponsibility, in refusing (for perhaps good reasons) to break the cycle of violence.

THE CRUCIFORM PEOPLE, THE STATE AND THE CHURCH

The cross provokes a strong hermeneutic of suspicion of Constantinian power. The Constantinian revolution was unfortunate, if perhaps inevitable, in co-opting Christianity to the power of empire. The crucifier assumed the

---

8. Clough and Stiltner, *Faith and Force*, 230.
9. Stevenson, *1914–1918*, 600.

mantle of the crucified, and the effects of that uncomfortable fit have skewed Christian social ethics ever since. Most perniciously, the concept of Christian territoriality arose, and Christendom became an entity to be defended by violence. Crusade replaced cruciformity. The myth of "Christian nations" hid the fact that there is no sociological entity which can properly bear the name Christian except the church (and, to a limited extent, certain parachurch organizations). This hermeneutic of suspicion of Constantinianism need not lead to a refusal by Christians to support movements which seek political power (for example, liberation theologians supporting the Sandinistas in Nicaragua). It would be foolish to deny that for the victims of society, a benevolent government is better than an oppressive tyrant. However, one should still retain a radically cruciform suspicion of power (both on the left and the right) and an awareness of the danger of its corruption. One of Yoder's main aims is to preserve the church from the trap of providing an open ended theological and sociological justification for the potential violence of the state.

If the cross entails a hermeneutic of suspicion of civil power, it should equally entail a hermeneutic of suspicion of the church, since it was an alliance between civil and religious authorities which crucified Jesus. The separation of the church from the world can be overemphasized, the relationship being better described as dialectical, and the boundaries between church and society often blurred. The church, like any other human institution, is corrupt and fallible, and falls foul of the temptations of illegitimate power. While it is unrealistic, given human sinfulness, to expect the church to be anything other than what it is, the inescapable essence of the task of the church is to be a foretaste of, and a witness to, the kingdom of God. There is a sense in which the prime (but certainly not the only) community for the exercise of Christian politics is the church. The church should be the setting in which the salvific values of the kingdom of God are promoted most energetically and seen most clearly.

It is a mistake to see the church as essentially other with regard to politics, as if it could stand outside politics and move politics from a position of grand detachment. However, attention needs to be given to the question of where the church positions itself vis-à-vis state power. Here, the liberation theologian's championing of a church of the poor is significant. A cruciform church is most effectively situated among (or at least in touch with and conscious of) the needs of the vulnerable. Whereas the church's relationship with political power has traditionally been from a position of equality and collegiality, a different approach is indicated. Speaking from the position of the vulnerable, and assuming the possibility of conflict, entails a critical yet participative approach to power which takes the perspective of the crucified rather than the crucifiers. Any engagement with and participation in structures of power must be done in terms of service rather than power seeking, with an awareness of the ever present danger of co-option. Withdrawal can of itself be a positive witness when the church refuses to collaborate with an oppressive state and takes sides with its victims.

POWERLESSNESS AND PERSUASIVE WITNESS

In the kenotic hymn in Philippians (Phil 2:5–11) Paul describes Jesus as rejecting control and choosing a powerlessness which culminated in the cross. Jesus' choice is paralleled by the prior decision of God, whose chosen power is that of suffering love. God chooses to restrain the divine power, abstaining from any coercion which might destroy human freedom, and, ultimately the possibility of loving relationships. This restraint, although based on God's free choice, is not totally contingent, given both God's nature of love and the necessity, for human freedom, for God to remain to some extent distanced from creation. The church aims to share in this pattern of divine love, revealed to its greatest extent in the cross of Jesus, and seeks to live in a self-giving, nonviolent, self-sacrificial love which best witnesses to the divine character. Hence the church should not use coercion as a strategy, but should rely on the persuasive power of its witness —the more consistent the witness, the stronger the persuasive power. However, while the church *qua* church should not use coercion, there is no reason why the individual Christian, acting as an agent of a beneficial state, should not use a degree of coercion, provided that this coercion is exercised within the limits of love. It is important to recognize that the power of the state is not normally constituted by the sword of lethal violence but rather by a more limited, if potentially coercive, police action.

The church in twenty-first-century Britain seems to be moving into a position of imposed and involuntary powerlessness. Such cruciform powerlessness is not to be sought as an ideal in itself, but is nevertheless a situation from which good things can come and which can release spiritual resources otherwise fettered by a reliance on the short cuts of power and force. This theme will be developed in the final chapter.

The Crucified People—Metaphor and Reality

The phrase crucified people sheds light both on the crucifixion of Jesus and on contemporary suffering, conveying the shocking enormity of that suffering and linking it with Christology. By such a linkage, it emphasizes both the innate dignity and value of humanity and the ways in which that dignity and value are violated by political and economic oppression, which is analogous to crucifixion. The crucified people are a constant throughout world history, the grim and continuing story of executioner and victim, of powerful and powerless. It is, however, important to stress the metaphorical nature of the language used. As with any metaphor, there is not a complete correspondence between the language used and the reality described. If this is forgotten, it could seem that the negative is being unduly privileged to the exclusion of a fuller description of a people's existence. The whole reality of the crucified people is not described by this metaphor; joy, community, cooperation, faith, and love co-exist with the crucifixion. If this whole reality is neglected, there is a danger that the crucified people motif can reduce people to passive and dependent objects that have terrible things done to them rather than subjects who make their own history. Another way of avoiding this danger—and the danger of a depowering negativity—is to remember that to call people crucified in a Christian context always implies the possibility of resurrection.

The phrase crucified people is, however, more than a metaphor. It describes the continuation in space and time of the sufferings of Christ, and his solidarity with those who suffer. The parable of the Sheep and the Goats (Matt 25: 31–46) illustrates this solidarity, as does Paul's enigmatic phrase ". . . completing what is lacking in Christ's afflictions" (Col 1:24, NRSV). This, as has previously been discussed, raises the question of the extent of the crucified people. If it is those who choose to bear the cross, its extent will be limited to Christians. If it is those who stand in the place where Jesus stood and are killed for the same reasons as Jesus, then its extent is far wider. As far as it can be recovered, the sociology of Jesus' first adherents indicates caution about drawing boundaries too tightly—Ched Myers suggests that "the community of discipleship is in one sense distinct, its group boundaries embrace the socially outcast—in utter contrast to the Pharisaic program of identity through separation."[10] As has been suggested, Rahner's use of the phrase anonymous Christians may perhaps be found useful. God's solidarity with suffering is not restricted to those who bear the name Christian, and the concept of the anonymous crucified might express the link between those who consciously and willingly bear the cross of Christ and those who have it thrust upon them.

---

10. Myers, *Binding*, 157.

THE CRUCIFIED PEOPLE AND SALVATION

While the theme of the crucified people links well with Christology, the link with soteriology is less well established. Much depends on how salvation is defined, and, as mentioned above, there are significant differences not only between liberation theology and more traditional theologies but also between Protestant and Catholic understandings of salvation. Care is needed with the language used, especially by liberation theologians, lest salvation be understood as being simply coterminous with social justice. Equally, more traditional theology must be aware of the possibility that salvation can be represented as hardly touching the earth at all, but detached from the reality of human struggle and the concreteness of sin. At the heart of salvation is a gift of God given in absolute grace through Christ, which restores a right relationship both between God and humanity and between human beings. That gift has to be appropriated, and that appropriation produces the fruits of justice, peace, restored relationships, and healing. Others can mediate salvation, but Jesus is the only definitive savior. How then can the crucified people be described in soteriological terms? Do the crucified people save others, or are they simply recipients of the saving love of God? It is perhaps best to describe the crucified people as: first, a vivid sign of the need for salvation; second, a sign that that salvation is in process; and third, the *locus* where the saving work of God is especially evident and present.

The crucified people stand as an open wound of humanity, and provide a shocking revelation of the sinful reality of the world and hence its need for salvation; the scandal of the cross and the scandal of poverty are intimately linked. In that sense they enable repentance and conversion by dispelling ignorance, bringing to consciousness as nothing else can the stark fact of human sin. They bear the sin of the world as an exposed nerve bears the pain of the body. In their struggles for liberation and in the love, solidarity and compassion they display within that struggle they demonstrate that salvation is at work, and offer those hard won values both to the rest of the world in general and to other crucified peoples in particular.

The theme of the crucified people certainly does not need a Marxist interpretation for its validation. It is, however, interesting that parallels can be found in Marx's view of the working class. Terry Eagleton writes:

> The working class for Marx is in one sense a specific social group. Yet because it signifies for him the wrong which keeps so many other kinds of wrong in business (imperial wars, colonial expansion, famine, genocide, the plundering of Nature, to some extent racism and patriarchy) it has a significance far beyond its own sphere. In this sense, it represents the scapegoat in ancient

societies, which is cast out of the city because it represents a universal crime, but which for just the same reason has the power to become the cornerstone of a new social order.[11]

THE CRUCIFIED PEOPLE, IDEOLOGY AND IDOLATRY

Theologically, the crucified people demonstrate the reality of Jesus, in the sense that they are the most vivid parallel possible in the present world to the historical crucifixion of Jesus. By demonstrating that reality, they prevent God from being seen idolatrously as a dispassionate monarch, rather than as a "fellow sufferer who understands."[12] The ever present temptation to idolatry is most effectively overcome by the cross, which rules out any easy interpretation of the divine as conforming to, and thereby buttressing, structures of human power. If the cross, and the incarnation in general, are to be interpreted most accurately in the present world, the crucified people provide the most illuminating context for that interpretation. Their suffering forms a definitive place of encounter with the God who shares that suffering and seeks to abolish it.

An attention to the theme of the crucified people can also help preserve theology from the Marxist charge against Christianity of forming a misleading ideology. Ideology, in the Marxist account, is described by Scott as follows: "Ideas have a particular function: either as a contribution to the explanation of our situation and so to overcoming or transcending this situation or as a contribution to the mystification or misconstrual of our situation."[13] Marxism accuses theology of "a capacity to mystify or obscure the 'real' social relations of contemporary capitalist society"[14] thereby preserving the power of the dominant classes in society. According to this charge, the ideological effect of Christianity is "autonomous individualism or, at best, an intersubjectivity."[15] This, according to Marxist analysis, has a doubly pernicious result—the suffering classes are prevented from accurately recognizing their true situation, and those who analyze society are given a misleading short cut by an over-general and non-historical doctrine of sin. If everything can simply be ascribed to sin there is a diminished need for social analysis.

---

11. Eagleton, *Marx*, 166.
12. Whitehead, *Process*, 350.
13. Scott, *Theology*, 15.
14. Scott, *Theology*, 64.
15. Scott, *Theology*, 60.

The theme of the crucified people provides a robust answer to these criticisms. First, the identification within Christian theology of a theological and sociological category of people as crucified by analyzable socio-economic and political factors sheds light upon, rather than mystifies their oppressed situation. This is not a short cut, avoiding socio-political analysis, but an added layer of analysis. Mere individualism is explicitly renounced—the people are crucified as a people, and not merely as individuals. Second, the self-recognition by the oppressed as crucified people enhances, rather than diminishes, their knowledge of their situation. Since domination often requires the consent of the dominated, through ignorance of their true potential, the self-consciousness of a people as being crucified helps to dispel that ignorance and provides potential for resurrection in what Foucault described as "the insurrection of subjugated knowledges."[16]

EXCURSUS—THE CRUCIFIED PEOPLE AND JUST WAR

Usually, Yoderian pacifism is criticized and just war theory defended, from the point of view of an Augustinian realism. This debate can usefully be illuminated by the theme of the crucified people. Jonathan Glover, in *A Moral History of the Twentieth Century*, describes the bombing of Cambodia by American forces in the escalation of the Vietnam War:

> To these political decisions, physical and psychological distance made their familiar contribution. Roger Morris, a member of Kissinger's staff, later described the deadened human responses. 'Though they spoke of terrible human suffering reality was sealed off by their trite, lifeless, vernacular: "capabilities," "objectives," "our chips."'[17]

To adduce the reality of the crucified people militates against such psychological distancing. For a Christian, the reality of suffering is concentrated when seen through the focus of the suffering Christ. Glover comments that "central to the moral imagination is seeing what is humanly important."[18] To recognize Christ the victim in those who suffer through war both brings home to the observer the shockingness of that suffering and elevates it as a matter of divine importance. Of course, such suffering is shocking in itself without reference to Christ—a Kantian ethic argues against using people as means to an end, in the form of cannon fodder for a cause. But the crucified

---

16. Foucault, *Power/Knowledge*, 81.
17. Glover, *Humanity*, 301.
18. Glover, *Humanity*, 401.

people theme concentrates and magnifies both the divine and human horror of such actions.

One of the most vigorous recent defenses of the just war theory, especially with regard to the proportionality criterion, has been made by Nigel Biggar in *In defence of war* and it may be useful to engage here with some of Biggar's arguments, which constitute a very energetic defense of just war theory and, in particular, Britain's actions in the First World War. I am aware that Biggar's work is only one in a number of recent defenses of just war theory, but his discussion is particularly sharply focused and invites response, especially from what might be a new angle, that of the crucified people.

Biggar argues, along with mainstream just war theory, that the benefits of violence must be proportionate to the harm such violence causes, but concedes that "there is one point where the pacifist case presses hard on just war reasoning: namely on the requirement of proportion."[19] His discussion centers on the First World War, and especially the Somme, where a death toll of over three hundred thousand lives resulted in minimal military gain. The criterion Biggar uses is in accord with traditional just war theory:

> A political decision to embark on a war and to keep prosecuting it, and a military decision to launch and continue an operation, are both required to appear proportionate, according to what one may reasonably expect the decision makers to have known at the time.[20]

This, of course, begs the huge question of the value the politician or general places on human life, which, in reality, can vary enormously, and where considerations such as the crucified people can play a huge role for the Christian. War, according to Biggar, is "worth it" if according to reasonable estimate it will result in a just peace, but the just war theory "rules out military operations that appear to be imprudently expensive of human lives." However, the criteria for imprudent expense appear in the end to be purely pragmatic rather than moral:

> Finally, granted sufficiently just cause the only quantity of military casualties at which belligerence as a whole becomes disproportionate is that which is unsustainable—whether in terms of human resources, military morale, or political support.[21]

Biggar asks if it is possible to establish a point at which rising casualties should have caused Britain to ask for a cessation of hostilities: "I believe

19. Biggar, *In Defence*, 60.
20. Biggar, *In Defence*, 113.
21. Biggar, *In Defence*, 148.

we can . . . when the rate of casualties outran the supply of replacements, or when it demoralized sufficient troops to the point of mutiny, or where it undermined domestic political support for the war."[22] It seems, then, that morally, if not pragmatically, anything goes in terms of human cost if one believes one's cause to be just. This seems to reduce the principle of proportionality to a calculation of what one can get away with in terms of size of population, or what the public are willing to bear, rather that weighing the horror of human life destroyed against a possible future good. Is there some point where one might say that the end, even if good, is not worth the sacrifice of human life? With regard to the Somme, because a war may be just at its outset (a historically debatable question) that fact does not justify its prosecution by all means, even if they are militarily and politically possible. An interesting and penetrating question is raised in Clough and Stiltner's discussion of just war theory: "Has there ever been a time when a nation has renounced a means of fighting a war, because, though it would be the only means of securing victory, it would contradict just war principles?"[23]

In the course of his argument Biggar quotes AJ Coates's critique of the attritional character of the battle of the Somme, as involving "an industrial and mechanical process in which the distinction between the human and the material element is systematically suppressed."[24] This suppression of "the distinction between the human and the material element" is precisely the point where the motif of the crucified people puts a huge question mark over much modern industrialized warfare. However, Biggar argues that "something can be worth buying even when one pays over the odds for it."[25] But what is the actual cost, and who actually pays? Cui bono the slaughter? National interest, as some might claim? We will return to the question of national interest later. Biggar's overwhelming criterion, if a war is considered just at its outset, is that of military success. This, however, may be to ignore the fact that there are moral stages in the conduct of a war, from actions that involve relatively small human cost to those that involve the massacre of whole populations. So it is not simply a question of whether or not a war is just, but whether it is sufficiently just to merit the cost. Here a contrast can perhaps be made between the First World War, a clash of empires, a war for control of political and economic resources between imperial powers, and the Russian "Great Patriotic War," a war of annihilation. Biggar comments, "Many people have thought and do think that it can be

---

22. Biggar, *In Defence*, 143.
23. Clough and Stiltner, *Faith and Force*, 74.
24. Biggar, *In Defence*, 127.
25. Biggar, *In Defence*, 129.

right to defend justice at the cost of sacrificing human life."[26] The problem here is, however, whose justice are we defending? Individual nation states rarely make good moral policemen. It is unrealistic in the extreme to suppose that foreign policy is based on impartial justice rather than national interest (with the possible exception of wars of humanitarian intervention). A perceived national interest, and even a desire for justice, can easily override proportionality. John Keegan (quoted by Biggar) comments, "The principle of the sanctity of international treaty, which brought Britain into the war, scarcely merited the price eventually paid for its protection."[27] Again, the "price worth paying" is to be seen in the light of the crucified people who are sacrificed in the process. Biggar, however, argues for the "incommensurability" of the goods and evils involved: "There is no common currency in terms of which they can all be measured and weighed against each other to produce a reliable answer."[28]

But, surely, this is what the proportion criterion of the just war theory is about—assessing, measuring, and weighing—unless it is in reality the case that once a justifiable war has been declared, in effect all actions *in bello* are justifiable.

If it is difficult to make such assessments for the near future, it is even more difficult to make assessments for the middle distance and far future. Biggar argues that "non resistance in 1914 would have produced neither a just peace nor a stable one."[29] However, the Versailles peace treaty, imposed by the victorious powers, can hardly be said to have been just, and ushered in a period of radical instability culminating in the Second World War.

We return to the question raised earlier of who, or what, benefited from the enormous price paid in human crucifixion in the First World War. Presumably, the war was fought in the national interest, or, as some put it, for the nation's honor. But whose interest? That of the millions whose lives were ended or ruined by the war? Those who benefited politically or economically from the Allied victory? Those who were defended from German militarism, only to be exposed to an even worse militarism twenty years later? The motif of the crucified people radically questions what national interest means. Jonathan Glover writes perceptively of the First World War:

> It was also a trap created by the bizarre interaction of different strands of prevailing beliefs; in some a nationalistic Social Darwinism, in others a morality which made an absolute of

---

26. Biggar, *In Defence*, 140–41.
27. Biggar, *In Defence*, 145.
28. Biggar, *In Defence*, 146.
29. Biggar, *In Defence*, 139.

honour. What these very different beliefs had in common was the way they stunted the moral imagination. Instead of attention being directed to people and what war would do to their lives, it was turned to the abstraction of the nation. The survival of the nation in the evolutionary struggle, the refusal to accept an insult to the nation, the avoidance of the nation being humiliated or dishonoured, seemed of supreme importance. Nations as imaginary people were put before the real people who made them up.[30]

The idolatry of the nation state, which has tyrannized over human history for so long, and so often been supported by religious nationalism, is undercut by the crucified people.

Finally, the theme of the crucified people can contribute to a discussion concerning the just war criterion of right intention. Biggar argues that "the focussing of moral concern on the motivation and intention of an act, rather than on its effects, is crucial for the justification of the use of lethal force."[31] The most obvious problem is that such an argument would excuse members of the SS, who believed themselves to be engaged in a virtuous fight for western civilization against the Marxist barbarians who would obliterate their country. The actions they perceived as brave and noble brought about the perpetuation of an evil regime and, ultimately, the holocaust. The just war criterion of right intention has to face up to the fact of human sinfulness and exercise a hermeneutic of suspicion on motives which may well be conditioned by nationalism, selfishness, and pride rather than Christian love. More particularly, with regard to the crucified people, weight needs to be placed not so much on the inner intention of a violent act, but on its actual effects on suffering humanity—the crucified people of that situation.

All this is not to write off just war theory, which, in some form or other, is the only realistic Christian alternative to pacifism. However, traditional just war theory, designed for supposedly Christian nations who could be expected to look to the gospel for guidance, has been overtaken by the fact that wars are now waged by non-Christian nations, by nations whose Christian heritage is rapidly fading, or by traditionally Christian nations in alliance with those whose avowed values are certainly not Christian (for example, the alliance with the Soviet Union in the Second World War). It is, however, necessary to seek clarifications and to introduce factors which must be brought into the equation if the just war criteria are not simply to be used as a tool to justify whichever war is felt to be in the national interest

---

30. Glover, *Humanity*, 199.
31. Biggar, *In Defence*, 29.

and whatever means are used to fight it. Too often, just war theory has been used as an *ex post facto* justification, rather than as an actual tool in the decision making process both *ad bellum* and *in bello*. David Clough, again, asks the pertinent question: "Has there ever been a nation prepared to suffer unilateral disadvantage for moral reasons?" and suggests that the just war theory has to provide "this kind of constraint in practice." Otherwise "just war theory is just a moral fig leaf for immoral wars."[32]

---

32. Clough and Stiltner, *Faith and Force*, 75.

Chapter 9

Hope, Eschatology, and the Cross

I now turn to wider questions of providence, power, and eschatology in the light of the cross. In this chapter we continue to focus on the crucified Jesus, but also consider the impact of his resurrection from the dead. What difference to Christian politics does it make to hope in a crucified and risen savior? I begin by exploring the place of hope in the theologies of our interlocutors.

A) YODER—THE CROSS, THE CHURCH, AND THE POLITICAL PROVIDENCE OF GOD

An Ethic of Faith and Hope

One of the most important elements in the theology of Yoder's cross-based pacifism is the centrality of eschatological hope and of faith in the resurrection. In chapter 4 of *Politics of Jesus*, "God will fight for us," the holy war tradition in the Old Testament is interpreted as a call for Israel to trust in God, who "fights" for his people, and not in their own armed strength. Yoder's is an ethic of active faith in God and trust in his appointed strategy, and the seeming risk of faith in a God whose purposes are active in history is accepted as the ethical norm.

The resurrection of the crucified Christ is central to that faith and hope, in opening up hitherto unsuspected possibilities and confirming the rightness of the way (of the cross) chosen by Jesus. This is no arbitrary or short term choice, but corresponds to the divine pattern of working within history—a vulnerable love that is willing to be crucified. The resurrection demonstrates both the rightness of that choice and the fact that the universe is indeed open to such cruciform action. In a major passage summing up the argument at the centre of *Politics of Jesus*, Yoder writes that the resurrection pre-empts a choice between "crucified agape" and (violent) "effectiveness" since "in the light of the resurrection crucified agape is not folly (as it seemed to the Hellenizers to be) and weakness (as the Judaizers believe) but the wisdom and the power of God."[1] If politics is the art of the possible, the resurrection immeasurably extends the accepted boundaries of the possible. Since the victory of God takes place through the divine act of resurrection, neither calculations of cause and effect nor reliance on control or violent self defense can have the last word. The last word lies with the God who raises the crucified Jesus from the dead, thus opening up unforeseen possibilities and instilling courage for faithful discipleship.

Yoder thus postulates a particular form of causality, through the action of God, of which the resurrection of the crucified is the major example. His christological pacifism is based throughout on the character of God and the work of Jesus Christ. Therefore "the calculating link between our obedience and ultimate efficacy has been broken, since the triumph of God comes through resurrection and not through effective sovereignty or assured survival."[2] This must beg the question: how does resurrection actively take place within history, except in 33 CE? It is easier to read crucifixion into political history in terms of the suffering of peoples than it is to interpret resurrection. Does Yoder mean a divine intervention, which God brings about in response to faithful people's obedience? Is it possible to point to such past interventions in history? Or is Yoder speaking more figuratively in terms of God's Spirit encouraging, directing, healing, and generally bringing good out of tragedy in honoring the faithfulness of God's people? The resurrection, as an event within as well as beyond history, is a sign of God ratifying a cruciform historical course of action, and thus acts as a hopeful indication to Christians that their acts corresponding to Jesus' life and character follow the grain of God's intentions. This must be received by faith—but perhaps the only true verification, for Yoder, is eschatological.

Yoder claims that his pacifism is based in realism, not a Niebuhrian realism but a reliance on the perceived reality of the nature of the universe when seen in the light of the cross and resurrection. If the cross and resurrection give ultimate meaning to history, the Christian can have hope that

1. Yoder, *Politics*, 109.
2. Yoder, *Politics*, 239.

what seems to be weakness will in the end turn out to be strength. Pacifism, on this account, may not necessarily be effective in the immediate situation, for the pacifist, the aggressor, or the victim. Its effectiveness is more long term, in the overall fulfillment of God's purposes. Yet signs of the eventual accomplishment of God's purposes are evident in the very act of peacemaking and nonviolence itself, in what can be described as the active inbreaking of God's kingdom, or as manifestations of the Spirit at work.

An Eschatological Ethic

It is instructive to compare Yoder's eschatological perspective with that of Niebuhrian realist or Constantinian theology. Yoder's view of the Christian faith is radically eschatological, looking for the inbreaking of God's kingdom and living in faithful anticipation of that inbreaking. By contrast, realism is more an ethic for the long haul, with no end in sight, save a distant heaven. It is centered around making the best of a bad job with human resources, in the belief that this is the responsibility to which God has called humanity. According to Yoder, any early Christian political eschatological hope was in effect neutralized by the establishment of a Constantinian Christendom. If Christian political success was measured in terms of holding the levers of power, there could be nothing more to expect. Politically, eschatology was realized in the Constantinian settlement, and the element of hope, in the sense of active divine involvement, was downplayed. Without this hope, and the "freedom for obedience" this brings, Constantinianism felt obliged to resort to violence, as the only option for change.[3] In contrast to the anthropocentricity of the Constantinian and realist analysis, Yoder's eschatological orientation is theocentric. His political eschatology focuses on the cross and the resurrection in equal measure, avoiding both a sense of hopelessness and also a facile evasion of the fact of suffering (it is no coincidence that Moltmann's first *magna opera* dealt first with hope, and then with the cross).

The church is the bearer of the new aeon, and points beyond the possibilities of the old aeon to another form of historical causation. In his 1994 epilogue to *Politics of Jesus*, changing his emphasis a little to include effectiveness and answering criticisms of irresponsibility, Yoder defends his pacifism against the realist accusation of sacrificing effectiveness and liberation in favor of moral purity and heavenly recompense. To trust in Christ means that "in Jesus we have a clue to what kinds of causation, what kinds of community building, which kinds of conflict management, go with the

---

3. As argued by Carter, *Politics*, 230.

grain of the cosmos."[4] Of that cosmos "Jesus is both the Word (the inner logic of things) and the Lord ('sitting at the right hand')." In other words, history does not need to be moved by the church. It is the church's ethical task to align itself with the divine movement of history, to witness to that without deviation from it, in the faith that this is where true long term effectiveness lies, since the world is "enclosed within . . . the sovereignty of the God of the Resurrection and the Ascension."[5]

Discerning the Presence in History of the Lamb Who Was Slain

Long term effectiveness, resting on the "Lamb who was slain," is the basis of Yoder's interpretation of the movement of history, and the political role of the church within it. For the church to fulfill its purpose it must correctly read and faithfully follow the pattern of God's action (in the sense of long term historical causation). Yoder argues that the church's calling is to be the "conscience and the servant within human society" and points to the necessity to discern "when and where God is using the Powers."[6] This task calls for wisdom to recognize God's working in history. As Yoder acknowledges, this is no straightforward task, given the danger of falling into what he describes as the "Sadducean or 'German Christian' temptation, to read off the surface of history a simple declaration of God's will."[7] Reading "the signs of the times" accurately is central to the church's political task—in other words, locating the interpretative key to history and its movement. "Jesus Christ is Lord," writes Yoder, "is a declaration about the nature of the cosmos and the significance of history, within which both our conscientious participation and our conscientious objection find their authority and their promise."[8] And, most significantly, the Christ who is Lord is the "Lamb who was slain," which gives us a clue to both the nature of the universe and the political (and individual) ethics by which the world must live. The "Lamb who was slain" is one of the primary images in Revelation, and it is in interpreting this apocalyptic imagery that Yoder provides his most cogent portrayal of the cruciform meaning of history. The biblical apocalypses, suggests Yoder, demonstrate

---

4. Yoder, *Politics*, 246–47.
5. Yoder, *Politics*, 246–47.
6. Yoder, *Politics*, 155.
7. Yoder, *Politics*, 155.
8. Yoder, *Politics*, 157.

how the crucified Jesus is a more adequate key to understanding what God is about in the real world of empires and armies and markets than is the ruler in Rome, with all his supporting military, commercial and sacerdotal networks.[9]

By extension, the crucified Jesus is a better model for Christian political ethics than is a church relying on an alliance with military, economic, and establishment power. The apocalypses attempt to describe God active in history, God working in past history and promising to be active in the present. How does that divine activity take concrete form in the power structures of the world? In an important passage, and one which sums up the thrust of *Politics of Jesus* as a justification for pacifism, Yoder writes that the Lordship of the "lamb that was slain" means that "the cross and not the sword, suffering and not brute power determine the meaning of history."[10] As a result of this, the Christian is called to be patient—an essential concept in Yoder's social ethics, combining both waiting and suffering. Yoder contrasts this patience with the more immediate realist criterion of effectiveness. The Christian can be patient—in other words, can wait in a potentially suffering hopefulness—and be obedient to God's call to nonviolence because the fundamental reality of history is on the Christian's side: "The triumph of the right, although it is assured, is sure because of the power of the resurrection and not because of any calculation of cause and effects, nor because of the inherently greater strength of the good guys." There is a different, divine causality which, if the church is to be faithful, it must respect: a causality not based on human power but on that of the cross and resurrection. All this is firmly rooted in Christology, in the historic pattern of the life and crucifixion of Jesus, whose choices, of "suffering servanthood rather than violent lordship, of love to the point of death rather than righteousness backed by power" form the inescapable pattern for the Christian. Pacifism, for Yoder, is in the end "right not because it works, but because it anticipates the triumph of the Lamb that was slain."[11]

Jesus himself is the key to the meaning of history—he is the criterion by which the moving of history is to be judged. Jesus is the prime example of the choice facing the Christian, between immediate effectiveness and long term obedience; the apocalyptic motif of the slain Lamb is inseparable from the political execution of Jesus by the Romans. Jesus could have aimed at success or effectiveness by an alliance with the forces of the zealots or some other power group; this was a genuine option, but was rejected. "The choice he made in rejecting the crown and accepting the cross was the commitment

---

9. Yoder, *Politics*, 246.
10. Yoder, *Politics*, 232.
11. Yoder, *Royal Priesthood*, 151.

to such a degree of faithfulness to the character of divine love that he was willing for its sake to sacrifice 'effectiveness.'"[12] This is not to be seen as a kind of backdoor route to effectiveness, since "Jesus excluded any normative concern for any capacity to make sure that things would turn out right." Yoder's intention throughout is to establish a political ethic concerned solely with faithfulness (i.e., faithful and consistent witness to the character of God), not with a calculation of consequences. This follows closely the imagery of Revelation, where the Lamb receives his praise from those who defeated the dragon "by the blood of the Lamb and by the word of their testimony [i.e., by martyrdom] for they did not cling to life even in the face of death."[13] (Rev 12:11, NRSV)

To conclude, Yoder describes the paradox, inherent in his work, of the dialectical relationship of faithfulness and effectiveness, of the long term effectiveness of a counter-intuitive neglect of short term consequences. Loving the enemy will in the long run be effective, because it follows the nature of God, yet effectiveness is not the reason why a Christian acts in such a way. The rejection of violence is counter-intuitive in the short term:

> It remains foolish like the cross of Jesus. Its only moral ground is the conviction that the cosmos is like that. Yet it is precisely people who think that about the cosmos who tend to get things done.[14]

B) BOFF AND SOBRINO—HOPE FOR THE VICTIMS

Boff—Hope for the Oppressed through the Cross and Resurrection

Although Boff and Sobrino grant a larger role to human endeavor in the moving of history than Yoder, eschatology in the sense of a hopeful faithfulness plays an equally important part in their theology and political spirituality. For Boff, the cross and resurrection give a meaning to suffering which is not wholly negative. Boff is aware of the danger of glorifying suffering per se, but can speak of Jesus transfiguring suffering into a positive spirituality of taking up the cross as a means of combating injustice. The self abandonment or de-centering involved in taking up the cross achieves an ultimate meaning which is made sure and manifest by the resurrection, the "fullness and

---

12. Yoder, *Politics*, 234.

13. Yoder, *Politics*, 235.

14. Yoder, unpublished paper presented at the AAR Section on Religion, Peace and War in Philadelphia, Novermber 18th, 1995.

manifestation of the Life that resonates within life and within death."[15] Moreover, the life of the resurrection is found not just after death, but "lies hidden in death itself," in the "life of love, solidarity, and courage that has so suffered and so died."[16] There is a unity between passion and resurrection, with the result that those "who have died in rebellion against the system of the world . . . are the risen ones. Insurrection for the cause of God and neighbor is resurrection."[17] Here Boff confuses (perhaps deliberately) the ways in which he writes of resurrection—the resurrection of Jesus, which he treats as having a historical and definitive nature, in that Jesus was raised by God as a validation of his nature and mission, and resurrection as meaning that those who die in the cause of liberation are risen because of the liberative nature of their death. Is Boff justified in running together these meanings of resurrection? It could be argued that this rather loose use of language confuses, rather than clarifies. Because of his radical empathy expressed in the cross, God takes the side of the oppressed: "God intervenes and justifies, in the risen Jesus, all the impoverished and crucified of history."[18] Again, Boff's use of the motif of justification is looser than the traditional Pauline sense. It might seem as if a person is put in a right relationship with God solely through his or her poverty, so that poverty and oppression replace faith as the channel of justification. Rather, he interprets this in terms of the resurrection giving meaning to the struggles for love and justice. "Their future is guaranteed. Justice, love, and our struggles to attain them only appear to have failed in the process of history. They shall triumph. Good, and good alone, shall reign."[19]

Boff thus interprets the resurrection retrospectively, in justifying and ratifying former actions (the liberative ministry of Jesus) and prospectively, as encouraging and strengthening future actions (the liberative ministry of Christians, and those who follow Christ's way). He represents the resurrection both as God's stamp of approval, or vindication, of Jesus and his liberative ministry, and also as a "matrix of liberative hope"[20] where death is not the ultimate reality. The resurrection is "the epiphany of the future that God has promised."[21] It is, however, significant that Boff identifies resurrection even within Christ's crucifixion, in terms of a total self giving that defeated death and all its power.[22] Again, there is a potentially misleading looseness of mean-

15. Boff, *Passion*, 132.
16. Boff, *Passion*, 132.
17. Boff, *Passion*, 132.
18. Boff, *Passion*, 133.
19. Boff, *Passion*, 133.
20. Boff, *Passion*, 66.
21. Boff, *Passion*, 67.
22. Boff, *Passion*, 65.

ing here. On the one hand, resurrection must be seen to be that of the crucified Christ, whom God raised to ratify his faithful self-surrender. In that sense resurrection arises from the midst of the crucifixion, and resurrection hope is offered to those crucified in the struggles of history. On the other hand, to identify crucifixion and resurrection too closely could obscure the sense of tragedy, cruelty, and (in a human sense) finality of crucifixion. Crucifixion has a dread (and theologically significant) reality apart from resurrection.

The timing of Boff's writing is important in understanding this aspect of his work, in which he attempts to use the crucifixion and resurrection to give meaning to the present sufferings and the lack of success of movements of political liberation. *Passion of Christ* (originally published in 1977) and *Way of the Cross* (originally published in 1978) were presumably written in the late nineteen seventies, following the defeat of Salvador Allende in Chile but prior to the Sandinista victory in Nicaragua, at a time when the tide of revolutionary optimism in Latin America was on the ebb. This is the background to such statements as: "Even in defeat they can give meaning to their lives . . . They can offer up their lives as a sacrifice to God."[23] He stresses the importance of hope for those who find it difficult, in the midst of the struggle, to envisage success. Human struggle is a history of many defeats, but the Christian can have a firm hope: "God has guaranteed final victory in the triumph of the Kingdom of love and goodness, but God allows the Way of the Cross with its suffering and seeming failure to go on from one century to the next."[24]

In other words, Boff is encouraging those working for justice and liberation to see their struggle in the context of a grand narrative, where even if they do not see the results, final success is assured.[25] Crucifixion, either of Jesus or of themselves, is not the end; the cross and the ensuing resurrection give meaning to the present struggle. There is a creative tension throughout Boff's thought. On the one hand the cross is a symbol of defeat, of suffering criminally imposed, in which God shares the victims' victimhood. On the other hand, the cross is a sign of hope, a hope resting on the very fact that God does share the victims' victimhood, and is therefore on the side of the those who suffer. And the crucifixion, as we have noted, is not to be seen in isolation from the resurrection, which "proves that the sacrifice of one's life out of love for the downtrodden and abused is not meaningless. It means sharing in the fullness of life and the definitive triumph of justice."[26]

---

23. Boff, *Way*, 82.
24. Boff, *Way*, 99.
25. Boff, *Way*, 99.
26. Boff, *Way*, ix–x.

Boff continues, "The Crucified One is the Living One. Those who are crucified today will also live." Here again Boff utilizes the idea of solidarity, which we encountered in our discussion of the crucified people. There is an identity between the crucified and the Crucified in both cross and resurrection. Moreover, the resurrection is a sign, embodied in the risen person of Jesus, of God's intentions, the point where the eschatological purpose of God breaks into history:

> The resurrection realizes the utopia of God's kingdom—not universally because of human rejection, but personally in the destiny of Jesus. In the person of Jesus, we glimpse what the cosmos and humanity are summoned to achieve, complete victory over everything that divides and threatens life . . . God was not defeated by the ability of human beings to reject him.[27]

This aspect of Boff's theology of the cross and resurrection is exemplified in his discussion of Metz's theology of *memoria passionis,* a subversive memory of those who have been defeated, oppressed and persecuted, "but whose memory can stir up dangerous visions, and launch new liberation movements."[28] This is the story of Jesus, and the task is simply to tell the story of the crucified victim. The present "negativity with no present meaning whatever," the meaningless suffering of the present victims, can have a glorious future revealed in the risen Jesus. Hence a *memoria passionis* becomes a *memoria resurrectionis*. Meaning is not solely the monopoly of the powerful; the resurrection reveals another kind of meaning, the future of those whose lot it has been to be the *massa damnata*, those forgotten by history. By retelling the story, by living the memory, the church functions as an "unmasker of totalitarian ideologies" and a conveyor of resurrection meaning to those who are oppressed.

Sobrino—The Crucified as Participating in Resurrection

In his "Theses for a historical Christology" from *Christology at the Crossroads* Sobrino's thesis 14 states that

> The cross is not the last word on Jesus because God raised him from the dead. But neither is the resurrection the last word on history because God is not yet 'all in all'. Christian existence in history draws its life from the dialectics of Jesus' cross and

---

27. Boff, *Way*, 124–25.
28. Boff, *Passion*, 108.

resurrection. This translates into a faith against unbelief, a hope against hope and a love against alienation.[29]

Although Sobrino's most original contribution to theology concerns the cross of Jesus and the crucified people, the cross is not the last word. The resurrection is central, as a historical triumph over injustice, an eschatological sign, and an existential question. In his collection of essays *Jesus in Latin America* he develops those three aspects. Chapter 7 is entitled "Jesus' resurrection from among the world's crucified," and stresses that "Jesus' resurrection is to be concrete, Christian good news and not abstract and idealistic good news."[30] It is the triumph, not simply of life over death, but of justice over injustice, of the unjustly victimized over their victimizers. Second, the resurrection is a sign of hope: "Jesus' resurrection is first and foremost hope for the crucified. God has raised a crucified one, and from this moment there is hope for the crucified of history."[31] Third, a searching question is posed by the resurrection: "Whether we too do not participate in the scandal of putting the just one to death—whether we are on the side of the murderers or on the side of the life-giving God."[32]

In his second work of Christology, *Christ the Liberator*, these themes are further developed. Resurrection is described in terms of hope in the providence of God—in an echo of Niebuhr, the impossible becomes possible, the crucified are taken down from the cross and given life. The task of the Christian in overcoming oppression is described in terms of giving analogous signs of the resurrection and the approaching kingdom.[33] This analogous giving of signs or, as Sobrino writes, "putting oneself at the service of the resurrection" involves "working continually, often against hope, in the service of eschatological ideals: justice, peace, solidarity, the life of the weak, community, dignity, celebration, and so on." Sobrino is careful to qualify these as only partial, but "these partial 'resurrections' can generate hope in the final resurrection, the conviction that God did indeed perform the impossible, gave life to one crucified and will give life to all the crucified."[34]

For Sobrino, the resurrection is both a historical and an eschatological reality. (At least, the disciples' faith in the resurrection is a historical reality—Sobrino seems to regard it as impossible, in terms of historical verification, to go beyond the fact of the disciples' faith.) Sobrino does, however, appear

---

29. Sobrino, *Christology*, 229.
30. Sobrino, *Latin America*, 148.
31. Sobrino, *Latin America*, 151.
32. Sobrino, *Latin America*, 150.
33. Sobrino, *Christ the Liberator*, 48.
34. Sobrino, *Christ the Liberator*, 49.

to believe in the resurrection as objective, rather than subjective truth and a present (and equally eschatological) reality for Jesus' disciples. This reality engenders hope, which allows the disciple, even when faced with crucifixion, to look to God for ultimate victory. This hope is of special relevance to the crucified people, since the historical circumstances of Jesus' death and resurrection show it to be not just a generalized victory over death, but specifically a victory of the victims over their oppressors. Sobrino would appear to share an inaugurated eschatology, in that he sees the kingdom as not yet present in history in its fullness, but as initiated in history by Jesus and lived out by his followers in hope, joy, and anticipation.

C) CONCLUSION

All three of our interlocutors take eschatology seriously in underpinning their political theologies, and in stressing the need for faith and hope in God who is active in history, most notably in the resurrection of Jesus Christ, the vindicated victim. All three wrestle with the difficulty inherent in applying eschatology to political theology—how do we interpret the similarities and differences, the continuities and discontinuities between the suffering and sinful present and the healed and triumphant future? How far can the ethics of the present mirror what we hope for in the future?

On the one hand, Luther is said to have remarked of the sinful present, "If the lion lies down with the lamb, the lamb must be replaced frequently."[35] A liberationist or a Niebuhrian would stress that a hard headed ethic must be formulated that fits both the reality of the present and the hoped for reality of the future. On the other hand, a Yoderian pacifist might argue, as David Clough, that "this relies heavily on interpreting the teaching of Jesus as not being wholly adequate for living during the already-but-not-yet, as needing a more realistic supplement . . . we cannot defer faithfulness to gospel teaching until the eschaton."[36]

Yoder's reliance on God, rather than the church, to move history in the right direction particularly rests on an active eschatological hope. Eschatology, for Yoder, is faith's projection into the future of the character of the world as designed and intended by God, where those who practice nonviolence and justice are working with the true grain of the universe, and not against it. The resurrection of the crucified Jesus opens up new possibilities by justifying the historical nonviolent acts of Jesus and offering his disciples power to follow in his steps.

35. Clough and Stiltner, *Faith and Force*, 33.
36. Clough and Stiltner, *Faith and Force*, 34.

For Boff and Sobrino, the resurrection of Jesus offers hope to those who are crucified within history. A criticism can, however, be made, especially of Boff: does he take history sufficiently critically as a means of revelation of the divine nature and purpose—a paradoxical criticism to make of a liberation theologian? He stresses, correctly, the "continuing history of crucifixion." But the problem with reading history as a continuing pointer to revelation lies in its potentially selective nature. The controversy between Barth and the "German Christians" such as Hirsch is a salutary example of the possible pitfalls. There are few problems with reading evidence for a crucified people from history. But that, by itself, gives limited hope. It is more difficult to read evidence in history for an analogous resurrection. History, the liberation theologian would argue, is overwhelmingly a story of unjust and repeated human suffering. It is possible to identify the passion and crucifixion of God in human suffering; it requires more subtle analysis to identify the resurrection acts of God in liberation. Despite its cosmic eschatological significance, as described by Paul and the book of Revelation, the gospel accounts of the resurrection stress the quietness, the unsensational nature, even the ordinariness of the risen Jesus. How is God's active power at work in history? How does the conjunction of the divine weakness as evidenced by the crucifixion and the divine power as evidenced by the resurrection bring about liberation? It could be argued that the two are not equivalent. The passion, whereby God is acted upon by humanity, and the resurrection, which is an act of God breaking into human history, may be thought of as belonging to different categories. As the language suggests, one is passive, the other active. To give human beings freedom, God's active power has necessarily to be restrained. Hence it is unreasonable to expect similar forms of evidence in history for crucifixion and resurrection. Boff, however, is still able to point to evidence of resurrection:

> The resurrection is a process that began with Jesus and that will go on until it embraces all creation. Wherever an authentically human life is growing in the world, wherever justice is triumphing over the instincts of domination . . . there the purpose of resurrection is being turned into a reality.[37]

The resurrection is an event which is part of, and yet transcends, history; a sign of the final purpose of God which was proleptically realized in the resurrection of Jesus but which has finally to be realized through the slow processes of crucifixion and resurrection in human history.

---

37. Boff, *Way*, 126.

Chapter 10

Power, Providence and the Cross

In this chapter we explore the themes of providence and power in the light of the cross. We begin by examining the doctrine of kenosis, which I regard as central to Yoder's theology, and which provides fruitful possibilities for a political ethic which will be more fully discussed in the next chapter. We then move to a consideration of Yoder's use of "Powers language," and end with a brief examination of the teaching of Boff and Sobrino on this theme.

A) YODER—THE CROSS, POWER AND PROVIDENCE

Yoder—Kenosis and Politics

Yoder builds his pacifist ethic on "the conviction that the cosmos is like that." Christian politics, therefore, according to Yoder, is an imitation of God's patient, kenotic, and cruciform relationship with the cosmos. Most important to Yoder's argument is his use of the kenotic hymn in Philippians 2. Yoder notes that although the initial *kenosis* lies further back behind the cross, in Jesus abandoning the privileges of the divine nature, yet in Paul's interpretation *kenosis* is radically cruciform: "The reference to humiliation becomes not simply 'human form' but the 'form of a servant', and this even to the extremity of death on a cross."[1] Yoder further notes that the equality with God rejected in the hymn is not a metaphysical attribute of the divine nature, but "providential control over events, the alternative being the

---

1. Yoder, *Politics*, 109.

acceptance of impotence."² Also rejected is the "claim to govern history."³ Yoder sees it as significant that the point in Philippians 2 at which the Christian is invited to follow the example of Christ is his rejection of sovereign exercise of power over the world: "What Jesus renounced was thus not simply the metaphysical nature of sonship, but rather the untrammeled sovereign exercise of power in the affairs of that humanity amid which he came to dwell."⁴ His kenotic acceptance of the form of servanthood and obedience unto death is "precisely his renunciation of lordship, his apparent abandonment of any obligation to be effective in making history move down the right track." This renunciation, this rejection of direct control over events, is judged by God to be a positive, rather than a negative, step in the fulfillment of the divine purposes: "This ancient hymn . . . one of the earliest extended snatches of Christian worship on record, is thus affirming that the dominion of God over history has made use of the apparent historical failure of Jesus as a mover of human events."⁵ Yoder thus suggests a philosophy of history "in which renunciation and suffering are meaningful." This is "profoundly linked with the person of Jesus" who in concrete historical circumstances rejected the zealot (or, for that matter, the collaborationalist) option. The hymn is not just about a Christ figure, coming down from heaven and returning thither, but about the historical Jesus and his political execution:

> The renunciation of the claim to govern history was not made only by the second person of the Trinity taking upon himself the demand of an eternal divine decree; it was made also by a poor, tired rabbi when he came from Galilee to Jerusalem to be rejected.⁶

Yoder's logic is this: Jesus' historical rejection of power and control mirrors God's refusal to exercise powerful control over history, and necessitates a corresponding political posture in the Christian. Yoder skillfully links the actual historical circumstances of Jesus' political choices and the historical causation of the cross with the grand narrative of God's ultimate purposes. The first two rejections of power and control—those by Jesus and by God—are, in my opinion, theologically valid. The consequences for human politics are not so firmly established. As we have already frequently noted, Yoder discounts an ethic of loving compromise for the sake of the immediate good of humanity in favor of a long term ethic of correspondence with the nature of God.

2. Yoder, *Politics*, 234.
3. Yoder, *Politics*, chapter 4 .
4. Yoder, *Politics*, 235.
5. Yoder, *Politics*, 236.
6. Yoder, *Politics*, 236.

The Cross as the Hermeneutical Key to God's Providential Action

Yoder uses the cross as the hermeneutical key for interpreting the New Testament as a whole, including passages which are otherwise interpreted in cosmological or incarnational terms. The cross reveals not simply the political events of first-century Palestine, but the whole shape of the divine interaction with the world. If Jesus is the definitive *logos* (as in John 1) his words and deeds reveal the pattern of the action of God in the whole of history. This is the fundamental Yoderian method, to draw eternal patterns from the historical circumstances of Jesus' life. We have already discussed how Yoder attempts to cross Lessing's ugly ditch at this point. The particular kenotic action of God in Jesus, in becoming vulnerable to the actions of humanity, is a sign of God's eternal nature. The self emptying of the creator in creating and suffering is paralleled and lived out historically by the crucified Jesus. The cross not only marks a point in the historical existence of Jesus, but reveals the nature of creation as a whole. The cross in Yoder is an interpretative sign of all divine action in history vis-à-vis humanity; God's whole relationship with humanity is cruciform and therefore, according to Yoder, non-coercive. This is seen particularly (but not exclusively) in the atonement. (It is a welcome characteristic of Yoder's overall theological method that the atonement, creation, and discipleship cannot be seen as self-contained units, but as deeply interrelated in God's cruciform dealings with humanity.) The cross is the supreme revelation of God's response to evil; in Jesus' forgiveness of the guilty, in his refusal to use violent or coercive means even in self defense, in the non-resistant way in which suffering was patiently born, we see revealed the whole character of God, the nature of divine providence, and the way of atonement.

The patience of God in the face of suffering (it is again useful to remember the dual aspects of patience as suffering and waiting) is most of all exemplified by the cross, and therefore indicates the same attitude for the believer. Yoder suggests that "the willingness to suffer is then not merely a test of our patience or a dead space of waiting; it is in itself a participation in the character of God's victorious patience with the rebellious Powers of his creation."[7] A coercive and violent seizure of power, even for the laudable aim of avoiding or diminishing suffering, is outlawed. Wright draws attention to the analysis of Yoder's method by Gayle Koontz, who notes that God, according to Yoder,

---

7. Yoder, *Politics*, 209.

persuades and suffers rather than determines; his providence is expressed by redemptive and suffering love rather than through the limitation, sustenance and control of humans . . . Yoder's theology revolves around how God responds to evil and his refusal to violate his creatures' freedom through coercive interventionism. . .It is the pattern of all the divine activity towards humankind . . .[8]

The persuasive power of suffering love in Yoder has (perhaps surprising) links with the idea of providence outlined in process theology, where a potentially changing God (suffering implying the capacity to be changed) persuades rather than compels.

Methodological and Ethical Criticisms

I regard the above as a meaningful and legitimate reading of God's providential working, and Yoder's theology is remarkably consistent in drawing out the implications of this reading. The question must, however, be asked whether it is justifiable to read off from a letting be of evil (to use McQuarrie's phrase[9]) in the divine working of providence a corresponding human letting be of evil in politics and society? Is Yoder's parallelism, in fact, a form of category mistake? One reason why God does not use coercion in atonement may well be, as Yoder argues, God's determination to exercise an agape which absolutely privileges and preserves freedom (although, as we have noted, by analogy, a parent is not bound by agape to preserve the absolute freedom of a child to harm him or herself—that freedom is limited by agape). On this account Yoder's letting be of evil may be transferable to human politics. But another reason could be that God forswears direct coercion to preserve the gap, necessary for a faith/love relationship, between the human and the divine (the Jewish doctrine of *zimzum*, as applied by Moltmann to Christian theology[10]). Were God to intervene too readily, for example in a more coercive atonement or providence, that necessary gap would be destroyed. Here the concern is more to preserve God's otherness than to privilege human freedom. It could also be argued that the fact that God refuses to exercise control over history might lead to the opposite conclusion to Yoder's—God draws back not so that Christians might follow that example, but so that Christians (alongside others) might have the freedom to assume real responsibility.

8. Wright, *Disavowing*, 94.
9. MacQuarrie, *Principles*, 183.
10. Moltmann, *God in Creation*, 88.

The criticism could also be made that God's ultimate freedom is compromised by Yoder's insistence on agape as demanding total freedom for humanity.[11] Against this criticism it can be argued that God's ultimate freedom is in any case always compromised by God's nature of love, and if love necessitates freedom and a certain measure of distancing, that is bound to restrict God's options in providence. This distancing argument can perhaps be answered by the fact that any such gap, while necessarily preserved for the sake of God's otherness is equally or even more necessarily preserved for the freedom of the human counterpart. The question remains, however, whether there is (or should be) a total parallelism and correspondence between God's action and human action, and whether there are some aspects of God's work that humans are not to copy in their entirety. A Yoderian would answer that what is to be imitated is God's character as revealed in the historical acts of Jesus, and the fact that God's character is of such a kind determines God's actions and therefore the actions of the Christian.

A more telling criticism, as has been previously argued, is the seeming complicity with evil which the non-resistant pacifist position might entail. Yoder is well aware that his doctrine of absolute divine respect for human freedom, as an essential component of agape, is subject to this criticism, but describes it in terms of patience, rather than complicity. A more severe criticism could be leveled against this patience when transferred to the human reaction to evil. A realist would argue that a person (or a nation) who is able to protect a victim from unjust aggression and yet does not is morally culpable, whereas a Yoderian pacifist certainly would subscribe to this view. There are real difficulties here, not least since the Yoderian doctrine, as has been previously argued, seems to contradict an important trend in Jesus' teaching; that sins of omission are of even greater weight than sins of commission. This points up the fundamental difference between the realist and the Yoderian—the latter's insistence on the absolute primacy of human freedom and divine patience, the overriding necessity for the Christian to witness to God's character, and the eschatological hope that following this course faithfully will ensure a sharing in God's ultimate triumph. The Yoderian holds that the Christian's duty is obedience and faithfulness, rather than a calculation of responsibility, and that it is through such an obedient and faithful community, the church, that God can work most effectively.

---

11. As argued by Pinches, "Christian Pacifism," 250.

Conflict with the Powers

It remains to examine another aspect of Yoder's political theology, the relationship between the cross and the Powers. Yoder devotes chapter 8 of *Politics of Jesus* to this theme, developing a theology of the cross as a critique and unmasking of the Powers, and hence of power itself. This requires a different kind of politics to the "domination system," to use Wink's phrase.[12] According to Murphy, "the most significant contribution that Yoder's reading of scripture makes to political analysis is his use of the Pauline doctrine of the 'principalities and powers.'"[13] This is perhaps overstating the case, as much work had already been done (by the time of the writing of *Politics of Jesus*) on this subject, primarily by Hendrikus Berkhoff in *Christ and the Powers* (Yoder in fact translated Berkhoff's seminal work, making it available to the English-speaking world). However, Yoder's exposition of the Powers adds significantly to his argument in *Politics of Jesus* and indicates ways in which the early Christians framed their language to interpret the impact of the crucifixion on the power structures of their day.

The Powers are necessary in the providence of God, as structures of regularity, system, and order without which human beings cannot live, but they have become absolutized and enslaving. Salvation has to deal with these Powers, not in the sense of abolishing them (since they are necessary for human existence) but by setting them in their proper place, with their sovereignty broken, yet holding together in Christ—fallen, yet redeemed. Yoder writes, "If then God is going to save his creatures *in their humanity*, the Powers cannot simply be destroyed or set aside or ignored."[14] The Powers as created by God are essential to the functioning of human society, as demonstrated, for example, by the benefits of Roman imperial rule in Palestine. But those same Powers become tyrannical and oppressive, as epitomized by the practice of crucifixion. And so it is necessary to break their sovereignty. This, argues Yoder, is what Jesus did, "concretely and historically, by living a genuinely free and human existence. This life brought him, as any genuinely human existence will bring anyone, to the cross." The death of Jesus was a direct result of his conflict with the Powers, symbolized by the Roman imperial and Jewish religious authorities, who acted in collusion to bring about his crucifixion. The positive side of the Powers—the peace, good government, order, and stability which the Roman Empire at its best provided,

---

12. Wink, *Engaging*.
13. Hauerwas et al., *Wisdom*, 49.
14. Yoder, *Politics*, 144.

and the religious devotion of both the Pharisees and Sadducees—were corrupted horrifically, leading to their collusion in judicial murder:

> Preaching and incorporating a greater righteousness than that of the Pharisees, and a vision of an order of social human relations more universal than the Pax Romana, he permitted the Jews to profane a holy day (refuting their own moral pretensions) and permitted the Romans to deny their vaunted respect for law as they proceeded illegally against him.[15]

It is interesting to observe Yoder postulating the cross as a form of entrapment, in causing the Powers to overreach themselves fatally—with echoes of earlier baited hook theories of the atonement. Murphy, in her chapter in Yoder's posthumous festschrift links his theology of the Powers with various traditional models of the atonement. She draws attention to the closeness of Yoder's doctrine of the atonement to the classic model, but points out that he "fills the gap left by the excision of a mythical Devil by means of the interpretation of the 'principalities and powers' described above."[16] Jesus frees humankind from these superhuman power structures "both by his example [and here the moral influence theory gets its due] and by stripping them of the illusion of absolute legitimacy, precisely because their most worthy representatives abused him in his innocence." Here again, the cross is central, as in the substitutionary model of atonement, but for different reasons: "Yoder does not ignore personal sinfulness, but he gives it neither the significance nor the inevitability that it has in Augustinian Christianity."[17] Yoder concentrates more on institutionalized sin—in other words, structural sin as interpreted by liberation theology.

One aspect of the corrupted Powers is their tendency towards a ruthless self-defensiveness when challenged as demonstrated by the events of Jesus' life and execution: "This they did in order to avoid the threat to their dominion represented by the very fact that he existed in their midst so morally independent of their pretensions."[18] Jesus by his very life challenged those pretensions, and by persisting in his moral consistency even to the point of death he gained a victory over them—and not only over the proximate Powers of the Roman and Jewish establishment, but over the Powers in general. The victory of the crucified Jesus over the Powers lay in his authentic humanity, free from the pretensions of the Powers, even when those Powers

---

15. Yoder, *Politics*, 144.
16. Hauerwas et al., *Wisdom*, 54.
17. Hauerwas et al., *Wisdom*, 54.
18. Yoder, *Politics*, 145.

threatened his life: "This authentic humanity included his free acceptance of death at their hands. Thus it is his death that provides his victory."

It is clear that Yoder (and other theologians, such as Berkhoff, who champion the Powers language) use the word triumph in a moral, rather than a physical sense. In the latter sense, the Powers triumphed over Jesus by crucifying him—in the former sense Jesus, by his death, won the victory. Yoder quotes Berkhoff in describing the Pauline theology (in Col 2:13–15, NRSV) of the victory of Christ over the Powers. Jesus "made a public example of them," by demonstrating, most vividly and radically in the crucifixion, their true nature: "Now that the true God appears on earth in Christ, it becomes apparent that the Powers are inimical to him, acting not as his instrument but as his adversaries."[19] Every power with which Jesus comes into contact has its pretensions exposed—the scribes, the Pharisees, and Pilate, representing religious law, personal piety, and secular justice, are unmasked by their complicity in the crucifixion. The power of illusion is the greatest weapon in the hands of the Powers—"their ability to convince men that they were the divine regents of the world, ultimate certainty and ultimate direction, ultimate happiness and the ultimate duty for small, dependent humanity." Now that the illusion is stripped away by the cross, it can be said that Christ has "disarmed" the Powers. The Christian who sees the public degradation of the Powers as revealed in the cross, and the divine justification of Christ in the resurrection, is freed from that most powerful illusion: "Unmasked, revealed in their true nature, they have lost their mighty grip on men. The cross has disarmed them: wherever it is preached, the unmasking and the disarming of the Powers takes place."[20]

The Church as Sharing in the Victory of the Cross over the Powers

The church is the body of people who have grasped this freedom from the dominion of the Powers and now live as a sign of that freedom.[21] The church itself both resists and attacks that dominion as it demonstrates in its fellowship how Christians can live freed from the Powers. The "weapons" the church bears are defensive: "Our weapon is to stay close to Him and thus to remain out of the reach of the drawing power of the Powers." As we have seen previously, the first task of the church in Yoder's political theology and action is, simply, to be the church. "The very existence of the church is its primary

19. Yoder, *Politics*, 146.
20. Yoder, *Politics*, 146.
21. Yoder, *Politics*, 147–48.

task. It is in itself a proclamation of the Lordship of Christ to the Powers from whose dominion the church has begun to be liberated." In this the cross is vital, since the church is the society formed by reconciliation brought about by the cross and bearing the marks of the cross in its ongoing life. It is a counter-cultural witness, a new humanity created by the cross and not the sword. (There are significant parallels here with the crucified people as martyrs/witnesses theme which we have noted in the theology of Sobrino.)

Another essential Yoderian theme emerges here: the primary social structure through which the gospel works to change other structures is the Christian community. Power is the good creation of God, and so Christians cannot opt out of the power structures of society entirely. Yoder's is not an ethic of Essene type withdrawal, but of a choice not to exercise certain types of power. The existence of a cruciform church that suffers through its ongoing stand against the Powers continues nothing less than the work of the crucified Christ. Just as the Powers were defeated by what Yoder calls the "concreteness of the cross," so they continue to be defeated by the church whose faithfulness and consistency mirrors that of Jesus: "The historicity of Jesus retains, in the working of the church as it encounters the other power and value structures of its history, the same kind of relevance that the man Jesus had for those whom he served until they killed him."[22] And, just as Jesus suffered at the hands of the Powers, so the church risks suffering when it stands against the Powers and empowers others to do so.

The Cross, Power, and the Powers

The question of power is central to Yoder's work and, as is his practice, he seeks to redefine its meaning. His exegesis of Powers language points towards such a redefinition. The Powers are real—otherwise Jesus would not have, very concretely, been crucified at their hands. And yet their power rests on a shaky foundation, which the cross exposes. This tension is both a strength and weakness in Yoder's work, which is shared by other theologians who talk the Powers language. From one perspective it makes little sense to herald the defeat of the Powers when they obviously continue to tyrannize. The concreteness of oppression is certainly not an illusion, and it would be grossly mistaken to deny that concreteness in the name of the illusory nature of the Powers. The cross reveals, in fact, both the continuing strength of the Powers and also their undermining. The strength of Yoder's Powers theology is to point to the potential, enabled by the cross, of victory over the Powers. The weakness is to tend to give an impression that such

22. Yoder, *Politics*, 158.

victory has already somehow been concretely achieved. Cullman's image of D-Day and VE-Day (in *Christ and Time*) is appropriate here: a decisive victory has been won, but the final victory is yet to be, and much struggle and suffering lies between.

Perhaps the most telling use of the language of Powers lies in its redefinition of divine power. Rather than power being understood as coercive, and at least potentially violent, divine power is interpreted in the light of the cross as uncoercive, persuasive, and creative. The radical nature of this shift, both theologically and practically, cannot be underestimated, since it undercuts many mainstream secular and religious doctrines of power. Pinches, in his exposition of Yoder's political theodicy, describes how "the cross of Christ is in fact a new definition of truth, both as power and as wisdom" and comments that "the truly powerful forces in history are perhaps those which stand clear of the coercive mainstream and call noncoercively, as Jesus did, for a transformation of the human spirit."[23] A vision of ultimate effectiveness is gained by recognizing this shift in the definition. The cross radically redefines power and how it can most effectively be accessed. According to Yoder, the view of power-as-destructive-force is futile and leads to an ethical blind alley.

B) BOFF AND SOBRINO ON THE QUESTION OF POWER

Liberation Theology and Power Language

One of the strengths of liberation theology has been its acknowledgment of the significance of power. The theologian's setting in the political and economic structures of power is, according to liberation theology, crucial for self understanding and shapes the very nature of the theology taught or written. For example, an insistence on the structural nature of sin, as against a purely individualistic doctrine, is a major emphasis of liberation theology. Overcoming the power to oppress and promoting the power to liberate is at the centre of the liberationist project. One criticism already noted is, indeed, that liberation theology does not go far enough in its critique of power; early forms of liberation theology may have given the impression of being interested in merely changing the power holders, rather than challenging the form and nature of political power itself. It is then, at first sight, puzzling that the kind of Powers language found in Yoder and more recently in Wink has not loomed larger in Latin American liberation theology. Perhaps this is due to the danger of syncretism in a culture where Catholicism sits

---

23. Pinches, "Christian Pacifism," 248.

alongside other religious movements in which powerful spirits are deemed to be an ever present force. It could be argued that this provides an opportunity to utilize such language, but possibly the risk of misinterpretation in this context would be too great.

Boff and Sobrino—Oppressive and Liberating Power

The fact that neither Boff nor Sobrino seem to use the language of the Powers does not mean that they do not seek to convey something similar in different ways. Boff, in *Church, Charism and Power*, discusses power within the church, rather than secular political or economic power, but his analysis is significant over a wider area. In chapter 5 he sketches a history of the early church, from its first three centuries as a movement lacking significant political power to its Constantinian rebirth as an institution not only allied with state power but incorporating the structures of state power into its continuing existence. Boff, like Yoder, sees the Constantinian revolution as a disaster—as the paganisation of Christianity, rather than the Christianization of paganism.[24] A major concept in Catholicism came, according to Boff, to be *potestas*—power exercised in a similar way to secular power, but worse since backed by divine sanction. This power, seen (and personally experienced) by Boff as oppressive, continues to this day, and leads to both a deadening centralization within the church and an unscrupulous defensiveness in relation to the world, exemplified by the concordat with Nazism. By contrast, the power of God is revealed in Jesus Christ, who "renounced power as domination; he preferred to die in weakness rather than use his power to subjugate people to his message."[25] It is significant that Boff here adduces the death of Christ as the prime example of a refusal of power, in terms strikingly similar to Yoder. The power of love, on which Jesus relied, is "fragile, vulnerable, conquering through its weakness and its capacity for giving and forgiveness."[26] Again, the emphasis on a cruciform power, in its chosen vulnerability, is striking.

Sobrino, too, links a Christian view of power with the ministry of Jesus and its culmination in the cross. In his "thesis 8" on the cross he questions what kind of power mediates God. Rather than the power exemplified by the Romans or their violent opponents, "the whole question of the true nature of power becomes acute when one views it in terms of Jesus' cross."[27] So-

---

24. Boff, *Church*, 50.
25. Boff, *Church*, 60.
26. Boff, *Church*, 59.
27. Sobrino, *Christology*, 209.

brino does not naively view power in a consistently negative light—to do so would, in his opinion, be to make a nonsense of belief in God, whose nature presupposes a form of power. The power that Jesus denies is "oppressive and authoritarian."[28] God's power is liberating power, a power which allows "human beings their freedom and responsibility for themselves." In a similar way to Yoder, Sobrino interprets the temptations of Jesus in terms of what sort of Messianic power he should exercise—"whether to carry this out with the power that controls history from outside or with immersion in history, with the power to dispose of human beings or with self-surrender to them."[29]

The distinction between a power from above, dominating and (at least potentially) oppressive, and a power from alongside, encouraging and suffering, is fundamental to Sobrino's theology of the cross. Power as such is not liberating, but some power is needed to bring about liberation. Sobrino argues from the point of view of "history's crucified who await salvation. They know that power is necessary for this. At the same time they mistrust pure power, since this always shows itself unfavorable to them in history."[30] As previously discussed, Sobrino recognized the need of the poor for a rescuer from outside (alterity) and a rescuer from alongside (affinity). This power from alongside is seen, paradoxically, in the weakness of the cross: "On Jesus' cross, in a first moment, God's impotence appeared. Of itself this impotence is not a cause of hope. But it lends credibility to the power of God that will be shown in the resurrection."[31] The impotence of the cross is something positive and salvific, the "expression of God's absolute nearness to the poor, sharing their lot to the end." The affinity aspect of salvation is, thereby, satisfied. God's power is not oppressive. Sobrino stresses the cross-demonstrated nearness of God to human beings. Without that nearness, he argues, "God's power in the resurrection would remain pure otherness and therefore ambiguous, and, for the crucified, historically threatening. But with that nearness, the crucified can really believe that God's power is good news, for it is love." The alterity is the inbreaking of divine power in the resurrection of the crucified.

C) CONCLUSION

There is certainly a difference in language used by Yoder, Boff, and Sobrino to describe the use and abuse of power. We have noted how liberation

28. Sobrino, *Jesus the Liberator*, 144.
29. Sobrino, *Jesus the Liberator*, 149.
30. Sobrino, *Latin America*, 152.
31. Sobrino, *Latin America*, 153.

theology largely avoids the Powers language of Berkhoff, Yoder, and Wink. However, there is much more shared ground in their teaching on the nature of the Powers (in the sense of sinful structures which extend beyond individual and personal sinfulness), the pretensions and oppressive nature of those Powers, and their undermining by the cross of Jesus. Yoder questions the nature of power and the relationship of the Christian with power more radically than do Boff and Sobrino, stressing (perhaps overstressing) the reluctance of Jesus to take power, and hence deducing the necessity for the church to refuse to accept the responsibility of power. Boff and Sobrino, on the other hand, helpfully point to the soteriological need of a power which combines both affinity and alterity. The sympathy of affinity is not, in itself, sufficient; a power which can actually rescue the vulnerable from their oppressors is also required.

Summary 4

Towards a Political Theology of the Cross—Hope and Power

The last two chapters have explored the cross in relation to hope and power. As before, I attempt now to outline elements arising from these chapters which I believe should be incorporated in a political theology of the cross.

HOPE, POWER, AND THE CROSS

The categories of hope and power are fertile ground for an exploration of the paradoxical nature of the cross. Perhaps the paradox can too easily be missed—the cross of Jesus is, in one sense, the epitome of hopelessness and powerlessness, as it was for tens of thousands of unfortunates in the Roman world. Politically, the cross was intended to humiliate, and to be a public demonstration of the dead end of rebellion against the imperial power.

The Roman world was notorious for its lack of hope, at least in the sense of hope for improvement of social conditions. The imperial ideology promoted hope, but only in a very general sense, as was displayed on the often fatuous slogans on imperial coinage. At the advent of a new emperor, especially after a time of war, a new age of peace and prosperity was often proclaimed. It is difficult to imagine any thinking person taking this seriously. One possible exception, about forty years before Jesus' birth, at the juncture between Republic and Principate, was Virgil's Messianic Eclogue, heralding the birth of a new ruler and a time of new hope after war, but by the early imperial period that Virgilian hope had turned to an Ovidian cynicism. A future golden age was so far off as to be totally unrealistic. In general, in the Roman world there was little conscious movement towards significant social reform, apart from minor efforts from some of the more humane emperors. Any sense of social progress, in a progressive liberal or Marxist sense, was absent. Hope was replaced by a static fatalism about social conditions.

This fatalism was reinforced through means of callous violence and the crushing exercise of power by the imperial authorities, whose interest lay in a passive acceptance of the status quo by the people of the empire. Any resistance to the imperial order led to the living death of labor in the mines or the tortured death of crucifixion. The acquisition of *imperium* (power) was the goal of political success, and once seized was exercised ruthlessly. The absolute powerlessness of the cross was the reverse side of the coin of the Roman idolization of elite political power, which kept the mass of the people without hope. To associate hope for the future with the cross would have seemed to Jesus' gentile contemporaries totally paradoxical. To the Jews, whose sense of social hope was in many ways more real and vibrant, the paradox would have seemed even greater. Their hopes rested on a Messianic future, and for a Messiah to be crucified was a contradiction in terms.

For the early Christians, these paradoxes could only be resolved by the resurrection. Therefore a contemporary political theology of the cross must incorporate a corresponding emphasis on the resurrection. Otherwise, the element of hope, essential for a balanced political theology, is missing.

A CRUCIFORM FAITH AS A PRECONDITION OF HOPE

One of the major differences between the Yoderian and realist is over the need for faith. The realist approach rests as much on wisdom and discernment as on faith. The Yoderian approach simply does not make sense without faith—faith in God who turns death to resurrection, faith that the universe is as it is, and that by going with the grain of the universe God's purposes will be forwarded. Yoder does not expect miraculous quick fixes, but sees God's involvement in terms of a long-term divine purpose, a divine pattern running through the processes of history. It is the church's task faithfully to imitate this divine pattern in a trustful reliance on a causality different from that of the crude categories of power and force. That faith constitutes the church in its political choice and stance. To be the church consistently, to bear the seeming folly of the cross of nonconformity, requires continuous acts of faith in the divine nature and the divine pattern within history. Faith seeks to be realistic, in the sense that the divine reality believed in is, in fact, the ultimate reality. Yoder claims that his realism, rather then Niebuhr's is, paradoxically, the true realism, because it is based on a christocentric faith in that divine ultimate reality. Hope projects that faith forwards into an expectation that reality is now, and will be in the future, congruent with the form that is seen in Jesus, and especially in his cross and resurrection.

How far is it possible to construct political policy on such faith and hope? The Yoderian would regard this as an illegitimate question, since it is not the task of the church, the primary Christian political body, to construct policy. Moreover, political policy is almost always short or medium term, and a Yoderian Christian politics takes the longer view. However, it is the church's task to recall the politician to that longer view as a measure of the rightness or otherwise of shorter term policies and the Christian politician's task to have that long view in mind in creating those short term policies.

READING CRUCIFIXION AND RESURRECTION IN HISTORY

Twentieth-century theology provides notable examples of (mis)reading contemporary history theologically. The seemingly triumphant convergence of liberal Protestantism in the early twentieth century with an optimistic secular belief in inevitable human progress was shattered by the First World War. The controversy in the 1930s (documented in Ericksen[1] and Reimer[2]) between the Nazi Hirsch and the socialist Tillich over recognizing "kairos moments" in history demonstrated how two theologians, beginning from similar theological presuppositions, could come to diametrically opposed political conclusions.

The danger of this conflation of revelation with contemporary history is compounded by a loose use of language to describe events in history, when words such as resurrection and justification have their meaning so far extended from their original usage as to cause a conceptual confusion. This tendency has been noted among liberation theologians, but is by no means restricted to them. The problem is that the opposite course, to confine such concepts either, at one extreme, to a divine realm above human life or, at the other, solely to events in Palestine in 33 CE is, first of all to diminish their relevance to the present and also to be untrue to their very nature. The crucifixion and the resurrection are both historical (in the sense of having happened at a certain time and in a certain place) and

1. Ericksen, *Theologians under Hitler*.
2. Reimer, *Debate*.

also meta-historical, because of the corporate nature of the Christ who is crucified and risen and the work of the Spirit which continues the reality of Christ in the present. In that sense Christ's crucifixion and resurrection *are* contemporary events, and their signs should be discernable in history. Every liberative, salvific, and humanizing change in human history is both an act of God and an event potentially open to socio-scientific examination.

How, then, does Jesus' resurrection give hope for an earthly, as well as a heavenly, future? Does the resurrection give an immediate hope, or a long term hope that in the end all will be well? The long term heavenly hope certainly has political relevance, in providing a *telos* for human endeavor, the vision of which can be worked back into current politics. It is not merely to be discounted as a distraction from earthly reality, since the hope in God of ultimate healing provides an incentive for a more proximate healing of the world. In the shorter term, one of the major themes in Paul is that of the power that raised Jesus from the dead being released into the world in a pattern of crucifixion and resurrection. This shorter term expectation, which can be described as partial vindications of the "Lamb who was slain," is the work of the Spirit, who strengthens the Christian as he or she follows the divine pattern of vulnerable love. Contemporary resurrection after crucifixion is not merely a metaphor, but is brought about by the same Spirit which raised Jesus from the dead.

In the light of this hope, can there be discernible progress within history towards the eschatological *telos*? The persistent presence of the crucified people within history would urge caution. It is misleading to speak of hope in the sense of an inevitable progress in history. Hope is for the short and medium term, in that God can bring the possibility of good things out of any "crucified" situation and will strengthen those who work in accordance with the divine pattern, and for the long term, in the sense of a heavenly hope. In the light of this hope, the realist prizes immediate effectiveness and puts off a purity of conscience to the long term (trusting to the mercy of God for forgiveness of the compromises thus entailed) but the Yoderian prizes immediate obedience in the expectation of long term effectiveness (and is willing to suffer the consequences in the meantime).

THE RELATIONSHIP BETWEEN CROSS AND RESURRECTION IN POLITICAL THEOLOGY

In the New Testament the cross and the resurrection are not seen as independent entities, but as inseparable. What relevance has this unity for political theology? First, the resurrection ratifies the meaning of the cross. Jesus' ways of nonviolence, his political choices which led to the cross, are given the divine stamp of approval. The cross is confirmed in its role of stripping away the illusory nature of the powers. Those who are willing to die like Jesus in a liberative cause can see themselves justified in the grand narrative of cross and resurrection. Second, the resurrection is not only the raising of someone who was dead, but also the vindication of a victim. There is, therefore, hope for victims of underserved suffering because God is on their side. The cross is a stark symbol of injustice, the resurrection of injustice overturned. Third, the resurrection opens up a hopeful future by setting free new power in the world, especially the potential for the crucified to be taken from their crosses and live. Whatever the situation of crucifixion, there can always be new possibilities of resurrection, thus engendering hope against hope. Fourth, the cross and the resurrection demonstrate both sides of salvation, alterity and affinity—affinity by the divine empathy with the crucified, alterity by the divine power that raised the crucified. God's radical empathy is not defeated by death but has the final victory. Last, the resurrection brings the future of hope into the present of crucifixion. A Christian, living in a state of crucifixion yet in the light of the resurrection, brings God's just future into present reality and recognizes analogous signs of resurrection. These signs, moreover, are not merely analogous, but are the working of the same Spirit by whom Jesus was raised from the dead.

KENOSIS AND THE CROSS

The kenotic hymn in Philippians is a significant text in a political theology of the cross. It is important to recognize the radically cruciform nature of this kenosis; the self-emptying of Christ would make sense if applied simply to the incarnation, but is immensely deepened by its application to the cross (as Paul recognizes in verse 8). The doctrine of kenosis describes the abandoning by Jesus of not just divine attributes, but also of the exercise of coercive power. Behind the kenotic Christ is the kenotic God, who similarly holds back from coercive control in the exercise of providence, choosing instead to work through a different paradigm. The cross, therefore, is the key to interpreting God's providential working. Persuasive patience replaces the power of dominion. God is revealed as uncoercive, vulnerable, liberative and creative, rather than coercively controlling.

This necessitates a radical redefinition of power—the difference between power from above, dominating and (potentially at least) oppressive, and power from alongside. Through this redefinition of divine power, which combines a restraint in the use of power and a willingness to suffer the consequences of that restraint, God's whole relationship with creation is seen as cruciform. It is that cruciform pattern that the church is called to imitate in order to conform and witness to the character of God. A fuller exploration of these themes is attempted in the two concluding chapters.

Chapter 11

The Cross and Political Power

The question of power is central to both theology and political ethics, to such an extent that it is impossible to construct a valid political theology without a realistic doctrine of power. In theology, the doctrine of providence attempts to explain and illustrate how God's power operates in the world. Creation and redemption are, at their root, doctrines of power, in the sense that they involve a divine ability to bring about change through the working of divine power. (I define power as the means of change used by its possessor in order to bring about a state of affairs closer to the possessor's intention.) Power is no less central in political ethics and forms a basic concept in analyzing the workings of national societies and international relationships. The earliest reflections on government in Greek political philosophy employ power terminology: democracy is the power, or *kratos*, of the *demos*, the people en masse; aristocracy is the power of the *aristoi*, the political elite established by birth. In the political culture contemporary with Jesus, a prime concept was *imperium*, the power of the person or nation which is given (or seizes) dominance over others. The language of power is fundamental to an understanding of contemporary politics. For example, the globalization process is increasingly regarded as involving a neo-imperialism of the north over the south, and American foreign policy is interpreted, with praise or blame, as establishing an American empire.[1] Imperialism, whether traditional or neo, exemplifies an imbalance in power relationships. The imperial power holder exercises economic or political domination over the (relatively) powerless

---

1. For an eloquent critique, see Nelson-Pallmeyer, *Saving*.

subject nation or community. This imbalance of power is not confined to international relationships. Questions of power and the consequences of its imbalance are involved in every area of human existence, from personal relationships to macro-economic transactions. Although the conservative political or structuralist sociological critique may see these imbalances as inevitable, harmonious, and creative, there is always the potential for such imbalances to become oppressive, and for the less powerful to become the suffering victims of those who hold the power.

The crucified Jesus is both a historical example and a potent symbol of this victim status. Historically, Jesus was the victim of both the imperial power of Rome and the national power structures of first-century Palestine. In devotion, the figure of the crucified Jesus has symbolized a victim both of human violence and of a divine decree interpreted, tragically, in terms of God the Father actively inflicting violence upon God the Son. In the light of the crucified and powerless Jesus, how can we formulate a Christian doctrine of power, both in terms of divine providence and political ethics? What sort of power is legitimate? How can the Christian concept of power be reformulated so as to be consistent with a crucified God? Is there a sense in which political power can parallel and be modeled upon the providential power of God, so that the grain of the universe as intended by God can be a guide to the well-being of human relationships, thus bringing the doctrine of providence and political ethics into convergence? What political ethic can be thus formulated? These are the questions explored in this chapter.

Our previous interlocutors have radically different attitudes to power, and to Christians exercising power. Yoder in effect rules out from a Christian political ethic the direct seeking of political power, as traditionally conceived. For him, the (literally) crucial power, on which, by faith, the Christian is to draw, is the eschatological power of God, as demonstrated historically in Jesus. The liberation theologians Boff and Sobrino, by contrast, have no such hesitation in encouraging the active use of political power in order to "remove the crucified from their crosses."

A) THE CROSS AS CRITICISM OF POLITICAL POWER

Dissonance and Applicability

It must be acknowledged at the outset that there is a striking dissonance in attempting to incorporate the cross, an instrument of oppression by the powerful over the powerless, into a theology of political power, unless that theology is primarily done from the perspective of the powerless. Indeed, political theology must start with an honest acknowledgment that Christianity and political power do not sit easily or naturally together. For the powerful to adopt the cross as a political symbol (the first and most notorious being Constantine) is a glaring contradiction in terms. Christian political thought has long suffered from this unresolved and frequently unnoticed dissonance. One tactic is to opt out of questions of political power. Yoder comes dangerously close to constructing a political theology which seeks to insulate the church from having to ask the awkward question: what sort of help might a Christian involved in politics receive from their faith, and, especially, from the cross, the hallmark of their faith? The most obvious Yoderian outcome is that of a sect entirely withdrawn from politics, a course which Yoder, nevertheless, eschews. Alan Billings, an Anglican priest who has served as Deputy Leader of Sheffield City Council and the South Yorkshire Police and Crime Commissioner, rightly insists on a realistic engagement with political power:

> the further Christianity is from the centre of power the more naïve its comments on the exercise of power are likely to be. If the Church is to contribute to public debate it needs some first hand acquaintance with the sorts of decisions politicians and soldiers have to make.[2]

However, such location within the centre of power can, paradoxically, reduce the sense of realism, if that location removes the politician from the perspective of those who are relatively powerless. Richard Harries uses the analogy of a log pile—for those sitting on the top (usually those with political power) the priority is the stability and security of the pile. For those at the foot of the pile, the need is to be free of the weight that is crushing them.[3] There is little doubt that a cruciform politics fits better with those who are situated at the foot of the pile, or on the periphery, outside of "Caesar's palace" than it does with those operating within the corridors of power. This sociological location of Jesus goes back beyond the crucifixion. Herzog describes Jesus' ministry as originating from the geographical, sociological and theological periphery of Jewish life "Jesus was a popular prophet whose roots were deeply embedded in Galilean village life . . . a peasant prophet who interpreted the Torah not as a representative of the great tradition emanating from Jerusalem, but as one who embodied the little tradition found in the villages and countryside of Galilee."[4]

---

2. Billings, *Dove*, 153.
3. Harries, *Guerrillas*, 44.
4. Herzog, *Jesus, Justice*, 70.

One of the chief differences between a Christian and an Islamic view of politics is that for the first three hundred years of its existence Christianity was a religion of the politically powerless, whereas almost from the beginning Islam was the religion of the rulers of the community or state. Where a nonviolent cruciform politics has been attempted by those who have entered the political process, there have certainly been successes, Gandhi and Martin Luther King being striking examples. But this has to be balanced by the confusion in pacifist politics in the 1930s, exemplified, in Britain, by the spectacle of the devoutly Christian pacifist Labour leader Lansbury being instructed by his realist colleague Ernest Bevin to "stop hawking his conscience around the conference table."[5] This led to Lansbury's resignation as Labour leader and Bevin's successful participation in the wartime coalition government and subsequent role as Foreign Secretary at the beginning of the Cold War. It is tempting to suggest that Lansbury's withdrawal from politics signified the only possibility for a consistent cruciform pacifism, thus corroborating Niebuhr's dismissal of pacifism as a useful minority vocation.

Nevertheless, the question of political power cannot be sidestepped so easily unless Christianity is indeed to withdraw into a sect mentality. An attempt must be made, *pace* Yoder, to find a place for a distinctively cruciform politics within the centers of political power as well as on the fringes. What might be described as a cruciform political epistemology is indicated—in other words, an attempt to understand politics from the point of view of the crucified people, the victims, those on the periphery, so that political decisions involving the exercise of governmental power may be informed by cruciform insights. This might be achieved in three ways. First, the starting point for cruciform politics must be the periphery. The "cruciform politician" (the verbal dissonance is striking, but must be held in tension unless political withdrawal is chosen) must begin from, or at least, relocate to, a position among those on the periphery, and not remain insulated within the established centers of power as a member of a political elite. Second, the cruciform politician must continually keep in touch with the periphery by physical, psychological, and economic location, and thereby exercise a continual hermeneutic of suspicion of political power, resisting the temptation to seek power for its own sake rather than for the benefit of the vulnerable and suffering. The creation of a political class, whether a traditional quasi aristocratic elite or a preponderance of career politicians detached from ordinary life and comfortable in power, is antithetical to a cruciform politics thus conceived. Thirdly, a cruciform politician must use the cross and the theologoumenon of the crucified people as a test to assess the validity of

---

5. Taylor, *English History*, 381–82.

policy—in other words, what the effect of policy decisions might be on the vulnerable, the crucified people.

The "Telos" of Political Power

The above criteria pose a more basic question: what is the goal, or *telos*, of political power, in the light of the cross and of the crucified people? The overarching principle is, as we have seen, and as has been eloquently propounded by liberation theologians, to "remove the crucified from their crosses." Perhaps it is too obvious to state, but the fundamental political task for the Christian has to be the diminution of suffering and oppression, and conversely the promotion of justice, freedom, wholeness, and flourishing. This perspective is, of course, not one peculiar to Christians, but the shocking fact of the cross and the crucified God at the centre of the Christian faith immensely concentrates this humanitarian protest against suffering. This *telos* for Christian politics does not exclude other elements, including (as Yoder stresses) bearing witness to the nature of God, but this is achieved both by the very act of "removing the crucified from their crosses" and by the methods used. Nor does this *telos* provide an exclusive agenda for the church, given its other roles alongside the political, such as worship, mutual upbuilding in fellowship, and evangelism. But for the church *qua* political body, and especially for the Christian involved in politics, the *telos* is all important.

The church, no less than other human institutions, falls under the judgment of that *telos*. There is a key division in interpretation within Christian political thought between an independent Jesus and a domesticated Jesus. The first stands, as it were, outside Christianity and questions the power structures of church and Christendom. The second stands within Christianity and questions those outside, whether contemporary Jewish authorities, Roman power structures, or modern governments. Perhaps, as Wilfred Owen wrote, to see Jesus "in no-man's land"[6] is the better perspective, allowing the crucified Jesus to critique all structures of power, both within the church and in society as a whole.

It might be argued that the above *telos* is all too obvious, and perhaps naïve. Does not all political action at least claim the intention of improving the human lot? This would, however, be to ignore the radical hermeneutic of suspicion (entailed by the cross) of political power, and the necessity, as mentioned above, for a cruciform political epistemology. Such a hermeneutic of suspicion needs to be consistent and thorough. In whose interests is political power actually sought and exercised? Is it, in reality, for personal or

---

6. Owen, *War Poems*, 68.

national self aggrandizement, to defend the vested interests of a particular class (of power holders)? The cross necessitated, among the earliest Christians, a radical questioning, even a reversal, of theological values, as they attempted to come to terms with the paradox of a crucified Messiah. Perhaps the huge scale of a similar redefinition of the aims of politics required by the cross has been greatly underestimated.

The European theologian who has most contributed to this cruciform redefinition is Jürgen Moltmann who, in his *Crucified God* points to a suffering, rather than a monarchical God, and draws the conclusion that the role of Christian politics is to use power to aid the suffering, alongside whom God also suffers, not to preserve present power structures supposedly corroborated by divine sanction. For Moltmann, the cross radically critiques any idolatry of political power (as in Luther's "*crux probat omnia*"[7]). The cross is seen as intrinsic to a Christian critical theory, parallel to the Marxism of the Frankfurt school, posing such questions as how can the false values of existing society, concealed by ideology, be exposed, so that there can be a transformation of the present structures of power. The cross, in Moltmann, performs an iconoclastic function, stripping bare any religiously corroborated illusions by which the present order of power is undergirded, since Jesus was crucified "in the name of the state gods of Rome who assured the Pax Romana."[8] The danger of political religion occurs where religion is used for social or national self-justification, to confirm the existing power structures and to absolutise those who rule (be they communist, capitalist, or fascist). The fact that Jesus died in powerlessness at the hands of the politically powerful means that religion can never be used as a sanction for political power. Any religious justification of political power from above (i.e., monarchical or hierarchical) is ruled out. This critique can be extended to a continuing hermeneutic of suspicion of all power.

The *telos* of "removing the crucified from their crosses" is another way of stating the necessity of seeing history from the perspective of the powerless rather than the powerful—in other words, those who actually suffer, rather than those who control (or attempt to control) the degree of that suffering. A Christian *telos* for politics must inevitably be victimological, and political power must be judged by how it affects its victims. The dominant criterion is that of social pain, as exemplified by the cross and the crucified peoples. Social pain, on this account, can never be a price worth paying for supposedly beneficial advances. Martin Hengel has usefully illustrated this aspect of the crucifixion in his analysis of how crucifixion might have been

7. Moltmann, *Crucified*, 7.
8. Moltmann, *Crucified*, 136.

regarded by different sections of Judean society. "The Palestinian peasant . . . saw in it the hated and feared instrument of repression employed by his Roman overlords." This is contrasted with the probable attitude of the inhabitants of the Hellenized cities, who will have regarded it as a horrible but nevertheless necessary "instrument for the preservation of law and order against robbers, violent men and rebellious slaves."[9] For the latter, the infliction of such social pain was a price worth paying for political stability and civilized well-being. A cruciform political theology denies that the creation of even a minority crucified people is justified in terms of a supposed future good. A modern illustration can perhaps be found in a conversation between a World Development Movement Group of which I was a member and their local MP, when discussing the possible long term benefits of globalization set alongside the social pain inflicted on large numbers of people in the (supposed) short term. It was pointed out that, with hindsight, the undoubted gains of the industrial revolution were achieved at a vast and unjustifiable social cost, and that a greater awareness of that cost could have greatly ameliorated the social pain without significantly diminishing the future good. Perhaps a similar analysis will be made of the contemporary globalization process by future economic historians. A cruciform theology, aware of the current social pain of a crucified people, and seeing economics from a victimological perspective, is a necessary corrective to the optimism of the ideology of globalization.

The traditional focus of the cross, theologically, has been God-orientated, in terms of salvation or theodicy. Without in any way diminishing that focus, a more human orientation is valuable in the analysis of power and the political process. This has been attempted in our discussion of the crucified people and the political criterion of the diminution of social pain. Where the divine and human orientations most fruitfully coincide is in the area of power, in a cruciform analysis of divine power and political power.

B) THE NATURE OF POLITICAL POWER

Next, I examine the nature of political power in a broad context. I note two aspects of political power to be identified, critiqued, and contrasted, and suggest a preliminary outline of a theology of power. All this is preparatory to the final section of this chapter, when I propose a theology of power with particular reference to the cross.

In addition to my definition of power at the beginning of this chapter, another general definition of power might be "the realization of possibilities

---

9. Hengel, *Crucifixion*, 79.

through the voluntary or coerced co-ordination of agents." This can be applied to the power of a physical human body as much as to the power associated with human relationships, including politics and government. It has already been suggested that power is the central concept in political analysis. For example, Bertrand Russell writes that "the fundamental concept in social science is Power, in the same sense in which Energy is the fundamental concept in physics."[10] Politics centers around the acquisition, distribution, and use of power. Tillich stresses that in pursuit of love, Christians should not be afraid of power, but should harness it in the work of love.[11] This is echoed by Martin Luther King, who states that "Power, properly understood, is the ability to achieve purpose . . . to bring about social, political, or economic changes. In this sense power is not only desirable but necessary in order to implement the demands of love and justice."[12] Love requires the dynamic energy of power to be effective, and power needs the discipline of love to be just. In the American Civil Rights struggle the quest for freedom was naturally overtaken by the demand for power, but King was careful to differentiate between the potential violence of Black Power and the nonviolence of collaborative and transformative power. Duncan Green, in an Oxfam study of "how active citizens and effective states can change the world" identifies four different forms of power:

> Power over: the power of the strong over the weak. This power is often hidden—for example, what elites manage to keep off the table of political debate; power to: meaning the capability to decide actions and carry them out; power with: collective power, through organisation, solidarity and joint action; power within: personal self confidence, often linked with culture, religion, or other aspects of collective identity, which influence what thoughts and actions appear legitimate or acceptable.[13]

Christine Hinze, to whose analysis this section is indebted, concentrates on the split between power *over* and power *to*.

Power Over

Power *over* can be described as the power of authority and control. It is hierarchical, structured, coercive, asymmetrical, and dominating. This idea of

---

10. Russell, *Power*, 10.
11. The theme of Tillich, *Love, Power and Justice*.
12. King, *Where Do We Go*, 37.
13. Green, *From Poverty*, 28–29.

power is central to Max Weber's analysis of politics and society. He defines power as *macht*, "the probability that one actor in a social relation will be in a position to carry out his own will despite resistance, regardless of the basis on which this probability rests," exercised as *herrschaft*, the "authoritarian power of command," "the probability that a command with a specific given content will be obeyed by a given group of persons."[14] Political power, as defined by Weber, is "the possession of a monopoly on the use of legitimate force within a given territory."[15] It is potentially backed by violence, and is an inevitable and inescapable phenomenon in human society, whatever the economic system which underlies it. It is interesting, given Yoder's disavowal of "responsibility" as a guide in Christian politics, that Weber distinguishes between *gesinnungsethik* (conviction, inspiration, ultimate ends, moral codes of love and compassion) and *verantwortungsethik* (ethic of responsibility based on desired political consequences).[16] On this analysis, for a responsible social ordering, a strong element of coercion backed ultimately by lethal force is necessary in order that society should hold together in the face of potentially disruptive and violent forces within it. Coercion is not necessarily overt; authority can be founded on convention, prestige, custom, or communal agreement. Potentially violent legitimate force is, however, the bedrock on which political power resides. This analysis of power has been prevalent in much early twentieth-century Christian political analysis. Power as superordination has been treated as basic to human social and political living, given the need to govern, justly and efficiently, large and complex nations and societies for the common good. For Niebuhr, the will to power is one of the chief sources of social sin, but legitimate superordinationist power is "the primary weapon for checking that sin."[17]

This superordinationist view of power has been criticized most fundamentally by Marx, who sees such asymmetrical relationships as the power of one class to dominate another, the power-exercising state being in the possession of the dominant class. Alienation arises when "people's communally generated transformative efficacy, or power *to* [see below], is wrested from them and re-introduced as an alien force, which is then experienced as dominative power over the community."[18] In the Marxist analysis, the possession of power by the mass of the people rather than by a controlling elite is the goal of politics, hence the Marxist warning that no matter what the

14. Hinze, *Comprehending*, 22.
15. Hinze, *Comprehending*, 29.
16. Hinze, *Comprehending*, 33.
17. Hinze, *Comprehending*, 85.
18. Hinze, *Comprehending*, 44.

ruling class gave to the workers in terms of better living and working conditions (as in the proto-welfare state of Bismarckian Germany) they would never give them power. In general, liberation theology seems to envisage democracy as the sharing of power by the mass of the people, in the sense of both governing and refusing to be dominated, and demands that this power sharing democracy should be extended to economics no less than politics. Power *over* can be criticized also in non-Marxist terms for its innate pessimism (which its defenders would, of course, describe as realism). To use the terminology of Radical Orthodoxy, original violence is presupposed, and society regarded as a scenario of conflict, tension, and grasping. Hinze points out that on the power *over* analysis, von Clausewitz' axiom, that war is simply politics carried on by other means, "is equally truthful when inverted."[19] The task of politics is to win the conflict, to impose one's (of course, beneficial) policies, and to defend them, ultimately by the use or threat of force.

Power To

Power *to*, in contrast to power *over* can be described as the power of transformative creativity. Hinze defines this mode of power as "effective capacity—power is primarily people's ability to effect their ends."[20] Such power is collaborative and non-hierarchical (or, at least, not necessarily hierarchical), involving the co-ordination of resources to achieve a goal. This may necessitate some elements of power *over*, but the emphasis is on shared growth and creativity, rather than dominion of one individual, group, class, or nation over another. If Weber is a prime example of a power *over* analysis, Hannah Arendt can serve as an example of promoting power *to*. She stresses the nature of power as capacity to effect creative change, tracing a wrong analysis of political power to Plato who "identified rule as constitutive of politics, mistaking relations of asymmetry and force for the heart of public life."[21] The essence of power is not the rule of one person or social group over another, but collaboration to achieve shared goals. Force and coercion are not the norm in social and political life, but a stop gap, which takes a decided second place to the power generated by the common consent of the people. Power is a shared strategy to enable human flourishing, rather than the coercive upholding of an asymmetrical structure. The power exercised

---

19. Hinze, *Comprehending*, 114.
20. Hinze, *Comprehending*, 5.
21. Hinze, *Comprehending*, 132.

by government does not exist for the sake of the government, but in service to the common good of the governed, who give that power by their consent.

The reaction against power *over* has been greatly strengthened by feminist social theory, through its critique of the masculinist dominance model in personal relationships and wider politics. Feminism "emphasizes transformative capacity and seeks ways to foster and enhance the collaborative and efficacious features of social and political relations,"[22] with a view of power that emphasizes "energy and competence rather than dominance."[23] The aim of power *to* is the enhancement of the capabilities of others, rather than the diminishment of their freedom, through empowering, interdependent, collaborative relationships. The purpose of power within a community is not to perpetuate structural differences, but to enhance the flourishing of each member in a creative and harmonious, rather than a conflictual and zero-sum, manner. Similarly, liberation theology stresses the liberative transformation of people from the status of being objects within a class-based hierarchy to that of subjects who develop their own powers in a context of mutual community. Power is realized when the previously powerless gain an energy and capability formerly denied them.

The chief criticism of power *to* is on the grounds of its perceived political naivety and unrealistic utopianism. Power *over* theorists such as Weber and Niebuhr certainly acknowledge the virtue of power *to*, but regard power *over* relationships as inevitable, given the fact of human inequality, and necessary, since even in mutual co-operation some authority is needed to bring about the co-ordination required to achieve goals. For Niebuhr, the sinfulness of humanity confines the practicability of power *to* within the realm of interpersonal relationships and eschatological aspirations. Justice in a fallen world needs power *over* relationships as a defense against individual and sectional threats to the common good. Against this, power *to* theorists argue that it is a mistake to make power almost synonymous with violence, since this omits much of the essence of power, and privileges what is only a comparatively small, and anomalous, element. Domination is sinful, and not therefore inherent to human wellbeing, and, although it may not be eliminated, should be minimized. Yet even power *to* is in itself ambivalent. Co-operative effectiveness can be used in collaboration for the greater good of a nation or community, but can also be turned to evil ends. For example, the holocaust would have been impossible without the SS's esprit de corps and the co-ordination of modern technology and transport.

22. Hinze, *Comprehending*, 164.
23. Hinze, *Comprehending*, 169.

The use of power and its dangers

It is clear that neither of the two above mentioned aspects of power is sufficient in itself to provide a total analysis of political power. For many Christian social ethicists the greatest problem with power *over* has been its maldistribution. Power *over* in itself is morally neutral; problems arise when that power is kept as the preserve of the few, exercised to perpetuate existing oppressive structures of power, and leaves the powerless at the mercy of the powerful. Whilst the holding of power is notoriously corrupting, powerlessness can also be morally corrupting, in terms of fatalism, despair, and self-destructive apathy. There is therefore religious justification for taking power from those who use it unjustly (a tradition going back to the Calvinist theory of revolution) and using it for the common good. Power is not to be sought *per se*, but as an instrument for social change and, even in a power structure of command and obedience, the presupposition is that of basic human equality between those who command and those who obey.

This critique is significantly broadened, especially in feminist writings, by questioning any justification for power *over*. It is admitted that there may be a need for a limited instrumental power *over*. This is, however, only provisional, temporary and fluid, as in parent-child relationships; it is strictly subservient to the goal of
co-coordinating resources for the common good; it is for the emergency rather than the norm. In other words, it provides safeguards against occasional threats rather than being the overriding social factor and serves to empower others, not to remove power from them. In political action, even when the aim is to gain power *over*, the means for this should be consistent with the end goal of a shared, creative, and mutual relationship of power *to* (as exemplified in the tradition of Gandhi and King). Walter Wink illustrates the differences between power *over* and power *to* by comparing the "domination system" with "God's domination free order." (The two roughly correspond to Hinze's distinction between power *over* and power *to*.) The contrast is drawn between a power to take life and to control destiny, and a power to support and nurture life; between domination and partnership; between win-lose and win-win; between competition and co-operation; between exploitation, greed, privilege or inequality, and sharing, sufficiency, responsibility, or equality; between domination hierarchies and actualization hierarchies; between the authoritarian and the enabling.[24] God's new order, and its embodiment in Jesus, is antithetical to the "domination system," and the conflict between the two, Wink believes, caused Jesus' death:

---

24. Wink, *Engaging*, 46.

"When the domination system catches the merest whiff of God's new order, by an automatic reflex it mobilizes all its might to suppress that order."[25]

A Preliminary Theology of Power

Hinze rightly suggests that there is no simple correspondence between Christian doctrines and power *over* or *to*.[26] Both elements of power are present in Christian conceptions of God, and in the doctrines of creation and redemption. Traditionally, the prevailing power-image of God has been that of dominance, with images of God as King, Lord, and Almighty. Feminist theologians have questioned the power-anthropology engendered by this one sided theology, and stressed the need for images of holy power as creative capacity, reciprocal and mutual power in addition to (or in place of) the traditional power *over* images.[27] This is of great significance not only for a doctrine of God but also for social ethics, since if God's normal way of exerting power is through human creatures, the character of the God exerting the power will radically affect the ways in which the human creatures are expected to exercise power. A misguided dynamolatry will inevitably have deleterious political consequences. Barbour writes that "divine love, like human love at its best, seeks neither [domineering] power over others nor [ineffective] powerlessness."[28] The theologian's task is to construct a doctrine of divine power which utilizes not only the traditional power-as-dominance images, but also "power as gentle efficacy" and creative empowering. A liberative theology rests on the divine power to energize God's creatures, both to realize their own liberation and to become instruments of God's liberating will for others. In constructing such a theology the cross, as we will see, is central.

C) THE CROSS, KENOSIS, AND POWER

The theological model which best expresses this liberative power of God is, I suggest, the kenotic. This model must accurately describes God's cruciform interaction with the world and provides the clearest indication of a Christian politics and a doctrine of political power in conformity with the cruciform character of God. While kenoticism may to some extent be valid

25. Wink, *Engaging*, 139.
26. Hinze, *Comprehending*, 286.
27. Hinze, *Comprehending*, 246–50.
28. Barbour, "God's Power," 15.

without the cross, it is immeasurably deepened and strengthened by the crucifixion. One proviso must first be made: Kenoticism is a diverse concept, and covers a wide gamut of usage; the metaphor of self-emptying can be used in various ways, including self-sacrifice, self-giving, self-limitation, etc. In developing this theme, I begin with a brief description of nineteenth and early twentieth-century kenoticism, then turn to more contemporary exegesis of the kenotic hymn in Philippians, and conclude with an adumbration of a cruciform kenoticism which will form the basis for a theology of a kenotic, cruciform God and a kenotic, cruciform political ethic. Yoder's use of the kenotic motif has already been noted. In the following description of kenoticism it should be noticed how much of Yoder's theology is fleshed out, especially with regard to the self limitation and patience of God.

Kenoticism, Philippians, and the Cross

Kenotic theology arose in Germany in the mid to late nineteenth century and in Britain in the late nineteenth and early twentieth centuries in answer to the christological problem of how to speak realistically of Christ's human life whilst maintaining his divinity. Given that Christ was truly human, with the limitations inherent in human life (limited knowledge, physical and psychological growth and development, etc.), how could the doctrine of the incarnation preserve the traditional duality in unity of humanity and divinity in one person? A doctrine of the incarnation had to be reformulated in the nineteenth-century context of the rise in historico-critical studies of Jesus revealing his limited knowledge, and of the increasing psychological research into human growth and development. If Christ retained the divine prerogatives, perfection, and powers of the eternal Son, how could he be truly human? The answer given by the German kenoticist Gottfried Thomasius, the English Charles Gore, and others, drawing on the Philippians hymn (Phil 2:5–11), was that God in Christ "emptied himself," i.e., took up a human existence with the necessary limitations of time, space, and knowledge, and lived a human life, including the human processes of growth and development. Divine attributes, such as omnipotence and omniscience were laid aside (or, at least, concealed). Moltmann usefully points out that this nineteenth-century kenoticism dealt not so much with Christ *who has become human* (i.e., the life of the historical Jesus) as Christ *in his becoming human* (i.e., the point at which Jesus entered history as a human being).[29] The divine logos retained the attributes which appertain to God's eternal inward nature—holiness, love, mercy, faithfulness—but renounced the external divine attributes

---

29. Moltmann, *God's Kenosis*, 137–51.

relating to the world—omnipotence, omniscience, omnipresence, etc. It is important to note that the kenotic doctrine arose not in opposition to incarnational Christianity, but in support of it. In more modern interpretation of kenoticism, Balthasar interprets the kenotic motif in trinitarian terms, in seeing the historical self-emptying of Jesus paralleling the eternal self giving of the Son to the Father.[30] In becoming a servant, Christ's divinity is not compromised, but rather reinforced, since his eternal relationship with the Father is played out in human history. Similarly, Coakley describes kenosis as "no longer understood as what Jesus does in order to become human, but rather what he does as a human in order to become God."[31]

In traditional kenoticism Christ is a pre-existent being who, in becoming incarnate, divests himself of divine attributes. More recent exegesis of Philippians 2 has questioned this account, locating Paul's focus in a kenosis within the life of Jesus rather than in a pre-incarnate decision. It has been argued that traditional kenoticism interpreted Philippians 2 in the light of subsequent patristic christological debate, and that Jesus' kenosis was not metaphysical, but ethical and socio-political. Dunn interprets Philippians 2 as speaking of the humanity of Jesus, whose sharing in the form of God denoted not pre-existence but the perfect likeness of God in the sense of the first Adam.[32] Moltmann comments that in Paul's account "Jesus did not take advantage of his superiority over virtually all humans in status and ability. Instead, he showed what the image of God truly is by serving others, by healing, forgiving, and submitting in love to the power of evil."[33] The emptying is not the incarnation in itself, but the humble and self giving course of Jesus' incarnate life, culminating in the cross. The kenosis, on this account, focuses much more on the cross than on the incarnation. McClendon draws attention to the political implications of such an interpretation, in pointing out that Christ's renunciations are meant to parallel Paul's own list in the previous chapter of Philippians—race, tribe, and status, all renounced for the sake of Christ. Jesus' choice not to grasp the "form of God" means "a rejection not of metaphysical perfections, but earthly temptations to kingship, in favor of identification with servants and outcasts, even though that identification would lead to his death."[34] This would clearly be very much in line with a Yoderian theology and also, given its emphasis on Jesus' self sacrifice, with a cruciform political theology.

30. In Balthasar, *Mysterium*.
31. Quoted in Weaver, *John Howard Yoder*, 232.
32. Dunn, *Christology*, 114–15.
33. Moltmann, *God's Kenosis*, 152.
34. McClendon, *Systematic Theology*, 268, and Murphy and Ellis, *Moral Nature*, 176.

Much modern exegesis of Philippians 2 is not, then, concerned so much with the metaphysics of the Trinity as with the structure of the incarnational narrative used by Paul to make an ethical point to his readers. For our purposes it is this narrative structure of the humiliation and exaltation of Christ which is important, rather than the precise starting point of that narrative. Even more important, the narrative structure is inescapably cruciform. Both traditional and modern interpretations describe a narrative of descent (or humiliation) and exaltation—it is simply that one (the traditional) starts further back than the other. Both end the downward movement with the cross, followed by the upward movement of the exaltation. On the traditional interpretation, taking the form of a slave included the act of the incarnation; compared to pre-existent divine glory any human limitation, even that of a king, would seem like slavery. But Paul (as the traditional interpretation agrees) goes far beyond this to describe a certain kind of cruciform incarnation. Philippians 2 is about more than simply becoming human; it is about a certain way of becoming human. There is a definite progress in the narrative of Philippians 2 from the humanity of Christ to a certain kind of humanity—a slave—ending with the particularly servile punishment (the *servile supplicium*) of the cross. In both interpretations, kenosis is inescapably cruciform in the narrative of descent to the lowest point, the crucifixion. Without the cross, the kenosis of the incarnation would lose much of its power. As has been argued previously, the cross is the radicalization of the incarnation; more incarnate than this God could not be, than to suffer the death of crucifixion. This is not to argue that cruciform and kenotic theologies are co-terminous; it is possible to have the one without the other, though both would lose considerable force. Hengel makes this point vigorously:

> The *thanatou de staurou* [death of the cross] is the last bitter consequence of the *morphen doulou labon* [taking the form of a slave] and stands in the most abrupt contrast possible with the beginning of the hymn with its description of the divine essence of the pre-existence of the crucified figure, as with the exaltation surpassing anything that might be conceived. . . . If it did not have *thanatou de staurou* at the end of the first strophe, the hymn would lack its most decisive statement.[35]

Kenosis is associated by Paul inextricably with the cross. Without the cross there would indeed be a kenosis in the incarnation (if that is what Philippians 2 is about) but it would be a much diminished kenosis, with a diminished political relevance.

35. Hengel, *Crucifixion*, 63.

The Cruciform and Kenotic Character of God

In addition to the differences in the exegesis of Philippians 2, there has been a significant shift in emphasis from the primarily christological concerns of the 19tth and early twentieth-century kenotic theologians to an attempt by late twentieth-century users of the kenotic motif to apply kenoticism to God's intrinsic nature, and in particular to God's providential relationship with creation. MacGregor describes a growing suspicion of kenoticism as a solution to the christological puzzle, but indicates an increasing openness to a kenotic understanding of the very being of God.[36] Brown, in a major survey of kenoticism, notes that kenosis "is now used primarily to say something about the character of God as such, and then only secondarily to imply something about the nature of Christ's incarnate life."[37] The emphasis has changed from looking at kenosis from above—the eternal divinity of Jesus given up in the incarnation—to a perspective from below—reading a kenotic God from the historical life of Jesus. Mitchell stresses that kenosis "puts the accent on the self giving behavior of Jesus and . . . reinvests that into the nature of transcendence."[38] Kenosis is interpreted as emphasizing "that it is the nature of divinity to empty itself out in love."

That the concept of kenosis has been expanded significantly beyond its original christological context is hardly surprising, given Jesus' role as the revealer in time of God's eternal essence and, indeed, Paul's use of the cross in "fostering a new kind of sociality that stands in contrast to structures of domination and division and to the religious values that legitimate such an order."[39] Christ, kenotic in either (or both) his incarnation or his earthly life (but especially his crucifixion) reveals an eternal divine kenosis. Robinson sees the human limitations of Jesus not as antithetical to divinity, but as a *plerosis* of divinity.[40] God, in freely restricting the divine power, is not less, but more, divine. God is seen as almighty in humility and self giving rather than as simply raw power. This emphasis on power as creative and loving self giving, rather than on power as dominance and control, is clearly paralleled by the distinction discussed above between power *over* and power *to*, and makes a significant difference to our understanding of both divine and political power.

---

36. MacGregor, *He Who Lets Us Be*, 71.
37. Brown, *Divine Humanity*, 221.
38. Mitchell, *Church*, 172.
39. Jennings, *Transforming*, 199.
40. Robinson, *Human Face*, 208.

The temporal actions of Jesus reveal the eternal kenotic nature of God's providential action. Moltmann in *The Trinity and the kingdom of God* draws attention to a long tradition in Anglican theology of linking a self-sacrificial God with the revelatory example of Christ. He quotes C.E. Rolt: "What Christ did in time, God does in eternity. His nature is the eternal self sacrifice of love. His suffering love is at the root of all evolution and all redemption."[41] Even earlier, F.D. Maurice interpreted the crucifixion in similar ways:

> The crucifixion of Jesus does not represent an emergency rescue package hastily put together to deal with the unforeseen consequences of human sin; it is a revelation of the eternal character of God, 'for the mind of the ruler of heaven and earth is a mind of self sacrifice; it is revealed in the Cross of Christ.'[42]

If the crucified Christ is, as Paul writes in Col 1:15–20, the pattern of creation, the source of all distinctively Christian discourse about God in his creation and providence, then it follows that the overall activity of God in creation and continuing providence is cruciform and kenotic. The Barthian movement in theology, of which Yoder was very much a part, championed the insight that the humiliation of the cross, far from denying Christ's divine nature, revealed God's fullness. The early Barth's *nein* to natural theology is famous. Yet, as the later Barth partially conceded, natural theology, when seen through the light of Christ, can shed light on the divine purposes. Hence there should be no contradiction between natural and revealed theology in a cruciform doctrine of providence. What we see definitively in the pattern of Christ's ministry, death, and resurrection, and what we read less definitively in the pattern of creation and providence, should be congruent. Peacocke, both a biochemist and a theologian, writes:

> Belief in Jesus the Christ as the self expression of God in the confines of a human person is entirely consonant with those conceptions of God, previously derived tentatively from reflection on natural being and becoming, which affirm that God, in exercising divine creativity, is self limiting, vulnerable, self emptying, and self giving—that is, supremely love in creative action.[43]

The kenotic creative and providential actions of God are universal, but are revealed in concentrated and definitive form in the actions of Jesus Christ. These actions took shape not in a vacuum, but in a political context where

41. Moltmann, *Trinity*, 31.
42. Bradley, *Power*, 172.
43. Peacocke, "Cost," 41.

questions of human political power were remarkably paralleled by questions of God's power in providence.

The cruciform and kenotic (therefore vulnerable) character of God necessitates an alternative way of interpreting power and political effectiveness, as we have seen in Yoder, Boff, and Sobrino. For Sobrino and Boff the pain and vulnerability of God continuing in (and reflected by) the crucified people is central to their political theology. For Yoder, a kenotic and cruciform doctrine of God revealed through Jesus' ministry and crucifixion is the basis for an eschatological doctrine of political effectiveness. In *For the Nations*, Yoder writes

> . . . the church's being shaken and moved, being vulnerable, defines or constitutes its participation in the travail of the Lamb who was slain and is therefore worthy to receive power and wealth and wisdom and might and honor and blessing. That suffering is powerful, and that weakness wins, is true not only in heaven but on earth. That is a statement about the destiny *not only of the faith community, but also of all creation*.[44]

The nature of the power of God, and therefore human political power, is radically questioned by the cross and by a cruciform doctrine of providence. The contrast between, to use Hinze's distinction, a dominating power *over* God and a vulnerable power *to* God is the basis for much of Moltmann's thesis in *The Crucified God*. Here the distinction is repeatedly made between the political consequences of a *theologia gloriae* and a *theologia crucis*. The concept of power is naturally and instinctively linked to God, and an image of power *over* is most closely associated with much of the biblical language (almighty, king, etc.) used to describe God. Hence the shock of a cruciform doctrine of God, which does not totally rule out power *over*, but admits suffering into that sovereignty and leads to a much greater emphasis on power *to*. Bonhoeffer, too, contrasts the natural human desire for divine power with the cruciform divine power revealed in Jesus: "Man's religiosity makes him look in his distress to the power of God in the world, and the Bible directs man to God's powerlessness and suffering."[45] If, as Hall points out, God's purpose is to bring us salvation through the "power of suffering love," then "no application of power in the usual [i.e., power *over*] sense can attain this object."[46] If power is interpreted as power *over*, the "weak" suffering of the power holder would seem to decrease that power, hence the unwillingness of

---

44. Yoder, *For the Nations*, 35. My italics.
45. Bonhoeffer, *Letters*, 361.
46. Hall, *Cross*, 79.

traditional theology to allow a doctrine of divine suffering.[47] But if power is interpreted as power *to*, there is a more integrated relationship between power and suffering, between vulnerability and creativity, between self sacrifice and transformation. This "weakness" inherent in suffering is paradoxically the divine strength in salvation, as Paul stresses in the Corinthian correspondence, especially in 1 Corinthians 1: 25 and 2 Corinthians 2: 9–10.

The Power and "Weakness" of God in the Light of the Cross

One of the most moving and powerful statements of divine cruciformity is found in the poetry of Studdert Kennedy (especially in the collection *The Unutterable Beauty*), inspired by the sufferings of the First World War. "*High and lifted up*," for example, is an angry counterblast against a conception of an invulnerable power *to* deity. Studdert Kennedy concludes: "For the very God of heaven is not power, but power of love."[48] A similar poetic statement can be found in "*Jesus of the Scars*" by Edward Shillito, also written in response to that war (most notably quoted by William Temple)

> The other gods were strong, but thou wast weak
> they rode, but thou didst stumble to a throne
> but to our wounds only God's wounds can speak
> and not a god has wounds, but thou alone.[49]

What does it mean to ascribe "weakness" to God? The term can cover a wide range of options from, on the one hand, a power *over* which allows itself in some areas to become vulnerable but retains what might be described as reserves of power, to a metaphysical weakness where the very being of God is totally contingent upon the response of creation. Adapting descriptions commonly used of the Trinity, a distinction may be made between the "essential weakness" and the "economic weakness" of God, the former seeking to describe God's metaphysical essence, and the latter seeking to describe God's relationship with creation. This is not an absolute distinction, as we will see, but can perhaps serve to clarify the concept of divine weakness. As examples of "essential weakness" I take Process Theology and the "weakness" theology of John Caputo, and to illustrate "economic weakness" the Lutheran tradition of which Bonhoeffer and Moltmann (Lutheran in his cross-theology, if not in his ecclesiastical allegiance) are a part.

---

47. As suggested by Hinze, *Comprehending*, 270.
48. Studdert Kennedy, *Unutterable Beauty*, 48.
49. Temple, *Readings*, 385.

It is sometimes difficult to penetrate Caputo's playful post-modernist talk of God as "event," and the boundaries between realism and non-realism are (deliberately) obscured, so it is virtually impossible to describe the "metaphysical" essence of God in Caputo's work. His "weakness theology" is, however, a fascinating combination of Derrida and the cruciform theology of Paul. Caputo describes a traditional "strong" church theology, complete with its images of God as king, divine rule, the control of history, hierarchy and powerful domination and contrasts this with a "weakness theology" which portrays God as a subversive and vulnerable promise for the future and a summons to justice. God is not a dominant power or even a metaphysical force, but a "weak" and vulnerable force which nevertheless claims us persuasively, persistently, and unconditionally. Caputo writes of the "power of powerlessness" and the "kingdom of weak forces."[50] God is a "weak force that lays claim to us unconditionally but has no army to enforce its claims." This "weak force" has political connotations:

> Suppose the sense of 'God' is to interrupt and disrupt, to confound, contradict, and confront the established human order ... Suppose God has no time for the hierarchical power structures that human beings impose upon one another and even less time for the power of God over human beings, which is actually the power that human beings exert 'in the name of God'[51]

Caputo locates the focal point of this "weak theology" on the cross:

> The weak force of God is embodied in the broken body on the cross ... The power of God is ... the power of powerlessness, the power of the call, the power of protest that rises up from innocent suffering and calls out against it, the power that says *no* to innocent suffering, and finally the power to suffer-with *(sym-pathos)* innocent suffering, which is perhaps the central Christian symbol.[52]

A more systematic, if less dramatic and provocative, approach to the "weakness" of God is that given by Process Theology, which understands the divine interaction with creation as involving persuasion rather than coercion. In the famous words of Whitehead, God is a "fellow sufferer who understands."[53] God, as an entity, is affected by other entities, and hence vulnerable to change, while remaining constant in character. Hence

50. Caputo, *Weakness*, 16.
51. Caputo, *Weakness*, 34.
52. Caputo, *Weakness*, 43.
53. Whitehead, *Process*, 350.

Whitehead's doctrine of God as dipolar, sympathetically responding to the world and experiencing the painful struggle endemic to creation, but still remaining God. Thus, for a process theologian, kenotic self restraint is not chosen by God, but is an integral part of the divine nature, which is limited and vulnerable in its very essence.

There is a sense, however, in which the distinction between essential and economic weakness, or necessity and contingency, is unreal. Process theology suggests that the kenotic limitation on divine power occurs from metaphysical necessity rather than through divine choice. But if God's essential nature is to be loving and creative, it is impossible that God could choose to be other than loving and creative. If love implies vulnerability, and God's freedom is freedom only to love, then God's vulnerability is not so much a choice as a necessity compelled by God's own nature. Or, to put this another way, divine omnipotence is not a power to do everything, but to act to the limits according to God's nature of love. So the omnipotence of God, with regard to creation, is to share the suffering of creation to the fullest extent. The humiliation of the cross is not a diminution of divine omnipotence, but its fullest outworking.

In the Lutheran tradition the cross is central to knowledge of God and therefore of God's power. In the Heidelburg thesis number 20 Luther wrote that "He deserves to be called a theologian who comprehends the visible and manifest things of God seen through suffering and the cross." This theme of a cruciform epistemology is emphasized by Bonhoeffer, who stresses the importance of knowing God as marginalized and excluded. Contrary to a god of the gaps epistemology, humanity knows God through what we experience in a prime and universal human category—suffering. For Bonhoeffer, a (potentially) suffering discipleship of a suffering God is the mark of Christian living by participating in the divine passion in the midst of ordinary life. "Man is summoned to share in God's sufferings at the hands of a godless world."[54] God does not help us by omnipotent power *over*, but by the power *to* manifest in creative suffering:

> God lets himself be pushed out of the world onto the cross. He is weak and powerless in the world, and that is precisely the way, the only way, in which he is with us and helps us. Matthew 8:17 makes it quite clear that Christ helps us, not by virtue of his own omnipotence, but by virtue of his weakness and suffering.[55]

---

54. Bonhoeffer, *Letters*, 361.
55. Bonhoeffer, *Letters*, 360.

Similarly, for Moltmann, God's power is limited by the nature of his creative love. Moltmann's political theology is predicated on the centrality of the cross in giving true knowledge of God's compassion, sympathy and fellow suffering. In his doctrine of creation he uses the Kabbalistic concept of *zimzum*, God's withdrawal of omnipotent power *over* in order to give room for the free flourishing of creation. God is powerful, but in the sense of power *to*, in giving power from the divine self to creation. "God does not create merely by calling something into existence . . . he 'creates' by letting be, by making room, and by withdrawing himself."[56] God's greatness is not compromised by such a withdrawal: "God never appears mightier than in the act of his self-limitation, and never greater than in the act of his self-humiliation."[57] This power involves the patience of suffering. As Moltmann continues, "God acts in the history of nature and of human beings through his patient and silent presence, by way of which he gives those he has created space to unfold, time to develop, and power of their own movement."[58] Nor is this patience simply uninvolved waiting, but God is gently at work, persuading and inviting a response, and suffering both the rejection of that offer and the pain of humanity as it suffers the consequences of that rejection. This forms a major theme of Moltmann's *The Trinity and the Kingdom of God* where (in chapter 2, entitled "The Passion of God") he outlines attempts to construct a model of divine action taking as its starting point the suffering of the cross, rather than, as in previous Christian tradition, the concept of impassibility. In addition to such diverse authorities as the Jewish Heschel, the Spanish Catholic Unamuno, and the Russian Orthodox Berdyaev, Moltmann draws on a strong tradition in Anglican theology (in the late nineteenth and early twentieth century) of God's passibility. Although Moltmann links this specifically with the Anglo-Catholic doctrine of Eucharistic Sacrifice, there are significant parallels with the contemporary emphasis on kenosis. We have seen how Moltmann particularly adduces *The World's Redemption* by C.E. Rolt, a specialist on the mystical theology of Dionysius the Areopagite. Rolt stresses that the omnipotence of God must be interpreted in the light of the cross, as the "almighty power of suffering love." The "cross on Golgotha has revealed the eternal heart of the Trinity," and the "historical passion of Christ reveals the eternal passion of God,"[59] self sacrifice being of the very essence and nature of God.

56. Moltmann, *God in Creation*, 88.
57. Moltmann, *God's Kenosis*, 148.
58. Moltmann, *God's Kenosis*, 149.
59. Moltmann, *Trinity*, 31–32.

Power, Weakness, and Love

Is it correct, then, to speak of God's "weakness"? If by weakness we mean helplessness and powerlessness, in terms of either power *over* or power *to*, such a description is grossly misleading. But if by weakness we mean vulnerability, kenotic humility, and restraint in exercising power, even on a power *over* model, weakness is a justifiable description, provided that weakness is interpreted economically and not essentially. From a power *to* perspective, such weakness is better interpreted as creative and vulnerable kenosis, self emptying, which, in the form of love, is an integral attribute of God. This weakness is certainly not helplessness, but the fullest and most effective compassion. God's nature of non-coercive love gives birth to a suffering creativity, the infinite and yet costly ability to give and share power. God is, as MacGregor puts it "self emptying being."[60] God's nature is to give self sacrificially in love, and that nature defines and limits the nature of the power God exercises. As feminist theology necessarily points out, God's power is not a magnification of normal human (masculinist) power; human power is redefined by the self-giving power of God.

In his cantata *Ani Maamin* (I believe) Eli Wiesel meditates on the shattering impact of the holocaust on the fate and faith of the Jewish people. God's deliverance comes six million deaths too late, and such a God seems powerless—a remorseful deity who can suffer but cannot enable. MacGregor states bluntly, in his kenotic theology *He who lets us be* that a powerless deity is useless to anyone. This problem has been discussed above in the debate concerning Yoder's priority of witness over (at least short term) effectiveness and in Sobrino's distinction between a God of affinity, a co-sufferer, and a God of alterity, a rescuer. A sufferer may well ask if God is powerful enough to do anything about their suffering, other than to sympathize. There is a risk of polarization between a theology of the suffering of God which may leave the sufferer untouched and unrescued, and a theology of controlling divine power which is both experientially unsustainable and results in an idolatrous and sub-Christian view of God.

The question of the effectiveness of divine power cannot be sidestepped. The traditional power *over* images of God's sovereignty and authority have clear connotations of effectiveness—but so do the power *to* images. If God's power does not sustain creation, promote creation's flourishing, and empower others, it cannot reasonably be designated as any kind of power at all. George Murphy wisely comments that kenosis "does not mean God's abdication, but God working in a way that is not recognizable to the theologians

---

60. MacGregor, *He Who Lets Us Be*, 179.

of glory."[61] Similarly, Polkinghorne draws the contrast: love without power means that God is a compassionate but impotent observer; power without love means that God is a cosmic tyrant.[62] How can a "weak" or power *to* God be transformative? The traditional Christian answer, in 2 Cor 12:9, speaks of strength made perfect in weakness. God's purposes come to fruition not despite suffering, but through it. Perhaps a better designation, beyond the power *over*/ power *to* dichotomy, is power *from alongside*, the power which is particularly demonstrated by a kenotic incarnation. There are clear similarities with Green's "power *with*."[63] God's power is seen as uncoercive, vulnerable, not controlling, and yet liberative, healing, and creative.

These questions are discussed here not so much in an attempt to discover an answer as to point up their relevance to political theology. A political theology modeled on power *to* may be more in accordance with God's cruciform nature and action. Weakness, however, in the sense of loss of power *over*, implies (at least in the short term) a lack of ability directly to protect the vulnerable or to decrease immediate suffering.

D) CONSTRUCTING A KENOTIC AND CRUCIFORM POLITICAL ETHIC

The Relationship between Divine Power and Human Power

In Yoder and the liberation theologians the strict distinctions between the doctrines of creation and atonement, of incarnation and redemption, are minimized. This accords with a general trend to see such doctrines not independently but as intimately related. A similar process can be seen in political theology: in Yoder, for example, his stress on an uncoerced response to love in his doctrine of atonement leads naturally to an avoidance of coercion in his political theology. In attempting to construct a kenotic and cruciform political ethic an important question must first be tackled: how far is it possible to model a political ethic on God's nature and character as expressed in the creation, incarnation and atonement? We have seen how divine power is not solely or chiefly power *over*, but power *to*—or more accurately, power *alongside*. Since it is at the heart of a Christian anthropology to see humanity in the image of God and created according to the divine plan and purpose, there should be some kind of relationship between divine power thus redefined and human power—at the very least, some parallelism

---

61. Murphy, *Cosmos*, 80.
62. Polkinghorne, "Kenotic Creation," 91.
63. Green, *From Poverty*, 28–29.

between God's action and Christian political ethics. Political ethics have at their centre the nature, use and distribution of power; hence the importance of the question of how far a Christian political ethic of power can mirror God's power in its nature and use. Is it possible to construct a political ethic of power which goes along the grain of creation as theistically interpreted?

I will argue that such an ethic can be constructed—with some important provisos. First, as Kant taught, in ethics "ought" implies "can." Is a kenotic ethic possible in a sinful and fallen political world? Niebuhrian realism would, as we have noted on many occasions, argue that a kenotic, cruciform ethic, may be the ideal, but needs to be adjusted if it is not to be irrelevant in a world of power *over*. As has been argued above, realism is not a blank cheque for abandoning any attempt to form a cruciform ethic, but the possibly harmful consequences of such an ethic cannot simply be ignored.

Second, is a parallelism between divine and human power obligatory? Does the correspondence have to be total between divine character and human ethics? The powerlessness of Jesus on the cross signals that divine power is of a certain type, but the crucifixion is not necessarily the exclusive paradigm of divine-human relationships. It may well be overwhelmingly decisive, but is not the only paradigm. To put the problem another way, is it axiomatic that the Christian has to imitate the cruciform nature of God in all circumstances? Or are there circumstances where faithfulness to God requires the Christian not to share in the cruciform divine nature? The problem of conflicting duties has already been mentioned in our discussion of Yoder, and is relevant here. There exists also the possibility that there may be parts of the divine personality which are solely divine and have no easy correspondence to human politics. We have to conclude that there is no automatically straightforward correspondence between Christian doctrine and questions of power.

This difficulty can be illustrated by twentieth-century attempts to build social ethics on certain aspects of Christian doctrine. For Moltmann, the trinitarian doctrine of God as a community of three equals, whose life consists of a self giving, cruciform love, provides a good indication for a social ethic of democratic socialism. For Caputo, a "strong" theology leads to militarism and violence, and so in order to promote peace and justice a "weak" theology is needed. It is a widely accepted maxim that if the object of worship is hierarchical or oppressive, the ensuing social ethic will probably be similarly hierarchical and oppressive. David Nicholls, in *Deity and Domination*, outlines a fascinating history of correspondence between images of God and concepts of political power, drawing attention to the potential pitfalls. For example the Nazi jurist Carl Schmitt argued, in his teaching about the "sociology of the concept" that the most important concepts in modern political and legal theory were "secularized theological concepts," both in their historical derivation and in their formal resemblances.[64] The danger in the mutual interrelationship is clear: erroneous theological concepts can lead to erroneous political theologies and secular ideologies, and vice versa. The difficulty, as Nicholls suggests, lies in avoiding the historical mistakes in such an *analogia entis*. He concludes:

> The attempt to find fixed criteria by which to assess the validity of the images used of God results in a wild goose chase ... [there are] no wholly objective criteria to which we can appeal that are free from the taint of cultural context.[65]

This gloomy prognosis can perhaps be confirmed by surveying some of the less beneficial ways in which the divine-human correspondence, especially with regard to the cross, has been used. For example, the kenotic imagery of sacrifice has been widely used to glamorize war and imperialism, especially in the early twentieth century. Rupert Brooke, with his seeming joy at the opportunity for self sacrifice in war ("Now God be thanked"), and hymns such as "O Valiant Hearts" take the theme of sacrifice and use it to support a militarist and nationalist ideology. There is indeed a sense in which the armies suffering the hell of the trenches could be said to form part of the crucified people (such imagery was not unknown in the war poets), and the poetry of Studdert Kennedy (significantly chosen by Moltmann as an outstanding pioneer of a theology of divine suffering) dramatically expresses God's suffering and sympathy. However, it is hard to avoid the conclusion that such language was frequently commandeered by those who sought to inculcate a spirit of sacrifice for dubious nationalistic ends. The misuse of cross/resurrection language can be illustrated equally by its use in post Versailles German Protestantism. Marsh notes that German protestants "would take comfort in imagining that the nation's defeat resembled Christ's humiliation on the cross ... God, in whom they kept faith, would resurrect the Fatherland from its ashes, restoring it to its former glory."[66]

All this is certainly not to argue that it is impossible to construct a social ethic which seeks to correspond to the character of God. To argue that there need be no such correspondence would remove such an ethic from any pretension of being called Christian. The problem is one of arbitrariness: how does one choose the particular aspect of God, or the particular aspect of Christian doctrine to which a Christian social ethic should correspond?

64. Nicholls, *Deity*, 241.
65. Nicholls, *Deity*, 232.
66. Marsh, *Strange Glory*, 60.

There are perhaps three criteria by which the validity of a cruciform, kenotic ethic, corresponding to the character of God, can be assessed. The first two are more associated with Yoder, the latter more with Sobrino and Boff.

The first criterion is that of revelation. The Christian belief is that the incarnate Jesus reveals the truth about God. In order to appreciate the aspects of the nature of God with most relevance to political ethics, it would seem reasonable to look to those aspects of the life of Jesus which connected most closely to the politics of his day. If Jesus lived a kenotic political life which ended with the inevitability of crucifixion, if Jesus renounced power *over* in favor of power *to* or *alongside*, then something definitive is revealed both about the nature of divine cruciform and kenotic power, and the kind of politics to which the Christian is committed in following Jesus at this point.

The second criterion is that of imitation. The moral character of God is revealed in Christ, and the Christian is called to imitate Christ as part of being in Christ. This imitation forms the social ethic which is an integral part of Christian discipleship. Yoder stresses that in the New Testament imitation of Christ is centered almost exclusively on the cross. There is no general concept of imitating random aspects of Christ's ministry; the only imitation in the New Testament being of the cross-bearing Christ, and hence of the particular kenotic use of power which this implies. This imitation leads to an ethic which aims to reflect the character of God, not just any aspect of the character of God, but his kenotic and cruciform nature.

The third criterion is that of vulnerability. If the previous criteria rested on contemplating Christ in his relation to first-century politics, this third criterion rests on contemplating Christ in his present sufferings in the crucified people. What is the effect of a doctrine of power on the present sufferings of Christ? What does the solidarity of Christ with the suffering have to say about the nature of power a Christian should seek to exercise?

In the following section I attempt to outline a cruciform, kenotic political ethic which seeks to correspond to the cruciform, kenotic character of God in accordance with the above criteria.

Kenosis as a Subversive Ethic

If the ultimate power, the divine, is cruciform and kenotic, all human pretensions to power are to some extent questioned and subverted. Kenosis parallels the ethic of reversal found in the Sermon on the Mount, and especially in the Beatitudes which illustrate what Kraybill described as the "upside down kingdom."[67] Hart describes the impact of Jesus as follows:

> The new world we see being brought into being in the gospels is one in which the whole grand cosmic architecture of prerogative, power and eminence has been shaken and superseded by a new, positively "anarchic" order: an order that is, in which we see the glory of God revealed in a crucified slave, and in which we are enjoined to see the forsaken of the earth as the very children of heaven.[68]

Jesus frequently spoke in power language, of a "kingdom of God," without overt irony. But the nature of that kingdom (where the first is last, and the meek inherit the earth) and the way of entering into it (as a little child) reveal a covert irony which is confirmed by the overall kenotic shape of his coming. Caputo captures this element in his description of the kingdom of God as "an anarchic field of reversals and displacements," and invites us to consider the name of God as describing "a disturbance or a holy disarray—a sacred anarchy, a hieranarchy."[69] Such a God cannot be a guarantor of any existing status quo, as in traditional conservatism, but stands as a radical question mark against the nature and use of power. This questioning of power does not necessarily abolish structures of power, but makes them accountable, both to those for whose benefit such structures exist (for example, in order to maintain the necessary organizations of a technological civilization) and to those whom such structures may, deliberately or inadvertently, exclude from power.

Roger Haydon Mitchell has formulated a compelling political ethic which he names "kenarchy," which etymologically and theologically combines rule and kenosis. He describes kenarchy as "the emptying out of power on behalf of others in contrast with exercising power over others" based on a divine politics, which is "not a dominating transcendence colonized by sovereignty but rather the gift of self emptying love or kenosis."[70] In *Discovering Kenarchy: Contemporary Resources for the Politics of Love* Mitchell and Arram attempt to envisage a politics flowing from such a kenotic vision, involving "emptying out power and encouraging the voices of the marginalized to find their place"[71] and "pouring out oneself as a gift for 'the other', whoever that

---

67. Kraybill, *Upside Down*.
68. Hart, *Atheist Delusions*, 174.
69. Caputo, *Weakness*, 14.
70. Mitchell, *Fall*, 6–7.
71. Mitchell and Arram, *Discovering*, 82.

'other' might be,"[72] the aim being the creation, as Arram puts it, of "a new inclusive humanity where the margins have become the centre."[73] In a (significantly) close echo of Yoder, Mitchell states that "kenarchy does not seek to immediately overturn the offending institution it confronts. Instead it seeks to overcome it by degrees in a loving rhythm of subversion and submission."[74]

In my outline of a possible kenotic ethic I make a rough division between a personal ethic of political kenosis, centered on a spirituality of kenotic political discipleship focusing on issues of lifestyle, and a social ethic of political kenosis, centered on a redefinition of power with the stress on nonviolence. I conclude with two provisos on the nature of such an ethic. I take as the most important arena for such an ethic the continuing crises of globalization, environmental degradation, poverty, and inequality in the world economy, seeking to indicate how such an ethic can be of use in this arena.

A Spirituality of Kenotic Political Discipleship

Murphy and Ellis, in *On the Moral Nature of the Universe* attempt to work out a kenotic political ethic on the basis of what accords with both God's kenotic nature and kenosis as demonstrated within creation. It is their political interpretation of kenosis which forms the basis for the discussion in the remainder of this chapter. Their ethic can be summed up as follows: "Self-renunciation for the sake of the other is humankind's highest good."[75] This ethic or (equally accurately) spirituality consists of self-sacrifice, other-centeredness, forgiveness, a willingness to accept suffering, and humility, exercised not merely privately but in relation to social and political life as a whole. We have already seen such a self-sacrificial cruciform spirituality in the writings of Boff and Sobrino in the context of Latin American discipleship and martyrdom. In a European context, Bonhoeffer, whose proclamation of Christian self sacrificial discipleship—"when Christ calls a man, he calls him to come and die"[76]—began as a metaphor and ended as a tragic reality, can serve as an example of such a political spirituality.

Such a kenotic ethic has been widely criticized, and with good reason. In its original Victorian and Edwardian forms[77] it has been interpreted as a product of the guilty consciences of wealthy members of the middle and

---

72. Mitchell and Aram, *Discovering*, 64.
73. Mitchell and Aram, *Discovering*, xi.
74. Mitchell and Aram, *Discovering*, 12.
75. Murphy and Ellis, *Moral Nature*, 118.
76. Bonhoeffer, *Cost*, 79.
77. See Bradley, *Power*, 161.

upper classes. Brown writes of early British kenoticism, "What one misses in all these writers is any real sense of the need to get alongside the person one seeks to benefit: instead of just handing out largesse, actually empowering the weak. Perhaps it was simply the overwhelming nature of the great contrast between God and ourselves that led them astray."[78] This criticism has been made particularly by feminist theologians, who have seen self-sacrificial kenosis as relevant to a predominantly male paradigm, and dangerous to women, for whom it leads to a self-destructive subordination.[79] According to this feminist critique, self development and self realization rank higher than self sacrifice. This criticism is valid as a warning against the ever present tendency for any spirituality to become corrupted in the interests of those holding power. It would be ironic in the extreme for a kenotic spirituality to be used as an instrument of confirming the powerless in their powerlessness, rather than as an encouragement for power sharing on a basis of equality. As we will see, kenosis is an insufficient ethic in itself if isolated from wider considerations.

However, this criticism does not fatally vitiate a kenotic ethic, if by means of such an ethic the overall aim is, in the words of the Magnificat, to "bring down the powerful from their thrones and lift up the lowly." (Luke 1:52, NRSV) In that task, self sacrifice, renunciation, suffering, and detachment from material reward may well be essential virtues. Brown sums up the positive effects of kenotic theology in "drawing the Church and its theologians away from the worship of power and into the glorious vision of divinity totally dedicated to the full flourishing of humanity and indeed all creation; power now properly moderated by creativity and love."[80] An intrinsic element of kenoticism is an individual's willingness to take responsibility for the interests of others, sometimes to the detriment of one's own interests, and a corporate willingness to seek a wider vision of political good, beyond the bounds of one's own interest group. If a general kenotic social ethic is indicated, there is also a need for a kenotic spirituality and a cruciform spiritual discipline to give that ethic support, impetus, staying power, and validity.

Kenotic Lifestyle Choices

In the light of the environmental crisis and the continuing destructive economic and political inequality between first and third worlds, a kenotic ethic is required from those at present enjoying a disproportionate share of

78. Brown, *Divine Humanity*, 190.
79. See Hampson's rejection of kenosis in Coakley, *Powers*, 3.
80. Brown, *Divine Humanity*, 265.

the world's resources, as indicated, for example, in the encyclical *Laudato Si*. This kenotic ethic would take the form of a voluntary self limitation in the use of resources, food and wealth. The link between kenosis and lifestyle has long been established. For example, in ecumenical theology of the nineteen seventies, Mar Ostathios, in an article headed *The rich must become poor voluntarily* wrote of the church and the Christian using Christ's kenosis as a pattern to follow in adopting a simpler lifestyle.[81]

I take as a historical example of this kenotic ethic the Lifestyle Movement of the nineteen seventies, the ethos of which has mushroomed in the contemporary upsurge of environmentalism, due to the crisis caused by global warming. Other similar examples were the evangelical "International Consultation on Simple Lifestyle" which grew out of the Lausanne Conference, and Roman Catholic concerns for lifestyle initiated by the encyclical *Populorum Progressio*.[82] The Lifestyle Movement arose chiefly under the aegis of Horace Dammers (Dean of Bristol Cathedral) who set out the principles of the movement in *Lifestyle, a Parable of Sharing*. The movement had its beginnings in the Church Leaders Conference in Selly Oak, Birmingham, in 1972, in the Commission on Man's [sic] Stewardship in God's World, where the following invitation was put to the conference:

> The Commission, convinced that environmental responsibility and social justice on a world scale demand changes in personal as well as national ways of life, recommends to each of its own members and invites all members of this Conference to pledge ourselves to a simplicity of life which is generous to others and content with enough rather than excess; and that each should privately review his or her life before God so as to implement this pledge, as necessary, by altered patterns of consumption.[83]

The links between environmental responsibility, social justice, and the lifestyle of the individual, the ideals of simplicity, enough and avoidance of excess, and private and personal responsibility for implementing the commitment were themes incorporated into the Lifestyle Commitment, which included the famous phrase used by the ecumenist / biologist Charles Birch, "I therefore propose to live more simply that others may simply live." The commitment is given to "change my own lifestyle as may be necessary . . . and to enjoy such material goods and services as are compatible with this commitment." Support is pledged "to such political and social action and to such economic policies as tend to conserve, develop, and redistribute the

---

81. Mar Ostathios, *Theology*, 104.
82. Details in Peet, "Lifestyle."
83. Dammers, *Lifestyle*, 106.

Earth's resources for the benefit of the whole human family." A percentage of income is to be given away, and participants are encouraged to join a Lifestyle cell or to form one. This simple lifestyle is not seen as the end, but as a means to an end, in a holistic framework which presupposes and includes political action; it is not, at least in intention, a privatized and individualistic venture. Ronald Sider, the author of *Rich Christians in an Age of Hunger*), the work which, more than any other, influenced evangelicals towards a simpler lifestyle, wrote that the purpose of a simpler lifestyle was "a desire for structural change to bring about a new kind of global community."[84] This was an attempt to answer the chief criticism of lifestyle movements, that they accept the existing economic order and power structure as basically sound and concentrate on the responsibilities and uses of economic power while ignoring the necessity for a more radical critique of the acquisition and maintenance of that power.

Lissner, a Dane working for the World Lutheran Federation, gave ten reasons for adopting a simpler lifestyle.[85] A simple lifestyle is an act "of faith; of self-defense (against over-consumption); of withdrawal (from the 'neurosis' of a materialist society); of solidarity; of sharing; of celebration; of provocation (a prophetic act); of anticipation (of a new era); of advocacy; and an exercise of purchasing power." Historically, the lifestyle movement arose in the nineteen seventies from a sense of disillusionment with the prevailing model for development, with its assumption of a shared interest between the wealthy and the poor (an assumption which is still prevalent in much development economics). A more conflictual model may well be indicated by a cruciform political theology, accompanied by an uneasiness about benefitting from an unjust economic system—in the sixties phrase, a desire to cease from being part of the problem, and become part of the solution. The environmental crisis has added weight to what might be called a Kantian criticism of the present maldistribution of the earth's resources, given the finite nature of these resources, the earth's finite capacity to deal with our waste, and an awareness that it is impossible for the whole of humanity to enjoy levels of consumption hitherto the norm in the richer nations without significant changes to the world's economic systems and modes of production. A Kantian ethic, by which a situation's moral acceptability rests on the rightness (and possibility) of its universalization, would seem to question the consumption of the rich, in the light of shortage of resources and the potential for conflict (military or economic) over them.

---

84. Sider, *Rich Christians*, 26–27.
85. Quoted in Dammers, *Lifestyle*, 81–82.

In this situation, some sort of a kenotic ethic would seem to be essential, for three reasons. First if (as seems overwhelmingly likely) the chief cause of the environmental crisis is over-consumption on behalf of the rich, some form of kenotic restraint is essential in order to remedy the situation. Second, one of the simplest arguments for a kenotic, simpler lifestyle, is the subsequent transfer of resources from the first world to the third, either through massively increased charitable giving—a course of action vigorously advocated by Peter Singer in *The Life You Can Save* or through socially useful forms of investment, such as micro credit schemes (as recommended, for example, by the Agra Covenant on Christian Capital[86]). This argument for a kenotic lifestyle circumvents the debate over whether the wealth of the first world is a contributory factor to the poverty of the third. Even if it could be demonstrated that first world wealth and third world poverty are not causally linked, the Christian would still have a responsibility to alleviate the suffering that exists. In the New Testament, and especially the teaching of Jesus (for example, Matt 25:31–46, Luke 10:25–37, and Luke 16:19–31) the rich are judged not so much for their part in directly and consciously causing suffering, but for their callous indifference to it and their refusal to use their wealth to alleviate it. A kenotic lifestyle, lived in awareness of the suffering of the crucified people, adopted by members of the first world would be an attempt to obey the teaching of Jesus at this point. Any charges of economic naivety, in that decreased first world demand entails global economic recession, could be countered by the fact that first world kenoticism would lead to increased third world investment and therefore beneficial economic activity.

As we have seen, one of the criticisms (perhaps, in practice, unjustified) of lifestyle movements has been their tendency to cultivate a privatized ethic, which ignores the need for structural change. This leads to the third reason for a kenotic lifestyle, that such a lifestyle gives integrity to political campaigning for such structural changes and brings about a shift in public attitudes which are usually a precursor to change. Syder adduces the example of the abolitionists of the nineteenth century, who would have had no case against slavery had they themselves kept slaves.[87] Elliot sees a significant role for the churches in the creation of an alternative consciousness which can bring about political change. This he sees as the "true task of the church in development"[88] advocating "centres of resistance"—small cells of people "who are discovering the interpenetration of

---

86. See Sider, *Rich Christians, Twentieth Anniversary*, 234–35.
87. Syder, "Theology in Development," 226.
88. Elliot, *Comfortable Compassion*, 117.

prayer and praxis in their own situation"—such as the base communities of Latin America and the Sojourners of the United States.[89] A kenotic theology could well form the basis for what Taylor called a "joyful resistance movement"[90] tackling environmental degradation and the persistence of poverty and inequality.

Kenotic Power as Em-powering

So far we have examined a mainly personal kenotic ethic and spirituality.

How might a kenotic ethic become capable of social and political embodiment? This begs the question of whether such an ethic is primarily for a relatively small number of committed individuals (i.e., a Yoderian disciplined church) or whether it is legitimate to extend such an ethic more widely. Whilst recognizing that the further it is removed from a committed minority grouping, the greater the inevitable dilution of a kenotic ethic, it would be paradoxical to argue that what is valid for one group in society is not applicable in any way to society as a whole. If the divine intention for humanity is some form of a kenotic ethic, modeled by the church, then it is legitimate to outline what a kenotic ethic might mean, and what social embodiment it might take, beyond the boundaries of the church.

I wish to examine this with particular reference to both political and economic power—two sides of the same coin, converging in the running, for example, of the IMF, World Bank, and other international economic organizations. In general terms, a kenotic doctrine of power aims to enable power in others through a degree, at least, of self-giving and self-sacrifice for the common good (the category of power *to*). As the Welsh socialist Aneurin Bevan is said to have remarked, the purpose of getting power is to be able to give it away. The logic of the cross, the "Son of Man came not to be served, but to serve, and to give his life a ransom for many" (Mark 10:45, NRSV) indicates a kenotic empowering through service and a renunciation of the power whose main object is domination. In the globalization debate, this would indicate a shift from coercive, dominating, centralized neo-imperialist power to an em-powering and enabling power, power to build up local strength and responsibility, power to enable others to fulfill their potential.

Murphy and Ellis describe four levels of economic activity, from non-kenotic to kenotic.[91] First, where the aim is totally self serving; sec-

89. Elliot, *Comfortable Compassion*, 180.
90. Taylor, *Enough*, 68.
91. Murphy and Ellis, *Moral Nature*, 122.

ond, where there is sharing in order to create new economic opportunities (where my sacrifice means, in the end, my gain in addition to the gain of others, for example, in microcredit loans); third, where there is pleasure from seeing someone else use a resource, even if it excludes me from certain goods or benefits (an example being the sacrifices made in family life); fourth, sacrifice for others, whose enjoyment will not contribute directly to my own happiness (for example, present sacrifices made for the environmental benefit of future generations).

Given the intrinsically and inevitably selfish character of liberal free market capitalism, which by its very nature is incapable of a kenotic instinct, the role of a kenotically influenced government would be to mould the course of the economic process by means of incentives and regulation towards a sharing and democratizing of economic power in the interests of those lacking that economic power. Here a paradox can clearly be seen: on a personal level, a kenotic spirituality or discipleship cannot be imposed by coercion or law, but can only be freely chosen. On a macro scale, a kenotic national or international ethic involves, where power is shared or devolved, a degree of coercion (or at least, governmental encouragement). This would mark a kenotic decision by society as a whole as to how it wishes its economy to operate. An example might be restrictions on carbon emissions, which would involve coercion in order to achieve a socially and environmentally desirable goal.

Similarly, Murphy and Ellis outline a scale of kenoticism in the political sphere, "a scale of attitudes and behavior, characterizing how political organizations relate to their members and the community, and a similar scale for a government's relations to its own citizens and to other states."[92] Murphy and Ellis suggest on the non-kenotic to kenotic scale: first, a centralized unilateral form of decision making enforced by tyrannical methods, with other groups dominated and brought into line by coercive methods; second, broadly democratic methods of majority decision making, but with the minority forced to accept the decision of the majority, power negotiations being undertaken with outside groups; third, participatory democracy, policy arrived at as general agreement, taking into account minority views, with methods of persuasion, negotiation, and accommodation used in relation to other groups; finally, consensus decision-making within the organization, and "true political kenosis in outside relations, opening oneself to the opposition and using methods that have the potential of transforming enemies into friends." Examples of the latter might be individual leaders such as Gandhi, King, Dolci—but, significantly, not national governments. It is doubtful whether in a large complex society such pure or true kenotic

---

92. Murphy and Ellis, *Moral Nature*, 132.

behavior, in the form of consensus decision making, is at all viable, at least in the functioning of national government.

However, a move towards kenoticism can certainly be made on what might be described as the structural and intentional levels. Structurally, policies such as the devolution of power, subsidiarity (a central component in Catholic social thinking) and federalism tend towards a kenotic power-sharing away from the centre and bring about local political enabling.

And if it is the intention of government not to govern in the interests of a small section of society or a dominating class, but to seek the common good, both for its own citizens and in international affairs, then that government can move in a kenotic direction, where power *to* gradually replaces power *over*. Problems occur when conflicts arise between the supposed good of its own citizens and the good of citizens of another nation. This poses the question whether a government can obey a kenotic international ethic to the (at least short term) detriment of its own citizens, for example in refraining from increased national prosperity in the interests of sharing prosperity with others or in refraining from environmentally damaging policies to protect nations at risk from rising sea levels (although, of course, a healthier environment is, in the long run, in the interests of all). A democratic government, elected on a kenotic manifesto, would be justified in pursuing such a policy. Whether or not such a situation would be possible could depend upon a change of consciousness in a kenotic direction in which a kenotic church might be a significant catalyst. In fact, it is unrealistic to expect the adoption of a kenotic national policy without such a witness from a committed minority, in which a kenotic and cruciform church could play a leading role.

Nonviolence as the Presumption

At the heart of a kenotic politics is the abandonment of expansionist self-aggrandizement, whether territorial, economic, or political. Expressed thus, a kenotic ethic cuts decisively across the grain of human history, a history of the waxing and waning of self-aggrandizing empires. It is important to recognize that a kenotic ethic calls for nothing less than a disposition and a policy diametrically opposed to this historical norm. Moreover, a kenotic ethic radically questions the ingrained custom of seeing one's nation state as the primary good, and the expansion of its wealth and power by whatever possible means as the primary aim of national policy—a tradition exemplified in its extreme by Machiavelli, but practiced throughout human history.

Murphy and Ellis go so far as to declare that the kenotic ethic "entails the proscription of violence"[93] and envisage a decreasing need for the violence of coercion as a kenotic ethic is applied: "A consistent policy of using the least coercive means possible in each social situation will affect the character of the individuals involved such that less coercion will be needed in future resolutions of conflict."[94] They adduce various different forms of coercion, beginning with the most kenotic, and ending with the least: persuasion by argument and, if necessary, by accepting suffering or self-sacrifice; nonviolent coercion, including indirect action through strikes or acts of non-cooperation; social coercion through ostracism or collective pressure; and finally, violent coercion.[95] They comment that "the factor that distinguishes the kenotic category of actions from other non-coercive forms of persuasion is the issue of suffering and of sacrificing oneself for the sake of the other."[96]

It is significant that, as in Yoder, the grounds for such non violence lie not so much in an inner logic of kenoticism as in an imitation of the character of God, who, in the historical cruciform paradigm given by Jesus, refused to resort to violence, and in his providential relationship with humanity does not violently coerce. Concern is therefore shown not merely for self defense, or for the defense of the neighbor, but for the good of the aggressor. There is a willingness to suffer in order to break a cycle of violence or, indeed, to prevent its initiation. A kenotic nonviolence renounces the right not only to attack, but to defend oneself if that self-defense oversteps the possibility of reconciliation. Such an ethic is certainly not passive or negative, in the sense of the mere avoidance of violence. Nor does such an ethic ignore the necessity to initiate and accomplish political change; it does, however, recognize that there are limits to the degree of coercion permissible in bringing about that change.

We return now to the basic difference between Yoderian (and Murphy and Ellis kenoticist) pacifism, and the Niebuhrian realist position, whose stance on the permissibility of violence is shared (reluctantly) by Boff and Sobrino. Given the competing duties argument inherent in any Christian discussion of violence, it is not clear why some degree of force, in terms of police action, should be totally excluded in a kenotic ethic. One can renounce self defense kenotically, but to renounce the defense of others may not be so easily justified. The nature, extent, and violence of the use of force

---

93. Murphy and Ellis, *Moral Nature*, 142.
94. Murphy and Ellis, *Moral Nature*, 151.
95. Murphy and Ellis, *Moral Nature*, 153–54.
96. Murphy and Ellis, *Moral Nature*, 156.

is certainly limited by a kenotic ethic, but force is not necessarily ruled out *per se*. Indeed, as Ellis points out, a kenotic ethic involves putting oneself at risk in the interests of others.[97] If the only way to defend those at risk is by force, it is, paradoxically, a relatively short step to a kenotically self sacrificial just war. It is important to recognize that both approaches rest on valid principles (and principles which can be justified by an appeal to the cross), the Yoderian pacifist imitating the kenotic action of God in Christ, and the liberation theologian being sensitive to the Christian's responsibilities towards the suffering, including their defense.

In practice, this tension is at least partially resolved by a kenotic spirituality which emphasizes the necessity for giving up revenge in favor of the long term benefits of peace, and of prioritizing reconciliation with the enemy over strict justice. Such a peacemaking theology has been developed, for example, by Shriver in *An Ethic for Enemies* and the *Forgiveness and Politics Study Project*, initiated by the British Council of Churches. In practical politics this approach has been most recently exemplified in South Africa, in the forgiveness and magnanimity demonstrated by Mandela, and the workings of the Truth and Justice Commission.

Two Provisos

The social theology of William Temple, which deeply influenced the setting up of the British welfare state, rested on four principles[98]—the freedom and dignity of each person; the social nature of persons; the principle of service; and the principle of sacrifice:

> The declaration of God's love for all in the life, self sacrificial death and resurrection of Jesus Christ will therefore mean that we shall be led to sacrifice ourselves in the service of others. This of course is extremely difficult and can scarcely be achieved directly and consciously. We have to forget ourselves.[99]

Suggate comments that "near the end of his life Temple dropped this fourth principle, not at all because it was unimportant but because he became increasingly aware that it was virtually impossible for large collective bodies, and especially nations, to practice sacrifice."[100] Is a kenotic ethic then really practicable?

97. Ellis, "Kenosis," 123.
98. As identified by Alan Suggate in Suggate, "Temple Tradition," 59–60.
99. Suggate, "Temple Tradition," 61.
100. Suggate, "Temple Tradition," 62.

The Niebuhrian objection to a kenotic politics is not that it is wrong, but that it is disastrously unfeasible, given the sinfulness of humanity, and likely to result in the further suffering of the vulnerable. This is a significant objection, and not simply to be countered by a Gandhian (or Yoderian) belief in prioritizing the purity of means, while leaving the ends to God. A kenotic ethic, according to the Niebuhrian, is certainly suitable for a highly committed minority, whose nonviolent witness would no doubt be valuable in pointing towards an ideal, but is totally unsuitable for the practical politics of governing a state, or establishing international order.

This is partially countered by my first proviso—that a kenotic ethic is not absolute. Brown states that "the attempt to follow Christ should not always take the kenotic path. Sometimes power is the right instrument to use. The difficulty lies in appropriate discernment."[101] There is a mean to be established between Yoderian kenotic risk and Niebuhrian responsibility. For example, a parent will, for the sake of a child's personal, social and moral development, allow a degree of risk, but that allowing of risk is not absolute; it is limited by their responsibility for the prevention of excessive harm. Here also we return to the theme which is basic to this subject—the necessity to construct a social ethic imitative of the character of God. It is essential to remember that the supreme and controlling attribute of God, on which all theology, political and otherwise, must be modeled, is not kenosis, but love. Kenosis may be the overriding way in which power is ideally exercised in love and forms the definitive way in which God interacts lovingly with creation, but kenosis is a concept secondary and subsequent to that of love. It may be argued that love in itself is an insufficient concept, and needs to be fleshed out by a kenotic incarnation which gives historical reality to that love, but love is still prior to any concept depending upon it. It is possible that love may sometimes override kenosis in divine providence, and therefore in a Christian politics.

This leads to my second proviso: kenosis in itself is not enough. It is a means, rather than an end. Jesus' kenotic advice to the rich young ruler was not simply "go, sell what you own, and follow me" (Mark 10:17–25, NRSV), but also "give the money to the poor." The command was not simply for the good of the rich young ruler's soul, in fulfilling an abstract kenotic demand, but for the good of the most vulnerable in the wider community. Likewise, kenosis does not consist of self-emptying or suffering for its own sake (or for the sake of the individual) but for the good of the world. Kenosis could lead to a self-absorbed blind alley unless coupled with a further vision for justice and the desire, actively "to remove the crucified from their crosses."

---

101. Brown, *Divine Humanity*, 264.

Chapter 12

The Cross, the Church, and the Crucified People

How can such a cruciform and kenotic social ethic be embodied in the community of the church? If Bonhoeffer is correct in his assertion, that the church is "Christ existing in community"[1] then political theology, ecclesiology, and Christology are inextricably entwined. Moltmann similarly declares that "every statement about the church will be a statement about Christ. Every statement about Christ will be a statement about the church."[2] What statement does the crucifixion make about the church, and the social ethics bound up with the resulting ecclesiology? In particular, how can a mainstream church in Britain, such as the Church of England or the Methodist Church, live out a political ethic marked by the cross, and act as social witness to the Crucified and the crucified? I am aware that the newer charismatic and evangelical churches are increasingly important in developing such a witness—a fine example of this is Christians against Poverty, which gained much of its impetus from the newer churches. But, although lessons can doubtless be drawn from and for the newer churches, it is the older churches upon which I intend to concentrate. In this concluding chapter I attempt to outline a theoretical framework for the political role of the mainstream British churches, with a briefer consideration of the position of the churches of America and beyond. In this I continue to draw on the insights of our three interlocutors,

1. Bonhoeffer, *Testament*, 65.
2. Moltmann, *Church*, 6.

in particular Yoder's vision of a cruciform minority church, and Boff and Sobrino's emphasis on the crucified people.

A) QUESTIONS OF DEFINITION—THE CRUCIFORM AND THE CRUCIFIED

The Church as the Body of Christ, and Therefore Cruciform

The leading image of the church in the New Testament, at least in the Pauline corpus, is that of the body of Christ. In that phrase, Christology and ecclesiology are combined in such a way that it is impossible to posit an ecclesiology that does not rest on a form of Christology. This insight has been seminal in twentieth-century Protestant political theology, for example in the Barthian christocentric doctrine of the church of the Barmen declaration, and the statement of Albrecht Schonherr, a former student of Bonhoeffer—"The church is not simply the church because it exists, but because it has to stand for the message of Jesus Christ. The church is the church of Jesus Christ only as long as it is the church of *Jesus Christ*."[3] The act of God in Christ constitutes the church—therefore there is a sequence of both correspondence and dependence between God, Christ, and the church. This is expressed by the more Catholic emphasis on the church as the body of Christ and therefore the extension of the incarnation. Gore, who was one of the pioneers in British theology of the kenotic theory and a leader in the movement towards a more left wing Anglo-Catholicism, wrote:

> The church embodies the same principle as the 'Word made flesh', that is, the expression and communication of the spiritual and divine through what is material and human . . . This life is none other than the life of the Incarnate. The Church exists to perpetuate in every age the life of Jesus, the union of manhood with God.[4]

It is, however, not sufficient for our purposes to describe the church as the body of Christ. The mode and meaning of the death of Christ indicate and necessitate the *cruciform* character of the church as his present body. It is highly significant that the christological definition of the church as the body of Christ in Pauline thought is rooted from the beginning in the concept of the suffering, crucified, people of God. At his conversion, Paul is convicted that by persecuting the Christian believers he is persecuting Christ

---

3. Barnett, *Soul*, 269.
4. Gore, *Incarnation*, 219.

himself.⁵ On this account, from the very outset, Paul sees the suffering church as Christ's persecuted body. The church's task is to embody Christ in the contemporary world and to create a continuing Christ-shaped community. Since Jesus' historical interaction with the society and the politics of his day led to his crucifixion, so that same vulnerability to suffering and persecution should inevitably be at least a possibility in the contemporary church's social and political witness. The church's cruciformity is an inescapable consequence of its nature as the body of Christ.

It is no exaggeration to state that the very genuineness of the church is recognized by such cruciformity. This is certainly not the sole or exclusive defining feature of the church; the church is a community of joy, of worship, fellowship, love, and service, with the distinctive marks of holiness, catholicity and apostolicity. The church is also, in the words of Geoffrey Paul, a "glorious mixture of saints and fatheads."⁶ Its historical and sociological reality is therefore bound to fall far short of its ideal nature, being inevitably corrupted by a sinful surrender to whatever temptations endanger it at any particular time. It is, however, significant that in New Testament ecclesiology (most notably in Paul's Corinthian correspondence, but also in Jesus' teaching in the Beatitudes) suffering is prominent as a distinguishing mark of the followers of Jesus. A Pauline *theologia crucis* leads inescapably to an *ecclesia crucis*, and a kenotic Christology to a kenotic ecclesiology. If the church's identity is found elsewhere than in the vulnerability of the crucified Christ, it foregoes its right to be called, in any meaningful way, the body of Christ. The prime contradiction of Christendom lies in the creation of an ecclesiology which obviates the need for vulnerability and therefore severs the link, in its sociological practice as a community, with the historical Jesus. A church which thus pretends to be the body of an uncrucified Jesus is living a lie. The church's essential cruciform vulnerability is well expressed in William Cavanaugh's reflections on the Chilean church under General Pinochet:

> The true body of Christ is wounded, marked by the cross. As the body of Christ, the church participates in the sacrifice of Christ, his bloody confrontation with the powers of this world. The church's discipline then is only the discipline of martyrdom, for Christ's body is only itself in its self-emptying. The church does not exist for its own sake; it is not predicated on its own perpetuation, as is the state. Its discipline is a constant dying to itself for the sake of others.⁷

5. As noted by Robinson, *Body*, 58.
6. Paul, *Pattern*, 135.
7. Cavanaugh, *Torture*, 27.

A note of caution and clarification must be introduced at this point. Certainly, a cruciform church must be a kenotic church. But kenotic does not mean losing identity or distinctiveness, as was perhaps the failing of the secular theologies of the nineteen sixties and nineteen seventies, where the church was to be somehow dissolved into a secular eschatology. Bradshaw describes a "liberation" ecclesiology where

> the church like her master is kenotic, she lives to give herself away, unsung and untriumphant, serving the interests of the kingdom wholly. She is not for herself but for others and the future of God . . . ultimately the church will merge into the greater kingdom of which she is an imperfect anticipation.[8]

There is much of value here. The church can never be an end in itself—its function is always to be looking, and serving, beyond itself, and to risk being broken in the process. But to postulate the necessary dissolution of the church into a secular utopia (uncannily parallel to the supposed withering away of the state under communism) is mistakenly to transpose a heavenly eschatology, where the church militant becomes the church triumphant, into continuing human history where, rather than dissolving away, the church's identity as a church remains crucial. In the same way that the kenotic Jesus gave himself away while retaining his identity, and God remains God while self emptying in Christ, so the kenotic church remains the church as it gives itself away.

A balance must be struck—there is, certainly, a danger in a form of kenoticism in which the church loses both its ecclesiological and christological identity. This danger must be acknowledged—but the history of the church demonstrates, at the very least, that the danger has moved more often in the other direction. Temptations to hierarchical power and the maintenance of a privileged position have too often outweighed the call to humble service. The church might be essential to God's purposes—but an overemphasis on ecclesiastical self-preservation risks losing sight of those purposes. The tension between these two poles plays a key role in Yoder's insistence on the centrality of the church for social ethics. The church must be a kenotic, not imperial church, but must maintain a strong identity—central in one sense, but peripheral in others. As Robinson and Cox insisted in the nineteen sixties, the church's role as servant might mean the necessity of abandoning "the security of its own structured institutions and existing in the structures of the world," since "a true servant does not live in his house

---

8. Bradshaw, *Olive Branch*, 222.

but that of others."⁹ On the other hand, if the church is to be, as the secular theologians rightly insisted, a catalyst for the brotherhood and sisterhood of humanity, there is a limit to which the church can lose its identity without also losing its message.

What, then, are the marks of a truly kenotic church? Most importantly, the church must reflect the kenotic Jesus in its manner of existence. If the church is to correspond in any sense at all to the incarnation, it must, in its own sociological reality, follow the pattern of Jesus as he related to the sociological reality that formed the context of his ministry. This has been a mark of renewal movements throughout the church's history. For example, in the Victorian era R.M. Benson, the founder of the Cowley Fathers, stated that "the essential nature of the church was to follow Christ and to be like him." If the church was to be an extension of the incarnation "it must be weak and conform its manner of life to such features of the Lord's incarnate life as vulnerability, homelessness, and poverty."¹⁰

Such a servant existence might be welcomed as a return to the early days of the church, before its life was corrupted by the worldliness of political power and hierarchy. However, the counter argument immediately arises—the church now is in a vastly different sociological and political setting, with two thousand years of history and tradition behind it. It is simply not possible to return to a supposedly uncorrupted state. The church must serve—but it is unrealistic to exclude the possibility that service might sometimes take place from within power structures as well as from outside. Kenoticism does not, of itself, automatically exclude a chaplaincy to power role.

In essence, the kenotic nature of the church is best expressed when it is thoroughly grounded in the reality of the people it primarily consists of and serves, in a potentially exposed and vulnerable existence. The process of secularization has meant that the church no longer has the protected enclaves it once possessed. This, although unsought, may well be a positive, rather than a negative factor, as was suggested in the nineteen sixties and seventies by Donald McKinnon, when secularization was beginning to accelerate, but when the church held a much more assured position in national life. In his Gore Lecture McKinnon concluded with some implications of kenosis to ecclesiology:

> What is cushioned is likely to be invalid. What encourages us to defend the security allegedly bestowed by our traditions puts our Christian understanding in peril . . . To live as a Christian in the world today is necessarily to live an exposed life; it is to be

9. Bradshaw, *Olive Branch*, 215.
10. Smith, *Benson*, 49.

> stripped of the kind of security that tradition, whether institutional or ecclesiological, easily bestows. We deceive ourselves if we suppose that we do not seek to hide ourselves away from the kind of exposure to which I am referring.[11]

To be conscious of the church's essentially kenotic character can be, at the very least, a protection from a self-regarding and self-serving ecclesiasticism.

Excursus—The Question of Disestablishment

The logic of my argument would seem to lead inexorably towards the disestablishment of the Church of England—and that is indeed a future for which I hope. A kenotic church does not sit well with what remains of the pomp and ceremony that has historically marked the ties between church and state in England.

The gulf is all too obvious between the crucified and powerless poor man of Nazareth and the appurtenances of state power and control. I do not intend to examine this question in any detail. The arguments are well aired, and, in any case, a sense of unreality pervades the whole question. The Church of England is to a great extent already disestablished, *de facto* if not *de iure*, and what remains is an increasingly irrelevant remnant of a previously significant bond. The Church of England is not now, and never was, "the people of England in its religious capacity," to use terms by which William Temple and others defended the establishment. The question is, as Colin Buchanan suggests, whether the Church of England, as a minority denomination, should retain its attenuated links to the state or begin a new existence as an NGO.[12]

It should be stressed that the argument has moved on significantly from the great battles of the past over disestablishment. Now, establishment is defined and defended in terms of service to the nation rather than power, as in the distinction between "high" and "earthed" establishment.[13] Donald MacKinnon, in his nineteen sixties broadside against the establishment, wrote of an

> addiction to the establishment . . . part of a built in inheritance of the Constantinian church whose status is guaranteed and which allows the manner of that guarantee (the exercise by the civil power of a measure of external compulsive authority) to

---

11. Connor, *Kenotic*, 99.
12. Buchanan, *Cut the Connection*.
13. As in Carr, *Say One*, 8.

invade the substance of her life ... a ground for boasting rather than an opportunity for presence; a status ensuring a counterfeit security rather than a way of assuring that there shall be no withdrawal from the actualities of human life.[14]

The force of that criticism has been lessened by the emphasis on establishment as service, as the old Constantinian ties between church and state have weakened. The established church in England is still tied to "The Establishment," but the ties are increasingly strained, nominal, and tenuous, although likely to be temporarily strengthened by events such as the coronation of a new monarch. The vital question is what message or sign does establishment or disestablishment give? What does it actually say and signify? A church still occupying a seat on the top table—or a church for the people with a responsibility of service for all?

Let us examine these arguments more closely; first, that a kenotic church must be a disestablished church. Historically, establishment has been inextricably associated with grand state occasions such as coronations, a prized chaplaincy to power, a privileged place in the life of the nation, ancient bonds with those who hold both political and economic power. Hastings, a sympathetic observer (and one who argued for the continuation of establishment) wrote that establishment "implies exclusivity or, at the very least, privilege and was of course meant so to imply."[15] That being so, to disestablish would indeed be to act kenotically as an act of faith that the church is essentially kenotic and cruciform and that establishment mars its true nature. Establishment inescapably involves a faint and lingering nostalgia for Christendom. Equally insidiously, establishment diminishes the distinctive message and being of the church, by interpreting it as the religious consciousness of the English people, rather than a church defined by revelation. (It is interesting to note the parallel here with the British Labour party—should it be an ideologically socialist party, or the political expression of the labor movement?) It is often suggested that establishment works against exclusivity and towards a truly popular church—but it is possible to be a community church without being established. Popular Catholicism in Liverpool and Welsh Nonconformity, to take two British examples, were far more people's churches than Anglicanism. An exclusive church is not necessarily disestablished, and an inclusive church not necessarily established.

The argument for the disestablishment of a kenotic church is thus political, sociological, and christological. An established church is continually in danger of endorsing political power structures which run counter

14. Connor, *Kenotic*, 94.
15. Hastings, *History*, 49.

to the Christian faith (not, again, that this is a temptation peculiar to an established church, given the concordat of the Roman Catholic and the accommodation of the German Evangelical church with Nazism). Sociological honesty compels an acknowledgment that the Church of England is no longer the church of the nation, and that any continued pretence to this is increasingly ridiculous. Christological consistency points in the same direction—if the church is the body of Christ, it must exhibit the characteristics of Christ—in particular Christ crucified—vulnerability and a location outside of the corridors of power, and serving alongside the crucified people. It is difficult, if not impossible for an established church to fulfill this role as the body of Christ. Theological integrity strongly indicates a severing of the ties of church and state and the rejection of the remnants of erastianism. The history of establishment, too, is a weight around the neck of the Church of England, and an often unacknowledged barrier to evangelism. The historical collusion between the established church and those holding power (for example the support of the oppressive political economy in the nineteenth century) has led to a folk memory of the church being "not for the likes of us," a church of the squirearchy and the prosperous. A kenotic, popular church must overcome this destructive history, and a significant factor in this would be disestablishment.

The kenotic case for disestablishment would, therefore, seem to be overwhelming. The argument, however, is perhaps not as clear cut as it may appear. If establishment is seen as service and service alone, might disestablishment be an abandonment of that service to become a self regarding, if purer, sect? Hastings, in his magisterial survey of twentieth-century British church history, concludes that

> both Christianity and English society would be further weakened without any real compensating advantage . . . [it would be] repudiating too much of its past history . . . [and derogating from its] responsibility for the whole of society.[16]

T.S. Eliot many years ago pointed to the dangers of disestablishing an already established church. What message would this give? That the Church of England was somehow withdrawing within itself? If disestablishment was seen as a self serving, and hence non-kenotic act, the impact both on evangelism and prophecy could be disastrous. The prevalent model for evangelism in the Church of England still rests on a lingering (if fading) attachment to the church through the occasional offices and what might be called the default nature of the church. A fringe of goodwill is built up, and evangelism

---

16. Hastings, *History*, 664.

consists in drawing in the fringe to a greater degree of conscious faith and commitment. It may be that this model for evangelism has to be rethought for a rapidly changing situation, but would the Church of England be wise in seeming to jettison what evangelistic opportunities it has? The church is hanging on (just) in many areas of national life—would disestablishment be the final nail in the coffin of an accelerating secularization? Against this, it can be argued that the fastest growing churches seem to be those churches or denominations which do not have, or do not choose to trade on, the traditional Anglican advantages. But doubts still remain concerning the impact of disestablishment, if it gives that message to the people of England that this is no longer their church, either actually or potentially. Similarly, it is possible that the church's prophetic ministry could be damaged if the Church of England is not seen as some sort of a national moral oracle—but, as argued elsewhere, it is a delusion to imagine that this is still the case, or has been in recent decades.

An interesting argument in favor of the retention of some form of establishment has come from representatives of other faiths. Modood argues from a Muslim perspective that "disestablishing the Church of England may have unexpected consequences: not only would it marginalise the Church of England, it would at the same time sideline all those who choose to take faith seriously whatever their religious allegiance."[17] An example of this may be found in the controversy over Archbishop Rowan Williams' remarks over sharia law, where Williams could be interpreted as using the privileges of establishment in a kenotic manner in order to forward the interests of another religious group. Similarly, from a Jewish perspective, Chief Rabbi Jonathan Sacks observed that disestablishment would symbolize "a significant retreat from the notion that we share any values and beliefs at all. And that would be a path to more, not fewer, tensions."[18] Establishment is represented as providing other religions with a shield against secularization—a worthy aim, but surely an insufficient argument of itself for a continuing establishment. Davie helpfully suggests a "weak establishment," where a "weak" established church uses the advantages of its past historic position to welcome, rather than exclude.[19]

So, *cui bono* disestablishment? If it is to give members of the church a sense of theological purity, while in reality diminishing its evangelistic and prophetic ministry, it would be a foolish and non-kenotic act. If it is to free the church from centuries of alignment with a certain type of political

---

17. Modood, "Establishment," 66.
18. Sacks, *Persistence*, 68.
19. Davie, *Paradox*, 97.

power and from a Constantinian bondage of which the shadow, if not the substance, remains; if it is, in the final analysis, to make the church more Christ-like, in terms of its political and sociological reality paralleling more closely the political and sociological reality of Jesus, then disestablishment would be a cruciform and kenotic act. The answer lies in how the church interprets and expresses its motives for establishment or disestablishment.

The Relationship between the Church and the Crucified People

Moltmann, in his systematic theology of the church, quotes Ignatius of Antioch's *Letter to the Smyrnaeans*: "Wherever Christ is, there is the catholic church."[20] (In the Latin translation the formula *ubi Christus, ibi ecclesia* originally reinforced the authority of bishops!) Christ's presence is located in the fellowship and mission of the institutional, visible church, in the sacraments and the worship. But he is present also in the poor: "This double presence is needed if it is to be the church of the crucified Christ whose appearance it awaits."[21] The crucified Christ is present both in his cruciform body, the church, and in his crucified body, the crucified people. There is a clear problem here for those who, like Yoder, stress the distinctiveness and the firm boundaries, enforced by discipline, of the believers' church, rather than the broader set of crucified people defined by suffering rather than belief. Is bearing the cross restricted to those who bear the name of Christ (defined here as the cruciform people) or can it refer more widely to those who have done to them what was done to Christ (the crucified people)?

I have suggested previously that Christ's solidarity with suffering is not restricted to those who bear the name Christian, and that the concept of the anonymous crucified might usefully express the link between those who consciously and deliberately bear the cross of Christ and those who unwillingly have it thrust upon them. One way of visualizing the relationship is as a Venn diagram consisting of two overlapping circles—one representing the cruciform people and another representing the crucified people. There are areas where there is no real overlap—on the one hand, where taking up the cross is purely voluntary, and on the other, where there is suffering, but no overt consciousness of sharing the crucifixion of Christ. But there is a large and growing area of overlap, especially since, as Jenkins points out, the increasing majority of Christians are from the poorer areas of the world, in the global south, and there is huge population growth in

---

20. Moltmann, *Church*, 129.
21. Moltmann, *Church*, 132.

many predominantly Christian countries (such as Uganda, the Philippines and Brazil).[22] The crucified people will thus not be coterminous with the church, but will approximate to it much more closely than previously. On this overlapping circles model, there is still a distinction between the cruciform and crucified peoples, but also a continuity and an ever increasing overlap. It may, at first sight, seem that there is little of this overlap in the predominantly middle class British mainstream churches, and compared to the gross disparities and deprivation in communities in the global south, British Christianity is, in general, economically prosperous. However, being disproportionately female and elderly (i.e., lower paid or no longer earning) the economic status of British Christians is probably well below the average in comparison with the population of Britain as a whole. Data is scarce, but this possibility is indicated by figures obtained through an exercise in the former Bradford diocese in the early 2000's to establish a fair diocesan share (the quota congregations contribute to the diocesan funds). This exercise, whereby individuals anonymously indicated their income, demonstrated that the earnings of congregational members were well below the national average (unpublished statistics from the former Diocese of Bradford). Perhaps this might reasonably be extrapolated for the country as a whole.

A formal parallel to this model of the continuity and discontinuity between the cruciform and the crucified can perhaps be seen in Aquinas' teaching on the relationship between baptism and martyrdom. Those who have not received baptism but share the suffering of Christ as martyrs (as may have been common in the persecutions in the early church) can be held as having received the sacramental *effect* of baptism in water without actually having received physical baptism.[23] Rahner, whose concept of anonymous Christians has been noted above with reference to the crucified people, suggests that "in martyrdom, what had previously been signified and made present through the sacramental sign of baptism is here simply fulfilled."[24] The martyrdom to which Aquinas refers is, of course, a conscious and willing witness to Christ, and it might be thought unreasonable to extend the sacramental effect of baptism to those individuals who unconsciously (and unwillingly) witness to Christ's sufferings through their own. However, when considering the crucified people as a whole, it is here that the continuing divine suffering is most made manifest and therefore stands as a continuing witness to the cross of Christ. It would be a mistake to draw the lines of demarcation too clearly, especially given the imprecise

22. Jenkins, *Next Christendom*, 104–7.
23. *Summa Theologiae* 3.66.11.
24. Rahner, *Death*, 102–3.

and provisional relationship in Jesus' teaching between the community of his followers and membership of the kingdom of God.

To sum up—Jesus stands within the church, as his body. Jesus stands outside the church, with the same potential message to it as to the religious people of his day, when it allies itself with the crucifiers. And Jesus stands both within and outside the church in the person of the crucified people.

B) UNCHOSEN CRUCIFORMITY

Chosen and Unchosen Cruciformity

In the remainder of this chapter I consider both types of cruciformity, chosen and unchosen. Chosen cruciformity can be seen in two ways—primarily as that of the Christian who seeks to take up the cross, but also as that of the non-Christian whose self-sacrificial service in the cause of "removing the crucified people from their crosses" parallels that of the Christian in performing the same task. This, as discussed above, has been a leading theme in Latin American liberation theology. Likewise, unchosen cruciformity can be interpreted in two ways: first, as has already been described, the unchosen cruciformity of the crucified people; and second, the unchosen cruciformity of the contemporary church in its marginalized situation in Britain and western Europe.

The Unchosen Cruciformity of British Christianity

In the 1930s Studdert Kennedy wrote of Jesus coming to Birmingham and simply being left out in the rain, weeping for Calvary.[25] In the nineteen sixties Archbishop Michael Ramsey made an equally disturbing observation concerning the Church of England: "It may be the will of God that our Church should have its heart broken."[26] Both describe the painful marginalization of the church in Britain, in Studdert Kennedy's case at a time when that marginalization was a shadow of the present situation. Compared to the physical suffering of the church under active persecution, it might seem a gross and tasteless exaggeration to describe this situation by the metaphor of crucifixion, but the unchosen weakness, marginalization, and powerlessness of the present church in Britain can perhaps go some way towards justifying its description as cruciform, at least in contrast to its previous

---

25. Studdert Kennedy, *Unutterable*, 34.
26. Hastings, *History*, 533.

Constantinian status. In her study of the Church of England under Margaret Thatcher, Eliza Filby goes as far as to describe the contemporary church with the phrase "the death of public Anglicanism."[27]

It is difficult to overestimate the revolution in political theology necessitated by this new situation, just as it is difficult to overstate the increasingly vulnerable position of the contemporary British mainstream churches. Most models of Christian political theology presuppose a strong, or at least a relatively strong, church. Even Moltmann, for all his radicalism, seems to presuppose a church numerically and sociologically strong enough to provide a powerful continuing political witness. Boff and Sobrino write against a background of a mass of people whose roots are firmly grounded in Christian practice and devotion. This is clearly no longer the case in Britain. Theology now has to be done "outside the city wall," to aid a weak church in a situation where Christendom is only a memory, or is preserved merely in rituals which have become increasingly empty and meaningless. In the recent symposium on Anglican social theology, this is widely recognized. Malcolm Brown contrasts the present situation with the sympathetic background against which William Temple wrote in the 1930s and early 1940s, and with the influential report *Faith in the City*, produced in 1985, with its "style and methods of a Royal Commission." That approach is no longer possible, since "Today's Church stands on shakier ground, its active membership ageing and diminishing and its place in the national consciousness often pushed to the margins."[28] Later in the symposium a similar conclusion is reached, describing a post-Christendom situation "in which the Church cannot presume that the political authorities or most of the population will share a Christian vision of society."[29] This is putting it mildly—it would be more realistic to presume that they will not share such a view, or, at least, not to any significant degree.

This decoupling from Christendom might indicate a more Yoderian theology—yet even Yoder, with his minority ecclesiology, presupposes a strong and disciplined church able to give a powerful witness. The changes to the future religious geography of Britain caused by both decline in numbers and the dangerously skewed age profile of most congregations, mean that such a witness will inevitably be weakened and diminished unless the very process of numerical decline, by a kind of Darwinian selection, increases the cohesion and discipline of the churches which remain. A more

---

27. Filby, *Mrs. Thatcher*, 311.
28. Brown, "Case for Anglican," 6.
29. Hughes, "After Temple?," 96.

sectarian future seems unavoidable, with the inevitable consequences for social ethics. Yoder writes

> It is one of the widely remarked developments of our century that now one dimension, now another, of the ecclesiastical experience and the ecclesiological vision once called 'sectarian' are now beginning to be espoused by some within majority communions.[30]

Yoder adduces Rahner preparing European Catholics for a diaspora existence, where it will no longer be a presupposition that the church can dominate a culture numerically or politically. Significantly, he also adduces the liberation theologian Juan-Luis Segundo's prophecy that "the church of the future needs to be a ministering, voluntary minority, instead of the mass."[31] In such a sect or diaspora existence, the task of political theology is to formulate a theology of divine power which coheres both with the cruciform God revealed in the scriptures and with the situation of weakness in which the church exists.

The Marginalization of the British Churches

The decline in institutional British Christianity has been well documented. The future of Methodism, statistically and demographically, seems grim. Numerical decline within the Church of England may be bottoming out, but the age profile of many churches is worrying. Here I draw especially upon the work of Grace Davie, a sociologist who is sympathetic to the Church of England but does not shrink from an uncomfortable analysis. In her earlier (1994) survey of British religious belief and practice Davie characterized British religion as "believing without belonging"[32] but even the diffuse penumbra of belief she described seems now to be shrinking. Hastings, in his history of the church in England in the twentieth century, writes that "between 1960 and 1985 the Church of England as a going concern was effectively reduced to not much more than half its previous size."[33] Davie comments twenty one years later, "Since then, erosion has by and large continued, though less abruptly than before."[34] This dramatic collapse

---

30. Yoder, *Priestly Kingdom*, 5.
31. Yoder, *Priestly Kingdom*, 5.
32. Davie, *Religion*, 5.
33. Hastings, *History*, 604.
34. Davie, *Paradox*, 50.

in Christian practice and observance is corroborated by current statistics. Davie notes:

> Statistically there can be little doubt about the trends; they go downward. Electoral roll figures, communicant numbers, baptisms per live births, confirmations, the proportion of marriages taking place in church, and, up to a point, funerals tell a similar story.[35]

The decline in more general Christian allegiance is evident in the difference between the 2001 and 2011 census. Davie describes:

> the decline in 'Christian' self identification, which fell from 72 per cent to 59 per cent . . . almost as striking is the growth in the percentage of people indicating that they have 'no religion'; this rose from 14 per cent to 25 per cent.[36]

This may, to some extent, be explained by a more critical self-identification, but the long term picture is not encouraging—in fact the age profile of Christian belief makes disturbing reading. Davie states that "In the oldest group polled [in the British Social Attitudes survey 1983–2011] one in two people identified as members of the Church of England; among the youngest that figure is one in twenty."[37] Davie concludes that "Growing numbers of British people, notably younger generations, are choosing to live their lives beyond the influence of organised religion."[38] This decline is regionally varied and countered, to some extent, by a rise in numbers joining independent and Pentecostal congregations, especially among immigrant communities, but it is difficult to disagree with Greenwood and Burgess in their statement that in Britain "the churches are facing the death of their current incarnation."[39]

This shrinking of institutional Christianity in Britain, at least in its present form, would seem to be incontestable. Both in terms of numbers and belief, this has serious consequences, not only for pastoral care, worship and evangelism, but also for political theology. If, as Davie argues, "nominal allegiance is by far the most prominent form of religious attachment"[40] then the possibility of the church having anything approaching a traditionally conceived hegemonic role is slim, since it is unlikely that the non (or infrequently) worshipping Christian will have their political beliefs significantly

35. Davie, *Paradox*, 49.
36. Davie, *Paradox*, 43.
37. Davie, *Paradox*, 48.
38. Davie, *Paradox*, 188.
39. Greenwood and Burgess, *Changing Society*, 15.
40. Davie, *Religion*, 49.

influenced by church teaching or formed in a distinctively Christian matrix. Christianity, except in a very diluted and incoherent shape, has very largely ceased to form the recognized foundation of cultural and social norms of society. Similarly, Bruce writes that "the Christian churches have lost their ability to shape popular thinking . . . [popular] images of the supernatural are no longer structured by Christian precepts. They are amorphous and idiosyncratic and have few, if any, behavioural consequences."[41]

There is not merely a disjunction between church and world. Linda Woodhead points to an empirical gap between views of the church hierarchy and laity:

> While statements issued by the Church have been broadly supportive of the existing system of benefits and necessity of the welfare state in something like its present form, poll findings indicate a greater suspicion of welfare claimants and less support for the welfare state.[42]

The question is asked:

> What if the trend towards individualism, utilitarianism and commodification has left a growing number of people without sufficient reference points and vocabulary to comprehend anything the churches might try to say into the social issues of the times? Clearly, if such is the case, the churches in England will need to be very different and to understand their role in the wider society in similarly different terms.[43]

Even worse, there is an increasing sense that traditional religion is not merely irrelevant, but immoral and damaging. It is a huge irony that in the widespread and growing resistance to homophobia in modern Britain many of those outside the churches have claimed, with some justice, to be acting in a more Christian manner than those within.

All this is not to argue that the churches in Britain have little or no social or political significance. Statistics from the 2000s showed that one in six of Britain's adults attended a church service at least once a month.[44] Moreover, the decline in institutional religion has to be set alongside wider sociological patterns, such as the widespread reluctance to join organizations or to take on responsibility for running them (membership of political parties being a quarter of the 1964 level, and ever decreasing, although the

---

41. Bruce, *Religion*, 71.
42. Rowlands, "Fraternal Traditions," 173.
43. Brown, "Anglican Social Theology," 185.
44. Barley, *Churchgoing*, 13.

"Corbyn surge" in membership of the Labour Party may have affected that trend).⁴⁵ Woodhead argues (using a minimalist definition of religious allegiance), that

> Many people write off the Church of England. But despite decline, Anglicans still make up a third of the population of Great Britain . . . And the Anglicans are not merely nominal. They believe, they practice, and—because they still identify as Anglican even though there is no longer any social pressure to do so—they belong.⁴⁶

Recent campaigns over international debt and trade justice might demonstrate some continuing influence on government by the churches—although the era of Temple and Tawney (whose Christian socialism shaped the welfare state for half a century) seems far distant from the contemporary situation. The present "exile" of the churches, to use Whitworth's phrase⁴⁷ sits in an uneasy dialectical relationship with the sometimes persistent remnants of Christendom. On the one hand, there is an increased willingness by government to use religious agencies to plug gaps in the welfare state. Davie points to "a growth rather than a decline in the presence of faith communities in the welfare provision of a modern western democracy, which is becoming more rather than less secular."⁴⁸ On the other hand, we are seeing what van den Heuvel described as the "humiliation of the church"—the fact that, as Medhurst and Moyser put it in their discussion on secularization, "organized expressions of religious life [have been] shunted aside from the mainstream of social, economic, and cultural life, and inherited religious beliefs have seemingly lost immediacy or plausibility for significant sectors of society."⁴⁹ Davie indicated "two relatively long term and seemingly contradictory processes, continuing secularization on the one hand, alongside increasing attention to religion in public life on the other."⁵⁰ There is a continuing tension between secularization and an attempt to co-opt the church into a "big society" framework, where the church is seen as a useful (and, it is hoped, an uncritical) aspect of civil society. What is certain is that the old Christendom, in the sense of the church as the "guardian of authoritative cultural norms" and as a base for shared values and societal unity, is over. Christian ideological hegemony can no longer be assumed; the churches

---

45. See Davie, *Paradox*, 64.
46. Davie, *Paradox*, 52.
47. Whitworth, *Prepare for Exile*.
48. Davie, *Paradox*, 208.
49. Medhurst and Moyser, *Church and Politics*, 18.
50. Davie, *Paradox*, 20.

have been forced (or, perhaps, eased) to the margins of "whole departments of life for which it once assumed the lion's share of responsibility."[51] Davie concludes ". . . the idea of a common narrative (of Christian liturgy or of Christian language and metaphor) becomes more and more tenuous almost by the day."[52] Given this loss of power and influence, this relocation of Christianity from within the gates of power to outside a city wall, a new strategy is required.

Loss and Gain

Such a strategy, taking into account the enforced cruciformity of the church in the sense of its powerlessness and marginalization, may well lead to a more faithful witness to the nature of God and to a political role more consistent with the pattern exemplified by Jesus' ministry and crucifixion. Bonhoeffer wrote of God, paradoxically, in two ways—both at the centre of life (i.e., not an imperialist God but equally not a "God of the gaps" or a *deus ex machina*[53] and pushed to the margins.[54] A cruciform church thus pushed to the margins better represents a crucified God pushed to the margins, since a powerful church can fall into the unconscious idolatry of attempting to represent a non–existent God of misconstrued power. The God revealed in Jesus is a crucified God, and is therefore represented by and witnessed to most accurately by a cruciform church.

The powerlessness of the church, in worldly terms, reveals itself not just in its position in national and civic life, but is also a daily fact of life for its ministers. All the minister has to offer, in worldly terms, seems little in comparison with what other professionals offer, in terms of the resources of medicine, legal knowledge, money from social services, etc. Compared to its past position of power and resource, this is a radically different situation. But it is not necessarily negative, and can direct the church to the source of its true power.

God's providential relationship with the world does not entail control or coercive direction, and for a church to represent God as controlling and powerful in this way is both spiritually and politically disastrous. Exile, or cruciformity, may be the church's best friend.[55] A recurring theme in the Old Testament is how, through the painful process of exile, God made the

51. Medhurst and Moyser, *Church and Politics*, 24.
52. Davie, *Paradox*, 5.
53. Bonhoeffer, *Letters*, 282.
54. Bonhoeffer, *Letters*, 360.
55. As argued in Whitworth, *Exile*, 97.

chosen people fit for purpose by making them totally vulnerable; it is not inconceivable that a similar process could be at work for the good in a cruciform church.

While considering the possible benefits of the weakness of the church, it is necessary to enumerate the potential dangers. First, although exile might be "the church's best friend," is such exile in the best interest of the society in which the church is called to serve as the leaven in the lump? Christendom certainly had its disadvantages, but it could well be argued that it provided at least a check against an even greater barbarism than European history has so far demonstrated.

Second, whereas a weak church may be a more purified body for the furthering of God's purposes, Davie asks "is there a minimum size beyond which an active minority is no longer effective in society?"[56] A church which is too small, fragmented, and marginalized could reach a point where it simply becomes irrelevant and virtually invisible. This points to a current dilemma, especially for the more liberal wing of the church in which intentional growth and overt evangelism have, in the past, tended to be looked upon with some suspicion. Filby suggests that there is "a fundamental dilemma concerning the role of the national church in a secular age: should the Church exist for the benefit of those who are not members of it?"[57] The problem is that the church on earth does not exist as a ministering body except as a community of those who choose to be members of it. To downgrade or neglect questions of evangelism, church growth or discipleship through fear of exclusiveness or erecting barriers incurs the danger of the church becoming a hollowed out institution which is too weak to make any beneficial impact on society.

Third, weakness and a sense of persecution may turn the church's political outlook into that of a selfish and self interested pressure group, concerned above all with self protection. Bartley draws a useful contrast between the persecution of the European churches in the pre-Christendom and post-Christendom eras.[58] Then, persecution involved torture and death; now, "persecution" involves exclusion from the mainstream and complaints over loss of privilege.

Fourth, and most significantly, a minority church is not necessarily a healthy witness of Christ to the majority society, if and when its morality is believed to fall below the standards of that society. Recent child abuse scandals are an obvious example. Increasingly recognized within the church

---

56. Davie, *Religion*, 75.
57. Filby, *Mrs. Thatcher*, 310.
58. Bartley, *Faith and Politics*, 128.

is the effect on wider society of the debate over gay relationships, where a defensive and embattled church can appear to be fighting on the wrong side against what many "in the world" would see as a more gracious morality.

Given these (substantial) reservations, the end of Christendom could provide a liberating opportunity for the British churches, in that the sociological actuality of the church better fits its theological and cruciform essence. It is foolishly unrealistic and theologically naive to envisage a church totally freed from corrupting political and cultural structures so that it somehow achieves its pure being. The church cannot exist in a vacuum, and its life is inevitably shaped in a dialectical interaction with the society in which it is placed. Nevertheless, any study of church history will provide examples of where that corruption has been almost overwhelming, and where attempts have been made (as is the nature of all movements of spiritual renewal) to return to a more purified essence. Yoder writes that the de-constantinianisation of the church need not be feared, but welcomed "as an opportunity for the free church to be the church—to live out its vocation as a visible people in the world bearing witness to the Lordship of Christ over the world."[59] The decline of civil religion where, for example, the Church of England risked becoming merely the amorphous religious expression of the British people, is a liberative opportunity, especially since that religion played a key role in the maintenance of a hierarchically structured society.

One sign of this healthy trend might be the increasing refusal of the British established churches automatically to support the state when it wages war. This questioning stance was negligible during the First World War, developed through the prophetic work of George Bell in the Second, and continued in the *Church and the Bomb* report during the Cold War. More recently we have seen Archbishop Runcie's refusal to turn the Falklands memorial service into a triumphalist celebration, the opposition of the Scottish churches to nuclear weapons, and the misgivings voiced by Archbishop Williams over the Iraq war. Hastings comments that the traditional structures of conservative English religion were put up "not only to fortify religion but to domesticate it . . . to sacralise society this much, secularize religion that much, effectively encapsulate the spirit within a given social and political order."[60] A cruciform, marginalized church is free from that overtly benign, yet inwardly corrupting control. Willingly to accept this enforced cruciformity, to welcome its challenges, and not to look back nostalgically to the old Christendom model, repeatedly to make the choice to take up the cross, is the only realistic option for the British churches,

---

59. Yoder, *Royal Priesthood*, 54.
60. Hastings, *History*, 586.

both pastorally and politically. Moreover, as Atherton suggests, seeking to include the marginalized and empowering them in actively shaping a reinvigorated democratic political economy responsive to basic human needs is "a major way the churches can extricate themselves from their own increasing marginalisation, whether imposed by society or induced by their own self absorption."[61]

The American Difference

If the United States and Britain are two nations divided by a common language, it is equally true that they are divided by a common religion. Both are historically Christian nations, but provide very different contexts for the formulation of a political theology. I will at this point attempt to outline some of these differences. Later in this chapter, I will suggest some ways in which a cruciform theology can be of special relevance to the United States.

The most obvious difference is the comparative numerical strength of American Christianity. Mark Chaves states that "Americans are still more pious than people in any Western country, with the possible exception of Ireland."[62] A national survey in 2008 showed religious service attendance to be 37 percent, and Chaves suggests that the percentages who "know God exists" (64), classify themselves as "born again" (36), and who "pray several times a week" (69), have barely changed since the 1980s.[63] Long term statistics are difficult to access, as the United States census does not include religious identity, but it is clear that in terms of church attendance and allegiance the United States is in a different league compared to Britain. Two minor caveats may be mentioned. First, there is a huge diversity in Christian expression in the United States, as befitting the *e pluribus unum*—there is no single religious narrative, but a variety of Christianities. Historically this differs from the *cuius regio eius religio* tradition in Europe, but in practice the present British religious situation is similarly fragmented, if to a lesser degree. Secondly, as Chaves suggests, "If there is a trend, it is a trend towards less religion."[64] Although Chaves insists that there is no very dramatic resurgence or decline, there is a downward trend in those believing in God (99 percent in the 1950s to 92 percent in 2008).[65] The total number of self identifying Christians dropped from 84 percent in 1990 to 77 percent in

---

61. Suggate, "Temple Tradition," 49.
62. Chaves, *American Religion*, 1.
63. Chaves, *American Religion*, 2.
64. Chaves, *American Religion*, 110.
65. Chaves, *American Religion*, 111.

2001, with a similar rise in those, especially younger people, who do not identify with religion at all (8 percent in 1990 to 14 percent in 2001). These figures indicate a numerical strength far in excess of anything in Britain or western Europe, with the concomitant temptations towards the exercise of direct political power. However, they are possible signs that the differences may slowly be decreasing.

> The second difference is the comparative strength in the United States of conservative religion. In the British context I include under the category of mainstream churches such as the Church of England, the Roman Catholic Church, the Church of Scotland, and the Methodist Church. Of their equivalents in the United States the Roman Catholic Church can certainly be described as mainstream, but the Episcopal Church, the Presbyterian Church, and the Methodist Church (all comparatively theologically liberal) have been overtaken in numerical terms by churches espousing a more conservative theology and political outlook. The Methodists, Episcopalians, Presbyterians, and Church of Christ were once numerically dominant within Protestantism, but their influence reached its zenith in the heyday of the social gospel, and has been in decline since. Chaves states that Since 1972 the percentage of Americans affiliated with theologically more liberal, mainline denominations has steadily declined while the percentage affiliated with more conservative, evangelical denominations increased slightly until the early 1990s and has remained stable since then. By 2008 twice as many people claimed affiliation with conservative denominations as with theologically more liberal ones—28 to 14 percent.[66]

Phillips claims that "The mainline Protestant denominations declined, partly by taking cultural and political positions on war, society and civil disobedience that were too liberal for their congregations."[67] What has this to say about Yoder's call for nonconformity? Perhaps such a call reached congregational leaders more effectively than it reached congregations themselves. Phillips comments: "Evangelical, fundamentalist and Pentecostal denominations began the new millennium verging on juggernaut status . . . the old mainline churches have been culturally and institutionally displaced by a new plurality; yesterday's supposed fringes are taking over American Protestantism's main square."[68] It is interesting that a certain conservative ecumenism in political and social ethics (notably on the issues of abortion

66. Chaves, *American Religion*, 87.
67. Phillips, *Theocracy*, 117.
68. Phillips, *Theocracy*, 101.

and gay rights) has grown between groups which, theologically, are far apart—between Pentecostalists and Calvinists, and even more dramatically, between mainstream Christians and the Church of the Latter Day Saints.[69] Mainstream Christianity in Britain can be characterized by an oscillation between a mild liberalism and mild conservatism in theology and political outlook—the contrast between this and the strength of American religious conservatism is striking. In Britain, the revivalist tradition was an important factor in the past—the Methodist, Welsh, and Ulster revivals were significant religious and social movements. The American revivalist tradition of the Great Awakenings, with their emphasis on conversion and moral campaigns has a greater contemporary power, and American conservative Christianity breathes the spirit of even earlier movements, such as the Puritans and Scots Covenanters. The eagerness of American Christianity to organize itself for effective moral campaigns, often with a socially conservative agenda sets it apart from mainstream British Christianity.

One consequence of this is what has been called the theologization of American politics.[70] In contrast to the notorious comment by Alistair Campbell on Tony Blair, "We don't do God," Tom DeLay, as Republican house majority leader, explicitly stated his political mission in religious terms, "God is using me all the time, everywhere, to stand up for a biblical world view in everything I do and everywhere I am. He is training me."[71] Similarly, Phillips, in his significantly entitled *American Theocracy* quotes Arthur Schlesinger describing George W. Bush as "the most aggressively religious president in American history . . . He is endeavoring to remold the American presidency, hitherto a secular office, into a 'faith based' presidency."[72] Phillips defines theocracy as "a polity where the leader is believed to speak for God or believes himself to speak for God."[73] Lacorne, a French scholar of political science, contrasts American secularism, which officially disallows religious establishment but in practice allows a huge amount of religious influence in political life, with French laicite, which seeks to keep religion and politics very much at arms length. He traces this to two predominant narratives in early American history—those of the secular enlightenment and the neo-puritans, and concludes: "Seen from France, evangelical Protestantism appeared to have successfully invaded the American public sphere, at the same time that old Europe, swept along

69. As suggested by Beal, *Religion*, 89.
70. Phillips, *Theocracy*, 237.
71. Lacorne, *Religion*, 138.
72. Phillips, *Theocracy*, xxxiv.
73. Phillips, *Theocracy*, xxxvii.

by powerful secularizing forces, was every day moving further away from its Christian roots."[74] In the task of formulating a political theology, the contextual difference between the United States and Europe should not be minimized or, for that matter, exaggerated. Barack Obama's "faith friendly secularism" is not far removed from the recent attempts of British governments to co-opt the churches into such programs as the "big society."

The American difference manifests itself most of all in the alignment of conservative religion in the United States with one party, the Republican. Again, the difference should not be exaggerated. In Germany, for example, the Social Democrats were traditionally secular, and the Christian Democrats greatly influenced by Catholic social theology. In Britain, the Church of England was dubbed the Conservative party at prayer, although this tag seems now to belong to a past age. In the United States, in contrast, the alignment is very real. Beal, in 2008, stated that 58 percent of Evangelicals are declared Republicans, with only 12 percent Democrats,[75] and Phillips comments that "The 2000 and 2004 presidential elections marked the transformation of the GOP into the first religious party in US history."[76] Perhaps this is an exaggeration, but conservative movements such as the Moral Majority and Christian Coalition were almost exclusively aligned with the Republicans. Chaves summarizes this tendency:

> Actively religious Americans are more politically and socially conservative than less religious Americans. Active churchgoers support more restrictions on legal abortion, endorse more traditional gender roles, and vote Republican more often than less religious people. These differences have existed since the 1970s, but some of them have increased since then, creating a tighter link between religiosity and some kinds of political and social conservatism.[77]

This tendency, moreover, is made still more significant by the increasing predominance of conservative religion in the United States, as suggested above, and the relative decline of the more religiously and socially liberal churches.

The consequences of this for a leftward leaning Yoderian or liberationist theology are disturbing. The church's distinctive witness seems increasingly to be aligned with political and social conservatism. Rather than

---

74. Lacorne, *Religion*, 124.
75. Beal, *Religion*, 38.
76. Phillips, *Theocracy*, x.
77. Chaves, *American Religion*, 94.

challenging conservative forces within society, religion (as it has for centuries within Christendom) seems increasingly to be reinforcing them.

To sum up: Britain and the United States are hugely different in the relationship of religion to politics. In some areas such as increased secularization, perhaps, there may be some convergence, but the differences are at present more striking. What would seem to be the preserve of a conservative minority in Britain is much more the norm in the United States.

C) CHOSEN CRUCIFORMITY

A Corporate Taking up of the Cross

Taking up the cross is not primarily for the individual, but for the community of which the individual is a member, as part of a communal, corporate commitment in a cruciform church. Before discussing what form this taking up of the cross could take, it might be useful again to sum up what is meant by a cruciform church. A cruciform church is one which has a minority status—it is not the state church of the majority; it operates in a context of political weakness; it does not have, or aspire to, Constantinian power; it exists as an exposed nerve to suffering; it consists of, or is in close touch with, the crucified people; and it seeks to witness to the crucified Christ (and his current embodiment) by word and action.

Such a church attempts to shape its political ethic by Jesus' incarnational social and political exemplarity (the historic political actions of Christ which led to the cross) and seeks a cruciform imitation of the character of a crucified God in the context of a crucified world.

This is the ideal, but this ideal must be worked out in the reality of a mixed and sinful body of people whose commitment to that ideal is variable and often unfocussed. Yoder's vision of a highly disciplined and tight knit church is, in the Anglican context, neither theologically desirable nor sociologically possible (although contraction, especially if it involves a diminution of a penumbra of occasional worshippers, will inevitably make church membership more closely defined). One of the strengths of the Church of England has been its inclusivity, where the boundary lines between church and kingdom of God have not been too tightly drawn, and it would be dangerous to abandon that balance in favor of a more disciplined, but more rigidly exclusive body.

Church Action on Poverty, a national ecumenical Christian social justice charity committed to tackling poverty in the UK, identifies five aspects of what it might mean for a British church to be a church of the poor:

- It is interested in *building the kingdom*, not growing the church.
- It *listens attentively* to voices from the margins and works to be *visibly present* to the community around it.
- It *expects to be challenged and changed* by its neighbours, especially by people on the margins.
- It puts an emphasis on *sharing food and hospitality*.
- It is *hungry and thirsty for justice*.[78]

I hope to have demonstrated that building the kingdom and growing the church are not in competition, and that a church which neglects growth might find itself simply unable to build the kingdom. That apart, the above statement indicates an inspiring vision for a local church seeking to exercise a cruciform ministry.

I describe chosen cruciformity, the corporate taking up of the cross, using two images: first, the Isaianic image of the suffering servant; second, the metaphor of a woman in labor. Together these may convey the sometimes painful but potentially creative political witness which is the task of a cruciform church.

The Suffering Servant—Solidarity

The servant songs of Isaiah 53 describe a figure (interpreters differ on the figure's historical, corporate, or symbolic status) which combines the roles of solidarity, prophecy, and martyrdom. The Servant stands in solidarity with the people of Israel (to such an extent that the servant figure has, in some interpretations, been thought to represent the exiled community); speaks a message from God to the contemporary society from a situation of affinity and solidarity; and undergoes suffering, death, and eventual vindication. New Testament scholarship is divided as to how deeply the suffering servant figure affected Christ's self understanding or the early church's interpretation of him (see the discussion in *Jesus and the Suffering Servant* by Bellinger and Farmer) but it is not difficult to see the parallels between Christ and the servant. No less clear are the parallels with Christ's body, the cruciform church.

Just as the Suffering Servant displays solidarity through his location with the exiled people of Israel, the social and political location of the cruciform church is essential to its identity. In the Christendom model, the church's location has been alongside and in a collegial relationship with

78. "Church of the Poor," paras. 6–10. Italics original.

those in power. A cruciform church, by contrast, is located with the crucified rather than the crucifiers, in solidarity with those who suffer under power rather than those who exercise it. This can be seen as a variant on Bonhoeffer's call for Christians to "share in God's sufferings at the hands of a godless world."[79] The Christendom temptation is to operate within the structures of power as insiders exercising, at best, an ameliorating chaplaincy to power, at worst, an inquisitorial theocracy. The cruciform role is to stand outside the structures of power, or if, as may sometimes be necessary through historical circumstances, the Christian or the church is positioned within those structures, still to take a guiding perspective from those situated on the outside. This political, social and psychological location is crucial to the political witness of a cruciform church, and involves a deep attentiveness to suffering. This attentiveness can, undoubtedly, be attained by those located within the structures of power, but the temptation to become insulated by those structures and to treat power as an end in itself can often be fatal to such attentiveness. As has been previously mentioned, because of such solidarity Christian political involvement is on the basis of affinity (salvation from inside) rather than alterity (salvation from a distance). Moreover, solidarity with the suffering means that political neutrality is not possible; the Christian is called to take sides and not to maintain a bland even handedness. The church in England, with its tradition of moderation, and with its foot in the camps both of governors and governed has not always taken this to heart. The assumption that every mainstream ideology is basically well meaning and well intentioned can be dangerously short sighted. In the 1920s, at the time of the bitter dispute between miners and mine owners, William Temple refused to back the miners when the mine owners refused mediation, seeing the role of the church as finding consensus and bringing reconciliation. Adrian Hastings wisely observes:

> [What if] reconciliation is impossible because one set of fellows is sitting firmly on the backs of the other set? Until they are got off, talk of reconciliation must be empty. In some sense liberation has to come first, but to help with that can mean an at least temporary commitment to one side and to particular policies, not just general principles. If the churchmen were not willing to go so far because it was not their own job they could better have stayed out of the whole thing.[80]

All this is not naively to minimize the problems of moral decision making in the complexities of modern economic and political systems. Rather, it

79. Bonhoeffer, *Letters*, 361.
80. Hastings, *History*, 191.

is first to determine the rightness or otherwise of economic decisions by their short and long term effects on the most vulnerable, as experienced from their perspective, and second to exercise a prophetic and critical discernment based on that perspective. For the British churches, this can work in two interrelated ways. First, with the rolling back of the welfare state, overturning a political consensus (inspired by such Christian socialists as Temple and Tawney) which has lasted since at least 1945, the churches have an increasing role to play in pointing to and standing alongside Britain's crucified people. Localism is an ideal much lauded, and the fact that the church is present with (and often consists of) the poor and marginalized, in ways in which other organizations are not, facilitates solidarity and adds force to its critique. It is significant that possibly the most effective instance of post war Anglican intervention into politics, *Faith in the City*, gained its moral authority largely because of the presence of the church among the powerless in the inner city and urban estate parishes, and not because of the church's association with the powerful. Second, the churches in Britain, with their strong links to sister churches in the global south, and through their missionary societies and relief organizations, are in a better position to realize this solidarity with the poor abroad than any other institution within British society. This intra-national and international solidarity does not occur naturally, automatically, or easily, but it forms the basis for any meaningful British political theology.

The Suffering Servant—Prophecy and Martyrdom

The Suffering Servant spoke God's message as a prophet, from a location in solidarity with the people of Israel. Similarly, the role of a cruciform church is to exercise a prophetic ministry based on such solidarity. An important aspect of this role is to "unmask the interiorities"[81] of social and political systems by demonstrating their outward effects on the most vulnerable. These interiorities are brought to light in two ways: first, by having their effects not only made visible but also widely publicized by the church as it stands in solidarity and continuity with the vulnerable; and second, by being analyzed in the light of the gospel of a crucified and vulnerable God. This deeper prophetic role stands alongside the church's ongoing dialogue with government and secular authority.

Perhaps one task for a cruciform church can be the development of what might be called a subversive language, based on a "dangerous memory of suffering" (to use Metz's phrase), bringing the often forgotten history of

---

81. Nancey Murphy's phrase in Gingerich and Grimsrud, *Transforming*, 37.

the suffering into sharper focus by associating it with that of Jesus Christ. The conscious sharing of that suffering, both historic and contemporary, forms part of the church's witness, and provides a form of language to describe what the rest of society finds difficult to express. The church, as a language community that speaks not a totally separate language but one with its own distinctive history, marks, and emphases, is well placed to articulate such a witness. Bretherton summarizes Hauerwas' vision for the church as being "to open new horizons, provide new languages of description and embody alternative practices."[82]

In addition to the role of prophet in solidarity with the people, the Suffering Servant fulfilled this martyr role in witnessing to the truth of God through suffering. The location of a cruciform church, alongside and attentive to the suffering, brings its own vulnerability. A cruciform church witnesses to Jesus, both the risen Christ present in and among the faithful and the crucified presence of Christ in and among those who suffer. This witness can be from a position of safety or of minor discomfort, but can also take the form of suffering when that witness is rejected by an unbelieving or oppressive society. As we have previously seen, the concept of martyrdom can usefully be extended from the traditional form of suffering on account of explicit faith in Jesus to a wider form of suffering as a result of witnessing on behalf of the present crucified people and taking up Jesus' historic project of the kingdom of God. These related concepts of martyrdom, both "Christian" and "Jesuanic," have played, as we have seen, an increasing role in Latin American liberation theology.[83]

The task facing churches in Britain may well be to develop the wisdom to discern the difference between martyrdom for the right reasons (a willingness, if necessary, to go against the grain of society's expectations for the sake of others, and to pay the penalty for such a stance) and martyrdom for the wrong reasons (for example standing up for the perceived interests of an embattled and minority church or espousing a social conservatism whose Christian justification is contested). It is a tragedy, for example, that some sections of the mainline British churches see themselves as fulfilling a martyr role in their opposition to equal marriage, when a large proportion of Christians within those same churches regard equal marriage as consonant with the gospel and, indeed, embodying gospel values. Perhaps this illustrates, at the very least, the difficulties of presupposing a Yoderian church where the social witness is necessarily united and distinctive in all aspects of faith and morality.

82. Bretherton, *Christianity*, 54.
83. For example Okura et al., *Rethinking Martyrdom*.

The Cruciform Church as a Woman in Labor—An Agent of Change

The image of a woman in labor can convey the sometimes painful process of new creation which belongs to the political role of the cruciform church. Cruciform weakness does not mean withdrawal or ineffectiveness. The church may have relinquished the Christendom model of responsibility for society, but, as Yoder stresses[84] his critique of the Christendom view of social ethics does not posit the two alternatives, responsibility or withdrawal. A post-Christendom church continues to have, as a prime element of its mission, a responsible involvement in society, even if that responsibility is exercised from below rather than from above. Yoder writes of the original disciples:

> There are thus about the community of disciples those sociological traits most characteristic of those who set about to change society: a visible structured fellowship . . . a clearly defined lifestyle distinct from that of the crowd . . . The distinctness is not a cultic or ritual separation, but rather a nonconformed quality of (secular) involvement in the life of the world.[85]

Similarly, he writes that "Only a continuing community dedicated to a deviant value system can change the world."[86] The church's political responsibility is not diminished by its marginalization or by its primary focus on being the church, since an integral part of being the church is a love which encompasses the whole of society and which therefore necessitates political involvement. This political involvement, marked by (to use Yoder's terms) nonconformity and deviance from oppressive value systems, risks conflict and therefore the possibility of the cross—a possibility which forms the dramatic background to much of the writing of the liberation theologians.

A primary role of the church is to give birth, or at least to act as a catalyst, to new liberative human possibilities. The politically creative role of the church is a necessary adjunct to a cruciform doctrine of power and the kenotic ethic which flows from it, as discussed in the previous chapter. A kenotic ethic, and the creation of a community increasingly marked by such an ethic, cannot be imposed by law or coercion, but can only be a voluntary choice—and in a democracy the critical mass of voluntary choices shapes the policy of the government. The role of the church is, then, that of a persuasive exemplar, giving birth to increasingly kenotic possibilities.

---

84. Yoder, *Royal Priesthood*, 63.
85. Yoder, *Politics*, 39.
86. Yoder, *Nevertheless*, 136.

Hinze writes, "Since a group has no real capacity for reflective or moral self-transcendence, leaders never have warrant to agapaically sacrifice the multiple interests of their own constituencies."[87] One of the main political roles of a cruciform church is to embody and enhance such moral self-transcendence, in order that society may move in a kenotic direction. To use Gramscian terms, it is the task of such a church to promote a gradual cruciform and kenotic counter-hegemony, neither by coercion (which is not possible, even if it were desirable) nor by sheer weight of numbers, but by (potentially suffering) servant witness. The birth of such a gentle counter-hegemony may not be without pain or sacrifice, since it will cut across the grain of society's expectations or challenge vested interests, which will fight back. The relevance of this political role is growing, especially in western Europe. If MacIntyre is correct to assert in *After Virtue* that the unifying metanarratives of society have all but collapsed, and that new and smaller scale moral communities are needed,[88] the church, even if a small minority, can have a significant part to play in forwarding its own kenotic and countercultural metanarrative by its prophetic being and actions. To use Richard Niebuhr's *Christ and Culture* categories, Christ may best be seen in creative and painful tension with culture, the cross symbolizing the labor pains of that process. Moreover, it seems that (at least in Britain) the prevalent ideology favors a shrinkage of the state as a provider of social goods. This will result in an increased need for voluntary organizations such as churches to fill the gap. As Filby points out, "Religious organizations are invited to make a contribution to civil society but it is on condition that they operate within the rules of tolerance and pluralism."[89] A kenotic political spirituality is perhaps more able to negotiate such a territory than a church which hankers after a revived Christendom.

The Cruciform Church as a Woman in Labor—A Sign of Hope

The birth of a child is a sign of hope for the future, of new possibilities coming into being. If, according to the Yoderian analysis, ecclesiology is the starting point for social ethics, the pattern of existence of the church is both a model for the present and a foretaste of the ultimate divine intention for the world. God's intention for human social interaction is prefigured in the church, which is a sign both of present witness and future hope. This statement must, of course, be set uncomfortably alongside the continuing

87. Hinze, *Comprehending*, 93.
88. MacIntyre, *After Virtue*, 263.
89. Filby, *Mrs. Thatcher*, 330.

imperfection and sinfulness of the existing church, exemplified painfully by Yoder's own actions, but the ideal cannot be set aside. A cruciform church is inextricably caught in tension between the pessimism of the cross and the hope of the resurrection. The cross indicates an almost Hobbesian pessimism about politics and liberative human possibilities in general, given the sinful nature of human power structures illustrated so dramatically, and so dreadfully, by the crucifixion of Jesus. There is no necessary progress in history; that is a nineteenth-century liberal or Marxist concept, and not Christian, at least in terms of relatively short term progress on earth. In a Christian reading of history, resurrection will be followed by further crucifixion, and so on. The aims of the church in the light of this necessary but realistic pessimism are limited, if essential: to take the crucified from their crosses, but with the expectation that they or others may probably be put back there again. The political task of the church is to stand again and again alongside the vulnerable, pointing to the divine sympathy exemplified in the cross and the hope offered by the resurrection. This resurrection hope means that the present situation of injustice and suffering does not always have to continue—there is no fatalistic necessity against which it is impossible and pointless to struggle—but the force of sin shown by the crucifixion means that such hope cannot be an easy optimism in an almost automatic movement of history. This is certainly not a counsel for despair, as might be represented by conservatives in their pessimism over the possibilities of human progress. Rather it is a recognition that earthly hope is not for a decisive once-and-for-all breakthrough to a new utopia, but for the continuing possibility of the removal of the crucified from their crosses and for the promise of divine power in accomplishing that task. The kingdom of God does not advance inexorably; the persistence of the crucified people throughout history decisively denies that illusion.

Hope, then, this side of heaven, is limited and temporary but nonetheless real. The cruciform church is to be a sign of that hope, a model and bearer of renewed human possibilities. Hope, shaped by the cross and resurrection, is not facile or unrealistic, but based on the unchanging divine purposes and character which it is the church's task to live out and to which the church bears witness. There is no automatic, easy causality in moving history since history cannot be moved except by slow and painful steps. Rather, a politics informed by the political actions of Jesus proposes a cruciform causality radically different from the violence of the world. The church is thus both a sign of that hope and a participant in making that hope a reality. The church, in its life of worship, fellowship, love, and evangelism, becomes a context where these present practices and future possibilities are explored, clarified, and shared, where an ethic of reliance upon the character of God and the promised Holy Spirit can be lived out. Such a church may not have the numbers or strength coercively to bring about change, as was attempted by the Christendom project (which failed both theologically and historically), but can be the matrix of wider transformation through its witness and example, and through its cruciform contradictions of the powers of the world. Sharon Welch entitles her feminist theology of liberation "Communities of Resistance and Solidarity."[90] This could usefully be extended to the church as a community of solidarity with the crucified people, of resistance to the crucifiers (risking crucifixion in the process), and of hope in the resurrection of the crucified.

D) CONCLUSION

The Church under the Roman Empire and Today

It is clear that the church in Europe appears to be moving into a post-Christendom situation. The option of returning to a pre-Christendom situation is, of course, impossible, as the centuries of Christendom have, for good or ill, left their mark. But Christendom is dead. At best, the churches cannot presume the co-operation of governments which share Christian presuppositions, and, at worst, find themselves at odds with the basic tenets of those governments. Parallels with the early church, powerless under an imperial system, become ever more apparent. The church's task, as a minority organization, is to explore and live out different ways of expressing a redeemed humanity against the backdrop of empire. Warren Carter points to five strategies adopted by the pre-Constantinian church:

1. The empire is of the devil
2. Rome's world is under judgment
3. In the meantime—acts of transformation
4. In the meantime—alternative communities
5. Submitting to, praying for, and honoring the empire[91]

   A social ethic for today for a similarly minority church majors on 3 and 4, while modifying the absolute pessimism of 1, remembering the realities of 2, and practicing 5 wherever possible, without compromising the gospel.

---

90. Welch, *Communities*.
91. Carter, *Roman Empire*, 16–17.

The Future of a Cruciform Church in Britain

Part of my aim in sketching a political role for a cruciform church arises from my recent role as a long serving Anglican Vicar and Methodist Minister in two villages on the fringe of the Bradford/Leeds conurbation. Here, the marginalization of the church is evident, even in communities where there is much goodwill. Given the age profiles of the congregations, it is probable that the religious geography of these communities, and of much of the surrounding area, will be significantly different in a few years time. The church will still be present, in the form of groups of committed Christians, living and witnessing in the local community, but the future of the church as a powerful institution, with an assured and integral place in society, would seem to be precarious. This undeniable institutional decline is uncomfortable both for those in positions of leadership who have to manage a shrinking and therefore pressurized organization, and also for those at the grass roots who feel marginalized and powerless in the face of sociological factors beyond their control. However, grim pessimism is a temptation to be avoided by those who believe in a God of resurrection hope. In 1832, the famously pessimistic assessment of the Church of England given by Thomas Arnold "The church, as it now stands, no human power can save"[92] was overtaken by the subsequent Anglican revival. The church will continue, but in a different form. Jenkins uses an analogy from astronomy in describing the smaller, but more focused bodies which will probably constitute the future for the churches in Europe: "When a star collapses, it becomes a white dwarf—smaller in size than it once was, but burning much more intensely. Across Europe, white dwarf faith communities are growing within the remnants of the old mass church."[93] For such a church, the vision of a new, cruciform, way of doing politics, eschewing control (which is impossible anyway) and concentrating on bearing a consistent and faithful witness to Christ crucified and risen is a useful pointer to a realistic political role. This is not to minimize the dangers inherent in institutional decline and marginalization. A critical choice faces the church: to embrace a cruciform redefinition of power and witness, or through panic, confusion or resigned pessimism to retreat into a defensive and fearful siege mentality. How the church in Britain deals with its marginalization will be crucial for its internal nature and external political role.

---

92. Edwards, *Leaders*, 30.
93. Jenkins, "Europe's Christian Comeback," para. 2.

Lessons for the Worldwide Church

If the church in Britain and Europe is moving away from a Constantinian role vis-à-vis political power, that is certainly not true for the church worldwide. Jenkins draws attention to the ways in which the churches of the global south are increasing in terms of numbers, spiritual dynamism and political power and influence.[94] This is a time both of great opportunities and potential pitfalls. In particular, Jenkins points to an increasing tendency for communities or nations to define themselves by their religion, especially on the dangerous fault line between Christianity and Islam in Africa, Indonesia, and the Philippines.[95] The sad consequences of such identification of Christianity with nationalism are amply demonstrated by a reading of European history. At this critical juncture, it would be particularly tragic if churches of the global south repeated the mistakes of the European churches and attempted a Christendom-type social theology. It is to be hoped that the churches of the global south, as they emerge into a new era of independence, confidence and strength, can resist the temptation to use their new found power in a way which has been shown in Europe, by hard experience, to be both a political dead end and a spiritual hazard. The adoption of a cruciform doctrine of power would be a useful corrective to this danger.

Cruciformity and the American Churches

A numerically strong church brings with it a temptation to a Constantinian role, and at present, in contrast to the European churches, the American churches are remarkably strong, at least in terms of numbers. How can a cruciform political theology speak to their situation? The starting point must be that the United States has in its own history reminders of the crucified people. The dispossession and genocide of Native Americans and the historical enslavement and present disadvantage of African Americans are facts with which contemporary American Christianity has still to come to terms. This, of course, is not exclusive to the United States—Australia had its genocide of the Aboriginal inhabitants, Germany its *shoah*, and Britain a shameful record of the slave trade and imperial exploitation.

What sets the United States apart in the contemporary world, and the point at which a cruciform political theology speaks perhaps most strongly, is the tension within American Christianity between, on the one hand, a privatization and official non-establishment of religion and, on the other,

---

94. Jenkins, *Next Christendom*, chapter 5.
95. Jenkins, *Next Christendom*, chapter 8.

a sense of America's special divine calling. Jefferson's wall of separation between church and state, although porous and often challenged (in the form, for example of current conservative crusades over issues such as prayer in schools), has been a hallmark of American Christianity since colonial days. Yet alongside this religious privatization there has been an underlying notion among some sections of American Christianity that America is a specially chosen people, a "city on a hill," with a national calling to a particular, favored and even redemptive role under God's providence—what Phillips describes as "a theological version of manifest destiny."[96] This idea, extrapolated from the biblical covenant with Israel, of a contemporary nation having a special role, as a force to do God's will, is highly dangerous (especially when that nation is a superpower) and can lead to a pernicious lack of self awareness of national sin. Add to that an apocalyptic theology which sees events in the Middle East as evidence of the end times, and warnings against Christians trying to move history in the right direction gain even more relevance. In the light of a cruciform theology, the danger of nation-as-church can be seen in two ways. From the liberationist perspective, it is the crucified people, and not the nation, that has a special role in God's purposes. From the Yoderian perspective, it is the church, the community of belief, and not the nation, that has a special role in God's purposes. The temptations to a misuse of power within some forms of American Christianity can best be countered by a more cruciform doctrine of power. At the very least, it might help the churches to tread the fine line between witnessing and party political campaigning, and to distinguish between the quest for justice and national self-righteousness.

The Political Role of a Cruciform Church

The political role of the church can be described in general terms as the shaping, by its words and actions, of a liberative vision of what it is to be human, in imitation of the character and workings of God as seen through the lens of Jesus Christ. In particular, the church can witness to a redefinition of power and its uses, by exercising a two-fold critique. First, the critique must be inward, recognizing that a marginalized church is not necessarily less likely to misuse power than a dominant church, but may do so in very different ways. A dominant church will try to exercise power over society as a whole; a marginalized church may seek to exercise a crude power internally, as it pulls up drawbridges against the world. Second, the critique must also be outward, challenging a totalitarian use of power both in society as a

---

96. Phillips, *American Theocracy*, 207.

whole and in religion in particular. A totalitarian exercise of religious power is an increasing phenomenon worldwide, and one of the tasks of a cruciform church is gently to counter such totalitarianism. This critique should not merely be verbal, but demonstrated by living out an alternative model of religion and power.

If Yoder can be said to provide the means to that end, Boff and Sobrino provide the content—the criteria by which a Christian politics can be judged—through their emphasis on the crucified people. Again, in very general terms, what differentiates a Christian politics from others is its interpretation of suffering. The dominant political doctrines of the twentieth century had at their heart a willingness to sacrifice huge numbers of human beings for the sake of the (supposed) greater good of other human beings, either in the present or the future. Nazism was prepared ruthlessly to eliminate what it saw as a Jewish and Slavic threat in order to create a better world for the Aryan *ubermensch*. Communism was willing to sacrifice millions of those who were seen as barriers to the revolution on the altar of industrialization and political repression in order to achieve utopia for the workers. The present dominating ideology, neo-liberal capitalism, has of course not indulged in such calculated slaughter and can point to significant economic success, at least where its rough edges are softened by the safeguards of social legislation and protection. But its controlling anthropology, of regarding human beings as mere units of production and consumption, has dangerously dehumanizing tendencies in its willingness to commit millions to a precarious and painful existence in order to achieve future economic benefit. Nazism and Communism are now discredited. Neo-liberal capitalism still seems to rest on the assumption that a certain amount of suffering, usually on the periphery, is a price worth paying for general future prosperity. The supposed "impossibility of making an omelette without breaking eggs" (a phrase first used by the journalist Walter Duranty, an admirer of Stalin, in a poem describing the supposedly justified human cost of building a communist society) could well be the motto of twentieth-century politics, and continues into the twenty-first. Such thinking, in the light of the cross, is revealed as not only anti humanitarian, but blasphemous. The "eggs" that are "broken" are the crucified people, with the value and dignity of people made in the image of God, loved by God, and revealed by the cross to be in solidarity with the crucified God. The crucifixion of Christ and the dehumanization of those who are thus written off are in close parallel. The church best exercises its political function in pointing to that cruciform parallel, in identifying with and, if necessary, defending the crucified, in standing in solidarity with them, and in bearing witness to the causes of their crucifixion.

In Conclusion—The Church as a Beatitude Community of Solidarity, Resistance and Hope

A cruciform church will seek to live out a spirituality of kenotic generosity. Such a spirituality bears a striking resemblance to that outlined in the Beatitudes of Matt 5:3–12 (NRSV). A cruciform church will be "poor in spirit." Whatever Jesus meant exactly by that enigmatic phrase, a cruciform church will know the poverty of lack of power and of marginalization. It will not be a proud and domineering church, but will be conscious of its own weakness. A cruciform church will "mourn." One of the roles of the church is to act (as the Jewish people have been described) as an exposed nerve of humanity consisting of or closely connected to the crucified people. Such a church will mourn, in that it will feel deeply the pain of the world. A cruciform church, unless it falls prey to self-delusion, cannot be other than "humble" or "meek," since the appurtenances of power will have been stripped away. A cruciform church will "hunger and thirst," not for power for itself, or for past glories, but for righteousness and justice. The political role of such a church will not be self-defensive, but will actively work for the rights of the other. A cruciform church will be "merciful." Such a church will be conscious of its own past responsibility and present potential for inflicting crucifixions, and so will be merciful to fellow sinners. A cruciform church will have the "pureness of heart" of having the external trimmings of power and success stripped away, in order to concentrate on its essential being and task. A cruciform church will, most of all, work for peace, in that it will seek to mirror God's character of peacemaker. Finally, a cruciform church will, by its very nature, be vulnerable to persecution, in seeking to do what the crucified God requires.

Bibliography

Bacevich, Andrew. *The New American Militarism: How Americans are Seduced by War.* Oxford: Oxford University Press, 2013.
Balthasar, Hans Urs von. *Mysterium Paschale.* Edinburgh: T. & T. Clark, 1990.
Barbour, Ian. "God's Power: A Process View." In *The Work of Love; Creation as Kenosis*, edited by John Polkinghorne, 1–20. London: SPCK, 2001.
Barley, Lynda. *Churchgoing Today.* London: Church House, 2006.
Barnett, Victoria. *For the Soul of the People: Protestant Protest against Hitler.* New York: Oxford University Press, 1992.
Barth, Karl. *Church Dogmatics III/4.* Edinburgh: T. & T. Clark, 1961.
Bartley, Jonathan. *Faith and Politics after Christendom.* Bletchley: Paternoster, 2006.
Beal, Timothy. *Religion in America: A Very Short Introduction.* Oxford: Oxford University Press, 2008.
Beilby, James, and Paul Eddy. *The Historical Jesus: Five Views.* London: SPCK, 2010.
Bellinger, William, and William Farmer, eds. *Jesus and the Suffering Servant: Isaiah 53 and Christian Origins.* Harrisburg, PA: Trinity Press International, 1998.
Berryman, Philip. *The Religious Roots of Rebellion.* London: SCM, 1984.
Biggar, Nigel. *In Defence of War.* Oxford: Oxford University Press, 2013.
Billings, Alan. *The Dove, the Fig Leaf, and the Sword.* London: SPCK, 2014.
Bishop, Peter. *A Technique for Loving: Non-violence in Indian and Christian Traditions.* London: SCM, 1981.
Boff, Leonardo. *Church, Charism and Power.* London: SCM, 1985.
———. *Ecclesiogenesis.* Maryknoll, NY: Orbis, 1986.
———. *Jesus Christ: Liberator.* Maryknoll, NY: Orbis, 1978.
———. *Passion of Christ, Passion of the World.* Maryknoll, NY: Orbis, 1987.
———. *Way of the Cross, Way of Justice.* Maryknoll, NY: Orbis, 1980.
Bonhoeffer, Dietrich. *The Cost of Discipleship.* London: SCM, 1959.
———. *Letters and Papers from Prison.* London: SCM, 1953.
———. *Testament to Freedom.* New York: Harper Collins, 1995.
Bonino, José Miguez. *Towards a Christian Political Ethics.* London: SCM, 1983.
Bradley, Ian. *The Power of Sacrifice.* London: Darton, Longman & Todd, 1995.
Bradshaw, Timothy. *The Olive Branch: An Evangelical Anglican Doctrine of the Church.* Carlisle: Paternoster, 1992.
Bretherton, Luke. *Christianity and Contemporary Politics.* Chichester: Wiley-Blackwell, 2010.

Brown, Andrew, and Linda Woodhead. *That Was the Church That Was*. London: Bloomsbury Continuum, 2016.
Brown, David. *Divine Humanity: Kenosis Explored and Defended*. London: SCM, 2011.
Brown, Malcolm. "Anglican Social Theology Tomorrow." In *Anglican Social Theology*, edited by Malcolm Brown, 175–89. London: Church House, 2014.
———. "The Case for Anglican Social Theology Today." In *Anglican Social Theology*, edited by Malcolm Brown, 1–28. London: Church House, 2014.
Buchanan, Colin. *Cut the Connection: Disestablishment and the Church of England*. London: Darton, Longman & Todd, 1994.
Bruce, Steve. *Religion in Modern Britain*. Oxford: Oxford University Press, 1995.
Burridge, Richard. *Imitating Jesus: an Inclusive Approach to New Testament Ethics*. Grand Rapids: Eerdmans, 2007.
Caputo, John D. *The Weakness of God*. Bloomington, IN: Indiana University Press, 2006.
Carr, Wesley, ed. *Say One for Me*. London: SPCK, 1992.
Carter, Craig A. *The Politics of the Cross. The Theology and Ethics of John Howard Yoder*. Grand Rapids: Brazos, 2001.
Carter, Warren. *The Roman Empire and the New Testament*. Nashville: Abingdon, 2006.
Cavanaugh, William T. *Torture and Eucharist*. Oxford: Blackwell, 1998.
Chatfield, Charles. *For Peace and Justice: Pacifism in America, 1914–1941*. Knoxville, TN: University of Tennessee Press, 1971.
Chaves, Mark. *American Religion: Contemporary Trends*. Princeton: Princeton University Press, 2011.
"What Does a 'Church Of the Poor' Look Like?" http://www.church-poverty.org.uk/churchofthepoorquestions/.
Clough, David L., and Brian Stiltner. *Faith and Force: A Christian Debate about War*. Washington, DC: Georgetown University Press, 2007.
Coakley, Sarah. *Powers and Submission*. Oxford: Blackwell, 2002.
"Notification on the Works of Father Jon Sobrino, SJ." http://www.vatican.va/roman_curia/congregations/cfaith/documents/rc_con_cfaith_doc_20061126_notification-sobrino_en.html.
Connor, Timothy G. *The Kenotic Trajectory of the Church in Donald MacKinnon's Theology*. London: Bloomsbury, 2011.
Cowling, Maurice. *Conservative Essays*. London: Cassell, 1978.
Crossan, John D. "Jesus and the Challenge of Collaborative Eschatology." In *The Historical Jesus: Five Views*, edited by James Beilby and Paul Eddy, 105–32. London: SPCK, 2010.
Cullmann, Oscar. *Christ and Time*. London: SCM, 1951.
Dammers, A. Horace. *Lifestyle, a Parable of Sharing*. Wellingborough: Turnstone, 1982.
Davie, Grace. *Religion in Britain: a Persistent Paradox*. Chichester: Wiley-Blackwell, 2015.
———. *Religion in Britain Since 1945*. Oxford: Blackwell, 1994.
Doerksen, Paul G. *Beyond Suspicion: Post-Christendom Protestant Political Theology in John Howard Yoder and Oliver O'Donovan*. Milton Keynes: Paternoster, 2009.
Dunn, James D. G. *Christology in the Making*. London: SCM, 1989.
Eagleton, Terry. *Why Marx was Right*. New Haven: Yale University Press, 2011.
Edwards, David L. *Leaders of the Church of England, 1828–1978*. London: Hodder & Stoughton, 1978.

Ellacuria, Ignacio, and Jon Sobrino, eds. *Mysterium Liberationis. Fundamental Concepts of Liberation Theology.* Maryknoll, NY: Orbis, 1994.
Elliot, Charles. *Comfortable Compassion?* London: Hodder & Stoughton, 1987.
Ellis, George F. R. "Kenosis as a Unifying Theme for Life and Cosmology." In *The Work of Love: Creation as Kenosis,* edited by John Polkinghorne, 107–26. London: SPCK, 2001.
Ericksen, Robert P. *Theologians under Hitler.* Yale: Yale University Press, 1985.
Filby, Eliza. *God and Mrs. Thatcher.* London: Biteback, 2015.
Forsyth, Peter T. *The Christian Ethic of War.* London: Longmans, 1916.
―――. *The Justification of God: Lectures for War time on a Christian Theodicy.* London: Independent, 1957.
Foster, Claude R. *Paul Schneider: The Buchenwald Apostle.* West Chester, PA: SSI Bookstore, 1995.
Foucault, Michel. *Power/Knowledge. Selected Interviews and Other Writings, 1972–1977.* New York: Pantheon, 1981.
Gingerich, Ray, and Ted Grimsrud, eds. *Transforming the Powers.* Minneapolis; Augsburg Fortress, 2006.
Glover, Jonathan. *Humanity: A Moral History of the Twentieth Century.* London: Pimlico, 2001.
Gore, Charles. *The Incarnation of the Son of God.* London: Murray, 1891.
Green, Duncan. *From Poverty to Power: How Active Citizens and Effective States Can Change the World.* Oxford: Oxfam International, 2008.
Greenwood, Robin, and Hugh Burgess. *Changing Society and the Churches: Power.* London: SPCK, 2005.
Gunton, Colin. *The Actuality of Atonement.* Edinburgh: T. & T. Clark, 1988.
Gutiérrez, Gustavo. *The Power of the Poor in History.* London: SCM, 1983.
Hall, Douglas J. *The Cross in Our Context.* Minneapolis: Fortress, 2003.
Harries, Richard. *Should a Christian Support Guerrillas?* Guildford: Lutterworth, 1982.
Hart, David Bentley. *Atheist Delusions: The Christian Revolution and Its Fashionable Enemies.* New Haven: Yale University Press, 2009.
Hastings, Adrian. *A History of English Christianity, 1920–1990.* London: SCM, 1991.
Hauerwas, Stanley. "In Defence of 'Our Respectable Culture': Trying to Make Sense of John Howard Yoder's Sexual Abuse." *ABC Religion and Ethics,* October 18, 2017. https://www.abc.net.au/religion/in-defence-of-our-respectable-culture-trying-to-make-sense-of-jo/10095302.
―――. "Stanley Hauerwas on John Howard Yoder." In *Radical Christian Writings,* edited by Andrew Bradstock and Christopher Rowland, 250–54. Oxford: Blackwell, 2002.
―――. *Vision and Virtue.* Notre Dame, IN: University of Notre Dame Press, 1981.
―――. *With the Grain of the Universe.* Grand Rapids: Brazos, 2001.
Hauerwas, Stanley, et al. *The Wisdom of the Cross: Essays in Honor of John Howard Yoder.* Grand Rapids: Eerdmans, 1999.
Hays, Richard B. *The Moral Vision of the New Testament.* San Francisco: Harper, 1996.
Hengel, Martin. *Crucifixion.* London: SCM, 1977.
Herzog, William. *Jesus, Justice, and the Reign of God.* Louisville: Westminster John Knox, 2000.
van den Heuvel, Albert H. *The Humiliation of the Church.* London: SCM, 1967.

Hinze, Christine Firer. *Comprehending Power in Christian Social Ethics*. Atlanta: Scholars, 1995.

Horsley, Richard A. *Jesus and the Politics of Roman Palestine* Columbia, SC: University of South Carolina Press, 2014.

Hovey, Craig. *To Share in the Body—a Theology of Martyrdom for Today*. Grand Rapids: Brazos, 2008.

Hughes, John. "After Temple? The Recent Renewal of Anglican Social Thought." In *Anglican Social Theology*, edited by Malcolm Brown, 74–101. London: Church House, 2014.

Jenkins, Philip. "Europe's Christian Comeback." *Foreign Policy*, June 12, 2007. https://foreignpolicy.com/2007/06/12/europes-christian-comeback/.

———. *The Next Christendom*. New York: Oxford University Press, 2007.

Jennings, Theodore W. *Transforming Atonement: A Political Theology of the Cross*. Minneapolis: Fortress, 2009.

Jersak, Brad, and Michael Hardin, eds. *Stricken by God? Non-violent Identification and the Victory of Christ*. Grand Rapids: Eerdmans, 2007.

King, Martin Luther, Jr. *A Testament of Hope: The Essential Writings of Martin Luther King Jr.* Edited by James Melvin Washington. San Francisco: Harper & Row, 1986.

———. *Where Do We Go From Here?* Boston: Beacon, 1967.

Kitamori, Kazoh. *Theology of the Pain of God*. London: SCM, 1965.

Kraybill, Donald B. *The Upside Down Kingdom*. Basingstoke: Marshall, Morgan & Scott, 1985.

Krehbiel, Stephanie. "The Woody Allen Problem: How Do We Read Pacifist Theologian (and Sexual Abuser) John Howard Yoder." *Religion Dispatches*, February 11, 2014. https://religiondispatches.org/the-woody-allen-problem-how-do-we-read-pacifist-theologian-and-sexual-abuser-john-howard-yoder/.

Lacorne, Denis. *Religion in America: A Political History*. New York: Columbia University Press, 2011.

MacGregor, Geddes. *He Who Lets Us Be*. New York: Paragon, 1987.

MacIntyre, Alasdair. *After Virtue*. Notre Dame, IN: University of Notre Dame Press, 1984.

MacKinnon, Donald. *The Stripping of the Altars*. London: Collins, 1969.

MacQuarrie, John. *Principles of Christian Theology*. London: SCM, 1966.

Marsh, Charles. *Strange Glory: A Life of Dietrich Bonhoeffer*. London: SPCK, 2014.

Martin, David. "The Christian, the Political and the Academic." *Sociology of Religion* 65.4 (2004) 341–56.

Mayhew, Peter. *A Theology of Force and Violence*. London: SCM, 1989.

McClendon, James W., Jr. *Systematic Theology*. Vol. 2, *Doctrine*. Nashville: Abingdon, 1994.

Medhurst, Kenneth N., and George H. Moyser. *Church and Politics in a Secular Age*. Oxford: Clarendon, 1988.

Mitchell, Roger Haydon. *Church, Gospel and Empire*. Eugene, OR: Wipf & Stock, 2011.

———. *The Fall of the Church*. Eugene, OR: Wipf & Stock, 2013.

Mitchell, Roger Haydon, and Julie Arram. *Discovering Kenarchy: Contemporary Resources for the Politics of Love*. Eugene, OR: Wipf & Stock, 2014.

Modood, Tariq. "Establishment, Multiculturalism and British Citizenship." *The Political Quarterly* 65.1 (1994) 53–73.

Moltmann, Jürgen. *The Church in the Power of the Spirit*. London: SCM, 1977.

———. *The Crucified God*. London: SCM, 1974.
———. *God in Creation*. London: SCM, 1985.
———. "God's Kenosis in the Creation and Consummation of the World." In *The Work of Love: Creation as Kenosis*, edited by J. Polkinghorne, 137–51. London: SPCK, 2001.
———. *The Trinity and the Kingdom of God*. London: SCM, 1981.
Moss, Candida. *The Myth of Persecution*. New York: Harper Collins, 2013.
Murphy, George L. *The Cosmos in the Light of the Cross*. Harrisburg, PA: Trinity, 2003.
Murphy, Nancey. "John Howard Yoder's Systematic Defense of Christian Pacifism." In *The Wisdom of the Cross: Essays in Honor of John Howard Yoder*, edited by Stanley Hauerwas et al., 45–68. Grand Rapids: Eerdmans, 1999.
Murphy, Nancey. "Social Science, Ethics, and the Powers." In *Transforming the Powers: Peace, Justice, and the Domination System*, edited by Ray Gingerich and Ted Grimsrud, 29–38. Minneapolis; Augsburg Fortress, 2006.
Murphy, Nancey. and George F. R. Ellis. On *the Moral Nature of the Universe*. Minneapolis: Fortress, 1996.
Myers, Ched. *Binding the Strong Man*. Maryknoll, NY: Orbis, 1988.
Nation, Mark T. *John Howard Yoder. Mennonite Patience, Evangelical Witness, Catholic Convictions*. Grand Rapids: Eerdmans, 2006.
Nelson-Pallmeyer, Jack. *Saving Christianity from Empire*. New York: Continuum, 2005.
Newbiggin, Leslie. *Foolishness to the Greeks: The Gospel and Western Culture*. London: SPCK, 1986.
Nicholls, David. *Deity and Domination*. London: Routledge, 1989.
Niebuhr, Reinhold. *Discerning the Signs of the Times*. London: SCM, 1946.
Niebuhr, H. Richard. *Christ and Culture*. New York: Harper & Row, 1951.
O'Donovan, Oliver. *The Desire of the Nations*. Cambridge: Cambridge University Press, 1996.
Okura, Teresa, et al., eds. *Rethinking Martyrdom (Concilium)*. London: SCM, 2003.
Mar Ostathios, Geevarghese. *Theology of a Classless Society*. London: Lutterworth, 1977.
Owen, Wilfred. *War Poems and Others*. London: Chatto and Windus, 1973.
Pascal, Blaise. *Pensees*. Harmondsworth: Penguin, 1966.
Pastoral Team of Bambamarca. *Vamos Caminando*. London: SCM, 1985.
Paul, Geoffrey D. *A Pattern of Faith*. Worthing: Churchman, 1986.
Peacocke, Arthur R. "The Cost of New Life." In *The Work of Love: Creation as Kenosis*, edited by John Polkinghorne, 21–42. London: SPCK, 2001.
Peet, John C. "The Lifestyle of the Rich and Development Issues." *Crucible* (October-December 1999) 351–66.
Phillips, Kevin. *American Theocracy*. London: Penguin, 2006.
Pinches, Charles. "Christian Pacifism and Theodicy: The Free Will Defense in the Thought of John H. Yoder." *Modern Theology* 5.3 (1989) 239–55.
Polkinghorne, John. "Kenotic Creation and Divine Action." In *The Work of Love: Creation as Kenosis*, edited by John Polkinghorne, 90–106. London: SPCK, 2001.
Preston, Andrew. *Sword of the Spirit, Shield of Faith*. New York: Anchor, 2012.
Rahner, Karl. *On the Theology of Death*. New York: Herder, 1961.
Reimer, A. James. *The Emmanuel Hirsch and Paul Tillich Debate*. New York: Edwin Mellen, 1990.
Rivkin, Ellis. *What Crucified Jesus?* London: SCM, 1984.
Robinson, John A. T. *The Body*. London: SCM, 1952.

———. *The Human Face of God.* London: SCM, 1973.
Rolt, Clarence E. *The World's Redemption.* London: Longmans, Green, 1913.
Rowlands, Anna. "Fraternal Traditions: Anglican Social Theology and Catholic Social Teaching in a British Context." In *Anglican Social Theology*, edited by Malcolm Brown, 133–74. London: Church House, 2014.
Russell, Bertrand. *Power: A New Social Analysis.* London: Allen & Unwin, 1938.
Sacks, Jonathan. *The Persistence of Faith.* London: Weidenfeld, 1991.
Scott, Peter. *Theology, Ideology and Liberation.* Cambridge: Cambridge University Press, 1994.
Scott, Peter, and William T. Cavanaugh, eds. *The Blackwell Companion to Political Theology:* Oxford: Blackwell, 2004.
Shriver, Donald W. *An Ethic for Enemies.* New York: Oxford University Press, 1995.
Sider, Ronald. *Rich Christians in an Age of Hunger.* London. Hodder & Stoughton, 1977.
———. *Rich Christians in an Age of Hunger, Twentieth Anniversary Edition.* London: Hodder & Stoughton, 1997.
Sider, Ronald, ed. *Lifestyle in the Eighties: An Evangelical Commitment to Simple Lifestyle.* Exeter: Paternoster, 1982.
Singer, Peter. *The Life You Can Save.* New York: Random House, 2009.
Slane, Craig J. *Bonhoeffer as Martyr: Social Responsibility and Modern Christian Commitment.* Grand Rapids: Brazos, 2004.
Smith, Martin L., ed. *Benson of Cowley.* Oxford: Oxford University Press, 1980.
Sobrino, Jon. *Christ the Liberator.* Maryknoll, NY: Orbis, 2001.
———. *Christology at the Crossroads.* London: SCM, 1978.
———. *Jesus in Latin America.* Maryknoll, NY: Orbis, 1987.
———. *Jesus the Liberator.* Royal Tunbridge Wells: Burns & Oates, 1994.
———. *The Principle of Mercy. Taking the Crucified People from the Cross.* Maryknoll, NY: Orbis, 1994.
———. *The True Church and the Poor.* London: SCM, 1984
———. *Where Is God? Earthquake, Terrorism, Barbarity and Hope.* Maryknoll, NY: Orbis, 2004.
———. *Witnesses to the Kingdom: The Martyrs of El Salvador and the Crucified Peoples.* Maryknoll, NY: Orbis, 2003.
Stalsett, Sturla. *The Crucified and the Crucified: A Study in the Liberation Christology of Jon Sobrino.* Berne: Lang, 2003.
Stark, Rodney. *The Rise of Christianity.* New York: Harper Collins, 1996.
Stevenson, David. *1914–1918: The History of the First World War.* London: Penguin, 2004.
Studdert Kennedy, Geoffrey A. *The Unutterable Beauty.* London: Hodder and Stoughton, 1947.
Suggate, Alan. "The Temple Tradition," In *Anglican Social Theology*, edited by Malcolm Brown, 28–73. London: Church House, 2014.
Syder, Martin R. "Theology in Development: English Christianity and the Third World, 1955–1990." MPhil diss., University of Leeds, 1991.
Taylor, Alan J. P. *English History, 1914–1945.* Oxford: Oxford University Press, 1965.
Taylor, John V. *Enough Is Enough.* London: SCM, 1975.
Temple, William. *Readings in St. John's Gospel.* London: MacMillan, 1945.
———. *Religious Experience and Other Essays and Addresses.* London: Clarke, 1958.
Tillich, Paul. *Love, Power and Justice.* New York: Oxford University Press, 1960.

Waltermire, Donald E. *The Liberation Christologies of Leonardo Boff and Jon Sobrino.* Lanham, MD: University Press of America, 1994.
Weaver, J. Denny. *John Howard Yoder Radical Theologian* Eugene, OR: Cascade, 2014.
Welch, Sharon D. *Communities of Resistance and Solidarity.* New York: Orbis, 1985.
Whitehead, Alfred N. *Process and Reality.* New York: Free Press, 1979.
Whitworth, Patrick. *Prepare for Exile.* London: SPCK, 2008.
Wiesel, Elie. *Ani Maamin.* London: Random House, 1973.
Wilkinson, Alan. *Dissent or Conform? War, Peace and the English Churches, 1900–1945.* London: SCM, 1986.
Williams, Daniel D. *The Spirit and the Forms of Love.* San Francisco: Harper & Row, 1968.
Wink, Walter. *Engaging the Powers.* Minneapolis, MN: Fortress, 1992.
Woolf, Greg. *Rome: An Empire's Story.* Oxford: Oxford University Press, 2012.
Wright, Nigel G. *Disavowing Constantine: Mission, Church, and the Social Order in the Theologies of John Howard Yoder and Jurgen Moltmann.* Carlisle: Paternoster, 2000.
Wright, N. T. *Jesus and the Victory of God.* Minneapolis: Fortress, 1996.
Yoder, John H. *Anabaptism and Reformation in Switzerland: An Historical and Theological Analysis of the Dialogues between Anabaptists and Reformers.* Kitchener: Pandora, 2004.
———. *The Christian Witness to the State.* Newton, KS: Faith and Life, 1964.
———. *Discipleship as Political Responsibility.* Scottdale, PA: Herald, 2003.
———. *For the Nations: Essays Evangelical and Public.* Grand Rapids: Eerdmans, 1997.
———. *Nevertheless: The Varieties and Shortcomings of Christian Pacifism.* Scottdale, PA: Herald, 1971.
———. *The Original Revolution.* Scottdale, PA: Herald, 1972.
———. *The Politics of Jesus.* 1st ed. Grand Rapids: Eerdmans, 1972.
———. *The Politics of Jesus.* 2st ed. Grand Rapids: Eerdmans, 1994.
———. *Preface to Theology: Christology and Theological Method.* Elkart, IN: Co-op Bookstore, 1982.
———. *The Priestly Kingdom: Social Ethics as Gospel.* Notre Dame, IN: University of Notre Dame Press, 1984.
———. *The Royal Priesthood: Essays Ecclesiastical and Ecumenical.* Scottdale, PA: Herald, 1998.
Zimbelman, Joel. "The Contribution of John Howard Yoder to Recent Discussions in Christian Social Ethics." *Scottish Journal of Theology* 45.3 (2009) 367–99.

www.ingramcontent.com/pod-product-compliance
Lightning Source LLC
Chambersburg PA
CBHW061430300426
44114CB00014B/1623